Road Atlas France

Contents

2 – 10	Driving in France
11	Regional map of France
12	Distance chart
13	Key to map pages
14 – 49	Road maps 1:700 000
50 – 52	City through–route maps
50	Lyon
51	Marseille, Paris
52	Strasbourg, Toulouse
53 – 72	Index to place names

Driving in France

French drivers tend to be quite aggressive and the high incidence of road deaths has become a cause for national concern. There are speed restrictions for drivers who have held their licence for less than 2 years (110 km/h on motorways, 100 km/h on dual carriageways and 80 km/h on ordinary roads). Seatbelts are compulsory for both front and rear. Children under 10 should travel in the back, if possible. Babies and young children should be restrained appropriately, with a booster seat (**siège réhausseur**) or babyseat (**siège pour bébés**).

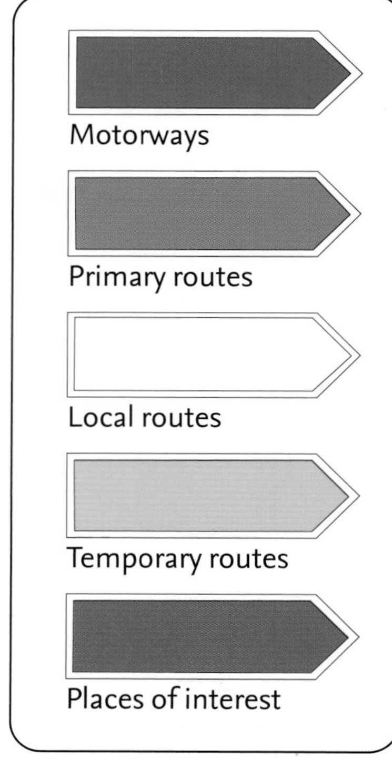

Motorways

Primary routes

Local routes

Temporary routes

Places of interest

▲ **French road signs are colour-coded**

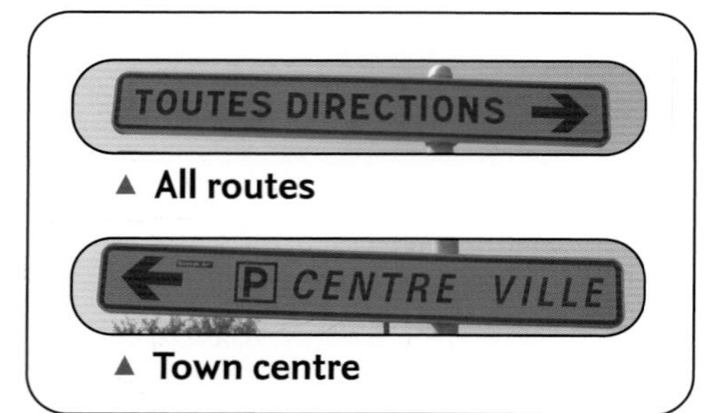

▲ **All routes**

▲ **Town centre**

built up area	**50** km/h
ordinary roads	**90** km/h
dual carriageway	**110** km/h
motorway	**130** km/h

▲ **Speed restrictions**

▼ **Route for heavy vehicles**

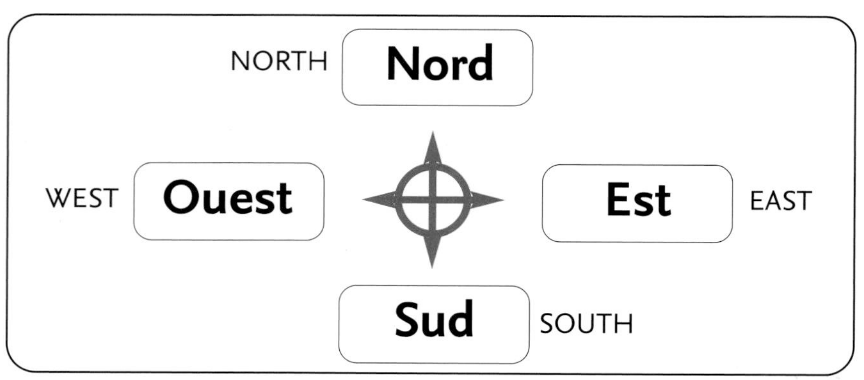

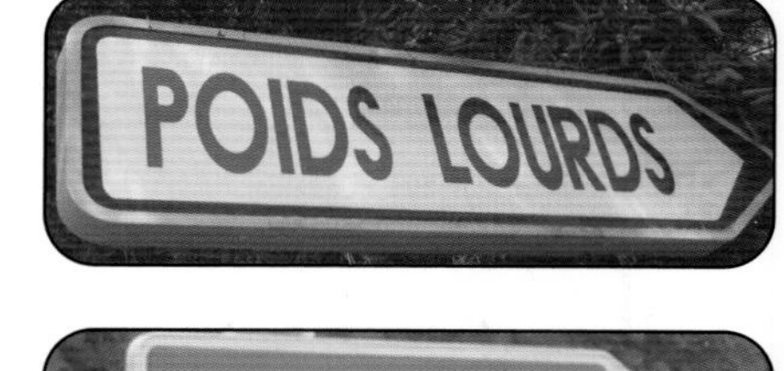

▲ **Other routes**

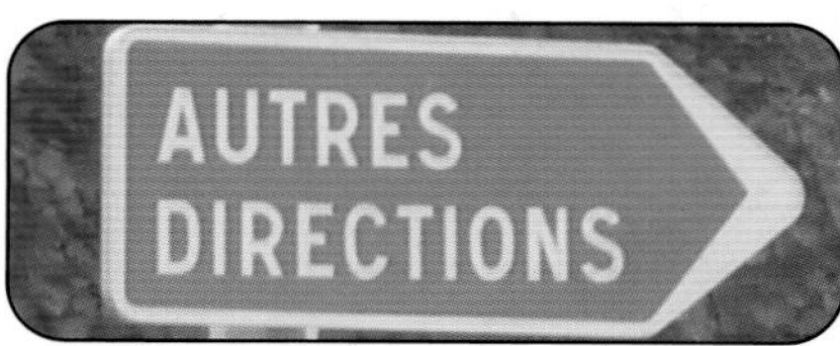

NORTH **Nord**

WEST **Ouest**   **Est** EAST

Sud SOUTH

▲ **Direction indicators**

we are going to...
nous allons à...
nooz a-loñ a...

is the road good?
est-ce que la route est bonne?
ess kuh la root ay bon

is the pass open?
est-ce que le col est ouvert?
ess kuh luh kol ayt oo-vehr

which is the best route?
quel est le meilleur itinéraire?
kel ay luh may-yuhr ee-tee-nay-rehr

can you show me on the map?
pouvez-vous me montrer sur la carte?
poo-vay voo muh moñ-tray soor la kart

do we need snow chains?
est-ce qu'il faut des chaînes?
ess keel foh day shen

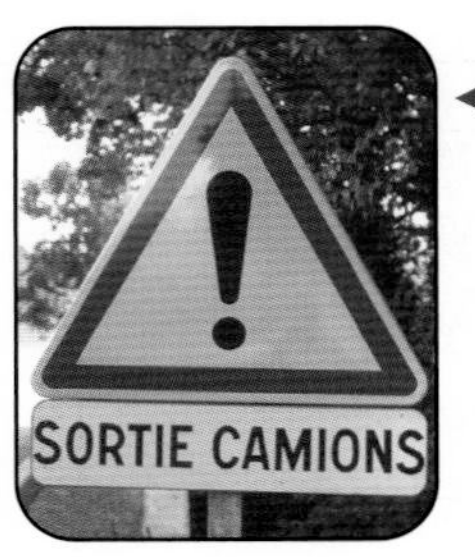

◄ Lorry exit

▼ School exit

DANGER *Sortie École*

SORTIE CAMIONS

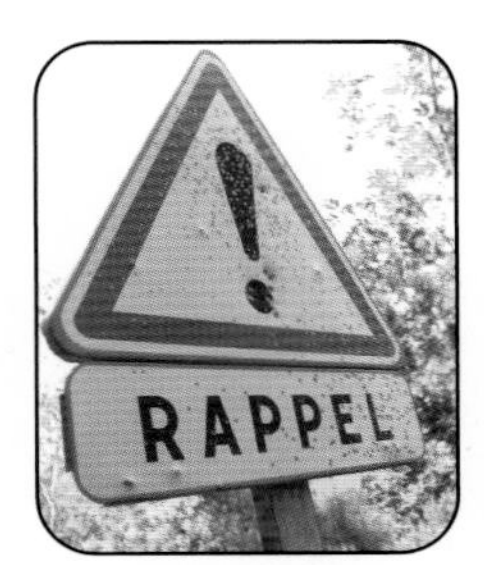
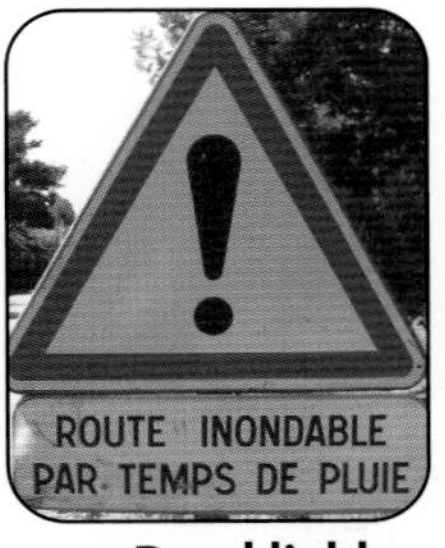

▲ **Road liable to flooding** ▲ **Danger**

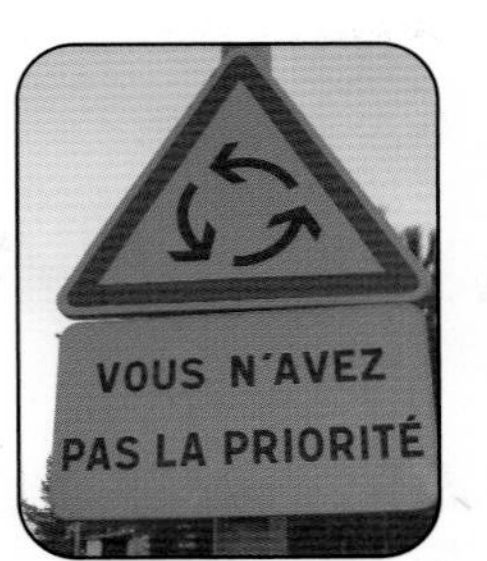
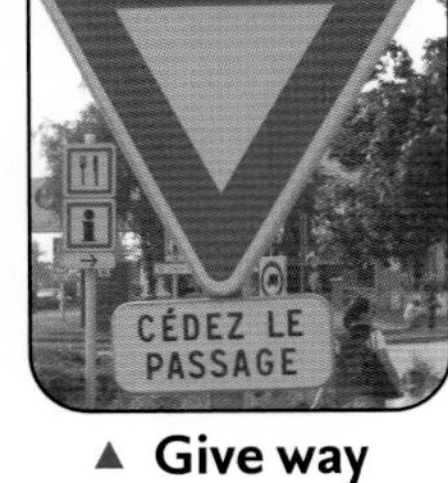

▲ **You do not have priority.** The traffic on the roundabout has priority. ▲ **Give way**

Warning that the crossroads (**carrefour**) is a roundabout (in France roundabouts are ▼ fairly new).

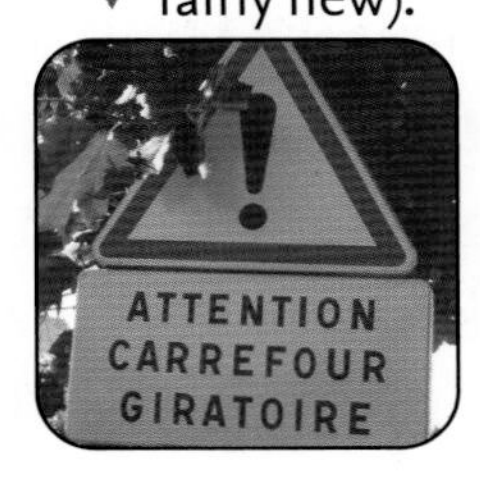
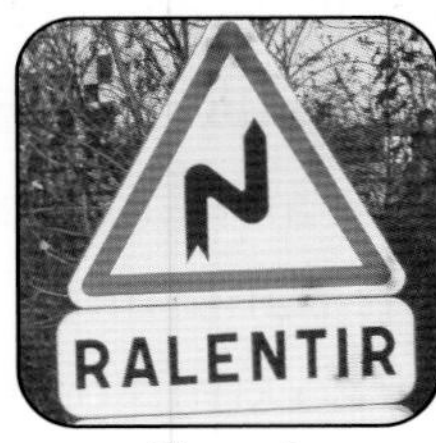

▲ **Slow down**

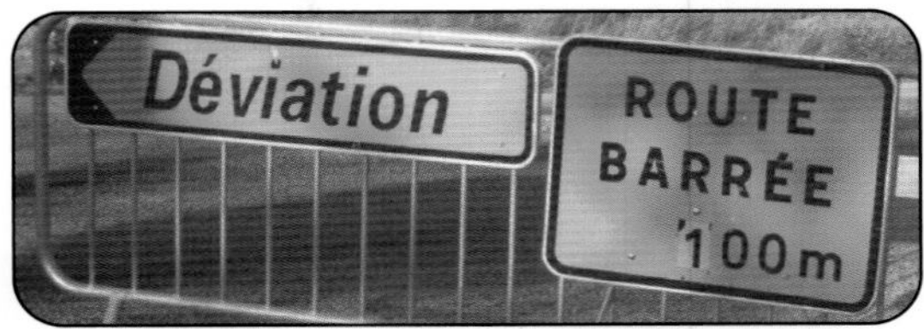

▲ **Detour**   **Road closed** ▲

Follow the yellow detour signs to rejoin your route.

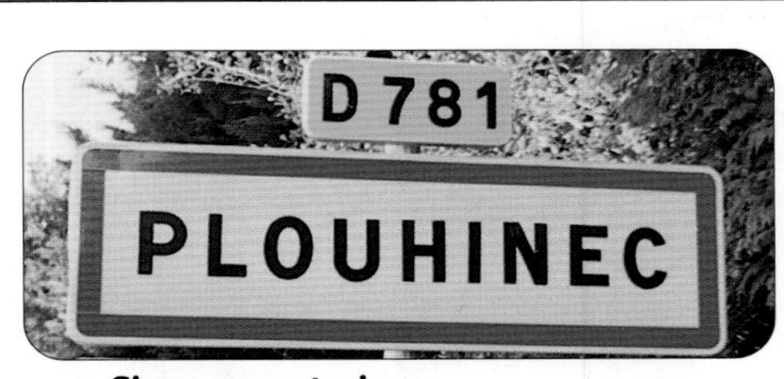

▲ **Signs on entering**
▼ **and leaving town**

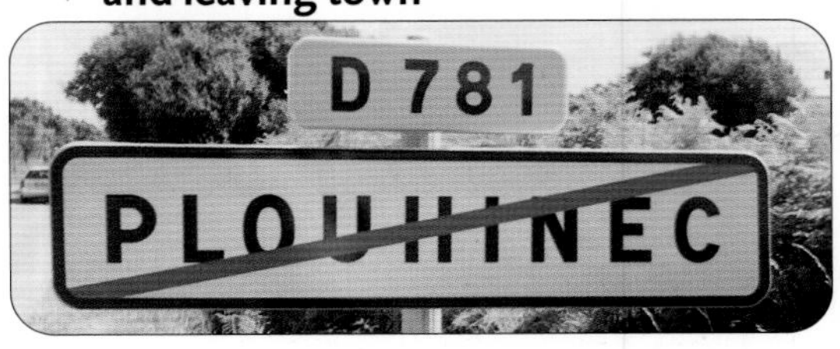

is this the road to…?
c'est bien la route de…?
say byañ la root duh…

I am sorry, I did not know
je suis désolé, je ne savais pas
zhuh swee day-zo-lay zhuh nuh sa-vay pa

do I have to pay the fine straight away?
est-ce qu'il faut payer l'amende tout de suite?
ess keel foh pay-ay la-moñd toot sweet

how do I get to…?
pour aller à…?
poor a-lay a…

Although some portions of motorways are free around cities, you have to pay a toll if travelling over long distances. You get a ticket when you join the motorway. On leaving it you hand the ticket in at the **station péage** and the amount to pay is flashed up on an illuminated sign. Remember it is the front passenger who pays if you have a right-hand-drive car. Take care over speeding: limits are lowered in wet weather – by 20 km/h on motorways and 10 km/h on other roads.

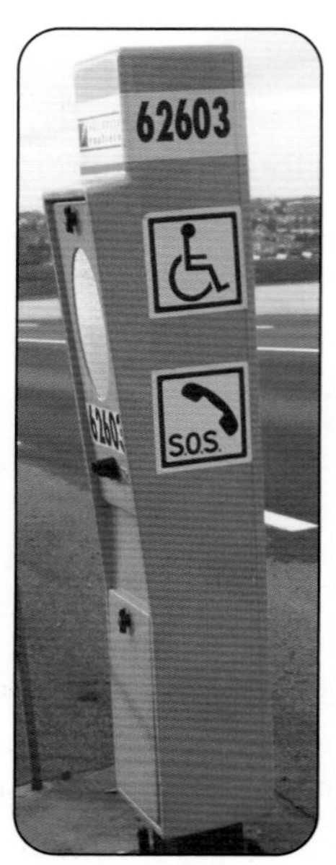

▲ Motorway emergency phone

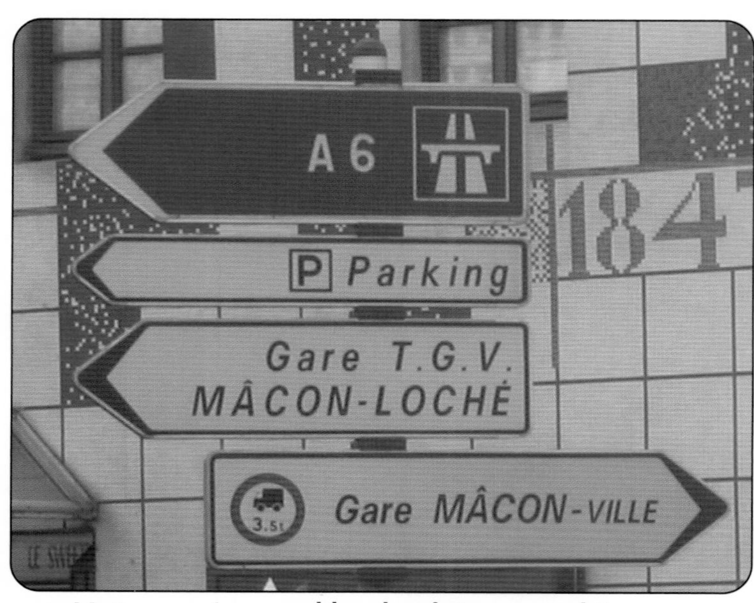

▲ Motorway signs are blue; local signs are white

▼ Motorway junction/exit

The motorway routes sign posted here ▼ are toll-paying (**péage**).

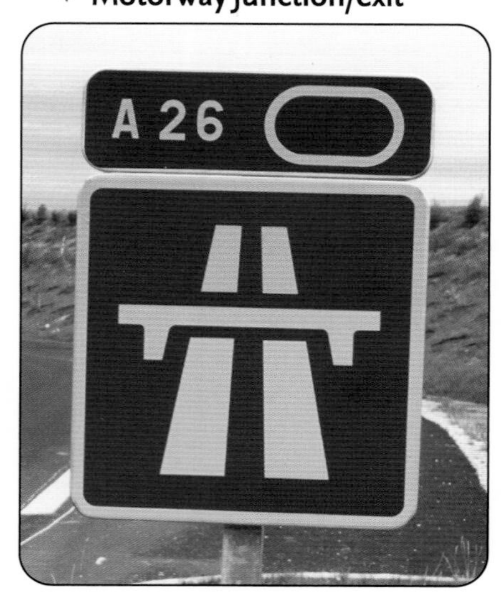

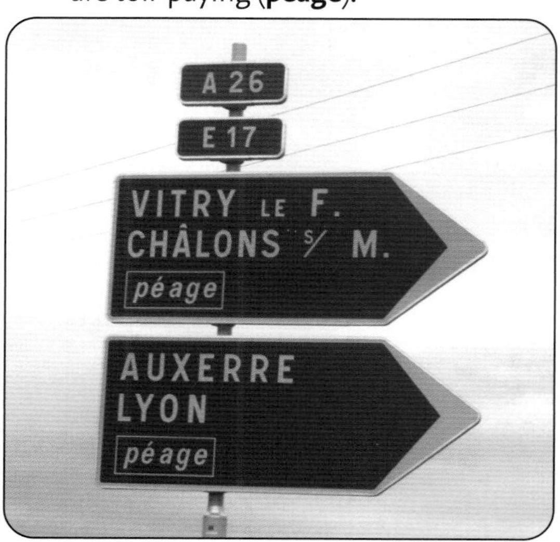

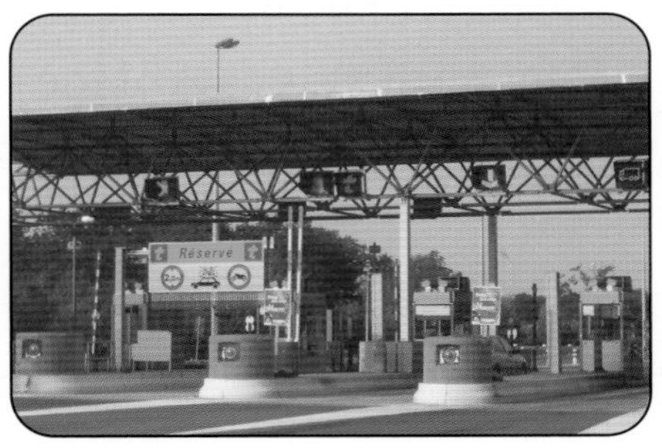
▲ Toll station

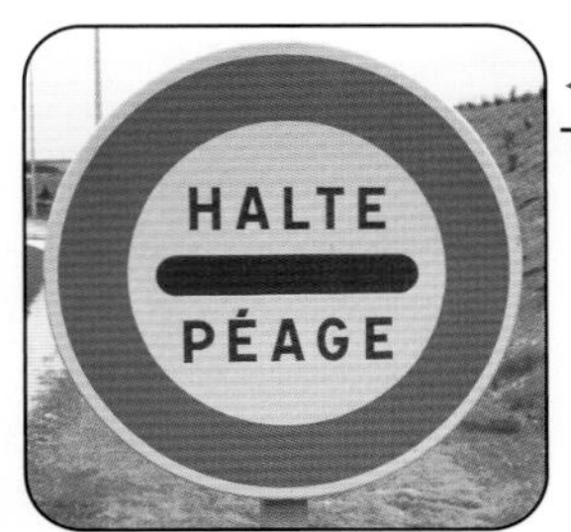
◄ **Stop**
Toll station

▼ **Motorway services are located every 30–40 km**

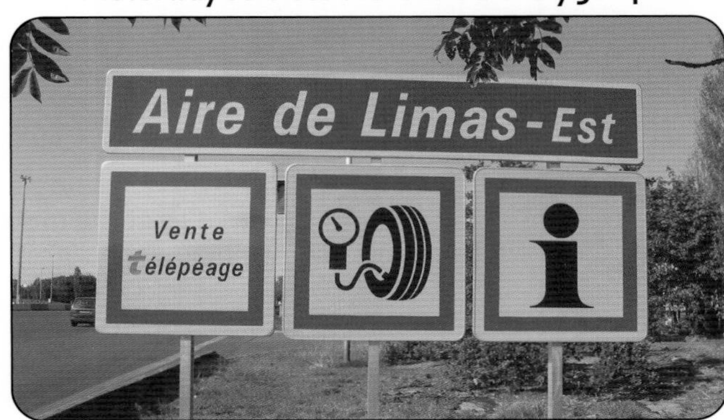

If you break down on the motorway

If you break down on the motorway, first you should put on your hazard lights and place the warning triangle about 30 m behind the car. You should alert the police on emergency number 17 stating your exact location. If you are using an emergency SOS phone (located every 2 km along the motorway) they will know your location. The police will arrange for a recovery vehicle to come to you.

my car has broken down
ma voiture est en panne
ma vwa-toor ay oñ pan

what do I do?
qu'est-ce que je dois faire?
kess kuh zhuh dwa fehr

I am on my own (female)
je suis seule
zhuh swee suhl

my children are in the car
mes enfants sont dans la voiture
mayz oñ-foñ soñ doñ la vwa-toor

the car is near junction number...
la voiture est près de la sortie numéro...
la vwa-toor ay pray duh la sor-tee noo-may-roh...

it's a blue Fiat Uno
c'est une Fiat Uno bleue
say ooñ fyat oo-noh bluh

registration number...
numéro d'immatriculation...
noo-may-roh dee-mat-ree-koo-las-yoñ...

In Paris, you generally pay to park. Outside Paris, in some parts of many towns, parking is only allowed on one side of the road. The system is that for the first 15 days of the month, parking is on the side of the road with odd house-numbers. During the second half of the month, parking is on the even-numbered-house side.

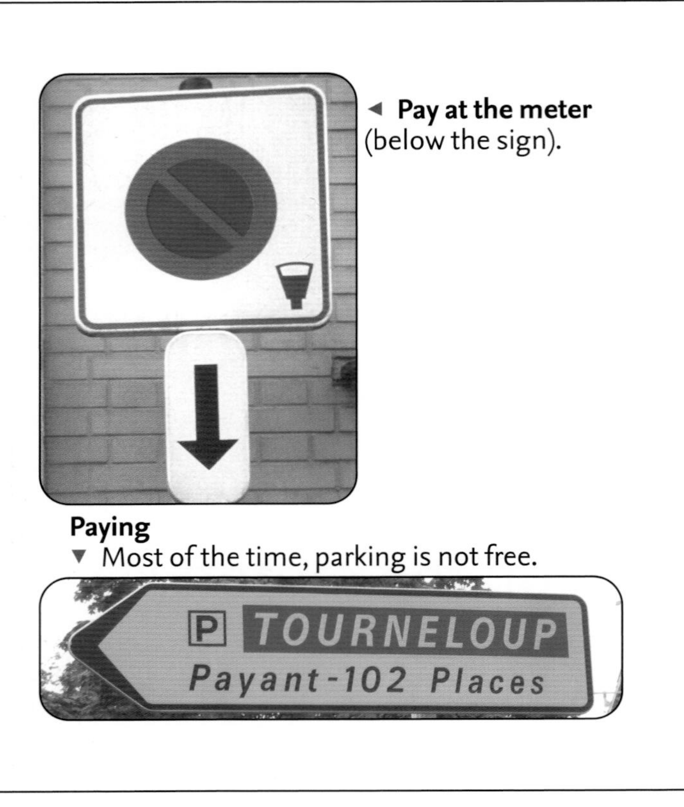

◄ **Pay at the meter** (below the sign).

Paying
▼ Most of the time, parking is not free.

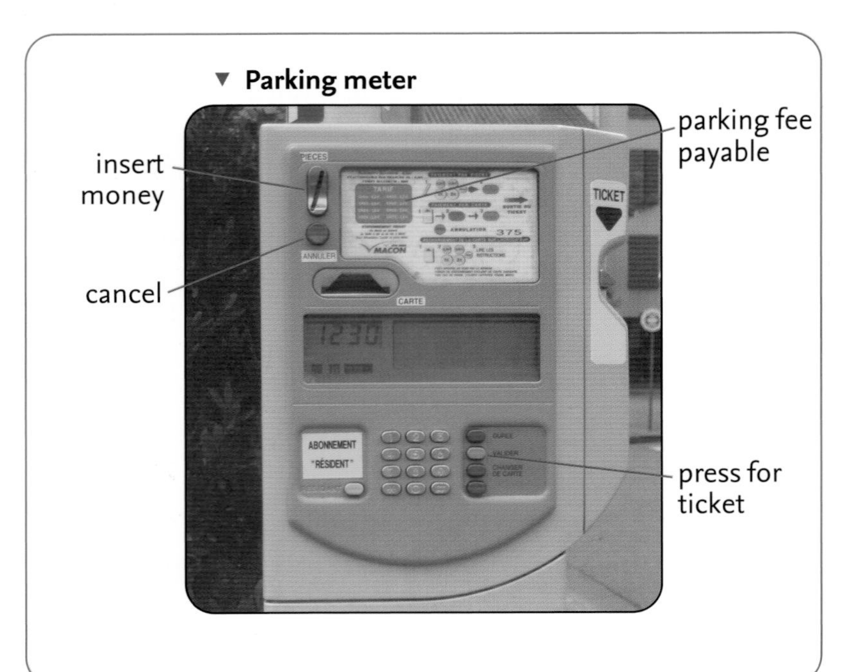

Parking meter ▼

insert money

cancel

parking fee payable

press for ticket

▲ **Only 3 minutes**

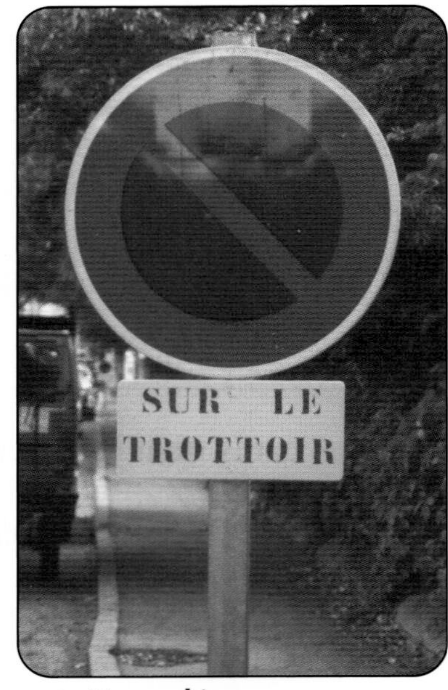

▲ **No parking on the pavement**

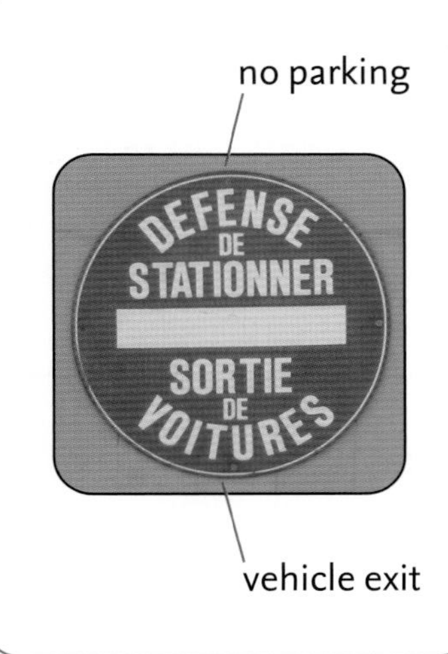

no parking

vehicle exit

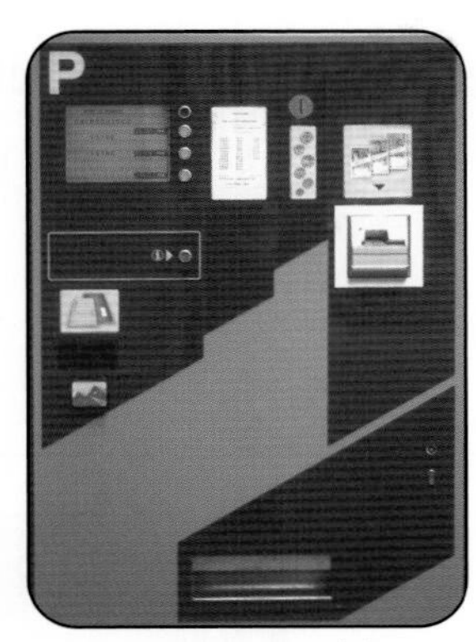

▲ Newer parking machines take notes and let you choose the language for your transaction.

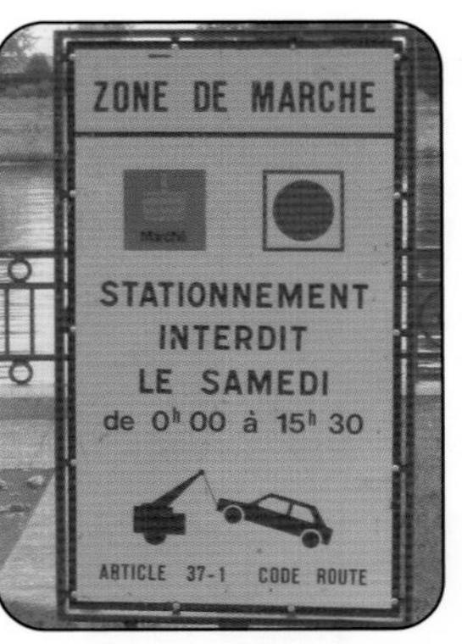

▲ No parking on Saturdays, market day

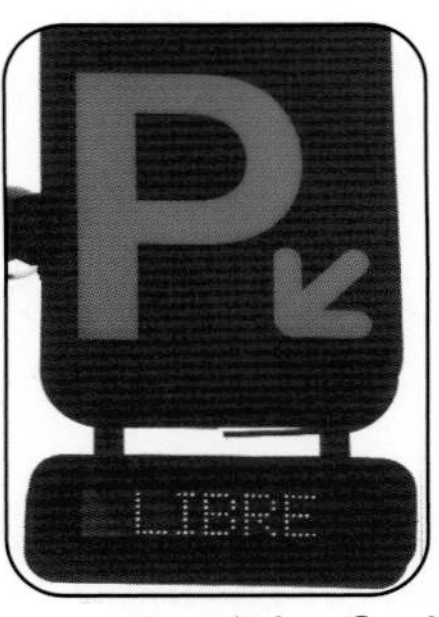

▲ Don't be fooled: **libre** means there are spaces, not that parking is free.

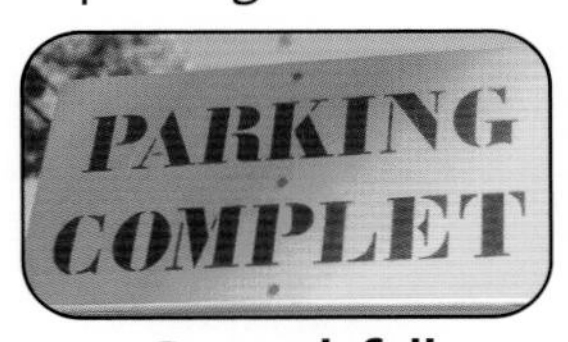

▲ **Car park full**

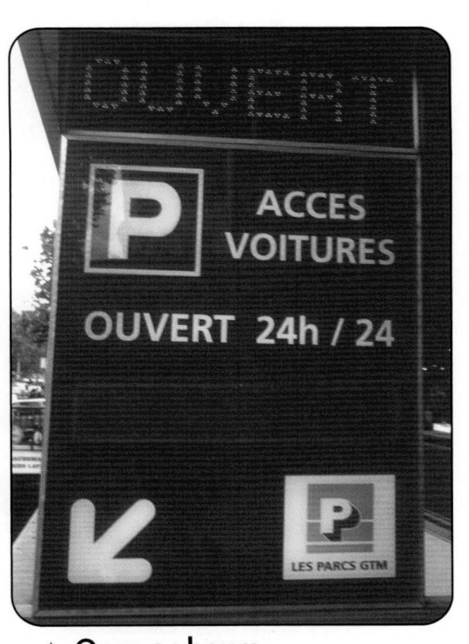

▲ **Open 24 hours**

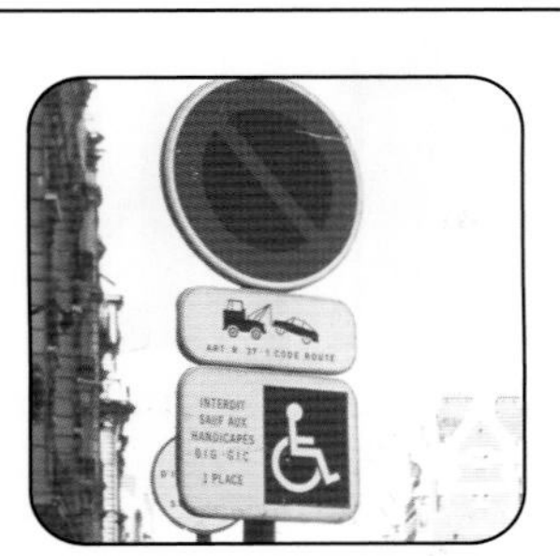

▲
Disabled parking places
▼

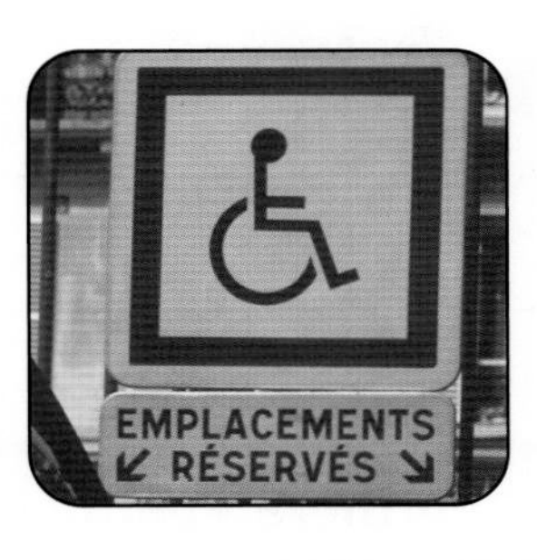

I am looking for a car park
je cherche un parking
zhuh shehrsh uñ par-keeng

can I park here?
est-ce que je peux me garer ici?
ess kuh zhuh puh muh ga-ray ee-see

the ticket machine doesn't work
l'horodateur ne marche pas
lo-ro-da-tuhr nuh marsh pa

do I need to pay?
il faut payer?
eel foh pay-ay

how long for?
pour combien de temps?
poor koñ-byañ duh toñ

Petrol stations in small towns are generally manned, but closed Sundays and in the evenings. The big towns have 24-hour petrol stations and you can buy petrol at some large supermarkets.

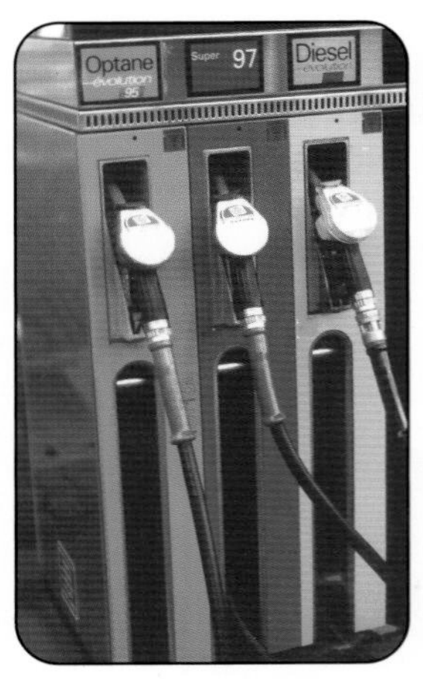

◄ **Petrol pumps are colour-coded**
You will find the pump number at the side

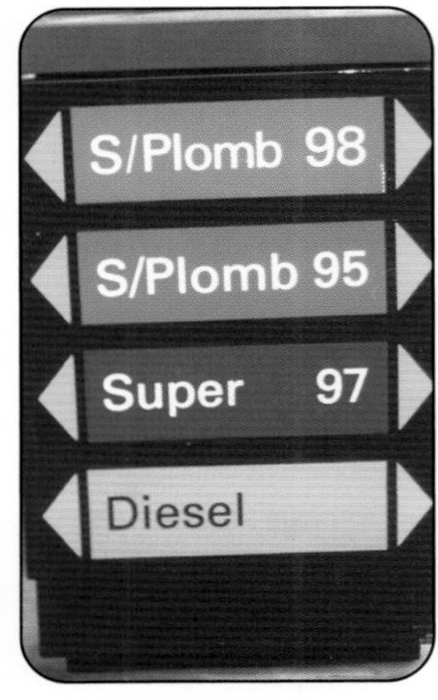

◄ Colour-coding matches the pump handle: green for unleaded (**sans plomb**), blue for super and yellow for diesel. The figure to the right (98, 95, 97) refers to the octane rating. Most cars run on the lower rating. The higher one is for powerful cars or towing cars.

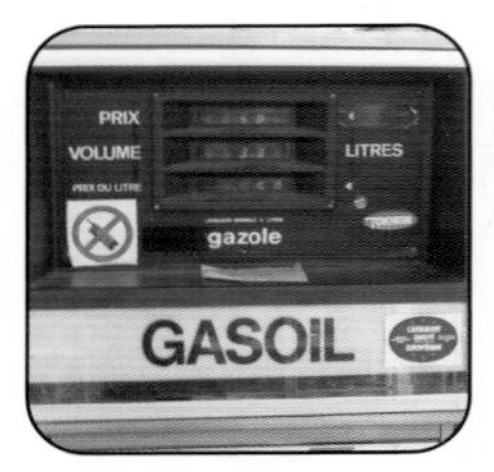

◄ Diesel is also known as **gazoil** or **gazole**.

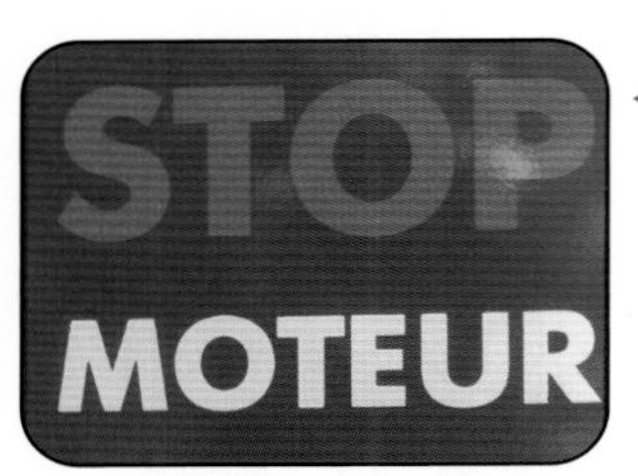

◄ **Turn off engine**

is there a petrol station near here?
est-ce qu'il y a une station-service près d'ici?
ess keel ee a oon stass-yoñ sehr-vees pray dee-see

fill it up please
le plein s'il vous plaît
luh plañ see voo play

40 euro worth of unleaded petrol
quarante euro d'essence sans plomb
ka-roñt uh-roh dess-oñss soñ ploñ

pump number...
pompe numéro...
poñp noo-may-roh...

I'd like to wash the car
je voudrais laver la voiture
zhuh voo-dray la-vay la vwa-toor

how much is that?
c'est combien?
say koñ-byañ

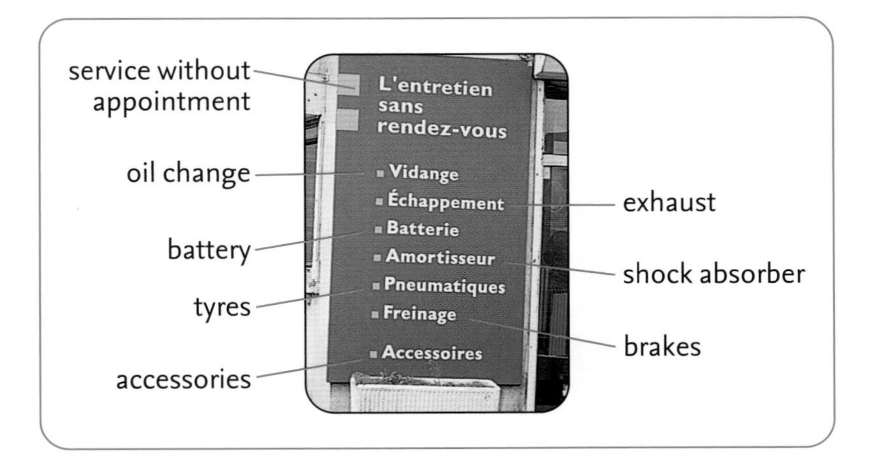

service without appointment — L'entretien sans rendez-vous

oil change — Vidange

exhaust — Échappement

battery — Batterie

shock absorber — Amortisseur

tyres — Pneumatiques

brakes — Freinage

accessories — Accessoires

You should carry a red warning triangle in case of breakdown. It is also advisable to carry a first-aid kit in the car. You will have no trouble in France finding a **garage** to do repairs.

I have broken down
je suis en panne
zhuh swee oñ pan

the car won't start
la voiture ne démarre pas
la vwa-toor nuh day-mar pa

I have a flat tyre
j'ai un pneu crevé
zhay uñ pnuh kruh-vay

the battery is flat
la batterie est à plat
la ba-tree ayt a pla

I need tyres
j'ai besoin de pneus
zhay buh-zwañ duh pnuh

I have run out of petrol
je suis en panne d'essence
zhuh swee oñ pan dess-oñss

where is the nearest garage?
où est le garage le plus proche?
oo ay luh ga-razh luh ploo prosh

something is wrong with...
il y a un problème avec...
eel ee a uñ pro-blehm a-vek...

the ... is not working
le/la ... ne marche pas
luh/la ... nuh marsh pa

the ... are not working
les ... ne marchent pas
lay ... nuh marsh pa

can you repair it?
vous pouvez le réparer?
voo poo-vay luh ray-pa-ray

how long will it take?
ça va prendre combien de temps?
sa va proñdr koñ-byañ duh toñ

when will it be ready?
ça sera prêt quand?
sa suh-ra pray koñ

how much will it cost?
combien ça va coûter?
koñ-byañ sa va koo-tay

can you replace the windscreen?
pouvez-vous changer le pare-brise?
poo-vay voo shoñ-zhay luh par-breez

please check...	**the oil**	**the water**	**the tyres**
vous pouvez vérifier...	l'huile	l'eau	les pneus
voo poo-vay ve-ree-fyay...	*lweel*	*loh*	*lay pnuh*

Emergency

The emergency number is 17 for the police (15 for an ambulance and 18 for the fire brigade). You will see either **Police** or **Gendarmerie** (in smaller towns and villages). You should report all thefts or crimes to them.

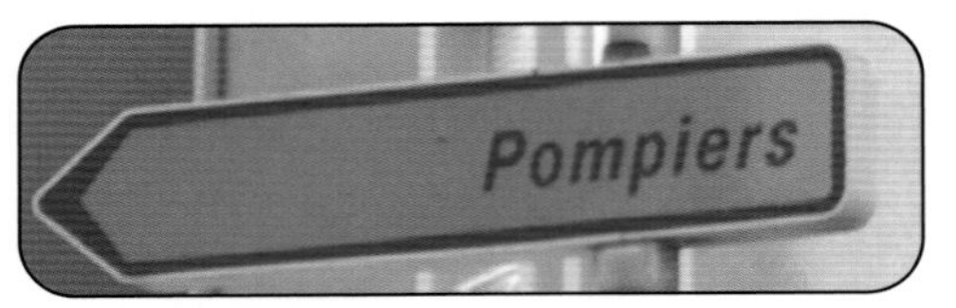

▲ Fire station

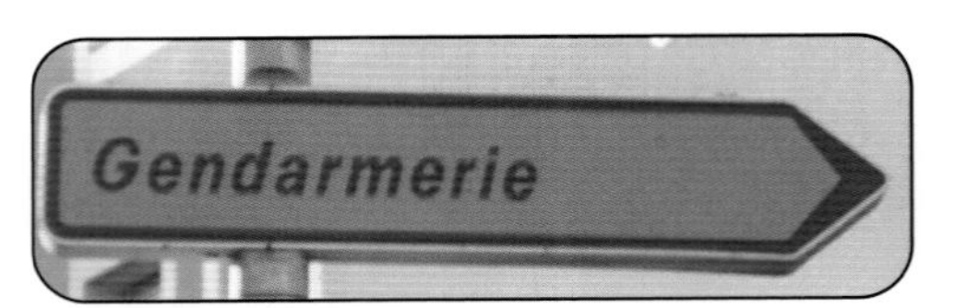

▲ Local police

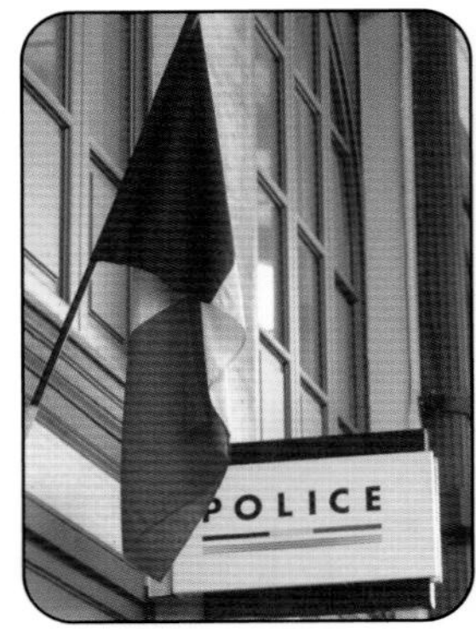

▲ Police station

help!
au secours!
oh suh-koor

can you help me?
vous pouvez m'aider?
voo poo-vay mah-day

please call...
s'il vous plaît! appelez...
seel voo play ap-lay...

the police
la police
la po-leess

an ambulance
une ambulance
oon oñ-boo-loñss

fire!
au feu!
oh fuh

please call the fire brigade!
s'il vous plaît! appelez les pompiers!
seel voo play ap-lay lay poñ-pyay

my ... has been stolen
on m'a volé mon/ma...
oñ ma vo-lay moñ/ma...

I want to report a theft
je veux signaler un vol
zhuh vuh seen-ya-lay uñ vol

here are my insurance details
voici mon assurance
vwa-see moñ a-soo-roñss

please give me your insurance details
votre assurance s'il vous plaît
votr a-soo-roñss seel voo play

where is the police station?
où est la gendarmerie?
oo ay la zhoñ-darm-ree

I would like to phone...
je voudrais appeler...
zhuh voo-dray ap-lay...

my car has been broken into
on a forcé ma voiture
on a for-say ma vwa-toor

I need a report for my insurance
il me faut un constat pour mon assurance
eel muh foh uñ koñ-sta poor mon a-soo-roñss

Regional map of France

▼ Tourist information

French Tourist Office
178 Piccadilly
London
W1J 9AL

Web address: www.franceguide.com
Tel. no.: 0906 8 244 123

Capital city: **Paris**

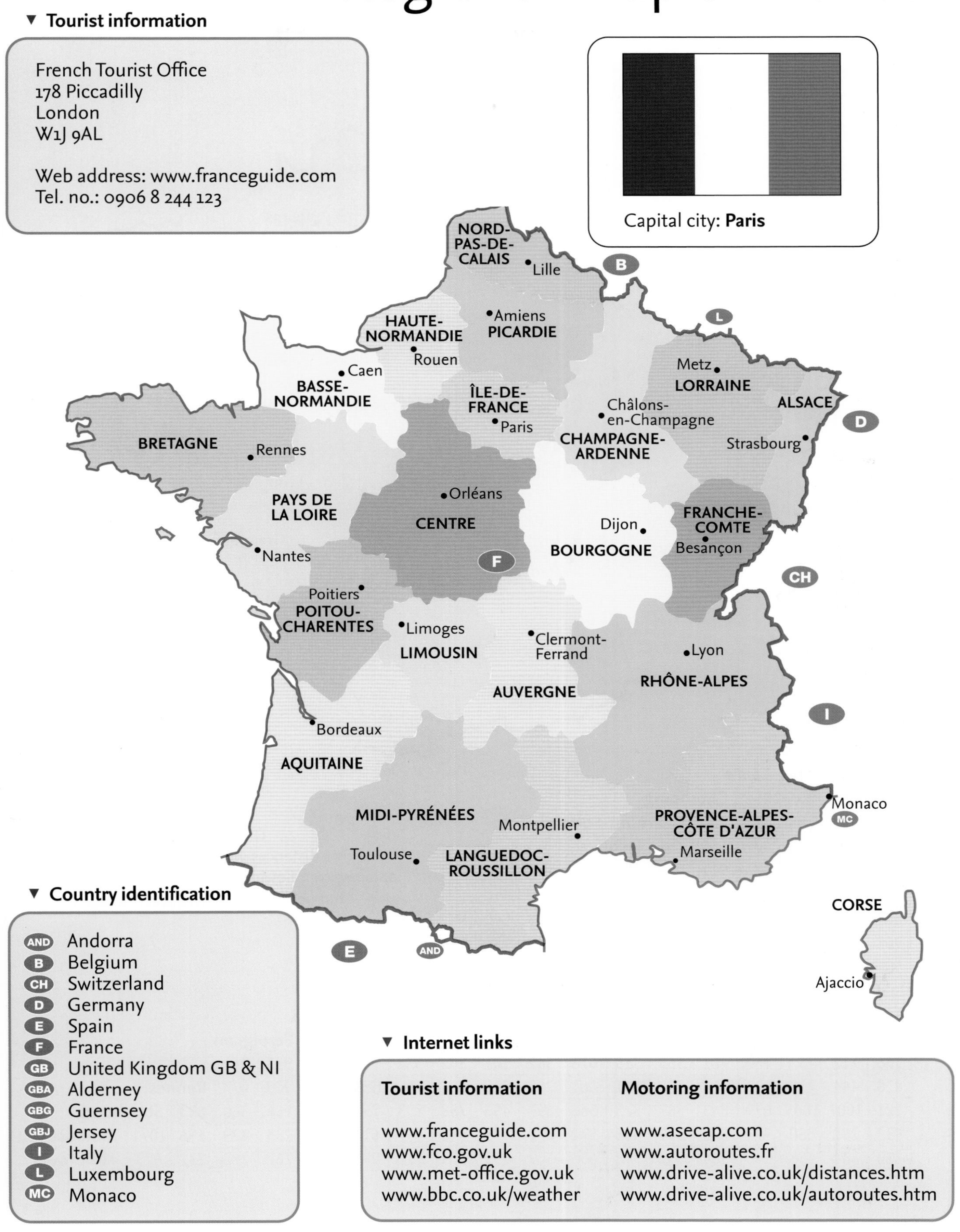

▼ Country identification

AND	Andorra
B	Belgium
CH	Switzerland
D	Germany
E	Spain
F	France
GB	United Kingdom GB & NI
GBA	Alderney
GBG	Guernsey
GBJ	Jersey
I	Italy
L	Luxembourg
MC	Monaco

▼ Internet links

Tourist information	Motoring information
www.franceguide.com	www.asecap.com
www.fco.gov.uk	www.autoroutes.fr
www.met-office.gov.uk	www.drive-alive.co.uk/distances.htm
www.bbc.co.uk/weather	www.drive-alive.co.uk/autoroutes.htm

Distance chart

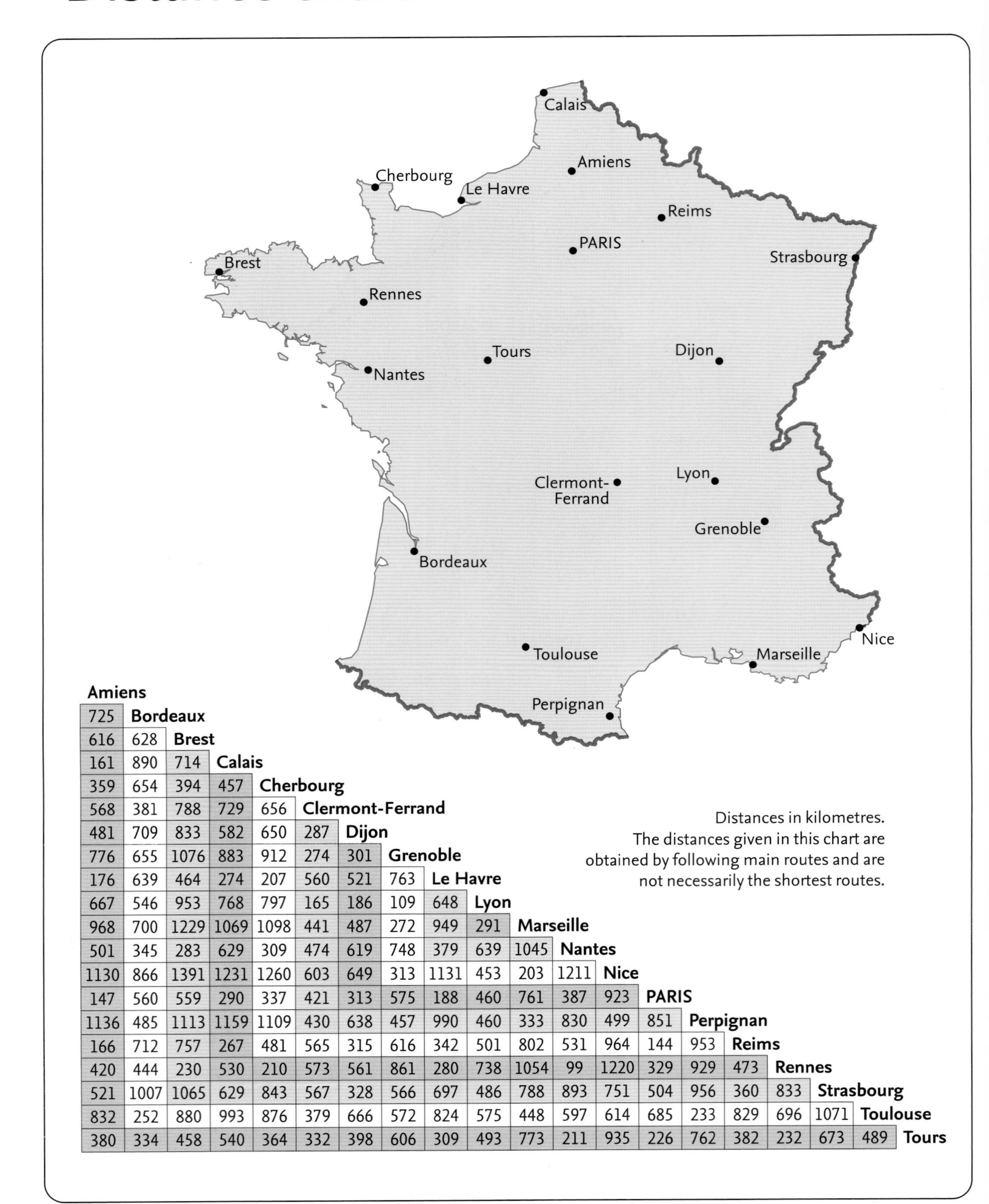

Distances in kilometres.
The distances given in this chart are
obtained by following main routes and are
not necessarily the shortest routes.

Amiens																		
725	**Bordeaux**																	
616	628	**Brest**																
161	890	714	**Calais**															
359	654	394	457	**Cherbourg**														
568	381	788	729	656	**Clermont-Ferrand**													
481	709	833	582	650	287	**Dijon**												
776	655	1076	883	912	274	301	**Grenoble**											
176	639	464	274	207	560	521	763	**Le Havre**										
667	546	953	768	797	165	186	109	648	**Lyon**									
968	700	1229	1069	1098	441	487	272	949	291	**Marseille**								
501	345	283	629	309	474	619	748	379	639	1045	**Nantes**							
1130	866	1391	1231	1260	603	649	313	1131	453	203	1211	**Nice**						
147	560	559	290	337	421	313	575	188	460	761	387	923	**PARIS**					
1136	485	1113	1159	1109	430	638	457	990	460	333	830	499	851	**Perpignan**				
166	712	757	267	481	565	315	616	342	501	802	531	964	144	953	**Reims**			
420	444	230	530	210	573	561	861	280	738	1054	99	1220	329	929	473	**Rennes**		
521	1007	1065	629	843	567	328	566	697	486	788	893	751	504	956	360	833	**Strasbourg**	
832	252	880	993	876	379	666	572	824	575	448	597	614	685	233	829	696	1071	**Toulouse**
380	334	458	540	364	332	398	606	309	493	773	211	935	226	762	382	232	673	489	**Tours**

Key to map pages

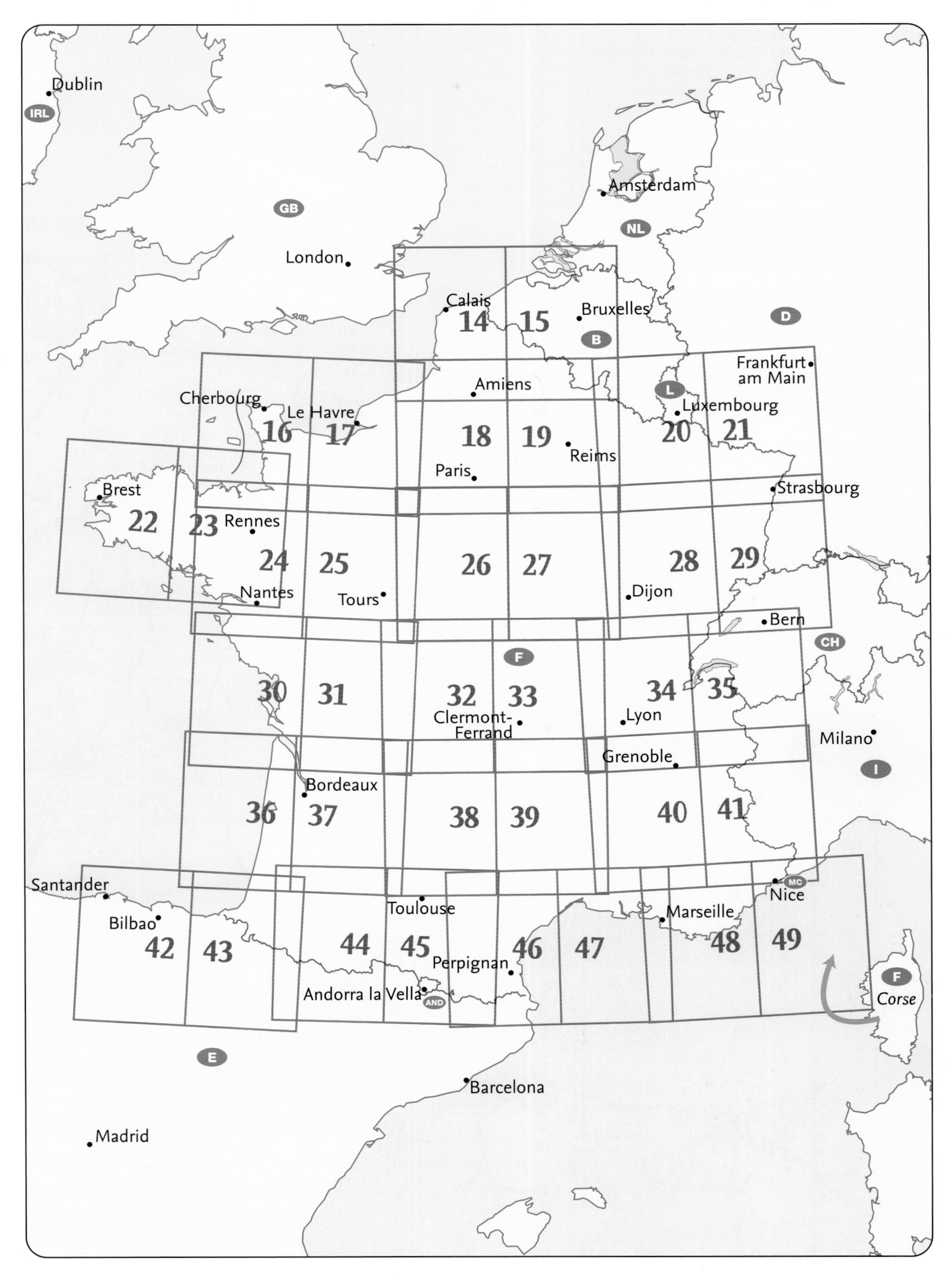

Dublin
IRL
GB
London
Amsterdam
NL
Calais
14
15
Bruxelles
B
D
Frankfurt am Main
Amiens
L
Luxembourg
Cherbourg
Le Havre
16
17
18
19
Reims
20
21
Paris
Brest
Strasbourg
22
23
Rennes
24
25
26
27
28
29
Nantes
Tours
Dijon
Bern
CH
F
30
31
32
33
34
35
Clermont-Ferrand
Lyon
Milano
Grenoble
I
Bordeaux
36
37
38
39
40
41
Santander
MC
Nice
Toulouse
Marseille
Bilbao
42
43
44
45
46
47
48
49
Perpignan
F
Corse
Andorra la Vella
AND
E
Barcelona
Madrid

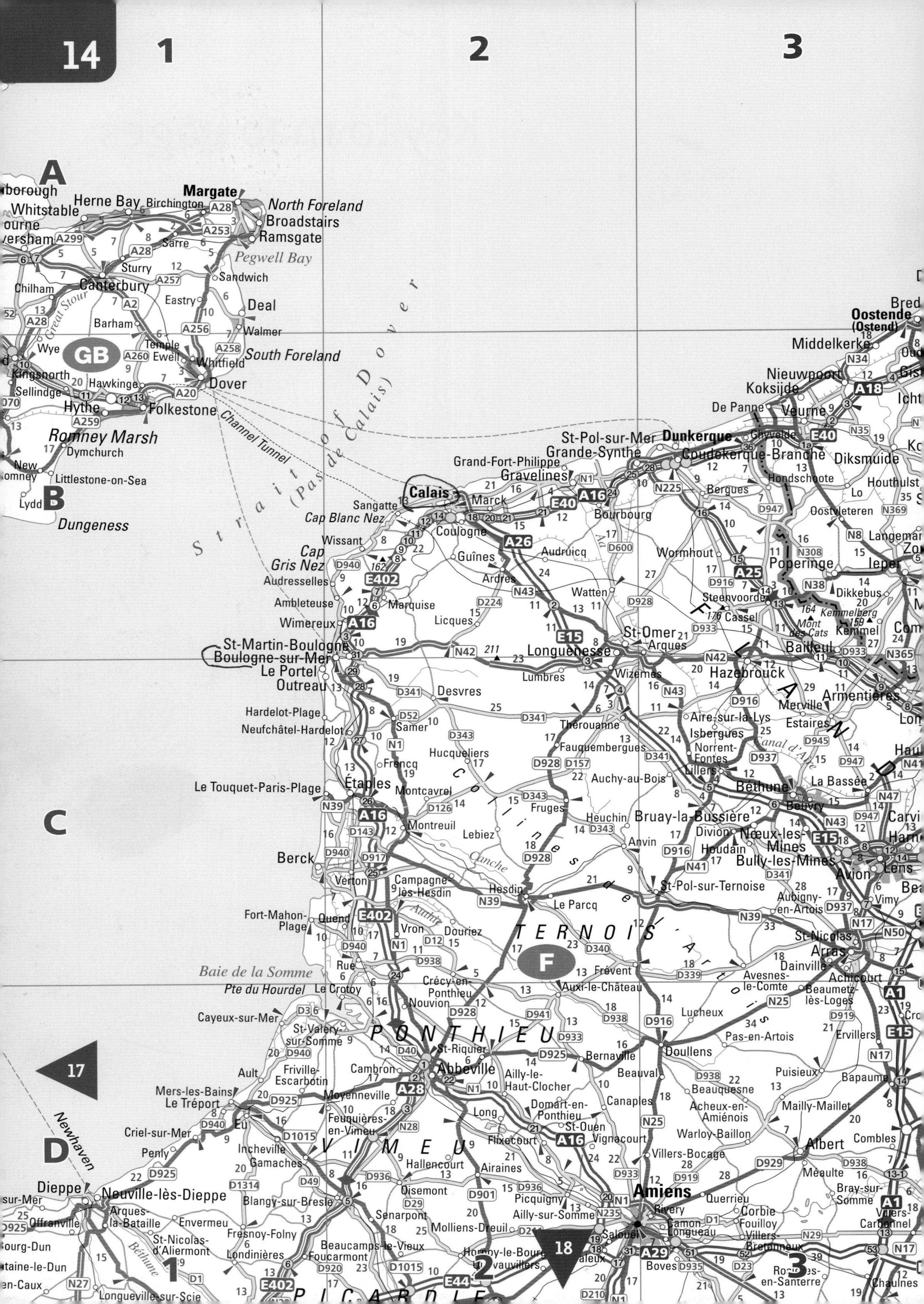
1
2
3
A
B
C
D
Margate
Herne Bay
Birchington
North Foreland
Whitstable
Broadstairs
Ramsgate
Sarre
Pegwell Bay
Sturry
Sandwich
Canterbury
Chilham
Eastry
Deal
Barham
Walmer
GB
Wye
Temple Ewell
Whitfield
South Foreland
Kingsnorth
Hawkinge
Dover
Sellindge
Hythe
Folkestone
Romney Marsh
Dymchurch
New Romney
Littlestone-on-Sea
Lydd
Dungeness
Channel Tunnel
Strait of Dover
(Pas de Calais)
Oostende
(Ostend)
Middelkerke
Nieuwpoort
Koksijde
De Panne
Veurne
St-Pol-sur-Mer
Dunkerque
Grande-Synthe
Grand-Fort-Philippe
Gravelines
Coudekerque-Branche
Diksmuide
Hondschoote
Houthulst
Bergues
Calais
Sangatte
Marck
Cap Blanc Nez
Coulogne
Bourbourg
Oostvleteren
Langemark
Wissant
Audruicq
Wormhout
Poperinge
Ieper
Cap Gris Nez
Guînes
Ardres
Audresselles
Watten
Steenvoorde
Dikkebus
Ambleteuse
Marquise
Cassel
Kemmelberg
Mont des Cats
Kemmel
Wimereux
Licques
St-Omer
Arques
Bailleul
St-Martin-Boulogne
Boulogne-sur-Mer
Longuenesse
Le Portel
Outreau
Lumbres
Wizernes
Hazebrouck
Desvres
Armentières
Hardelot-Plage
Neufchâtel-Hardelot
Samer
Thérouanne
Aire-sur-la-Lys
Merville
Estaires
Isbergues
Fauquembergues
Norrent-Fontes
Canal d'Aire
Frencq
Hucqueliers
Lillers
Auchy-au-Bois
La Bassée
Le Touquet-Paris-Plage
Étaples
Montcavrel
Béthune
Beuvry
Fruges
Montreuil
Heuchin
Bruay-la-Buissière
Lebiez
Nœux-les-Mines
Divion
Houdain
Bully-les-Mines
Anvin
Berck
Canche
Avion
Lens
Verton
Campagne-lès-Hesdin
Hesdin
Le Parcq
St-Pol-sur-Ternoise
Aubigny-en-Artois
Vimy
Fort-Mahon-Plage
Quend
Vron
Douriez
Authie
TERNOIS
St-Nicolas
Arras
Rue
F
Frévent
Dainville
Baie de la Somme
Avesnes-le-Comte
Achicourt
Pte du Hourdel
Le Crotoy
Crécy-en-Ponthieu
Auxi-le-Château
Beaumetz-lès-Loges
Nouvion
Cayeux-sur-Mer
Lucheux
Pas-en-Artois
St-Valery-sur-Somme
PONTHIEU
Ervillers
St-Riquier
Bernaville
Doullens
Ault
Friville-Escarbotin
Cambron
Abbeville
Aïlly-le-Haut-Clocher
Beauval
Puisieux
Bapaume
Mers-les-Bains
Le Tréport
Moyenneville
Beauquesne
Canaples
Feuquières-en-Vimeu
Long
Domart-en-Ponthieu
Acheux-en-Amiénois
Mailly-Maillet
Criel-sur-Mer
Eu
St-Ouen
Warloy-Baillon
Flixecourt
Vignacourt
Combles
Albert
Penly
Incheville
Gamaches
VIMEU
Hallencourt
Airaines
Villers-Bocage
Méaulte
Dieppe
Neuville-lès-Dieppe
Oisemont
Amiens
Bray-sur-Somme
Blangy-sur-Bresle
Picquigny
Querrieu
Rivery
Corbie
Arques-la-Bataille
Envermeu
Senarpont
Ailly-sur-Somme
Camon
Longueau
Fouilloy
Villers-Bretonneux
Fresnoy-Folny
Molliens-Dreuil
Salouël
St-Nicolas-d'Aliermont
Londinières
Beaucamps-le-Vieux
Foucarmont
Hornoy-le-Bourg
Boves
Rosières-en-Santerre
Chaulnes
Longueville-sur-Scie
PICARDIE
Newhaven
Béthune
17
18

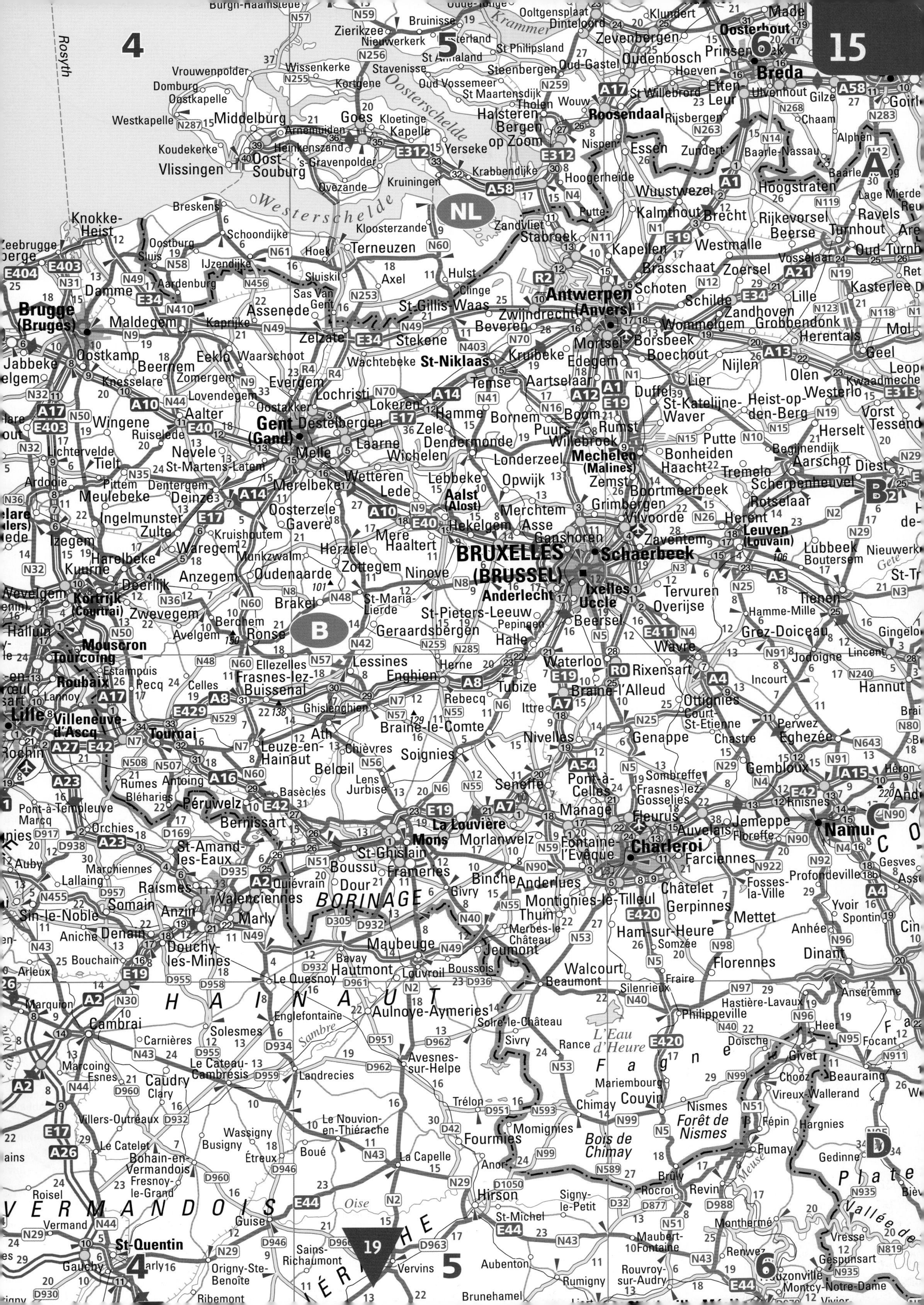
4
5
6
NL
B
A
B
C
D
Rosyth
Zierikzee
Nieuwerkerk
Bruinisse
Oltgensplaat
Dinteloord
Klundert
Zevenbergen
Made
Oosterhout
Breda
Oudenbosch
Prinsenbeek
St Philipsland
St Annaland
Vrouwenpolder
Wissenkerke
Stavenisse
Steenbergen
Oud-Gastel
Hoeven
Domburg
Oostkapelle
Kortgene
Oud Vossemeer
St Maartensdijk
Tholen
Wouw
St Willebrord
Etten-Leur
Ulvenhout
Gilze
Westkapelle
Middelburg
Goes
Kloetinge
Kapelle
Arnemuiden
Halsteren
Bergen op Zoom
Roosendaal
Rijsbergen
Chaam
Koudekerke
Heinkenszand
's-Gravenpolder
Yerseke
Nispen
Essen
Zundert
Baarle-Nassau
Baarle-Hertog
Alphen
Vlissingen
Oost-Souburg
Krabbendijke
Hoogerheide
Ovezande
Kruiningen
Wuustwezel
Hoogstraten
Oosterschelde
Westerschelde
Breskens
Knokke-Heist
Zeebrugge
Oostburg
Sluis
Schoondijke
IJzendijke
Terneuzen
Hoek
Kloosterzande
Zandvliet
Stabroek
Putte
Kalmthout
Brecht
Rijkevorsel
Ravels
Beerse
Turnhout
Lage Mierde
Westmalle
Kapellen
Brasschaat
Zoersel
Vosselaar
Oud-Turnhout
Aardenburg
Sluiskil
Axel
Hulst
Clinge
Schoten
Schilde
Lille
Kasterlee
Damme
Brugge (Bruges)
Maldegem
Kaprijke
Assenede
Sas Van Gent
St-Gillis-Waas
Zwijndrecht
Antwerpen (Anvers)
Zandhoven
Grobbendonk
Herentals
Mol
Beveren
Wommelgem
Borsbeek
Mortsel
Zelzate
Stekene
Jabbeke
Oostkamp
Beernem
Eeklo
Waarschoot
Wachtebeke
St-Niklaas
Kruibeke
Edegem
Boechout
Nijlen
Geel
Zomergem
Evergem
Temse
Aartselaar
Lier
Olen
Leopoldsburg
Knesselare
Lovendegem
Lochristi
Lokeren
Hamme
Bornem
Boom
Duffel
St-Katelijne-Waver
Heist-op-den-Berg
Westerlo
Kwaadmechelen
Aalter
Oostakker
Gent (Gand)
Destelbergen
Zele
Puurs
Rumst
Vorst
Tessenderlo
Wingene
Ruiselede
Dendermonde
Willebroek
Putte
Herselt
Nevele
Melle
Laarne
Wichelen
Londerzeel
Mechelen (Malines)
Bonheiden
Begijnendijk
Aarschot
Diest
Lichtervelde
Tielt
St-Martens-Latem
Merelbeke
Wetteren
Lebbeke
Opwijk
Haacht
Tremelo
Ardooie
Pittem
Dentergem
Lede
Aalst (Alost)
Zemst
Boortmeerbeek
Scherpenheuvel
Meulebeke
Deinze
Oosterzele
Merchtem
Grimbergen
Rotselaar
Ingelmunster
Zulte
Gavere
Hekelgem
Asse
Vilvoorde
Herent
Leuven (Louvain)
Izegem
Kruishoutem
Mere
Haaltert
Ganshoren
Zaventem
Lubbeek
Harelbeke
Waregem
Munkzwalm
Herzele
BRUXELLES (BRUSSEL)
Schaerbeek
Boutersem
Kuurne
Anzegem
Oudenaarde
Zottegem
Ninove
Tervuren
Tienen
Deerlijk
Wevelgem
Kortrijk (Courtrai)
Zwevegem
Brakel
St-Maria-Lierde
Anderlecht
Ixelles
Uccle
Overijse
Hamme-Mille
Halluin
Mouscron
Avelgem
Berchem
Ronse
Geraardsbergen
St-Pieters-Leeuw
Pepingen
Halle
Beersel
Grez-Doiceau
Tourcoing
Roubaix
Lannoy
Estaimpuis
Pecq
Celles
Ellezelles
Frasnes-lez-Buissenal
Lessines
Herne
Enghien
Tubize
Waterloo
Rixensart
Wavre
Jodoigne
Incourt
Hannut
Lille
Villeneuve-d'Ascq
Tournai
Ghislenghien
Rebecq
Ittre
Braine-l'Alleud
Ottignies
Court-St-Etienne
Perwez
Eghezée
Ath
Braine-le-Comte
Nivelles
Genappe
Chastre
Leuze-en-Hainaut
Chièvres
Soignies
Beloeil
Lens
Jurbise
Seneffe
Pont-à-Celles
Sombreffe
Gembloux
Rumes
Antoing
Bléharies
Basècles
Péruwelz
Frasnes-lez-Gosselies
Manage
Fleurus
Pont-à-Templeuve
Marcq
Orchies
Bernissart
La Louvière
Auvelais
Jemeppe
Namur
St-Amand-les-Eaux
Mons
St-Ghislain
Morlanwelz
Fontaine-l'Evêque
Charleroi
Floreffe
Farciennes
Boussu
Frameries
Binche
Anderlues
Châtelet
Profondeville
Gesves
Marchiennes
Lallaing
Raismes
Quiévrain
Dour
Givry
Fosses-la-Ville
Gerpinnes
Somain
Anzin
Valenciennes
BORINAGE
Montignies-le-Tilleul
Thuin
Mettet
Yvoir
Spontin
Sin-le-Noble
Marly
Merbes-le-Château
Ham-sur-Heure
Anhée
Aniche
Denain
Douchy-les-Mines
Maubeuge
Bavay
Jeumont
Somzée
Dinant
Bouchain
Hautmont
Louvroil
Boussois
Walcourt
Beaumont
Florennes
Arleux
Le Quesnoy
Silenrieux
Fraire
Marquion
Cambrai
Englefontaine
Aulnoye-Aymeries
Solre-le-Château
Philippeville
Hastière-Lavaux
Anseremme
Carnières
Solesmes
Sivry
Rance
L'Eau d'Heure
Heer
Focant
H A I N A U T
Marcoing
Esnes
Caudry
Clary
Le Cateau-Cambrésis
Landrecies
Avesnes-sur-Helpe
Doische
Givet
F a g n e
Villers-Outréaux
Trélon
Mariembourg
Couvin
Chimay
Beauraing
Chooz
Vireux-Wallerand
Le Catelet
Wassigny
Busigny
Étreux
Le Nouvion-en-Thiérache
Momignies
Fourmies
Bois de Chimay
Nismes
Forêt de Nismes
Fépin
Hargnies
Bohain-en-Vermandois
Fresnoy-le-Grand
Boué
La Capelle
Anor
Fumay
Gedinne
Roisel
Hirson
Signy-le-Petit
Rocroi
Revin
Brûly
Meuse
Oise
Guise
VERMANDOIS
Vermand
St-Michel
Monthermé
Vallée de
Plateau
Bièvre
St-Quentin
Gauchy
Origny-Ste-Benoîte
Sains-Richaumont
Vervins
Aubenton
Rumigny
Maubert-Fontaine
Rouvroy-sur-Audry
Renwez
Vresse
Gespunsart
Nouzonville
Montcy-Notre-Dame
Ribemont
Brunehamel
THIÉRACHE
Sambre
Gete
Krammer
19
E312
E313
E403
E404
E34
E17
E40
E19
E411
E42
E429
E420
E44
A1
A4
A7
A8
A10
A12
A13
A14
A15
A16
A17
A2
A21
A23
A26
A27
A54
A58
R0
R2
R4

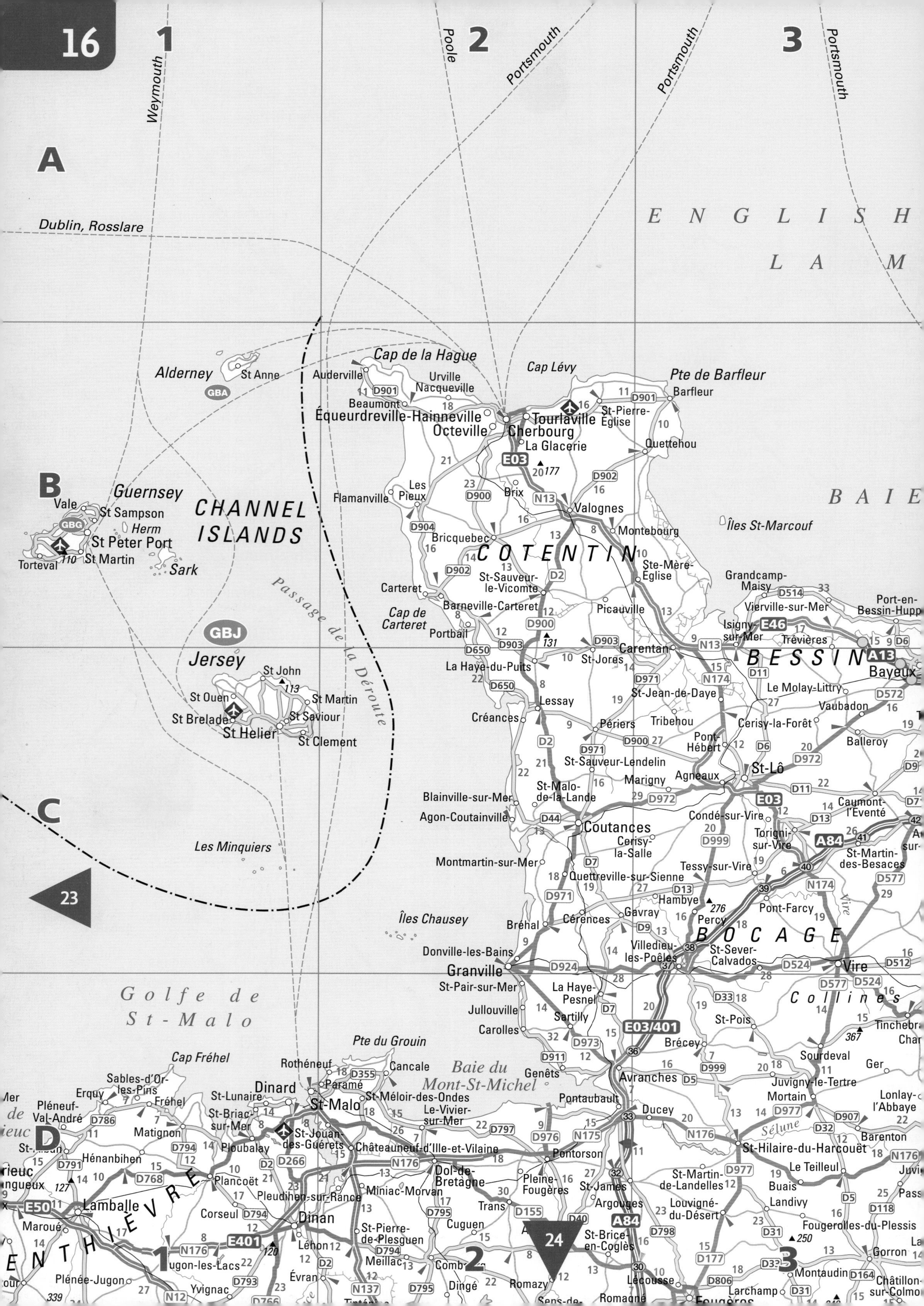

1 Weymouth 2 Poole Portsmouth Portsmouth 3 Portsmouth

A

Dublin, Rosslare

E N G L I S H
L A M

Cap de la Hague   Cap Lévy   Pte de Barfleur

Alderney   St Anne   Auderville   St-Pierre-   Barfleur
GBA   11 D901   Urville   16 D901   Église 11 D901
                                    Nacqueville   Cherbourg   10
                      Beaumont   18   Quettehou
            Équeurdreville-Hainneville   Tourlaville
                      Octeville   Cherbourg
                                    La Glacerie   E03
B   Vale   Guernsey   21   20 177
    St Sampson   23   Brix   D902
GBG   Herm   Les   D900   N13   16   Montebourg
    St Peter Port   Flamanville   Pieux   Valognes
Torteval 110 St Martin   16   8   Ste-Mère-
                        Sark   D904   13   Église
                                    Bricquebec   13
    CHANNEL   16   10
    ISLANDS   14   D902   D2   8   Grandcamp-
                          13   St-Sauveur-   Maisy   D514 33
GBJ   Carteret   le-Vicomte   Vierville-sur-Mer   Port-en-
                          Barneville-Carteret   12 D900   Isigny-   E46 Bessin-Hupp
    Jersey   St John   Portbail   12   131   D903   sur-Mer   15 9 D6
        113   D650   D903   10   Carentan   N13   A13
    St Ouen   St Martin   La Haye-du-Puits   10 St-Jores   14   BESSIN Bayeux
    St Brelade   St Saviour   22   8   N174   D572
    St Helier   St Clement   D650   Lessay   19   St-Jean-de-Daye   D11   Le Molay-Littry   19
                          Créances   9 Périers   Tribehou   D6   27   Cerisy-la-Forêt   Vaubadon
                                            D2   D971   D900 27   Pont-   12   Balleroy
                                        21   St-Sauveur-Lendelin   Hébert   20   D972   D9
                          Les Minquiers   22   Marigny   Agneaux   St-Lô   E03   D11
C 23   Blainville-sur-Mer   St-Malo-   16   D972   29   Condé-sur-Vire   14   Caumont-
                              D44   de-la-Lande   D999   20   D13   l'Eventé
                          Agon-Coutainville   13   Coutances   Cerisy-   Torigni-   A84   42
                          Montmartin-sur-Mer   D7   la-Salle   sur-Vire   40   26   A
                                        18 Quettreville-   D971   Tessy-sur-Vire   19   St-Martin-   D577
        Îles Chausey   sur-Sienne   19   27   D13   39   des-Besaces   N174
                          Bréhal   Cérences   D9   13 Hambye   276   Pont-Farcy   Vire   29
                                    9   16 Gavray   Percy   BOCAGE   19
                          Donville-les-Bains   14   Villedieu-   38   St-Sever-   D512
    Golfe de   Granville   D924   les-Poêles   37   Calvados   D524   Vire   16
    St-Malo   St-Pair-sur-Mer   28   28   D524
                                    La Haye-   D33 18   St-Pois   Collines   D577
                      Jullouville   Pesnel   D7   20   19   14   15
        Cap Fréhel   Carolles   32   Sartilly   E03/401   Brécey   367 Tinchebra
                      Rothéneuf   Cancale   Genêts   D973 12   36   D999   7   Sourdeval   Char
    Sables-d'Or-   D355   Baie du   D911   18   18   Juvigny-le-Tertre   Ger
    les-Pins   Paramé   Mont-St-Michel   Avranches   D5   16   Mortain   Lonlay-
    Erquy 7 Fréhel   St-Méloir-des-Ondes   D999   l'Abbaye
D   Pléneuf-   St-Lunaire Dinard   Le-Vivier-   Pontaubault   33   13 14 D977   Barenton   N176
    Val-André   St-Briac-   St-Malo   sur-Mer   Ducey   20   Séluine   St-Hilaire-du-Harcouët   D32
    D786   sur-Mer   8   22 D797   Pontorson   N175   N176   D907   Juvi
    Matignon 14   St-Jouan-   Châteauneuf-d'Ille-et-Vilaine   D976   15   32   St-Martin-   Le Teilleul   18
    Hénanbihen   des-Guérets   N176   Dol-de-   16   de-Landelles   D977   Buais   D5   25 Pass
    D794   Ploubalay   D266   Bretagne   Pleine-   St-James   19   Louvigné-   16   D118
    Plancoët   Pleudihen-sur-Rance   Miniac-Morvan   Fougères   Argouges   du-Désert   Landivy   Fougerolles-du-Plessis
    Corseul   D794   Trans   D155   A84   La
    Lamballe   Dinan   Cuguen   30   250   D798   D31   Gorron
    D12 Lugon-les-Lacs   Léhon   D795   D40   St-Brice-   D177   Montaudin   D164   Châtillon-
    Plénée-Jugon   Évran   Dingé   Comb   en-Coglès   D806   Larchamp   sur-Colmo
    339   D793   D766   Romazy   30   Romagné   Lécousse

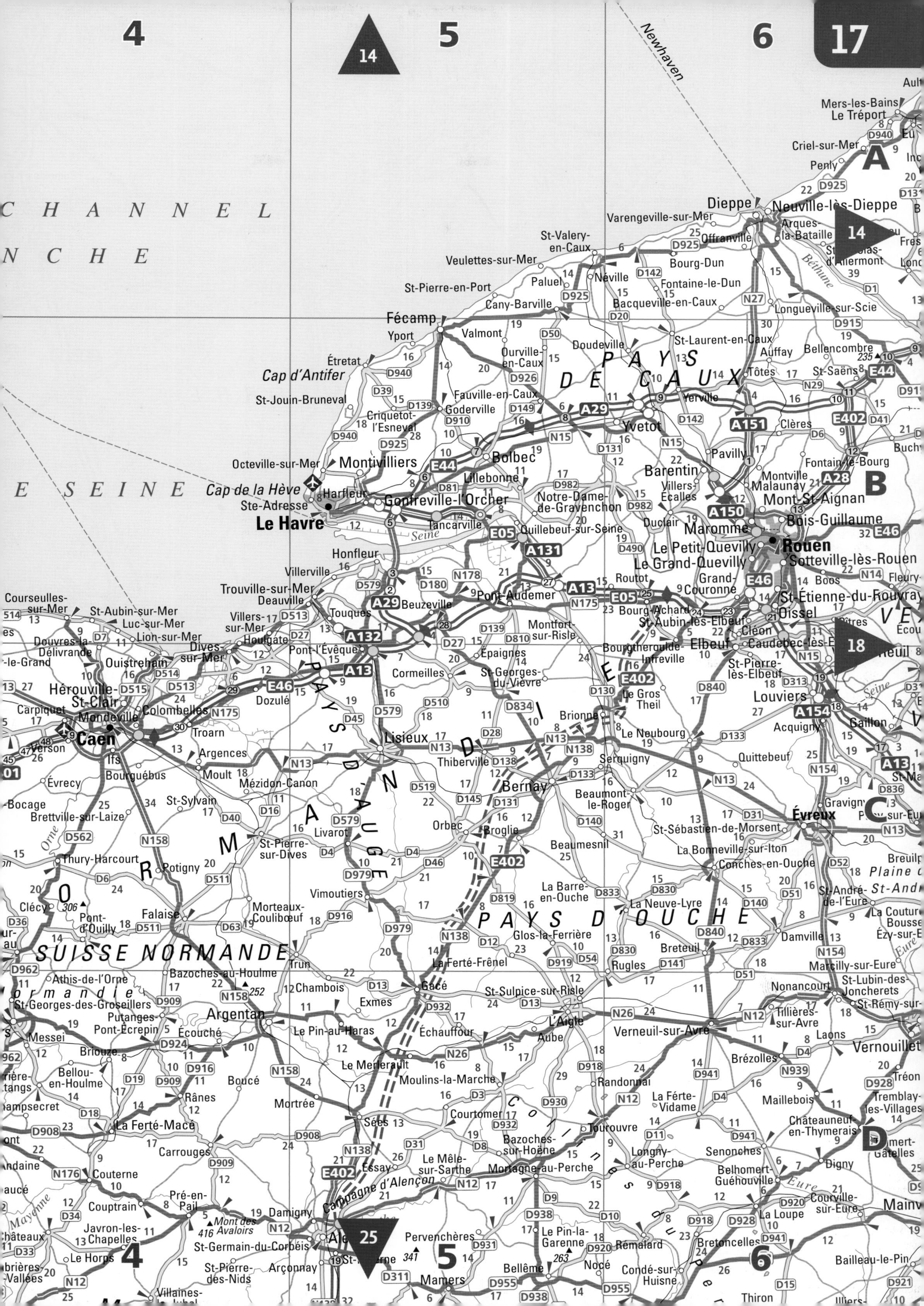

17
4
5
6
14
Newhaven
CHANNEL
NCHE
E SEINE
Mers-les-Bains
Le Tréport
Eu
Criel-sur-Mer
Penly
A
Dieppe
Neuville-lès-Dieppe
Varengeville-sur-Mer
Arques-la-Bataille
Offranville
St-Valery-en-Caux
Veulettes-sur-Mer
Bourg-Dun
Paluel
Néville
Fontaine-le-Dun
St-Pierre-en-Port
Bacqueville-en-Caux
Cany-Barville
Longueville-sur-Scie
Fécamp
Yport
Valmont
Doudeville
St-Laurent-en-Caux
Auffay
Bellencombre
Étretat
Ourville-en-Caux
Cap d'Antifer
PAYS DE CAUX
Tôtes
St-Saëns
St-Jouin-Bruneval
Fauville-en-Caux
Yerville
Criquetot-l'Esneval
Goderville
Yvetot
Clères
Bolbec
Pavilly
Fontaine-le-Bourg
Octeville-sur-Mer
Montivilliers
Barentin
Lillebonne
Montville
Malaunay
B
Cap de la Hève
Harfleur
Notre-Dame-de-Gravenchon
Villers-Écalles
Mont-St-Aignan
Ste-Adresse
Gonfreville-l'Orcher
Le Havre
Tancarville
Duclair
Maromme
Bois-Guillaume
Quillebeuf-sur-Seine
Seine
Honfleur
Le Petit-Quevilly
Rouen
Le Grand-Quevilly
Sotteville-lès-Rouen
Villerville
Routot
Grand-Couronne
Boos
Trouville-sur-Mer
Deauville
Pont-Audemer
Beuzeville
Bourg-Achard
St-Étienne-du-Rouvray
Courseulles-sur-Mer
St-Aubin-sur-Mer
Luc-sur-Mer
Lion-sur-Mer
Villers-sur-Mer
Touques
Houlgate
St-Aubin-lès-Elbeuf
Oissel
Montfort-sur-Risle
Cléon
Douvres-la-Délivrande
Dives-sur-Mer
Pont-l'Évêque
Épaignes
Bourgtheroulde-Infreville
Elbeuf
Caudebec-lès-Elbeuf
Ouistreham
Cormeilles
St-Georges-du-Vièvre
St-Pierre-lès-Elbeuf
Hérouville-St-Clair
Dozulé
Le Gros Theil
Louviers
Carpiquet
Mondeville
Colombelles
Brionne
Caen
Troarn
Lisieux
Le Neubourg
Acquigny
Gaillon
Verson
Argences
Thiberville
Serquigny
Quittebeuf
Ifs
Bourguébus
Moult
Évrecy
Mézidon-Canon
Bernay
Beaumont-le-Roger
Bocage
Brettville-sur-Laize
St-Sylvain
Orbec
Gravigny
Évreux
C
Livarot
Broglie
St-Sébastien-de-Morsent
Orne
St-Pierre-sur-Dives
Beaumesnil
La Bonneville-sur-Iton
Thury-Harcourt
Potigny
Conches-en-Ouche
Plaine
Vimoutiers
La Barre-en-Ouche
St-André-de-l'Eure
Clécy
Morteaux-Coulibœuf
La Neuve-Lyre
Pont-d'Ouilly
Falaise
PAYS D'OUCHE
Glos-la-Ferrière
Damville
SUISSE NORMANDE
Trun
La Ferté-Frênel
Breteuil
Rugles
Marcilly-sur-Eure
Athis-de-l'Orne
Bazoches-au-Houlme
Chambois
Gacé
St-Sulpice-sur-Risle
Nonancourt
St-Lubin-des-Joncherets
St-Georges-des-Groseillers
Putanges-Pont-Écrepin
Exmes
St-Rémy-sur-Avre
Argentan
L'Aigle
Tillières-sur-Avre
Messei
Écouché
Le Pin-au-Haras
Échauffour
Verneuil-sur-Avre
Aube
Laons
Vernouillet
Briouze
Le Merlerault
Brézolles
Bellou-en-Houlme
Bouce
Moulins-la-Marche
Randonnai
Tréon
Rânes
Mortrée
La Ferté-Vidame
Maillebois
Tremblay-les-Villages
La Ferté-Macé
Sées
Courtomer
Tourouvre
Châteauneuf-en-Thymerais
D
Carrouges
Bazoches-sur-Hoëne
Longny-au-Perche
Senonches
Gâtelles
Couterne
Essay
Le Mêle-sur-Sarthe
Mortagne-au-Perche
Digny
Belhomert-Guéhouville
Campagne d'Alençon
Eure
Courville-sur-Eure
Pré-en-Pail
Couptrain
Damigny
Mont des Avaloirs
Javron-les-Chapelles
Mayenne
Le Pin-la-Garenne
La Loupe
Alençon
Pervenchères
Rémalard
Bretoncelles
Le Horps
St-Germain-du-Corbéis
Bailleau-le-Pin
St-Pierre-des-Nids
Arçonnay
Bellême
Noce
Condé-sur-Huisne
Mamers
Villaines-la-Juhel
Thiron
COLLINES DU PERCHE
PAYS D'AUGE
NORMANDIE
A13
A29
A28
A131
A132
A150
A151
A154
E05
E44
E46
E402
N13
N12
N26
N138
N158
N175
N154

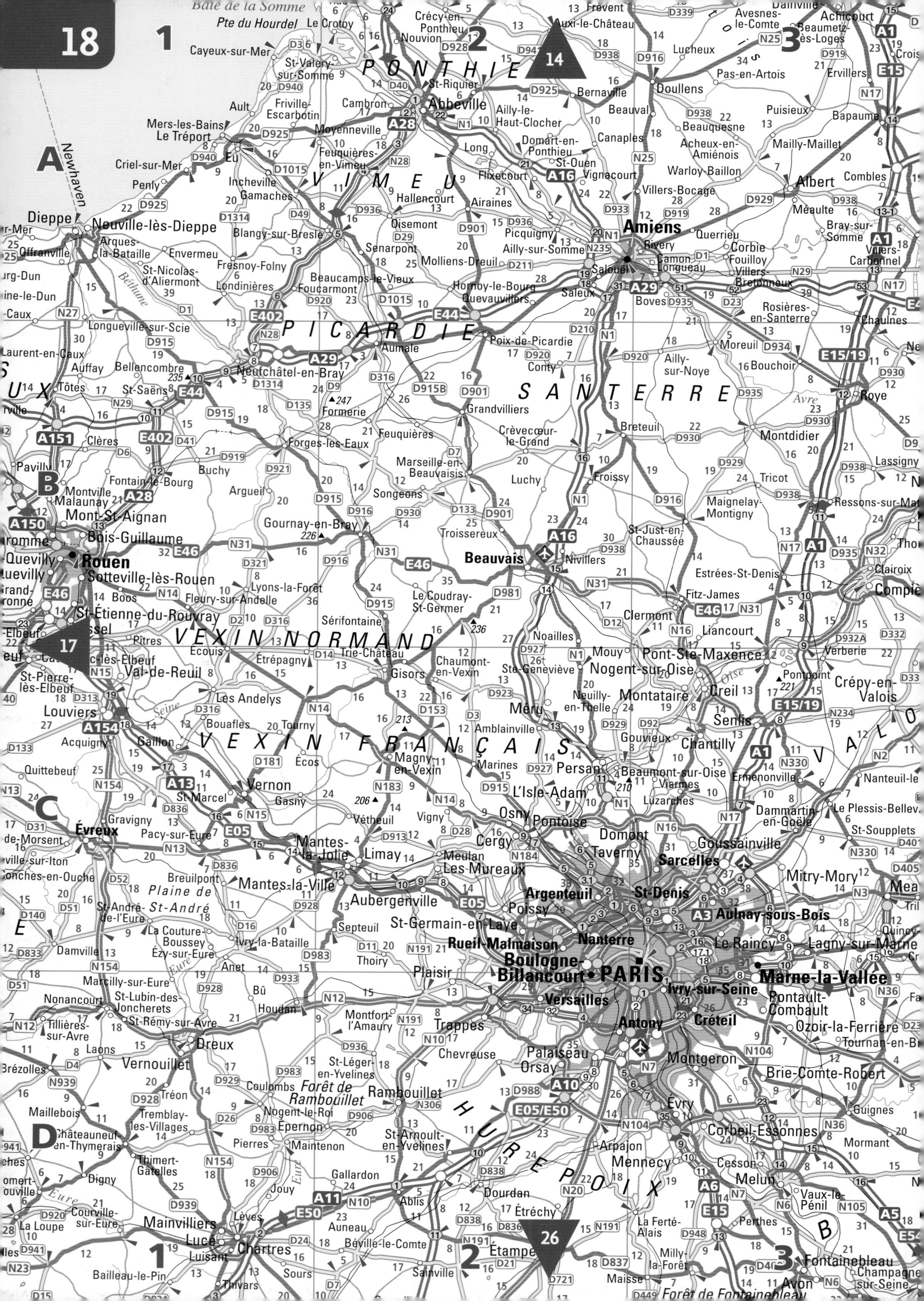

18
1
2
3
A
B
C
D
14
17
26
Baie de la Somme
Pte du Hourdel
Le Crotoy
Cayeux-sur-Mer
St-Valery-sur-Somme
Crécy-en-Ponthieu
Nouvion
PONTHIEU
Auxi-le-Château
Frévent
Avesnes-le-Comte
Achicourt
Beaumetz-lès-Loges
Lucheux
Pas-en-Artois
Ervillers
Doullens
Bernaville
St-Riquier
Abbeville
Cambron
Friville-Escarbotin
Ault
Mers-les-Bains
Le Tréport
Moyenneville
Feuquières-en-Vimeu
Aily-le-Haut-Clocher
Domart-en-Ponthieu
Beauval
Canaples
Beauquesne
Acheux-en-Amiénois
Puisieux
Bapaume
Mailly-Maillet
Newhaven
Criel-sur-Mer
Eu
Penly
Incheville
Gamaches
VIMEU
Hallencourt
Long
Flixecourt
St-Ouen
Vignacourt
Warloy-Baillon
Albert
Combles
Villers-Bocage
Dieppe
Neuville-lès-Dieppe
Offranville
Arques-la-Bataille
Envermeu
Blangy-sur-Bresle
Oisemont
Airaines
Picquigny
Ailly-sur-Somme
Amiens
Querrieu
Méaulte
Bray-sur-Somme
Rivery
Camon
Longueau
Corbie
Fouilloy
Villers-Bretonneux
Villers-Carbonnel
Fresnoy-Folny
St-Nicolas-d'Aliermont
Londinières
Senarpont
Molliens-Dreuil
Salouël
Saleux
Boves
Béthune
Beaucamps-le-Vieux
Foucarmont
Hornoy-le-Bourg
Quevauvillers
Rosières-en-Santerre
Chaulnes
Longueville-sur-Scie
PICARDIE
Aumale
Poix-de-Picardie
Conty
Moreuil
Ailly-sur-Noye
Bouchoir
Auffay
Bellencombre
Neufchâtel-en-Bray
Tôtes
St-Saëns
Formerie
Grandvilliers
SANTERRE
Roye
Avre
Clères
Forges-les-Eaux
Feuquières
Crèvecœur-le-Grand
Breteuil
Montdidier
Lassigny
Buchy
Fontaine-le-Bourg
Montville
Malaunay
Argueil
Marseille-en-Beauvaisis
Songeons
Luchy
Froissy
Tricot
Maignelay-Montigny
Ressons-sur-Matz
Mont-St-Aignan
Bois-Guillaume
Rouen
Gournay-en-Bray
Troissereux
Beauvais
St-Just-en-Chaussée
Nivillers
Estrées-St-Denis
Clairoix
Compiègne
Sotteville-lès-Rouen
Lyons-la-Forêt
Fleury-sur-Andelle
Boos
St-Étienne-du-Rouvray
Le Coudray-St-Germer
Sérifontaine
Clermont
Fitz-James
Liancourt
VEXIN NORMAND
Pîtres
Écouis
Étrépagny
Trie-Château
Gisors
Chaumont-en-Vexin
Noailles
Mouy
Ste-Geneviève
Nogent-sur-Oise
Pont-Ste-Maxence
Verberie
Pontpoint
Crépy-en-Valois
St-Pierre-lès-Elbeuf
Val-de-Reuil
Les Andelys
Louviers
Seine
Bouafles
Tourny
Méru
Neuilly-en-Thelle
Montataire
Creil
Senlis
Chantilly
Gouvieux
Amblainville
VEXIN FRANÇAIS
VALOIS
Acquigny
Gaillon
Écos
Magny-en-Vexin
Marines
Persan
Beaumont-sur-Oise
Viarmes
Ermenonville
Nanteuil-le-Haudouin
Quittebeuf
Vernon
St-Marcel
Gasny
L'Isle-Adam
Luzarches
Dammartin-en-Goële
Le Plessis-Belleville
Évreux
Gravigny
Pacy-sur-Eure
Vétheuil
Vigny
Osny
Pontoise
Domont
Goussainville
St-Soupplets
Mantes-la-Jolie
Limay
Meulan
Les Mureaux
Cergy
Taverny
Sarcelles
Mitry-Mory
Conches-en-Ouche
Breuilpont
Plaine de St-André
Mantes-la-Ville
Aubergenville
Argenteuil
St-Denis
Aulnay-sous-Bois
St-André-de-l'Eure
La Couture-Boussey
Ézy-sur-Eure
Ivry-la-Bataille
Septeuil
St-Germain-en-Laye
Poissy
Nanterre
Le Raincy
Lagny-sur-Marne
Damville
Anet
Thoiry
Rueil-Malmaison
Boulogne-Billancourt
PARIS
Marne-la-Vallée
Marcilly-sur-Eure
Bû
Plaisir
Ivry-sur-Seine
Nonancourt
St-Lubin-des-Joncherets
Houdan
Montfort-l'Amaury
Trappes
Versailles
Antony
Créteil
Pontault-Combault
Ozoir-la-Ferrière
Tillières-sur-Avre
St-Rémy-sur-Avre
Dreux
Tournan-en-Brie
Brézolles
Laons
Vernouillet
St-Léger-en-Yvelines
Chevreuse
Palaiseau
Orsay
Montgeron
Brie-Comte-Robert
Tréon
Coulombs
Forêt de Rambouillet
Rambouillet
HUREPOIX
Évry
Guignes
Maillebois
Tremblay-les-Villages
Nogent-le-Roi
Épernon
St-Arnoult-en-Yvelines
Corbeil-Essonnes
Mormant
Châteauneuf-en-Thymerais
Pierres
Maintenon
Arpajon
Mennecy
Cesson
Thimert-Gâtelles
Digny
Gallardon
Jouy
Dourdan
Melun
Vaux-le-Pénil
Eure
Courville-sur-Eure
La Loupe
Mainvilliers
Lèves
Lucé
Luisant
Chartres
Ablis
Auneau
Étréchy
La Ferté-Alais
Perthes
Béville-le-Comte
Étampes
Milly-la-Forêt
Fontainebleau
Champagne-sur-Seine
Bailleau-le-Pin
Thivars
Sours
Sainville
Maisse
Forêt de Fontainebleau
Avon

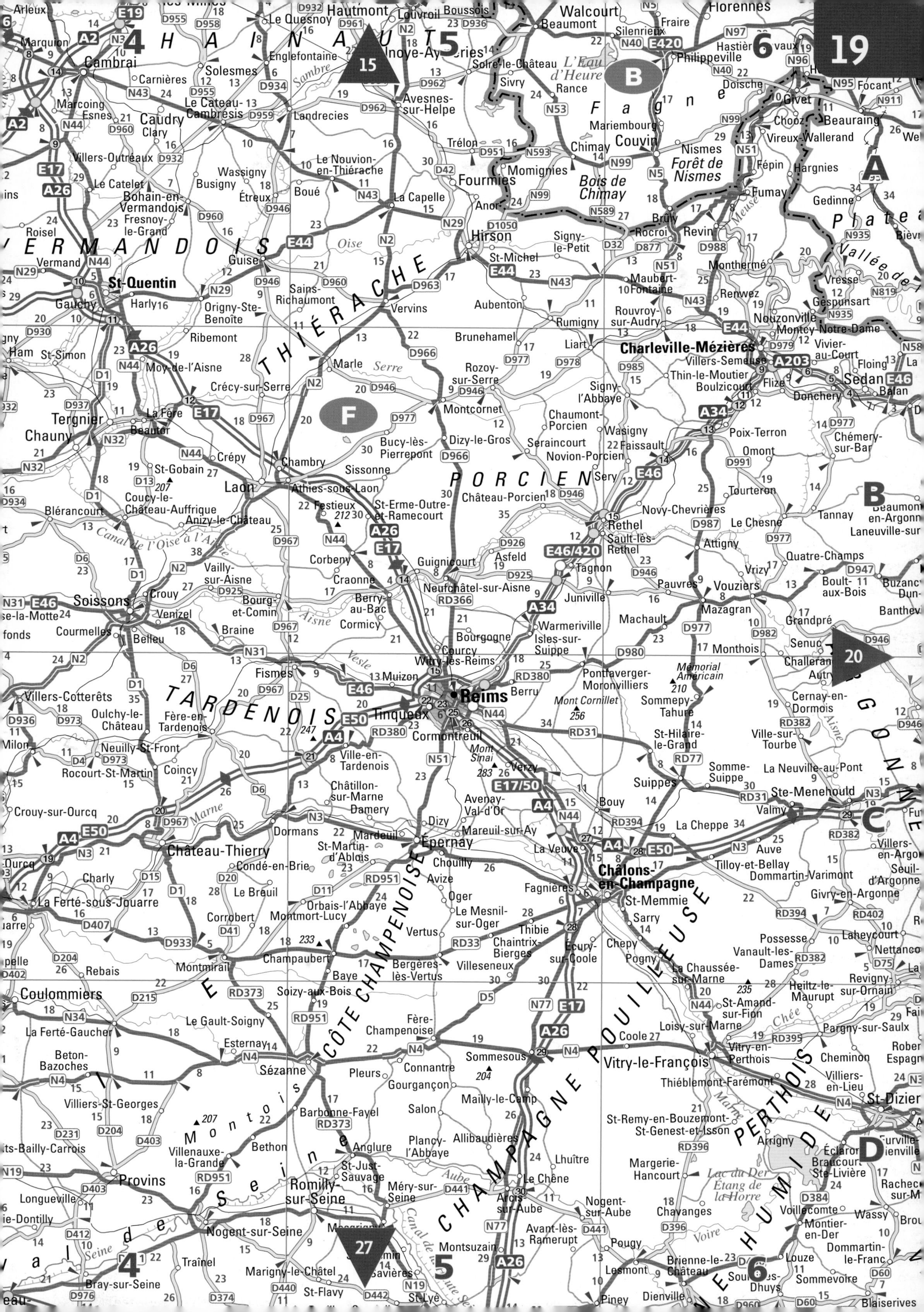
19
HAINAUT
Arleux
Marquion
Cambrai
Carnières
Solesmes
Le Quesnoy
Englefontaine
Hautmont
Louvroil
Boussois
Sambre
Marcoing
Esnes
Caudry
Clary
Le Cateau-Cambrésis
Landrecies
Avesnes-sur-Helpe
Villers-Outréaux
Le Catelet
Bohain-en-Vermandois
Fresnoy-le-Grand
Wassigny
Busigny
Étreux
Boué
Le Nouvion-en-Thiérache
La Capelle
Fourmies
Trélon
Anor
Momignies
Chimay
Bois de Chimay
Couvin
Nismes
Forêt de Nismes
Mariembourg
Fagne
Walcourt
Beaumont
Silenrieux
Florennes
Fraire
Philippeville
Hastière
Solre-le-Château
L'Eau d'Heure
Sivry
Rance
Doische
Givet
Chooz
Beauraing
Focant
Vireux-Wallerand
Fépin
Hargnies
Fumay
Gedinne
Plateau
Vallée de
Revin
Rocroi
Brûly
Signy-le-Petit
Hirson
St-Michel
Monthermé
Vresse
Gespunsart
Nouzonville
Montcy-Notre-Dame
Renwez
Maubert-Fontaine
Rouvroy-sur-Audry
Rumigny
Aubenton
Liart
Charleville-Mézières
Villers-Semeuse
Vivier-au-Court
Floing
Sedan
Balan
Donchery
Flize
Thin-le-Moutier
Boulzicourt
Poix-Terron
Omont
Chémery-sur-Bar
Roisel
VERMANDOIS
Vermand
St-Quentin
Gauchy
Harly
Guise
Oise
Origny-Ste-Benoîte
Ribemont
Sains-Richaumont
Vervins
THIÉRACHE
Ham
St-Simon
Moy-de-l'Aisne
Marle
Serre
Brunehamel
Rozoy-sur-Serre
Signy-l'Abbaye
Crécy-sur-Serre
Montcornet
Chaumont-Porcien
Wasigny
Tergnier
La Fère
Beautor
Chauny
Crépy
St-Gobain
Bucy-lès-Pierrepont
Dizy-le-Gros
Seraincourt
Novion-Porcien
Faissault
Sery
Chambry
Laon
Sissonne
Athies-sous-Laon
PORCIEN
Château-Porcien
Tourteron
Tannay
Coucy-le-Château-Auffrique
Blérancourt
Anizy-le-Château
Festieux
St-Erme-Outre-et-Ramecourt
Novy-Chevrières
Rethel
Sault-lès-Rethel
Le Chesne
Beaumont-en-Argonne
Laneuville-sur
Canal de l'Oise à l'Aisne
Corbeny
Craonne
Guignicourt
Asfeld
Attigny
Quatre-Champs
Vrizy
Vouziers
Pauvres
Tagnon
Juniville
Boult-aux-Bois
Buzancy
Soissons
Crouy
Vailly-sur-Aisne
Bourg-et-Comin
Berry-au-Bac
Cormicy
Neufchâtel-sur-Aisne
Warmeriville
Isles-sur-Suippe
Machault
Mazagran
Grandpré
Venizel
Courmelles
Belleu
Braine
Aisne
Bourgogne
Courcy
Witry-lès-Reims
Monthois
Senuc
Challerange
Autry
20
Villers-Cotterêts
Fismes
Vesle
Muizon
Reims
Berru
Pontfaverger-Moronvilliers
Mémorial Américain
Mont Cornillet
Sommepy-Tahure
Cernay-en-Dormois
TARDENOIS
Oulchy-le-Château
Fère-en-Tardenois
Tinqueux
Cormontreuil
Ville-sur-Tourbe
St-Hilaire-le-Grand
Neuilly-St-Front
Rocourt-St-Martin
Coincy
Ville-en-Tardenois
Mont Sinaï
Verzy
Somme-Suippe
Suippes
La Neuville-au-Pont
Châtillon-sur-Marne
Damery
Avenay-Val-d'Or
Bouy
Ste-Menehould
Valmy
Crouy-sur-Ourcq
Marne
Dormans
Mardeuil
Dizy
Mareuil-sur-Ay
Épernay
La Cheppe
Auve
Château-Thierry
St-Martin-d'Ablois
Chouilly
Avize
La Veuve
Châlons-en-Champagne
Tilloy-et-Bellay
Dommartin-Varimont
Villers-en-Argonne
Seuil-d'Argonne
Charly
Condé-en-Brie
Le Breuil
Oger
Le Mesnil-sur-Oger
Fagnières
St-Memmie
Sarry
Givry-en-Argonne
La Ferté-sous-Jouarre
Orbais-l'Abbaye
Montmort-Lucy
Corrobert
Vertus
Thibie
Chaintrix-Bierges
Écury-sur-Coole
Chepy
Pogny
Possesse
Vanault-les-Dames
Laheycourt
Nettancourt
Rebais
Montmirail
Champaubert
Bergères-lès-Vertus
Villeseneux
Baye
La Chaussée-sur-Marne
Heiltz-le-Maurupt
Revigny-sur-Ornain
Coulommiers
Soizy-aux-Bois
St-Amand-sur-Fion
Chée
Le Gault-Soigny
Fère-Champenoise
Loisy-sur-Marne
Pargny-sur-Saulx
La Ferté-Gaucher
Esternay
Coole
Vitry-en-Perthois
Cheminon
Beton-Bazoches
Sézanne
CÔTE CHAMPENOISE
Pleurs
Connantre
Sommesous
Vitry-le-François
Villiers-en-Lieu
St-Dizier
Gourgançon
Thiéblemont-Farémont
Villiers-St-Georges
Mailly-le-Camp
CHAMPAGNE POUILLEUSE
Barbonne-Fayel
Salon
St-Remy-en-Bouzemont-St-Genest-et-Isson
PERTHOIS
Montois
Allibaudières
Arrigny
Éclaron-Braucourt-Ste-Livière
Villenauxe-la-Grande
Bethon
Anglure
Plancy-l'Abbaye
Margerie-Hancourt
Lac du Der
Étang de la Horre
Provins
St-Just-Sauvage
Lhuître
Le Chêne
Aube
Méry-sur-Seine
Arcis-sur-Aube
Nogent-sur-Aube
Chavanges
Voillecomte
Wassy
Longueville
Romilly-sur-Seine
Montier-en-Der
Nogent-sur-Seine
Avant-lès-Ramerupt
Pougy
Voire
Dommartin-le-Franc
CHAMPAGNE HUMIDE
Montsuzain
Seine
Traînel
Marigny-le-Châtel
Savières
Lesmont
Brienne-le-Château
Louze
Soulaines-Dhuys
Sommevoire
Bray-sur-Seine
St-Flavy
St-Lyé
Piney
Dienville
Blaiserives
Val de Seine
27
15

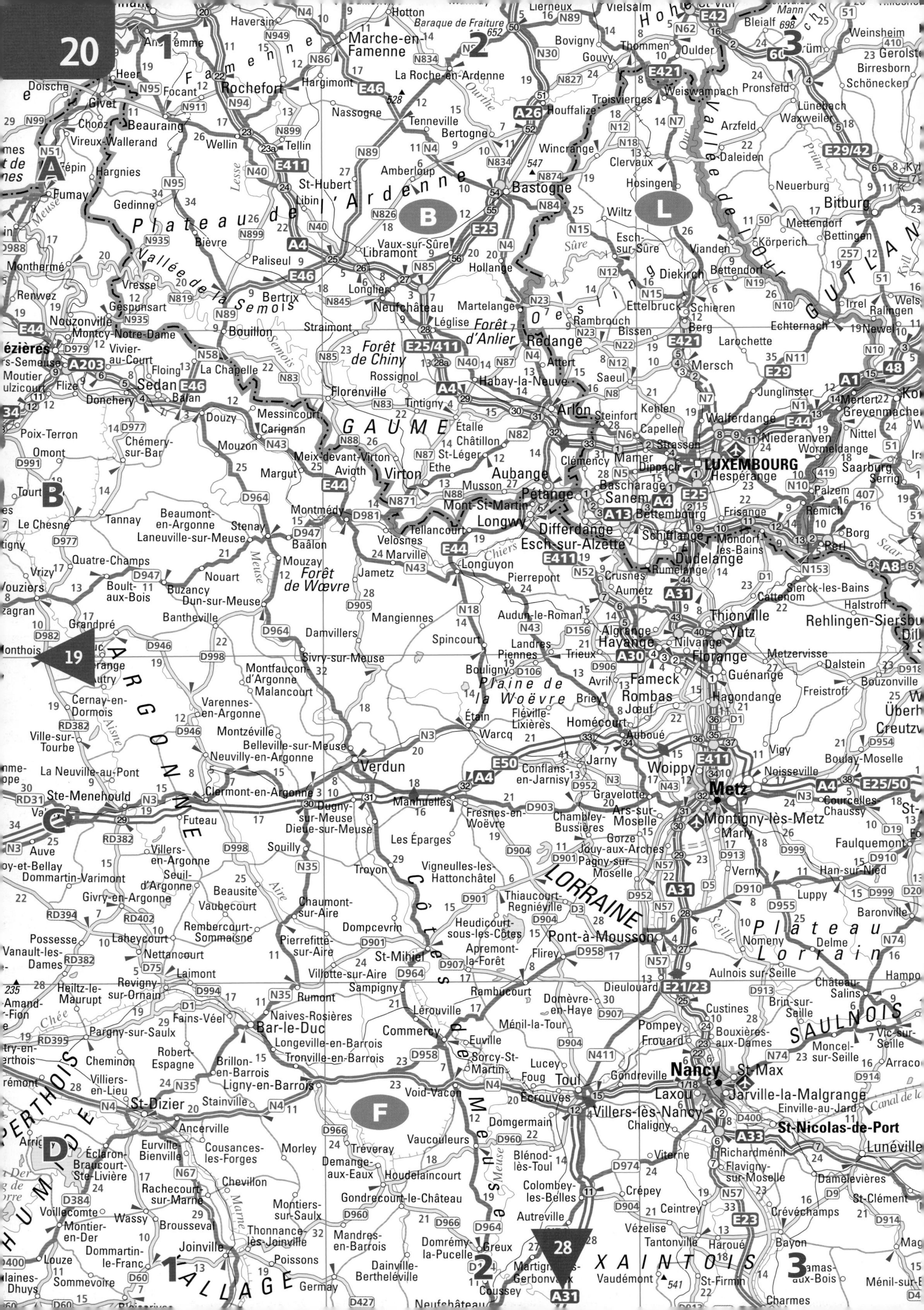
20
Haversin
Hotton
Baraque de Fraiture
Vielsalm
Marche-en-Famenne
Famenne
La Roche-en-Ardenne
Bovigny
Gouvy
Thommen
Oudler
Bleialf
Weinsheim
Prüm
Gerolstein
Birresborn
Schönecken
Heer
Doische
Focant
Rochefort
Hargimont
Nassogne
Ourthe
Houffalize
Troisvierges
Weiswampach
Pronsfeld
Givet
Chooz
Beauraing
Vireux-Wallerand
Wellin
Tellin
Tenneville
Bertogne
Wincrange
Clervaux
Arzfeld
Lünebach
Waxweiler
Daleiden
Fépin
Hargnies
Fumay
Gedinne
St-Hubert
Amberloup
Bastogne
Hosingen
Neuerburg
Bitburg
Libin
Plateau de l'Ardenne
Wiltz
Mettendorf
Bettingen
Körperich
Bièvre
Paliseul
Vaux-sur-Sûre
Libramont
Hollange
Esch-sur-Sûre
Vianden
Diekirch
Bettendorf
Monthermé
Vallée de la Semois
Vresse
Bertrix
Longlier
Neufchâteau
Martelange
Ettelbruck
Schieren
Irrel
Ralingen
Renwez
Gespunsart
Nouzonville
Montcy-Notre-Dame
Bouillon
Straimont
Léglise
Forêt d'Anlier
Rambrouch
Bissen
Berg
Echternach
Larochette
Mézières
Vivier-au-Court
Forêt de Chiny
Redange
Attert
Mersch
Flize
Floing
Sedan
Balan
La Chapelle
Rossignol
Habay-la-Neuve
Saeul
Junglinster
Mertert
Grevenmacher
Donchery
Florenville
Tintigny
Arlon
Steinfort
Kehlen
Walferdange
Poix-Terron
Chémery-sur-Bar
Douzy
Messincourt
Carignan
GAUME
Étalle
Châtillon
Capellen
Strassen
Niederanven
Nittel
Omont
Mouzon
Meix-devant-Virton
St-Léger
Clémency
Mamer
Dippach
LUXEMBOURG
Hesperange
Wormeldange
Saarburg
Serrig
Tourteron
Margut
Avioth
Virton
Ethe
Musson
Aubange
Pétange
Bascharage
Sanem
Mont-St-Martin
Longwy
Differdange
Bettembourg
Frisange
Palzem
Remich
Le Chesne
Tannay
Beaumont-en-Argonne
Stenay
Montmédy
Laneuville-sur-Meuse
Baâlon
Tellancourt
Velosnes
Esch-sur-Alzette
Schifflange
Mondorf-les-Bains
Dudelange
Borg
Perl
Quatre-Champs
Mouzay
Marville
Jametz
Forêt de Wœvre
Longuyon
Pierrepont
Crusnes
Aumetz
Rumelange
Vouziers
Boult-aux-Bois
Buzancy
Nouart
Dun-sur-Meuse
Sierck-les-Bains
Cattenom
Grandpré
Bantheville
Mangiennes
Spincourt
Audun-le-Roman
Landres
Algrange
Hayange
Thionville
Yutz
Rehlingen-Siersburg
Damvillers
Piennes
Trieux
Nilvange
Florange
Metzervisse
Dalstein
Bouzonville
Sivry-sur-Meuse
Montfaucon-d'Argonne
Malancourt
Bouligny
Plaine de la Woëvre
Avril
Fameck
Guénange
Freistroff
ARGONNE
Cernay-en-Dormois
Varennes-en-Argonne
Étain
Briey
Rombas
Jœuf
Hagondange
Ville-sur-Tourbe
Montzéville
Warcq
Fléville-Lixières
Homécourt
Auboué
Creutzwald
Belleville-sur-Meuse
Neuvilly-en-Argonne
Verdun
Conflans-en-Jarnisy
Jarny
Woippy
Boulay-Moselle
Vigy
La Neuville-au-Pont
Ste-Menehould
Clermont-en-Argonne
Dugny-sur-Meuse
Dieue-sur-Meuse
Manheulles
Fresnes-en-Woëvre
Gravelotte
Chambley-Bussières
Ars-sur-Moselle
Metz
Montigny-lès-Metz
Noisseville
Courcelles-Chaussy
Auve
Futeau
Villers-en-Argonne
Souilly
Les Éparges
Gorze
Marly
Faulquemont
Dommartin-Varimont
Seuil-d'Argonne
Beausite
Vaubecourt
Troyon
Vigneulles-lès-Hattonchâtel
Jouy-aux-Arches
Pagny-sur-Moselle
Verny
Han-sur-Nied
Givry-en-Argonne
Chaumont-sur-Aire
Thiaucourt-Regniéville
LORRAINE
Luppy
Baronville
Rembercourt-Sommaisne
Dompcevrin
Heudicourt-sous-les-Côtes
Pont-à-Mousson
Plateau Lorrain
Possesse
Laheycourt
Pierrefitte-sur-Aire
St-Mihiel
Côtes de Meuse
Apremont-la-Forêt
Flirey
Nomeny
Delme
Vanault-les-Dames
Nettancourt
Laimont
Villotte-sur-Aire
Aulnois sur-Seille
Revigny-sur-Ornain
Heiltz-le-Maurupt
Sampigny
Rambucourt
Dieulouard
Château-Salins
Rumont
Lérouville
Domèvre-en-Haye
Custines
Brin-sur-Seille
Fains-Véel
Naives-Rosières
Bar-le-Duc
Commercy
Ménil-la-Tour
Pompey
Frouard
Bouxières-aux-Dames
SAULNOIS
Vic-sur-Seille
Moncel-sur-Seille
Pargny-sur-Saulx
Longeville-en-Barrois
Euville
Robert-Espagne
Tronville-en-Barrois
Sorcy-St-Martin
Lucey
Toul
Gondreville
Nancy
St-Max
Cheminon
Brillon-en-Barrois
Ligny-en-Barrois
Foug
Laxou
Jarville-la-Malgrange
Einville-au-Jard
PERTHOIS
Villiers-en-Lieu
St-Dizier
Stainville
Void-Vacon
Écrouves
Villers-lès-Nancy
Ancerville
Domgermain
Chaligny
St-Nicolas-de-Port
Arrigny
Éclaron-Braucourt-Ste-Livière
Eurville-Bienville
Cousances-les-Forges
Morley
Tréveray
Vaucouleurs
Blénod-lès-Toul
Viterne
Richardménil
Flavigny-sur-Moselle
Lunéville
Demange-aux-Eaux
Houdelaincourt
Colombey-les-Belles
Dameleviéres
Rachecourt-sur-Marne
Chevillon
Gondrecourt-le-Château
Crépey
Ceintrey
Crévéchamps
St-Clément
Voillecomte
Montier-en-Der
Wassy
Brousseval
Montiers-sur-Saulx
Autreville
Vézelise
Dommartin-le-Franc
Joinville
Thonnance-lès-Joinville
Mandres-en-Barrois
Domrémy-la-Pucelle
Greux
Tantonville
Haroué
Bayon
Louze
Poissons
Dainville-Bertheléville
Martigny-les-Gerbonvaux
XAINTOIS
Vaudémont
St-Firmin
Gamas-aux-Bois
Ménil-sur-Belvitte
Sommevoire
VALLAGE
Germay
Coussey
Charmes
Neufchâteau
19
28

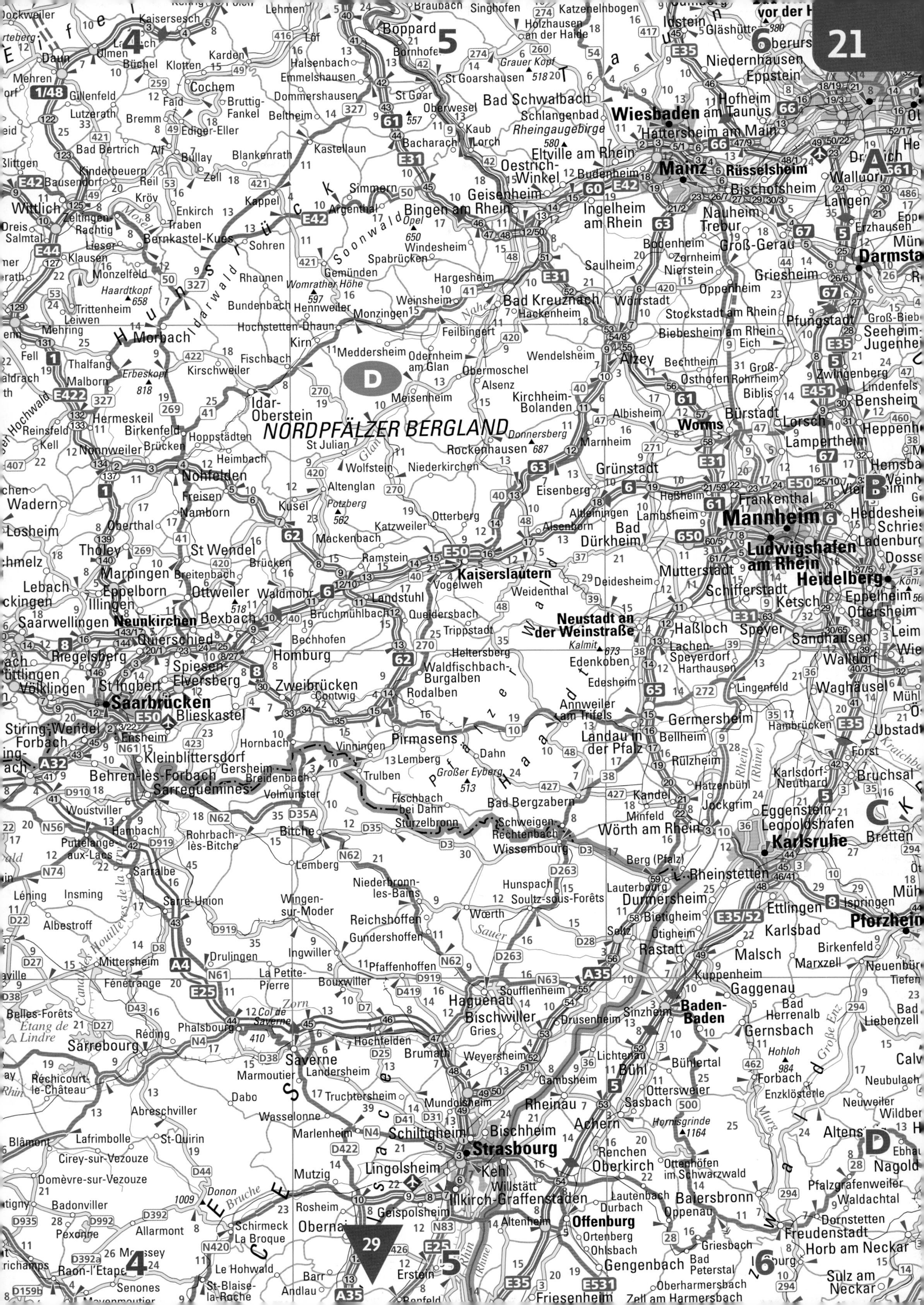
Daun
Ulmen
Kaisersesch
Büchel
Klotten
Karden
Cochem
Mehren
Gillenfeld
Lutzerath
Bremm
Bruttig-Fankel
Ediger-Eller
Bad Bertrich
Alf
Bullay
Zell
Kinderbeuern
Bausendorf
Reil
Wittlich
Zeltingen-Rachtig
Kröv
Enkirch
Traben
Bernkastel-Kues
Lieser
Klausen
Monzelfeld
Salmtal
Haardtkopf 658
Trittenheim
Leiwen
Mehring
Morbach
Thalfang
Erbeskopf 818
Malborn
Hermeskeil
Reinsfeld
Kell
Birkenfeld
Brücken
Nonnweiler
Hunsrück
Idarwald
Rhaunen
Sohren
Kappel
Simmern
Kirchberg
Kastellaun
Blankenrath
Argenthal
Soonwald
Gemünden
Womrather Höhe 597
Bundenbach
Hennweiler
Monzingen
Hochstetten-Dhaun
Kirn
Fischbach
Kirschweiler
Idar-Oberstein
Hoppstädten
Heimbach
Nohfelden
Freisen
Namborn
Oberthal
Wadern
Losheim
Tholey
St Wendel
Marpingen
Lebach
Eppelborn
Illingen
Ottweiler
Neunkirchen
Bexbach
Saarwellingen
Quierschied
Riegelsberg
Spiesen-Elversberg
St Ingbert
Völklingen
Saarbrücken
Blieskastel
Homburg
Bechhofen
Zweibrücken
Contwig
Hornbach
Forbach
Stiring-Wendel
Ensheim
Kleinblittersdorf
Behren-lès-Forbach
Sarreguemines
Gersheim
Breidenbach
Volmunster
Rohrbach-lès-Bitche
Bitche
Puttelange-aux-Lacs
Hambach
Sarralbe
Woustviller
Sarre-Union
Insming
Léning
Albestroff
Drulingen
Mittersheim
Fénétrange
Phalsbourg
Sarrebourg
Réding
Réchicourt-le-Château
Abreschviller
Dabo
Saverne
Marmoutier
Wasselonne
Lafrimbolle
St-Quirin
Blâmont
Cirey-sur-Vezouze
Domèvre-sur-Vezouze
Badonviller
Pexonne
Allarmont
Raon-l'Etape
Senones
Schirmeck
La Broque
Le Hohwald
St-Blaise-la-Roche
Mutzig
Rosheim
Obernai
Barr
Andlau
Erstein
Boppard
Braubach
Lehmen
Löf
Halsenbach
Emmelshausen
Dommershausen
Beltheim
St Goar
Oberwesel
Kaub
Lorch
Bacharach
St Goarshausen
Bad Schwalbach
Schlangenbad
Rheingaugebirge
Eltville am Rhein
Oestrich-Winkel
Geisenheim
Bingen am Rhein
Windesheim
Spabrücken
Hargesheim
Weinsheim
Bad Kreuznach
Hackenheim
Feilbingert
Meddersheim
Odernheim am Glan
Obermoschel
Alsenz
Meisenheim
NORDPFÄLZER BERGLAND
St Julian
Wolfstein
Niederkirchen
Rockenhausen
Donnersberg 687
Kirchheim-Bolanden
Altenglan
Kusel
Potzberg 562
Katzweiler
Otterberg
Mackenbach
Ramstein
Kaiserslautern
Landstuhl
Vogelweh
Bruchmühlbach
Queidersbach
Trippstadt
Waldmohr
Heltersberg
Waldfischbach-Burgalben
Rodalben
Pirmasens
Vinningen
Lemberg
Trulben
Dahn
Großer Eyberg 513
Pfälzer Wald
Haardt
Fischbach bei Dahn
Sturzelbronn
Schweigen-Rechtenbach
Wissembourg
Bad Bergzabern
Annweiler am Trifels
Landau in der Pfalz
Edenkoben
Edesheim
Kalmit 673
Neustadt an der Weinstraße
Weidenthal
Deidesheim
Bad Dürkheim
Grünstadt
Eisenberg
Altleiningen
Alsenborn
Wörrstadt
Alzey
Wendelsheim
Albisheim
Marnheim
Worms
Osthofen
Bechtheim
Wiesbaden
Mainz
Rüsselsheim
Hattersheim am Main
Hofheim am Taunus
Eppstein
Niedernhausen
Idstein
Taunus
Budenheim
Ingelheim am Rhein
Nauheim
Trebur
Groß-Gerau
Bodenheim
Nierstein
Oppenheim
Saulheim
Stockstadt am Rhein
Biebesheim am Rhein
Gernsheim
Eich
Biblis
Bürstadt
Lorsch
Lampertheim
Frankenthal
Mannheim
Ludwigshafen am Rhein
Heidelberg
Lambsheim
Mutterstadt
Schifferstadt
Speyer
Haßloch
Lachen-Speyerdorf
Harthausen
Germersheim
Bellheim
Rülzheim
Lingenfeld
Kandel
Wörth am Rhein
Hatzenbühl
Jockgrim
Minfeld
Karlsruhe
Eggenstein-Leopoldshafen
Rheinstetten
Berg (Pfalz)
Lauterbourg
Durmersheim
Bietigheim
Ötigheim
Rastatt
Ettlingen
Karlsbad
Malsch
Pforzheim
Bretten
Bruchsal
Forst
Karlsdorf-Neuthard
Waghäusel
Hambrücken
Walldorf
Wiesloch
Sandhausen
Ketsch
Oftersheim
Eppelheim
Ladenburg
Heddesheim
Schriesheim
Viernheim
Weinheim
Hemsbach
Heppenheim
Bensheim
Zwingenberg
Seeheim-Jugenheim
Pfungstadt
Griesheim
Darmstadt
Langen
Erzhausen
Walldorf
Dreieich
Bischofsheim
Gaggenau
Kuppenheim
Baden-Baden
Sinzheim
Bühl
Bühlertal
Gernsbach
Forbach
Hohloh 984
Ottersweier
Sasbach
Achern
Hornisgrinde 1164
Renchen
Oberkirch
Ottenhöfen im Schwarzwald
Baiersbronn
Freudenstadt
Oppenau
Lautenbach
Durbach
Offenburg
Ortenberg
Ohlsbach
Gengenbach
Bad Peterstal
Griesbach
Oberharmersbach
Zell am Harmersbach
Friesenheim
Kehl
Willstätt
Rheinau
Lichtenau
Strasbourg
Bischheim
Schiltigheim
Illkirch-Graffenstaden
Lingolsheim
Geispolsheim
Marlenheim
Truchtersheim
Mundolsheim
Brumath
Weyersheim
Gambsheim
Drusenheim
Haguenau
Bischwiller
Gries
Soufflenheim
Hochfelden
Landersheim
Bouxwiller
La Petite-Pierre
Ingwiller
Pfaffenhoffen
Reichshoffen
Gundershoffen
Niederbronn-les-Bains
Wingen-sur-Moder
Wœrth
Soultz-sous-Forêts
Hunspach
Seltz
Lemberg
Neuenbürg
Bad Herrenalb
Bad Liebenzell
Calw
Neubulach
Enzklösterle
Wildberg
Altensteig
Nagold
Pfalzgrafenweiler
Waldachtal
Dornstetten
Horb am Neckar
Sulz am Neckar
Schwarzwald
Rhein (Rhine)
Vosges
Alsace
Eifel
D
A
B
C
4
5
6
29

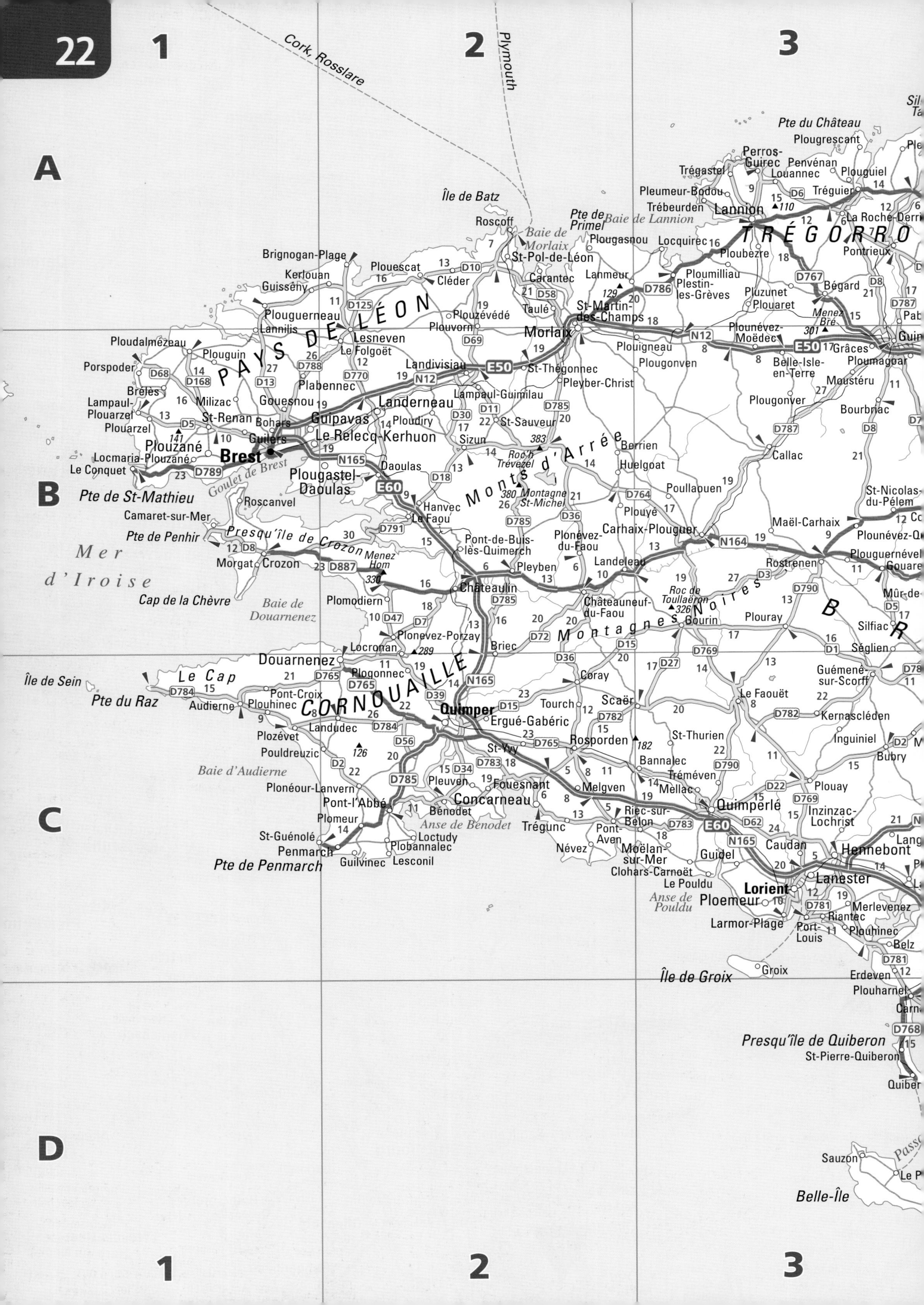
1
2
3
A
B
C
D
Cork, Rosslare
Plymouth
Pte du Château
Plougrescant
Perros-Guirec
Penvénan
Trégastel
Louannec
Plouguiel
Pleumeur-Bodou
Tréguier
Trébeurden
Lannion
La Roche-Derrien
Île de Batz
Roscoff
Pte de Primel
Baie de Lannion
Baie de Morlaix
Plougasnou
Locquirec
TRÉGORRO
Pontrieux
Brignogan-Plage
Plouescat
St-Pol-de-Léon
Ploubezre
Kerlouan
Cléder
Carantec
Lanmeur
Plestin-les-Grèves
Ploumilliau
Guissény
Bégard
Taulé
St-Martin-des-Champs
Pluzunet
Plouaret
Plouguerneau
Plouzévédé
Menez Bré
Lannilis
PAYS DE LÉON
Plouvorn
Morlaix
Plounévez-Moëdec
Ploudalmézeau
Lesneven
Plouigneau
Grâces
Plouguin
Le Folgoët
Plougonven
Belle-Isle-en-Terre
Ploumagoar
Porspoder
Landivisiau
St-Thégonnec
Pleyber-Christ
Moustéru
Brélès
Plabennec
Lampaul-Guimiliau
Lampaul-Plouarzel
Milizac
Gouesnou
Landerneau
Plougonver
Bourbriac
Plouarzel
St-Renan
Bohars
Guipavas
Ploudiry
St-Sauveur
Plouzané
Guilers
Le Relecq-Kerhuon
Sizun
Berrien
Callac
Locmaria-Plouzané
Brest
Roc'h Trévezel
Monts d'Arrée
Huelgoat
Le Conquet
Daoulas
Plougastel-Daoulas
Goulet de Brest
Pte de St-Mathieu
Roscanvel
Hanvec
Montagne St-Michel
Poullaouen
Plouyé
St-Nicolas-du-Pélem
Camaret-sur-Mer
Le Faou
Carhaix-Plouguer
Maël-Carhaix
Pte de Penhir
Presqu'île de Crozon
Pont-de-Buis-lès-Quimerch
Plonévez-du-Faou
Plounévez-Quintin
Mer d'Iroise
Morgat
Crozon
Menez Hom
Pleyben
Landeleau
Rostrenen
Plouguernével
Gouarec
Châteaulin
Roc de Toullaëron
Montagnes Noires
Cap de la Chèvre
Baie de Douarnenez
Plomodiern
Châteauneuf-du-Faou
Mûr-de-Bretagne
Gourin
Plouray
Silfiac
Plonevez-Porzay
Montagnes
Briec
Locronan
Séglien
Douarnenez
Plogonnec
Guémené-sur-Scorff
Île de Sein
Le Cap
Coray
Le Faouët
Pte du Raz
Pont-Croix
Audierne
Plouhinec
CORNOUAILLE
Quimper
Tourch
Scaër
Kernascléden
Landudec
Ergué-Gabéric
Plozévet
St-Yvy
Rosporden
St-Thurien
Inguiniel
Pouldreuzic
Bubry
Bannalec
Baie d'Audierne
Pleuven
Fouesnant
Tréméven
Plouay
Plonéour-Lanvern
Concarneau
Melgven
Mellac
Pont-l'Abbé
Bénodet
Riec-sur-Bélon
Quimperlé
Inzinzac-Lochrist
Plomeur
Anse de Bénodet
Trégunc
Pont-Aven
St-Guénolé
Loctudy
Névez
Moëlan-sur-Mer
Caudan
Hennebont
Penmarch
Plobannalec
Guidel
Lanester
Pte de Penmarch
Guilvinec
Lesconil
Clohars-Carnoët
Le Pouldu
Lorient
Anse de Pouldu
Ploemeur
Merlevenez
Riantec
Larmor-Plage
Port-Louis
Plouhinec
Belz
Groix
Île de Groix
Erdeven
Plouharnel
Presqu'île de Quiberon
St-Pierre-Quiberon
Sauzon
Belle-Île
E50
E60
N12
N165
N164
D789
D125
D770
D788
D785
D787
D786
D767
D782
D783
D784
D765
D790
D769
D887
D791
D781
D768

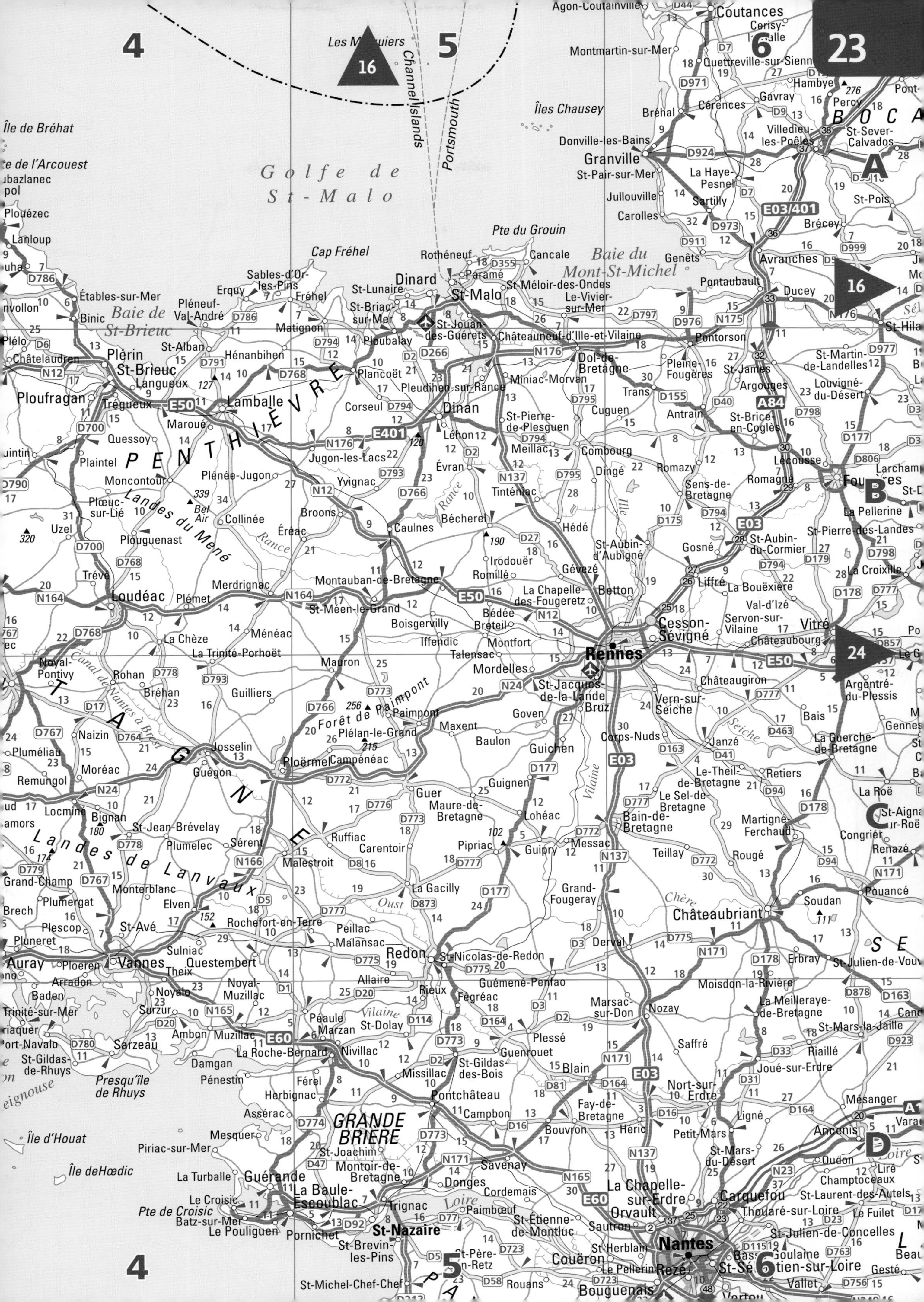
Golfe de St-Malo
Channel Islands
Portsmouth
Les Minquiers
Îles Chausey
Île de Bréhat
Baie de St-Brieuc
Cap Fréhel
Pte du Grouin
Baie du Mont-St-Michel
Coutances
Montmartin-sur-Mer
Quettreville-sur-Sienne
Hambye
Gavray
Percy
Cérences
Bréhal
Villedieu-les-Poêles
St-Sever-Calvados
Donville-les-Bains
Granville
St-Pair-sur-Mer
La Haye-Pesnel
Jullouville
Sartilly
Carolles
Brécey
St-Pois
Genêts
Avranches
Pontaubault
Ducey
Pontorson
St-Hilaire
St-Martin-de-Landelles
Louvigné-du-Désert
St-James
Argouges
St-Brice-en-Coglès
Lécousse
Fougères
Larchamp
La Pellerine
St-Pierre-des-Landes
St-Aubin-du-Cormier
Gosné
Liffré
La Bouëxière
La Croixille
Val-d'Izé
Servon-sur-Vilaine
Vitré
Châteaubourg
Cesson-Sévigné
Rennes
Argentré-du-Plessis
Châteaugiron
Vern-sur-Seiche
Bais
La Guerche-de-Bretagne
Janzé
Corps-Nuds
Le Theil-de-Bretagne
Retiers
Le Sel-de-Bretagne
Bain-de-Bretagne
Martigné-Ferchaud
La Roë
Congrier
Renazé
Teillay
Rougé
Pouancé
Soudan
Châteaubriant
Erbray
St-Julien-de-Vouvantes
Moisdon-la-Rivière
La Meilleraye-de-Bretagne
St-Mars-la-Jaille
Riaillé
Joué-sur-Erdre
Nozay
Marsac-sur-Don
Saffré
Nort-sur-Erdre
Ligné
Mésanger
Ancenis
Petit-Mars
St-Mars-du-Désert
Oudon
Champtoceaux
St-Laurent-des-Autels
Le Fuilet
Carquefou
Thouaré-sur-Loire
St-Julien-de-Concelles
La Chapelle-sur-Erdre
Orvault
Sautron
Nantes
St-Herblain
Rezé
Bouguenais
Couëron
Le Pellerin
Basse-Goulaine
St-Sébastien-sur-Loire
Vertou
Vallet
Gesté
Rothéneuf
Paramé
Cancale
St-Méloir-des-Ondes
Le Vivier-sur-Mer
Dinard
St-Lunaire
St-Malo
St-Briac-sur-Mer
St-Jouan-des-Guérets
Châteauneuf-d'Ille-et-Vilaine
Dol-de-Bretagne
Miniac-Morvan
Pleine-Fougères
Trans
Antrain
Cuguen
Combourg
Meillac
Dingé
Romazy
Sens-de-Bretagne
Tinténiac
Hédé
St-Aubin-d'Aubigné
Gévezé
Betton
La Chapelle-des-Fougeretz
Bécherel
Irodouër
Romillé
Bédée
Breteil
Montfort
Iffendic
Talensac
Mordelles
St-Jacques-de-la-Lande
Bruz
Goven
Guichen
Guignen
Lohéac
Guipry
Messac
Pipriac
Grand-Fougeray
Derval
Sables-d'Or-les-Pins
Erquy
Fréhel
Pléneuf-Val-André
Matignon
St-Alban
Hénanbihen
Ploubalay
Plancoët
Pleudihen-sur-Rance
Corseul
Dinan
Léhon
Évran
St-Pierre-de-Plesguen
Lamballe
Jugon-les-Lacs
Plénée-Jugon
Yvignac
Broons
Caulnes
Éréac
Montauban-de-Bretagne
St-Méen-le-Grand
Boisgervilly
Mauron
Paimpont
Plélan-le-Grand
Forêt de Paimpont
Maxent
Baulon
Campénéac
Ploërmel
Guer
Maure-de-Bretagne
Carentoir
Ruffiac
Malestroit
La Gacilly
Sérent
Plumelec
St-Jean-Brévelay
Bignan
Locminé
Moréac
Josselin
Guégon
Naizin
Remungol
Pluméliau
Rohan
Bréhan
Noyal-Pontivy
Guilliers
La Trinité-Porhoët
Ménéac
La Chèze
Merdrignac
Plémet
Loudéac
Trévé
Uzel
Plœuc-sur-Lié
Plouguenast
Moncontour
Collinée
Landes du Mené
Plaintel
Quessoy
Maroué
Trégueux
Ploufragan
Langueux
St-Brieuc
Plérin
Binic
Étables-sur-Mer
Châtelaudren
Plélo
Lanloup
Plouézec
Paimpol
Quintin
PENTHIÈVRE
BRETAGNE
Landes de Lanvaux
Grand-Champ
Monterblanc
Elven
Plumergat
St-Avé
Plescop
Pluneret
Auray
Ploeren
Vannes
Theix
Arradon
Baden
Sulniac
Questembert
Rochefort-en-Terre
Malansac
Peillac
Redon
St-Nicolas-de-Redon
Allaire
Rieux
Fégréac
Guémené-Penfao
Noyalo
Surzur
Noyal-Muzillac
Ambon
Muzillac
Sarzeau
St-Gildas-de-Rhuys
Presqu'île de Rhuys
Damgan
Pénestin
La Roche-Bernard
Nivillac
Péaule
Marzan
St-Dolay
Missillac
St-Gildas-des-Bois
Guenrouet
Plessé
Blain
Fay-de-Bretagne
Héric
Bouvron
Campbon
Pontchâteau
Férel
Herbignac
Assérac
GRANDE BRIÈRE
Mesquer
Piriac-sur-Mer
La Turballe
Guérande
St-Joachim
Montoir-de-Bretagne
Savenay
Donges
Cordemais
La Baule-Escoublac
Trignac
Le Croisic
Pte de Croisic
Batz-sur-Mer
Le Pouliguen
Pornichet
St-Nazaire
Paimbœuf
St-Étienne-de-Montluc
St-Brevin-les-Pins
St-Père-en-Retz
St-Michel-Chef-Chef
Rouans
Île d'Houat
Île de Hœdic
Loire
Vilaine
Rance
Oust
Chère
Seiche
Ille
E50
E401
E03
E60
A84
N12
N24
N137
N164
N165
N171
N175
N176
4
5
6
16
24
A
B
C
D

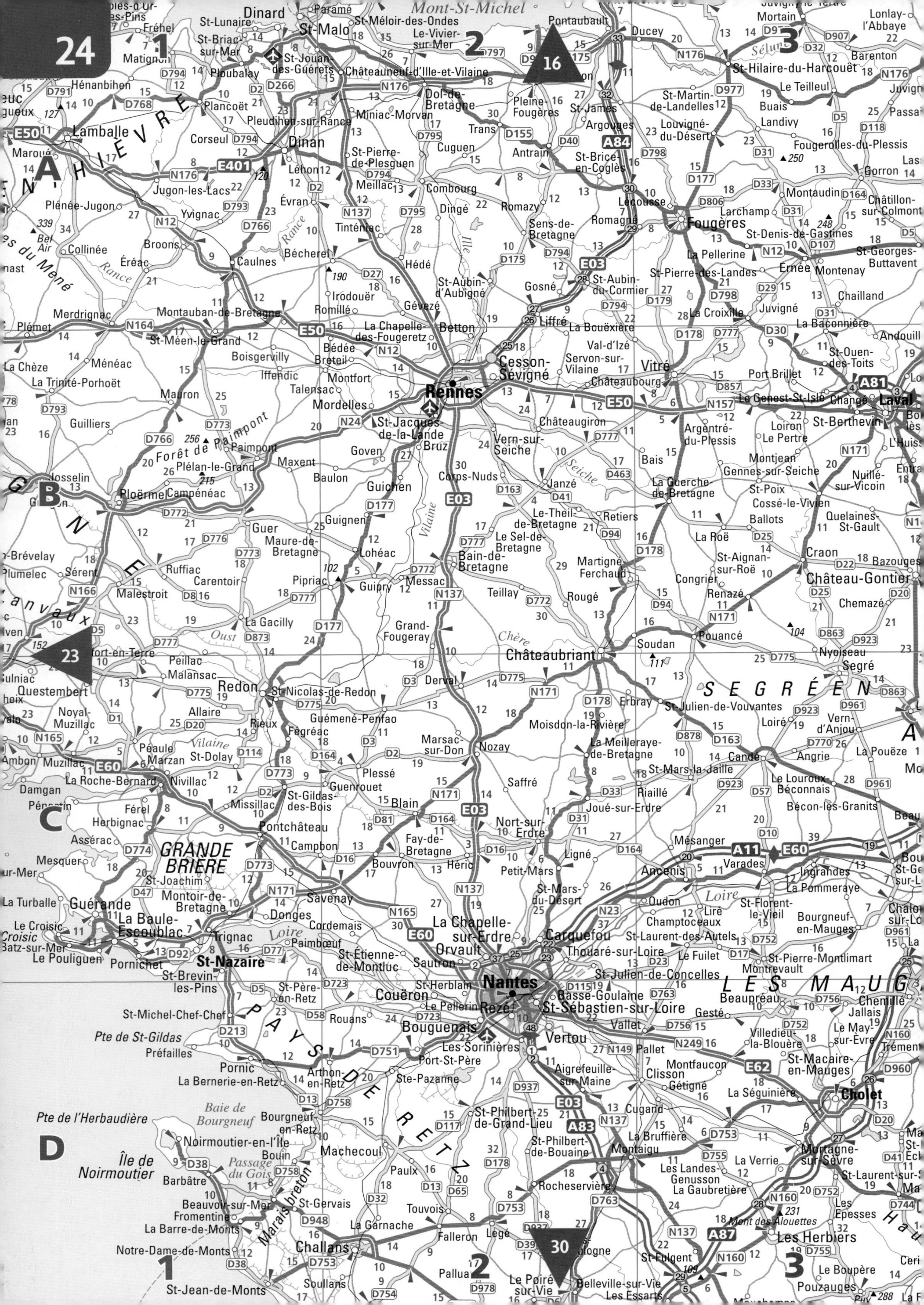
Dinard
St-Malo
Mont-St-Michel
Pontaubault
Ducey
Mortain
Lonlay-l'Abbaye
Fréhel
St-Lunaire
St-Briac-sur-Mer
Matignon
St-Jouan-des-Guérets
St-Méloir-des-Ondes
Le Vivier-sur-Mer
Châteauneuf-d'Ille-et-Vilaine
St-Hilaire-du-Harcouët
Barenton
Ploubalay
Hénanbihen
Plancoët
Pleudihen-sur-Rance
Dol-de-Bretagne
Miniac-Morvan
Pleine-Fougères
St-James
Argouges
St-Martin-de-Landelles
Le Teilleul
Buais
Landivy
Lamballe
Corseul
Dinan
Trans
Cuguen
Antrain
Louvigné-du-Désert
Fougerolles-du-Plessis
PENTHIÈVRE
Jugon-les-Lacs
Léhon
St-Pierre-de-Plesguen
Meillac
Combourg
St-Brice-en-Coglès
Gorron
Plénée-Jugon
Yvignac
Évran
Tinténiac
Dingé
Romazy
Sens-de-Bretagne
Lécousse
Fougères
Larchamp
Montaudin
Châtillon-sur-Colmont
Broons
Collinée
Éréac
Caulnes
Bécherel
Hédé
Romagné
St-Denis-de-Gastines
La Pellerine
Ernée
Montenay
St-Georges-Buttavent
Landes du Mené
Rance
Irodouër
St-Aubin-d'Aubigné
Gosné
St-Aubin-du-Cormier
St-Pierre-des-Landes
Chailland
Merdrignac
Montauban-de-Bretagne
Romillé
Gévezé
La Croixille
Juvigné
Plémet
St-Méen-le-Grand
La Chapelle-des-Fougeretz
Betton
Liffré
La Bouëxière
La Baconnière
Andouillé
Bédée
Breteil
Val-d'Izé
Ménéac
Boisgervilly
Cesson-Sévigné
Servon-sur-Vilaine
Vitré
St-Ouen-des-Toits
La Chèze
La Trinité-Porhoët
Iffendic
Montfort
Rennes
Châteaubourg
Port Brillet
Laval
Mauron
Talensac
Mordelles
Le Genest-St-Isle
Changé
St-Jacques-de-la-Lande
Châteaugiron
Argentré-du-Plessis
Loiron
St-Berthevin
Guilliers
Forêt de Paimpont
Paimpont
Goven
Bruz
Vern-sur-Seiche
Le Pertre
Bais
Montjean
Josselin
Plélan-le-Grand
Maxent
Baulon
Corps-Nuds
Janzé
La Guerche-de-Bretagne
Gennes-sur-Seiche
Nuillé-sur-Vicoin
Ploërmel
Campénéac
Guichen
St-Poix
Cossé-le-Vivien
Le Theil-de-Bretagne
Retiers
Ballots
Quelaines-St-Gault
Guer
Guignen
Le Sel-de-Bretagne
La Roë
Maure-de-Bretagne
Lohéac
Bain-de-Bretagne
Martigné-Ferchaud
St-Aignan-sur-Roë
Craon
Bazouges
Ruffiac
Sérent
Carentoir
Pipriac
Guipry
Messac
Congrier
Château-Gontier
Malestroit
Teillay
Rougé
Renazé
Chemazé
La Gacilly
Grand-Fougeray
Pouancé
Oust
Châteaubriant
Soudan
Noyant
Segré
Peillac
Malansac
Redon
St-Nicolas-de-Redon
Derval
Questembert
SEGRÉEN
Allaire
Guémené-Penfao
Erbray
St-Julien-de-Vouvantes
Noyal-Muzillac
Rieux
Fégréac
Moisdon-la-Rivière
Loiré
Vern-d'Anjou
Péaule
Vilaine
Marsac-sur-Don
Nozay
La Meilleraye-de-Bretagne
Candé
Angrie
La Pouëze
Muzillac
Marzan
St-Dolay
Plessé
St-Mars-la-Jaille
La Roche-Bernard
Nivillac
Guenrouet
Saffré
Riaillé
Le Louroux-Béconnais
Damgan
Missillac
St-Gildas-des-Bois
Blain
Joué-sur-Erdre
Bécon-les-Granits
Pénestin
Férel
Herbignac
Pontchâteau
Nort-sur-Erdre
Assérac
Campbon
Fay-de-Bretagne
Mésanger
GRANDE BRIÈRE
Mesquer
Bouvron
Héric
Petit-Mars
Ligné
Ancenis
Varades
Ingrandes
St-Joachim
La Pommeraye
Montoir-de-Bretagne
Savenay
St-Mars-du-Désert
Oudon
La Turballe
Guérande
Donges
St-Florent-le-Vieil
Liré
Bourgneuf-en-Mauges
Cordemais
La Chapelle-sur-Erdre
Champtoceaux
La Baule-Escoublac
Le Croisic
Trignac
Loire
Paimbœuf
Orvault
Carquefou
St-Laurent-des-Autels
Batz-sur-Mer
Le Pouliguen
Pornichet
St-Nazaire
St-Étienne-de-Montluc
Sautron
Thouaré-sur-Loire
Le Fuilet
St-Pierre-Montlimart
St-Brevin-les-Pins
St-Julien-de-Concelles
Montrevault
St-Père-en-Retz
St-Herblain
Nantes
LES MAUGES
Couëron
Basse-Goulaine
Beaupréau
Chemillé
Le Pellerin
Rezé
St-Sébastien-sur-Loire
St-Michel-Chef-Chef
Rouans
Geste
Jallais
PAYS DE RETZ
Bouguenais
Vallet
Pte de St-Gildas
Villedieu-la-Blouère
Le May-sur-Èvre
Préfailles
Les Sorinières
Vertou
Pallet
Trémentines
Pornic
Port-St-Père
Aigrefeuille-sur-Maine
Clisson
Montfaucon
St-Macaire-en-Mauges
La Bernerie-en-Retz
Arthon-en-Retz
Ste-Pazanne
Gétigné
Cholet
La Séguinière
Baie de Bourgneuf
Pte de l'Herbaudière
Bourgneuf-en-Retz
St-Philbert-de-Grand-Lieu
Cugand
Noirmoutier-en-l'Île
La Bruffière
St-Philbert-de-Bouaine
Montaigu
Mortagne-sur-Sèvre
Île de Noirmoutier
Bouin
Machecoul
La Verrie
Passage du Gois
Les Landes-Genusson
St-Laurent-sur-Sèvre
Barbâtre
Paulx
La Gaubretière
Marais breton
Rocheservière
Beauvoir-sur-Mer
St-Gervais
Mont des Alouettes
Les Epesses
Fromentine
Touvois
La Barre-de-Monts
La Garnache
Legé
Notre-Dame-de-Monts
Challans
Falleron
St-Fulgent
Les Herbiers
Soullans
Palluau
Le Poiré-sur-Vie
Belleville-sur-Vie
Les Essarts
Le Boupère
Pouzauges
St-Jean-de-Monts

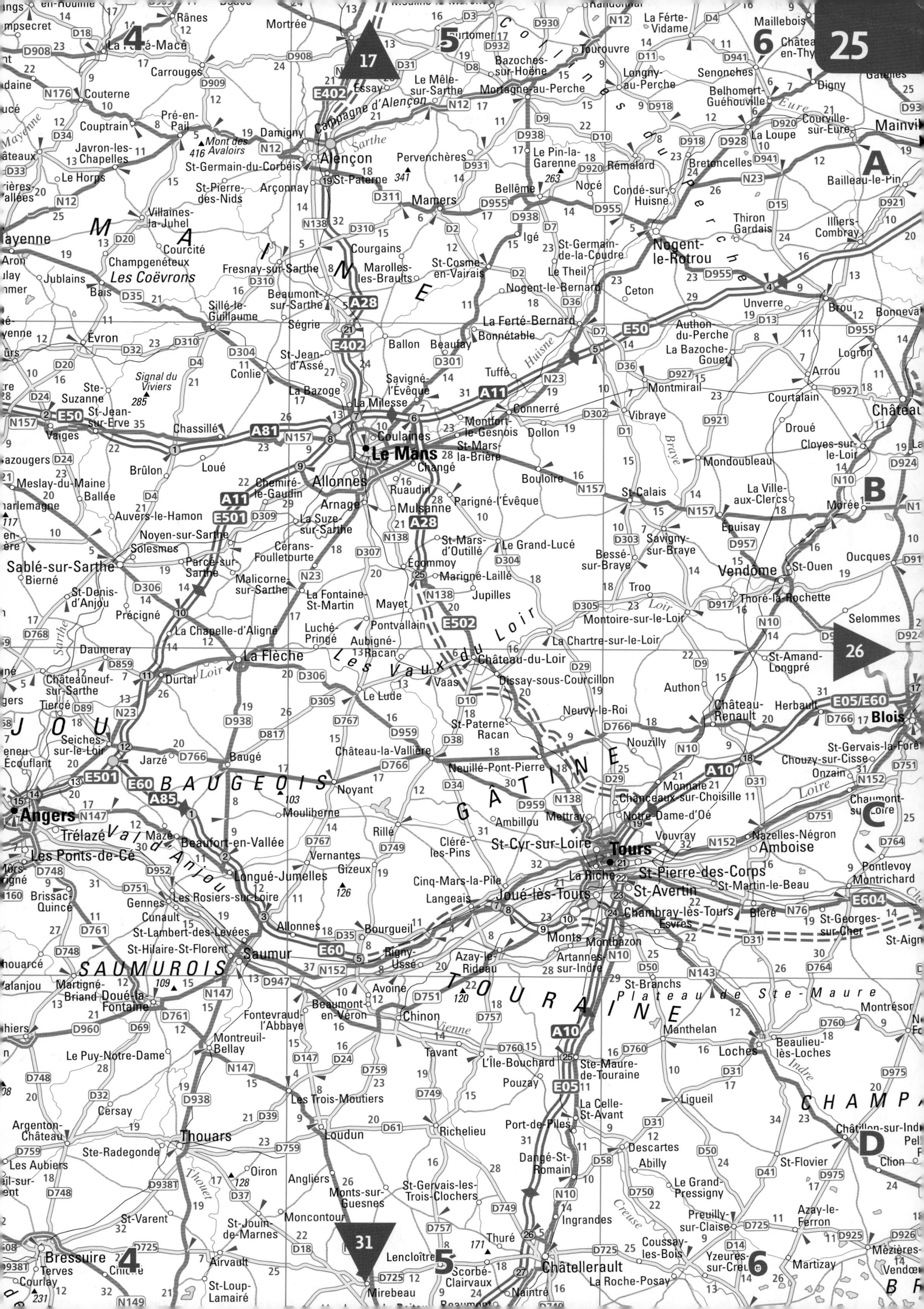

25
4
5
6
17
26
31
A
B
C
D
Rânes
Mortrée
La Ferté-Macé
Carrouges
Couterne
Pré-en-Pail
Couptrain
Javron-les-Chapelles
Mont des Avaloirs
416
Damigny
Alençon
St-Germain-du-Corbéis
Le Horps
Villaines-la-Juhel
St-Pierre-des-Nids
Arçonnay
St-Paterne
Essay
Campagne d'Alençon
Sarthe
Le Mêle-sur-Sarthe
Courtomer
Bazoches-sur-Hoëne
Mortagne-au-Perche
Pervenchères
341
Mamers
Tourouvre
La Ferté-Vidame
Longny-au-Perche
Maillebois
Château-en-Thymerais
Senonches
Digny
Belhomert-Guéhouville
Eure
Courville-sur-Eure
La Loupe
Bretoncelles
Le Pin-la-Garenne
263
Rémalard
Bellême
Noce
Condé-sur-Huisne
Bailleau-le-Pin
Thiron Gardais
Illiers-Combray
Nogent-le-Rotrou
Collines du Perche
Mayenne
Aron
Jublains
Bais
Les Coëvrons
Courcité
Champgenéteux
MAINE
Fresnay-sur-Sarthe
Courgains
Marolles-les-Braults
St-Cosme-en-Vairais
Igé
St-Germain-de-la-Coudre
Le Theil
Nogent-le-Bernard
Ceton
Sillé-le-Guillaume
Beaumont-sur-Sarthe
Ségrie
Évron
Ste-Suzanne
Signal du Viviers
285
Conlie
St-Jean-d'Assé
Ballon
Beaufay
Bonnétable
La Ferté-Bernard
Huisne
Authon-du-Perche
La Bazoche-Gouet
Unverre
Brou
Bonneval
Logron
Arrou
Courtalain
Châteaudun
St-Jean-sur-Erve
Vaiges
Chassillé
La Bazoge
La Milesse
Savigné-l'Évêque
Tuffé
Connerré
Montfort-le-Gesnois
St-Mars-la-Brière
Dollon
Montmirail
Vibraye
Droué
Cloyes-sur-le-Loir
Coulaines
Le Mans
Changé
Allonnes
Brûlon
Loué
Meslay-du-Maine
Ballée
Chemiré-le-Gaudin
Ruaudin
Arnage
Mulsanne
Parigné-l'Évêque
Bouloire
St-Calais
Mondoubleau
Braye
La Ville-aux-Clercs
Morée
Auvers-le-Hamon
Noyen-sur-Sarthe
Solesmes
La Suze-sur-Sarthe
Cérans-Foulletourte
St-Mars-d'Outillé
Le Grand-Lucé
Écommoy
Bessé-sur-Braye
Savigny-sur-Braye
Épuisay
Vendôme
St-Ouen
Oucques
Sablé-sur-Sarthe
Bierné
Parcé-sur-Sarthe
Malicorne-sur-Sarthe
La Fontaine-St-Martin
Marigné-Laillé
Jupilles
Troo
Thoré-la-Rochette
St-Denis-d'Anjou
Précigné
Mayet
Pontvallain
Montoire-sur-le-Loir
Selommes
Daumeray
La Chapelle-d'Aligné
Luché-Pringé
Aubigné-Racan
La Chartre-sur-le-Loir
St-Amand-Longpré
Châteauneuf-sur-Sarthe
Durtal
La Flèche
Les Vaux du Loir
Château-du-Loir
Vaas
Dissay-sous-Courcillon
Authon
Tiercé
Le Lude
St-Paterne-Racan
Neuvy-le-Roi
Château-Renault
Herbault
Blois
Seiches-sur-le-Loir
Jarzé
Baugé
Château-la-Vallière
Neuillé-Pont-Pierre
Nouzilly
St-Gervais-la-Forêt
Chouzy-sur-Cisse
Onzain
Écouflant
BAUGEOIS
Noyant
103
Mouliherne
Monnaie
Chanceaux-sur-Choisille
Notre-Dame-d'Oé
Chaumont-sur-Loire
Angers
Trélazé
Mazé
Val d'Anjou
Beaufort-en-Vallée
Rillé
GÂTINE
Ambillou
Mettray
Vernantes
Cléré-les-Pins
St-Cyr-sur-Loire
Tours
Vouvray
Nazelles-Négron
Amboise
Les Ponts-de-Cé
Longué-Jumelles
Gizeux
La Riche
St-Pierre-des-Corps
Pontlevoy
Montrichard
Brissac-Quincé
Gennes
Les Rosiers-sur-Loire
126
Cinq-Mars-la-Pile
Langeais
Joué-lès-Tours
St-Avertin
St-Martin-le-Beau
Cunault
St-Lambert-des-Levées
Allonnes
Bourgueil
Chambray-lès-Tours
Esvres
Bléré
St-Georges-sur-Cher
St-Hilaire-St-Florent
Saumur
Rigny-Ussé
Azay-le-Rideau
Monts
Montbazon
Artannes-sur-Indre
SAUMUROIS
109
Martigné-Briand
Doué-la-Fontaine
Avoine
Beaumont-en-Véron
120
TOURAINE
St-Branchs
Plateau de Ste-Maure
Montrésor
Chinon
Fontevraud-l'Abbaye
Montreuil-Bellay
Vienne
Tavant
L'Île-Bouchard
Ste-Maure-de-Touraine
Manthelan
Loches
Beaulieu-lès-Loches
Indre
Le Puy-Notre-Dame
Pouzay
Les Trois-Moutiers
La Celle-St-Avant
Ligueil
CHAMPAGNE
Cersay
Argenton-Château
Thouars
Loudun
Richelieu
Port-de-Piles
Descartes
Abilly
Châtillon-sur-Indre
Ste-Radegonde
Les Aubiers
Oiron
128
Thouet
Angliers
Monts-sur-Guesnes
St-Gervais-les-Trois-Clochers
Dangé-St-Romain
Le Grand-Pressigny
St-Flovier
Clion
St-Varent
St-Jouin-de-Marnes
Moncontour
Ingrandes
Creuse
Preuilly-sur-Claise
Azay-le-Ferron
Bressuire
Terves
Courlay
231
Chiché
Airvault
St-Loup-Lamairé
Mirebeau
Lencloître
171
Thuré
Scorbé-Clairvaux
Naintré
Châtellerault
La Roche-Posay
Coussay-les-Bois
Yzeures-sur-Creuse
Martizay
Mézières-en-Brenne
Vendœuvres
E50
A81
A11
A28
E402
E501
E502
A85
E60
A10
E05
E05/E60
E604

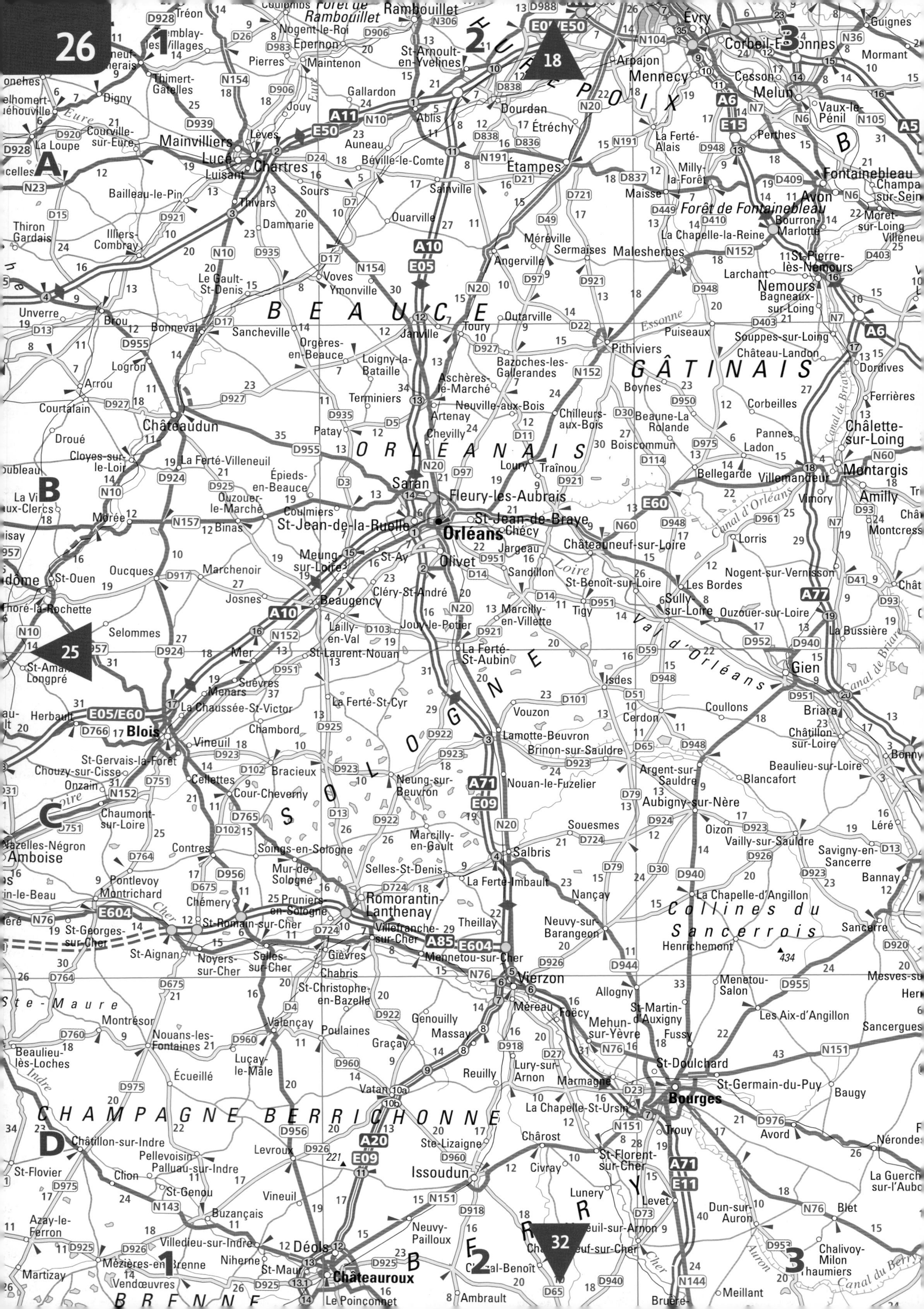

26
Rambouillet
Forêt de Rambouillet
HUREPOIX
Évry
Corbeil-Essonnes
Guignes
Mormant
Nogent-le-Roi
Épernon
Maintenon
Pierres
St-Arnoult-en-Yvelines
Arpajon
Mennecy
Cesson
Melun
Vaux-le-Pénil
Thimert-Gâtelles
DignY
Gallardon
Jouy
Ablis
Dourdan
Étréchy
La Ferté-Alais
Perthes
Courville-sur-Eure
La Loupe
Mainvilliers
Lucé
Lèves
Chartres
Luisant
Auneau
Béville-le-Comte
Étampes
Milly-la-Forêt
Fontainebleau
Avon
Bailleau-le-Pin
Sours
Sainville
Maisse
Forêt de Fontainebleau
Bourron-Marlotte
Moret-sur-Loing
Thivars
Dammarie
Ouarville
La Chapelle-la-Reine
Thiron Gardais
Illiers-Combray
Méréville
Sermaises
Malesherbes
St-Pierre-lès-Nemours
Angerville
Larchant
Nemours
Le Gault-St-Denis
Voves
Ymonville
Bagneaux-sur-Loing
Unverre
Brou
BEAUCE
Outarville
Bonneval
Sancheville
Janville
Toury
Pithiviers
Puiseaux
Souppes-sur-Loing
Château-Landon
Orgères-en-Beauce
Loigny-la-Bataille
Bazoches-les-Gallerandes
GÂTINAIS
Dordives
Logron
Arrou
Aschères-le-Marché
Boynes
Ferrières
Terminiers
Neuville-aux-Bois
Chilleurs-aux-Bois
Beaune-La Rolande
Corbeilles
Courtalain
Châteaudun
Artenay
Patay
Chevilly
Boiscommun
Pannes
Châlette-sur-Loing
Droué
ORLÉANAIS
Ladon
Cloyes-sur-le-Loir
La Ferté-Villeneuil
Loury
Traînou
Bellegarde
Villemandeur
Montargis
Épieds-en-Beauce
Saran
Amilly
Ouzouer-le-Marché
Coulmiers
Fleury-les-Aubrais
Vimory
Morée
Binas
St-Jean-de-la-Ruelle
St-Jean-de-Braye
Orléans
Chécy
Montcresson
Meung-sur-Loire
St-Ay
Olivet
Jargeau
Châteauneuf-sur-Loire
Lorris
St-Ouen
Oucques
Marchenoir
Sandillon
Loire
St-Benoît-sur-Loire
Nogent-sur-Vernisson
Josnes
Cléry-St-André
Les Bordes
Fréteval
Beaugency
Marcilly-en-Villette
Tigy
Sully-sur-Loire
Ouzouer-sur-Loire
Lailly-en-Val
Jouy-le-Potier
Val d'Orléans
La Bussière
Selommes
Mer
St-Laurent-Nouan
La Ferté-St-Aubin
Gien
St-Amand-Longpré
Suèvres
Ménars
Isdes
La Ferté-St-Cyr
La Chaussée-St-Victor
Vouzon
Cerdon
Coullons
Briare
Herbault
Blois
Chambord
Lamotte-Beuvron
Châtillon-sur-Loire
Vineuil
Brinon-sur-Sauldre
St-Gervais-la-Forêt
SOLOGNE
Bonny
Chouzy-sur-Cisse
Bracieux
Cellettes
Neung-sur-Beuvron
Argent-sur-Sauldre
Beaulieu-sur-Loire
Blancafort
Onzain
Cour-Cheverny
Nouan-le-Fuzelier
Aubigny-sur-Nère
Chaumont-sur-Loire
Léré
Souesmes
Oizon
Vailly-sur-Sauldre
Nazelles-Négron
Amboise
Contres
Soings-en-Sologne
Marcilly-en-Gault
Salbris
Savigny-en-Sancerre
Pontlevoy
Montrichard
Mur-de-Sologne
Selles-St-Denis
La Ferté-Imbault
Bannay
Chémery
Romorantin-Lanthenay
La Chapelle-d'Angillon
Nançay
Collines du Sancerrois
St-Georges-sur-Cher
St-Romain-sur-Cher
Pruniers-en-Sologne
Theillay
Neuvy-sur-Barangeon
Sancerre
Villefranche-sur-Cher
Henrichemont
St-Aignan
Noyers-sur-Cher
Selles-sur-Cher
Gièvres
Mennetou-sur-Cher
Chabris
Vierzon
Menetou-Salon
Mesves-sur-Loire
St-Christophe-en-Bazelle
Allogny
Ste-Maure
Montrésor
Méreau
Foëcy
St-Martin-d'Auxigny
Les Aix-d'Angillon
Genouilly
Mehun-sur-Yèvre
Valençay
Poulaines
Massay
Fussy
Sancergues
Nouans-les-Fontaines
Graçay
Beaulieu-lès-Loches
Luçay-le-Mâle
Lury-sur-Arnon
St-Doulchard
Écueillé
Reuilly
Marmagne
Vatan
Bourges
St-Germain-du-Puy
Baugy
CHAMPAGNE BERRICHONNE
La Chapelle-St-Ursin
Trouy
Châtillon-sur-Indre
Levroux
Ste-Lizaigne
Chârost
Avord
Nérondes
Pellevoisin
St-Florent-sur-Cher
St-Flovier
Clion
Palluau-sur-Indre
Issoudun
Civray
La Guerche-sur-l'Aubois
St-Genou
Vineuil
Lunery
BERRY
Buzançais
Levet
Dun-sur-Auron
Blet
Azay-le-Ferron
Neuvy-Pailloux
Villedieu-sur-Indre
Déols
Chalivoy-Milon
Mézières-en-Brenne
Niherne
St-Maur
Châteauroux
Thaumiers
Martizay
Vendœuvres
Le Poinçonnet
Ambrault
Meillant
BRENNE
Canal d'Orléans
Canal de Briare
Canal du Berry
18
25
32

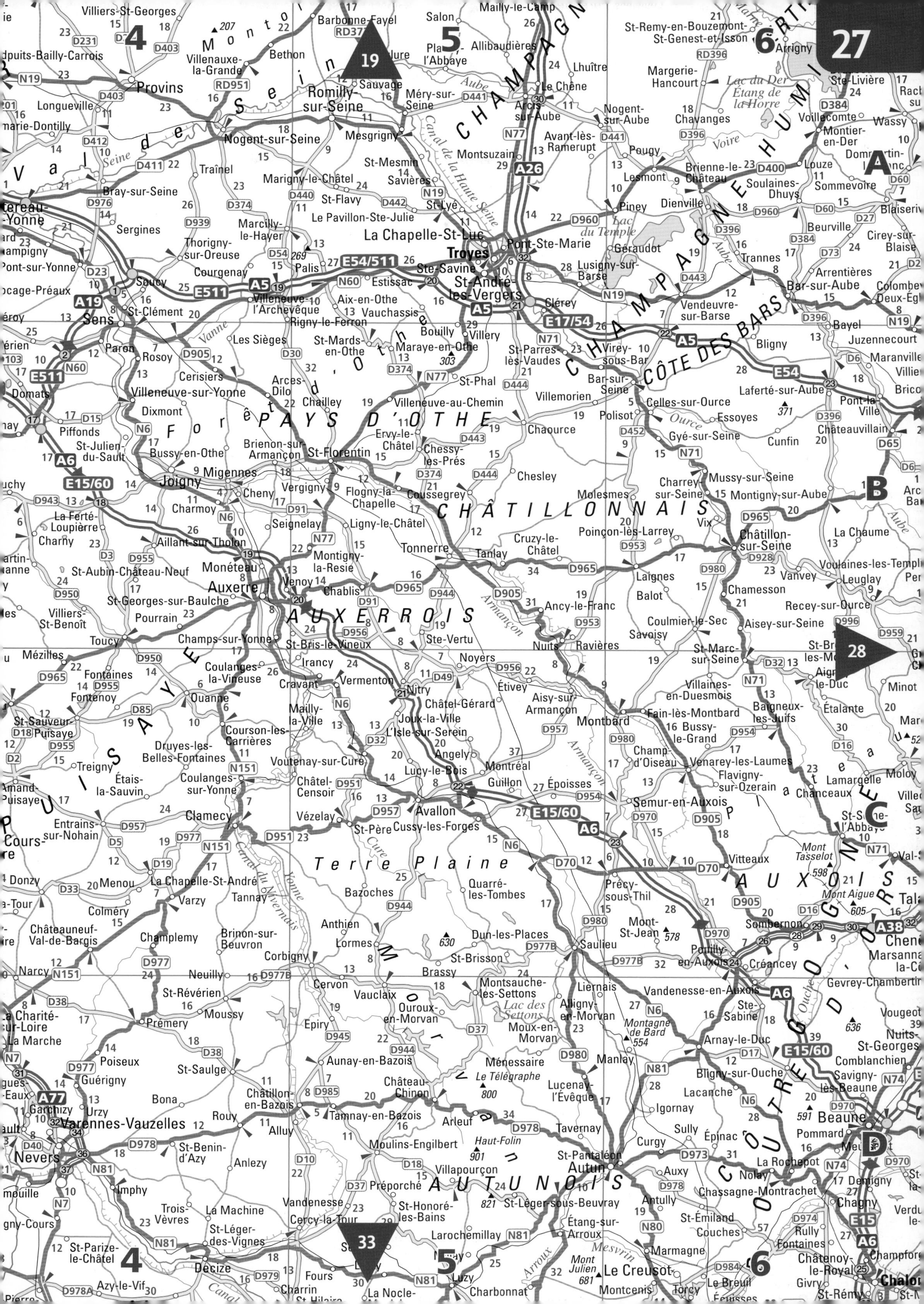
4
5
6
19
28
33
A
B
C
D
Villiers-St-Georges
Montois
Barbonne-Fayel
Salon
Mailly-le-Camp
St-Remy-en-Bouzemont-St-Genest-et-Isson
Arrigny
Provins
Villenauxe-la-Grande
Bethon
Plancy-l'Abbaye
Allibaudières
Lhuître
Margerie-Hancourt
Lac du Der Étang de la Horre
Ste-Livière
Longueville
Sauvage
Romilly-sur-Seine
Méry-sur-Seine
Le Chêne
Arcis-sur-Aube
Nogent-sur-Aube
Chavanges
Voillecomte
Wassy
Montier-en-Der
Nogent-sur-Seine
Mesgriny
CHAMPAGNE
Avant-lès-Ramerupt
Pougy
Voire
Montsuzain
Canal de la Haute Seine
Val de Seine
Traînel
St-Mesmin
Savières
Brienne-le-Château
Lesmont
Soulaines-Dhuys
Sommevoire
Bray-sur-Seine
Marigny-le-Châtel
St-Flavy
St-Lyé
Piney
Dienville
Le Pavillon-Ste-Julie
Blaiserive
Sergines
Marcilly-le-Hayer
La Chapelle-St-Luc
Lac du Temple
Beurville
Thorigny-sur-Oreuse
Troyes
Pont-Ste-Marie
Géraudot
Trannes
Cirey-sur-Blaise
Pont-sur-Yonne
Courgenay
Palis
Ste-Savine
St-André-les-Vergers
Lusigny-sur-Barse
Arrentières
Bar-sur-Aube
Soucy
Estissac
Vendeuvre-sur-Barse
Colombey-les-Deux-Églises
Sens
St-Clément
Villeneuve-l'Archevêque
Aix-en-Othe
Vauchassis
Rigny-le-Ferron
Clérey
Bayel
Les Sièges
St-Mards-en-Othe
Bouilly
Villery
Maraye-en-Othe
St-Parres-lès-Vaudes
Virey-sous-Bar
Bligny
Juzennecourt
Paron
Rosoy
Vanne
CÔTE DES BARS
Maranville
Cerisiers
Arces-Dilo
St-Phal
Bar-sur-Seine
Laferté-sur-Aube
Villeneuve-sur-Yonne
Dixmont
Chailley
Villeneuve-au-Chemin
Villemorien
Pont-la-Ville
Piffonds
Forêt d'Othe
PAYS D'OTHE
Ervy-le-Châtel
Polisot
Celles-sur-Ource
Ource
Essoyes
Châteauvillain
St-Julien-du-Sault
Bussy-en-Othe
Brienon-sur-Armançon
St-Florentin
Chessy-les-Prés
Chaource
Gyé-sur-Seine
Cunfin
Joigny
Migennes
Cheny
Vergigny
Flogny-la-Chapelle
Coussegrey
Chesley
Molesmes
Charrey-sur-Seine
Mussy-sur-Seine
Montigny-sur-Aube
La Ferté-Loupière
Charmoy
CHÂTILLONNAIS
Vix
Seignelay
Ligny-le-Châtel
Poinçon-lès-Larrey
Châtillon-sur-Seine
La Chaume
Charny
Aillant-sur-Tholon
Montigny-la-Resle
Tonnerre
Tanlay
Cruzy-le-Châtel
Voulaines-les-Templiers
St-Aubin-Château-Neuf
Monéteau
Venoy
Chablis
Laignes
Vanvey
Leuglay
Auxerre
Balot
Chamesson
Recey-sur-Ource
St-Georges-sur-Baulche
Ancy-le-Franc
Villiers-St-Benoît
Pourrain
AUXERROIS
Armançon
Coulmier-le-Sec
Aisey-sur-Seine
Savoisy
Toucy
Champs-sur-Yonne
St-Bris-le-Vineux
Ste-Vertu
Nuits
Ravières
St-Marc-sur-Seine
Mézilles
Irancy
Noyers
Coulanges-la-Vineuse
Fontaines
Cravant
Vermenton
Nitry
Étivey
Villaines-en-Duesmois
Aignay-le-Duc
Minot
Fontenoy
Ouanne
Châtel-Gérard
Aisy-sur-Armançon
Fain-lès-Montbard
Baigneux-les-Juifs
Étalante
St-Sauveur-en-Puisaye
Mailly-la-Ville
Joux-la-Ville
Montbard
Bussy-le-Grand
Courson-les-Carrières
L'Isle-sur-Serein
Druyes-les-Belles-Fontaines
Angely
Champ-d'Oiseau
Venarey-les-Laumes
Treigny
Vouteney-sur-Cure
Montréal
Lamargelle
Moloy
PUISAYE
Étais-la-Sauvin
Coulanges-sur-Yonne
Châtel-Censoir
Lucy-le-Bois
Guillon
Époisses
Flavigny-sur-Ozerain
Chanceaux
St-Amand-en-Puisaye
Avallon
Semur-en-Auxois
Clamecy
Vézelay
St-Père
Cussy-les-Forges
St-Seine-l'Abbaye
Entrains-sur-Nohain
Cosne-Cours-sur-Loire
Cure
Mont Tasselot
Terre Plaine
Vitteaux
Canal du Nivernais
Yonne
AUXOIS
Donzy
Menou
La Chapelle-St-André
Tannay
Bazoches
Quarré-les-Tombes
Précy-sous-Thil
Mont Aigue
Varzy
Colméry
Sombernon
Châteauneuf-Val-de-Bargis
Champlemy
Brinon-sur-Beuvron
Anthien
Dun-les-Places
Mont-St-Jean
Chenôve
Lormes
St-Brisson
Saulieu
Pouilly-en-Auxois
Créancey
Marsannay-la-Côte
Narcy
Corbigny
Neuilly
MORVAN
Brassy
Gevrey-Chambertin
Cervon
Montsauche-les-Settons
Liernais
St-Réverien
Vauclaix
Vandenesse-en-Auxois
Moussy
Ouroux-en-Morvan
Lac des Settons
Alligny-en-Morvan
Ste-Sabine
Vougeot
La Charité-sur-Loire
La Marche
Prémery
Epiry
Moux-en-Morvan
Montagne de Bard
Nuits-St-Georges
Arnay-le-Duc
Ménessaire
Manlay
Comblanchien
Poiseux
St-Saulge
Aunay-en-Bazois
Le Télégraphe
Bligny-sur-Ouche
Savigny-lès-Beaune
Guérigny
Château-Chinon
Lucenay-l'Évêque
Lacanche
Garchizy
Bona
Châtillon-en-Bazois
Urzy
Tamnay-en-Bazois
Arleuf
Igornay
Beaune
Varennes-Vauzelles
Rouy
Alluy
Tavernay
Pommard
Haut-Folin
Sully
Épinac
Curgy
Nevers
St-Benin-d'Azy
Moulins-Engilbert
Meursault
Anlezy
St-Pantaléon
La Rochepot
Nolay
Autun
Villapourçon
Auxy
Demigny
Magny-Cours
Imphy
Préporché
AUTUNOIS
Chassagne-Montrachet
Chagny
Trois-Vèvres
La Machine
Vandenesse
St-Honoré-les-Bains
St-Léger-sous-Beuvray
Antully
Verdun-sur-le-Doubs
St-Léger-des-Vignes
Cercy-la-Tour
Larochemillay
Étang-sur-Arroux
St-Émiland
Couches
Rully
Fontaines
St-Parize-le-Châtel
Decize
Marmagne
Châtenoy-le-Royal
Mesvrin
Arroux
Mont Julien
Le Creusot
Champforgeuil
Azy-le-Vif
Fours
Luzy
Charbonnat
Montcenis
Torcy
Le Breuil
Givry
St-Rémy
Chalon-sur-Saône
Charrin
La Nocle-Maulaix
CÔTE D'OR
CÔTE DE NUITS
Ouche
Bernon
A5
A6
A19
A26
A38
A77
E15
E15/60
E17/54
E54
E54/511
E511
N6
N7
N19
N60
N71
N77
N80
N81
N151

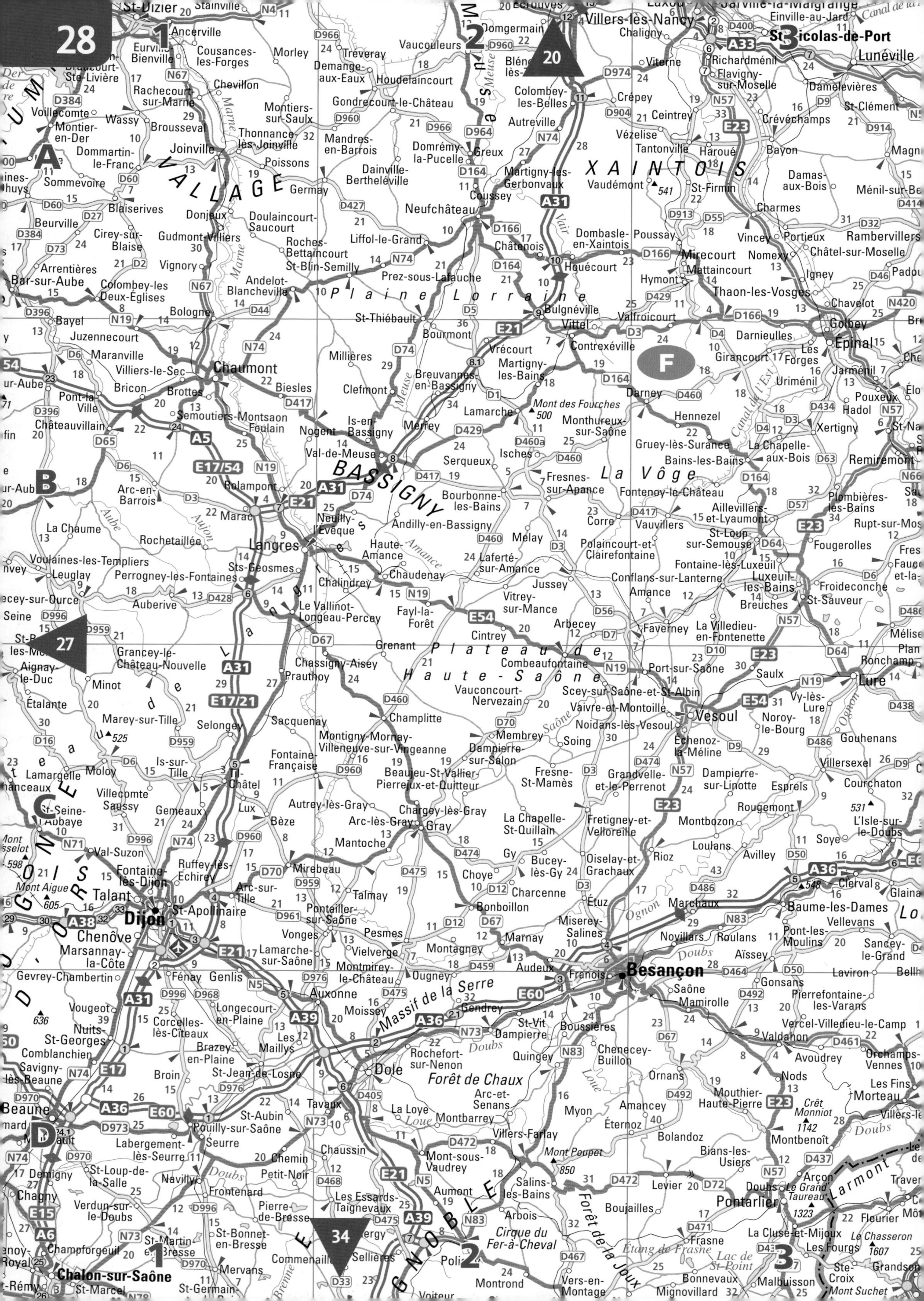
28
St-Dizier
Stainville
Ancerville
Eurville-Bienville
Cousances-les-Forges
Morley
Tréveray
Demange-aux-Eaux
Vaucouleurs
Domgermain
Ecrouves
Villers-lès-Nancy
Chaligny
Laxou
Jarville-la-Malgrange
Einville-au-Jard
St-Nicolas-de-Port
Lunéville
Canal de la Marne au Rhin
Blénod-lès-Toul
Richardménil
Flavigny-sur-Moselle
Viterne
Ste-Livière
Rachecourt-sur-Marne
Chevillon
Houdelaincourt
Gondrecourt-le-Château
Colombey-les-Belles
Crépey
Dameleviéres
St-Clément
Voillecomte
Montier-en-Der
Wassy
Brousseval
Montiers-sur-Saulx
Thonnance-lès-Joinville
Mandres-en-Barrois
Domrémy-la-Pucelle
Greux
Autreville
Vézelise
Ceintrey
Crévéchamps
Tantonville
Haroué
Bayon
Dommartin-le-Franc
Joinville
Poissons
Dainville-Bertheléville
Martigny-les-Gerbonvaux
XAINTOIS
Vaudémont
541
St-Firmin
Damas-aux-Bois
Magnières
Ménil-sur-Belvitte
Sommevoire
VALLAGE
Germay
Coussey
Neufchâteau
Charmes
Blaiserives
Beurville
Donjeux
Doulaincourt-Saucourt
Liffol-le-Grand
Vair
Dombasle-en-Xaintois
Poussay
Vincey
Portieux
Rambervillers
Châtel-sur-Moselle
Cirey-sur-Blaise
Gudmont-Villiers
Roches-Bettaincourt
Châtenois
Mirecourt
Nomexy
Arrentières
Vignory
St-Blin-Semilly
Prez-sous-Lafauche
Houécourt
Mattaincourt
Hymont
Igney
Padoux
Bar-sur-Aube
Colombey-les-Deux-Églises
Andelot-Blancheville
Plaine Lorraine
Thaon-les-Vosges
Chavelot
Bulgnéville
Valfroicourt
Bayel
Bologne
St-Thiébault
Bourmont
Vittel
Golbey
Juzennecourt
Contrexéville
Darnieulles
Épinal
Maranville
Villiers-le-Sec
Chaumont
Millières
Vrécourt
Martigny-les-Bains
Girancourt
Les Forges
Jarménil
Bar-sur-Aube
Pont-la-Ville
Bricon
Brottes
Biesles
Clefmont
Breuvannes-en-Bassigny
Uriménil
Darney
Pouxeux
Hadol
Éloyes
Châteauvillain
Semoutiers-Montsaon
Foulain
Nogent
Is-en-Bassigny
Meuse
Merrey
Lamarche
Mont des Fourches
500
Monthureux-sur-Saône
Hennezel
Canal de l'Est
Xertigny
Val-de-Meuse
Serqueux
Isches
Gruey-lès-Surance
La Chapelle-aux-Bois
Bains-les-Bains
Remiremont
BASSIGNY
Arc-en-Barrois
Rolampont
Bourbonne-les-Bains
Fresnes-sur-Apance
La Vôge
Fontenoy-le-Château
Plombières-les-Bains
Aube
Aujon
Marac
Neuilly-l'Évêque
Andilly-en-Bassigny
Corre
Vauvillers
Aillevillers-et-Lyaumont
Rupt-sur-Moselle
La Chaume
Rochetaillée
Langres
Haute-Amance
Amance
Melay
Polaincourt-et-Clairefontaine
St-Loup-sur-Semouse
Fougerolles
Voulaines-les-Templiers
Leuglay
Perrogney-les-Fontaines
Sts-Geosmes
Chalindrey
Chaudenay
Laferté-sur-Amance
Jussey
Fontaine-lès-Luxeuil
Conflans-sur-Lanterne
Luxeuil-les-Bains
Froideconche
St-Sauveur
Recey-sur-Ource
Auberive
Le Vallinot-Longeau-Percey
Fayl-la-Forêt
Vitrey-sur-Mance
Amance
Breuches
Seine
St-Broing-les-Moines
27
Cintrey
Arbecey
Faverney
La Villedieu-en-Fontenette
Mélisey
Grancey-le-Château-Nouvelle
Aignay-le-Duc
Chassigny-Aisey
Prauthoy
Grenant
Plateau de Haute-Saône
Combeaufontaine
Port-sur-Saône
Saulx
Ronchamp
Lure
Minot
Étalante
Vauconcourt-Nervezain
Scey-sur-Saône-et-St-Albin
Vy-lès-Lure
Marey-sur-Tille
Selongey
Champlitte
Vaivre-et-Montoille
Noidans-lès-Vesoul
Vesoul
Noroy-le-Bourg
Sacquenay
Membrey
Saône
Soing
Échenoz-la-Méline
Gouhenans
525
Montigny-Mornay-Villeneuve-sur-Vingeanne
Dampierre-sur-Salon
Villersexel
Is-sur-Tille
Fontaine-Française
Beaujeu-St-Vallier-Pierrejux-et-Quitteur
Fresne-St-Mamès
Grandvelle-et-le-Perrenot
Dampierre-sur-Linotte
Esprels
Courchaton
Lamargelle
Moloy
Til-Châtel
Chanceaux
Villecomte
Saussy
Lux
Autrey-lès-Gray
Chargey-lès-Gray
La Chapelle-St-Quillain
Rougemont
531
St-Seine-l'Abbaye
Gemeaux
Bèze
Arc-lès-Gray
Gray
Fretigney-et-Velloreille
Montbozon
L'Isle-sur-le-Doubs
Mantoche
Loulans
Soye
Mont Afrique
Val-Suzon
Ruffey-lès-Echirey
Mirebeau
Gy
Bucey-lès-Gy
Oiselay-et-Grachaux
Rioz
Avilley
598
Mont Aigue
605
Fontaine-lès-Dijon
Arc-sur-Tille
Talmay
Choye
Charcenne
Cléval
Glainans
Talant
Dijon
St-Apollinaire
Pontailler-sur-Saône
Bonboillon
Étuz
Ognon
Marchaux
Baume-les-Dames
Chenôve
Vonges
Pesmes
Marnay
Miserey-Salines
Novillars
Roulans
Vellevans
Pont-les-Moulins
Sancey-le-Grand
Marsannay-la-Côte
Lamarche-sur-Saône
Vielverge
Montagney
Audeux
Besançon
Aïssey
Gevrey-Chambertin
Fénay
Genlis
Montmirey-le-Château
Ougney
Franois
Doubs
Laviron
Belleherbe
Auxonne
Massif de la Serre
Gendrey
Saône
Mamirolle
Gonsans
Pierrefontaine-les-Varans
Longecourt-en-Plaine
Moissey
Vougeot
636
Nuits-St-Georges
Corcelles-lès-Cîteaux
Les Maillys
Brazey-en-Plaine
St-Vit
Dampierre
Boussières
Vercel-Villedieu-le-Camp
Valdahon
Orchamps-Vennes
Comblanchien
Savigny-lès-Beaune
St-Jean-de-Losne
Rochefort-sur-Nenon
Dole
Quingey
Chenecey-Buillon
Avoudrey
Broin
Forêt de Chaux
Ornans
Nods
Les Fins
Morteau
Beaune
Tavaux
Arc-et-Senans
Mouthier-Haute-Pierre
Crêt Monniot
1142
St-Aubin
La Loye
Loue
Montbarrey
Myon
Amancey
Villers-le-Lac
Pouilly-sur-Saône
Seurre
Éternoz
Meursault
Labergement-lès-Seurre
Chaussin
Villers-Farlay
Bolandoz
Montbenoît
Chemin
Mont-sous-Vaudrey
Mont Poupet
850
Bians-les-Usiers
Demigny
St-Loup-de-la-Salle
Navilly
Petit-Noir
Salins-les-Bains
Levier
Arçon
Le Grand Taureau
1323
Larmont
Chagny
Frontenard
Les Essards-Taignevaux
Aumont
Forêt de la Joux
Doubs
Pontarlier
Verdun-sur-le-Doubs
Pierre-de-Bresse
Boujailles
Arbois
Fleurier
Champforgeuil
St-Martin-en-Bresse
St-Bonnet-en-Bresse
Chemin
34
Cirque du Fer-à-Cheval
Frasne
La Cluse-et-Mijoux
Le Chasseron
1607
Chalon-sur-Saône
Mervans
Commenailles
Sellières
Poligny
Étang de Frasne
Lac de St-Point
Les Fourgs
Ste-Croix
Grandson
St-Rémy
St-Marcel
St-Germain-du-Plain
Voiteur
Montrond
Vers-en-Montagne
Bonnevaux
Mignovillard
Malbuisson
Mont Suchet
Brenne
GNOBLE

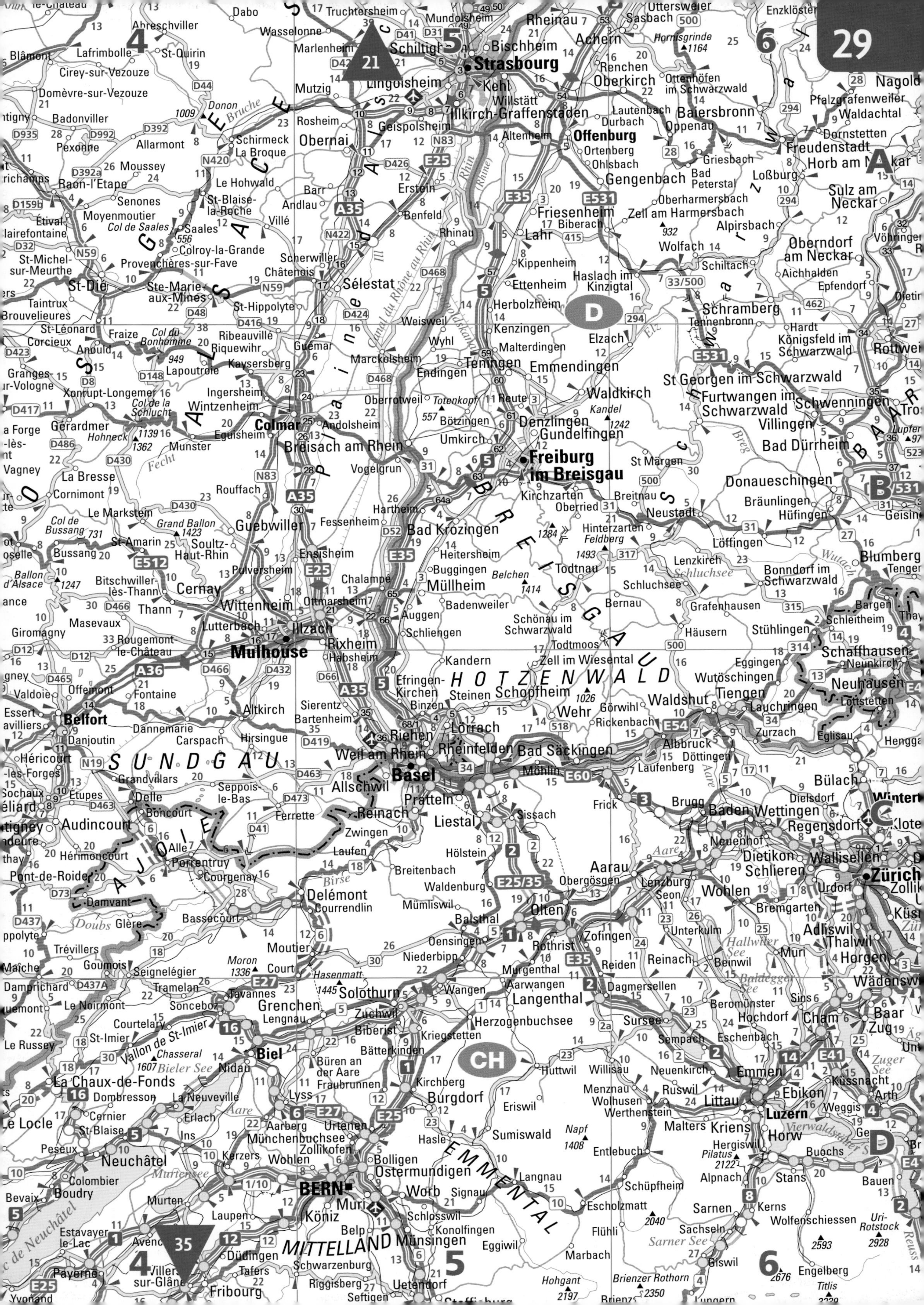
Dabo
Truchtersheim
Mundolsheim
Rheinau
Achern
Sasbach
Ottersweier
Enzklösterle
Abreschviller
Wasselonne
Marlenheim
Schiltigheim
Bischheim
Hornisgrinde
1164
Nagold
Blâmont
Lafrimbolle
St-Quirin
Strasbourg
Renchen
Oberkirch
Ottenhöfen im Schwarzwald
Pfalzgrafenweiler
Cirey-sur-Vezouze
Mutzig
Lingolsheim
Kehl
Willstätt
Waldachtal
Domèvre-sur-Vezouze
Illkirch-Graffenstaden
Lautenbach
Baiersbronn
Dornstetten
Badonviller
Donon
1009
Bruche
Rosheim
Geispolsheim
Durbach
Oppenau
Freudenstadt
Pexonne
Allarmont
Schirmeck
La Broque
Obernai
Altenheim
Offenburg
Ortenberg
Griesbach
Horb am Neckar
Moussey
Ohlsbach
Bad Peterstal
Loßburg
Raon-l'Etape
Le Hohwald
Erstein
Gengenbach
Sulz am Neckar
Senones
St-Blaise-la-Roche
Barr
Andlau
Friesenheim
Oberharmersbach
Etival
Moyenmoutier
Col de Saales
556
Saales
Villé
Benfeld
Rhinau
Biberach
Zell am Harmersbach
Alpirsbach
Clairefontaine
Colroy-la-Grande
Lahr
932
Oberndorf am Neckar
St-Michel-sur-Meurthe
Provenchères-sur-Fave
Scherwiller
Châtenois
Kippenheim
Wolfach
Schiltach
Aichhalden
St-Dié
Ste-Marie-aux-Mines
Sélestat
Ettenheim
Haslach im Kinzigtal
Epfendorf
Taintrux
Brouvelieures
St-Hippolyte
Herbolzheim
Schramberg
Tennenbronn
St-Léonard
Fraize
Col du Bonhomme
Ribeauvillé
Weisweil
Kenzingen
Elzach
Hardt
Corcieux
Anould
Riquewihr
Guémar
Wyhl
Malterdingen
Königsfeld im Schwarzwald
Rottweil
949
Lapoutroie
Kaysersberg
Marckolsheim
Endingen
Teningen
Emmendingen
Granges-sur-Vologne
Xonrupt-Longemer
Ingersheim
Oberrotweil
Totenkopf
557
Reute
Waldkirch
St Georgen im Schwarzwald
Furtwangen im Schwarzwald
Schwenningen
Col de la Schlucht
1139
Wintzenheim
Colmar
Andolsheim
Bötzingen
Denzlingen
Kandel
1242
Villingen
Gérardmer
Hohneck
1362
Munster
Equisheim
Breisach am Rhein
Umkirch
Gundelfingen
Bad Dürrheim
Vagney
La Bresse
Vogelgrun
Freiburg im Breisgau
St Märgen
Donaueschingen
Cornimont
Rouffach
Kirchzarten
Oberried
Breitnau
Bräunlingen
Le Markstein
Hartheim
Neustadt
Hüfingen
Col de Bussang
731
Grand Ballon
1423
Guebwiller
Fessenheim
Bad Krozingen
1284
Hinterzarten
Feldberg
Löffingen
Bussang
St-Amarin
Soultz-Haut-Rhin
Ensisheim
Heitersheim
1493
Todtnau
Lenzkirch
Schluchsee
Blumberg
Ballon d'Alsace
1247
Bitschwiller-lès-Thann
Pulversheim
Cernay
Buggingen
Belchen
1414
Müllheim
Bonndorf im Schwarzwald
Thann
Wittenheim
Chalampé
Ottmarsheim
Badenweiler
Bernau
Grafenhausen
Bargen
Schleitheim
Giromagny
Masevaux
Rougemont-le-Château
Lutterbach
Illzach
Auggen
Schliengen
Schönau im Schwarzwald
Häusern
Stühlingen
Mulhouse
Rixheim
Habsheim
Todtmoos
Schaffhausen
Neunkirch
Kandern
Zell im Wiesental
Eggingen
Valdoie
Offemont
Fontaine
Efringen-Kirchen
HOTZENWALD
Wutöschingen
Neuhausen
Essert
Belfort
Altkirch
Sierentz
Bartenheim
Steinen
Schopfheim
1026
Waldshut
Tiengen
Lauchringen
Lottstetten
Danjoutin
Dannemarie
Carspach
Hirsingue
Binzen
Lörrach
Wehr
Görwihl
Rickenbach
Zurzach
Eglisau
Héricourt
SUNDGAU
Riehen
Weil am Rhein
Rheinfelden
Bad Säckingen
Albbruck
Döttingen
Laufenberg
Hengga
Grandvillars
Seppois-le-Bas
Allschwil
Basel
Möhlin
Bülach
Sochaux
Etupes
Delle
Boncourt
Ferrette
Reinach
Pratteln
Frick
Brugg
Dielsdorf
Montbéliard
Audincourt
AJOIE
Alle
Liestal
Sissach
Baden
Wettingen
Regensdorf
Zwingen
Laufen
Hölstein
Neuenhof
Dietikon
Wallisellen
Hérimoncourt
Porrentruy
Courgenay
Breitenbach
Aarau
Obergösgen
Lenzburg
Schlieren
Zürich
Pont-de-Roide
Delémont
Courrendlin
Birse
Waldenburg
Seon
Wohlen
Urdorf
Zollikon
Damvant
Mümliswil
Olten
Bremgarten
Bassecourt
Glère
Doubs
Balsthal
Unterkulm
Adliswil
Thalwil
Moutier
Oensingen
Rothrist
Zofingen
Hallwiler See
Muri
Horgen
Trévillers
Niederbipp
Reiden
Reinach
Beinwil
Maîche
Goumois
Seignelégier
Moron
1336
Court
Hasenmatt
1445
Murgenthal
Aarwangen
Dagmersellen
Baldegger See
Wädenswil
Damprichard
Tramelan
Tavannes
Solothurn
Wangen
Langenthal
Sins
Cham
Baar
Le Noirmont
Sonceboz
Grenchen
Lengnau
Zuchwil
Beromünster
Hochdorf
Zug
Courtelary
Biberist
Kriegstetten
Herzogenbuchsee
Sursee
Eschenbach
St-Imier
Vallon de St-Imier
Chasseral
1607
Bieler See
Biel
Nidau
Bätterkinden
Sempach
Le Russey
Büren an der Aare
CH
Huttwil
Willisau
Neuenkirch
Emmen
Zuger See
Küssnacht
La Chaux-de-Fonds
Dombresson
La Neuveville
Lyss
Fraubrunnen
Kirchberg
Burgdorf
Menznau
Ruswil
Littau
Ebikon
Arth
Le Locle
Cernier
St-Blaise
Erlach
Aare
Aarberg
Urtenen
Eriswil
Wolhusen
Werthenstein
Luzern
Weggis
Peseux
Neuchâtel
Ins
Kerzers
Münchenbuchsee
Zollikofen
Hasle
Sumiswald
Napf
1408
Malters
Kriens
Horw
Vierwaldstätter See
Colombier
Boudry
Murtensee
Wohlen
Bolligen
Ostermundigen
EMMENTAL
Entlebuch
Hergiswil
Pilatus
2122
Buchs
Bevaix
Murten
BERN
Worb
Signau
Langnau
Alpnach
Stans
Bauen
Lac de Neuchâtel
Laupen
Muri
Köniz
Schüpfheim
Escholzmatt
Kerns
Estavayer-le-Lac
Avenches
Belp
Schlosswil
Konolfingen
2040
Sarnen
Wolfenschiessen
Uri-Rotstock
2928
Flühli
Sachseln
Sarner See
MITTELLAND
Münsingen
Eggiwil
2593
Payerne
Villars-sur-Glâne
Düdingen
Tafers
Schwarzenburg
Marbach
Giswil
Engelberg
Fribourg
Riggisberg
Seftigen
Uetendorf
Hohgant
2197
Brienzer Rothorn
2350
2676
Titlis
Yvonand
Plaine d'Alsace
VOSGES
ALSACE
Schwarzwald
BREISGAU
BAAR
Canal du Rhône au Rhin
Rhin (Rhein)
21
35

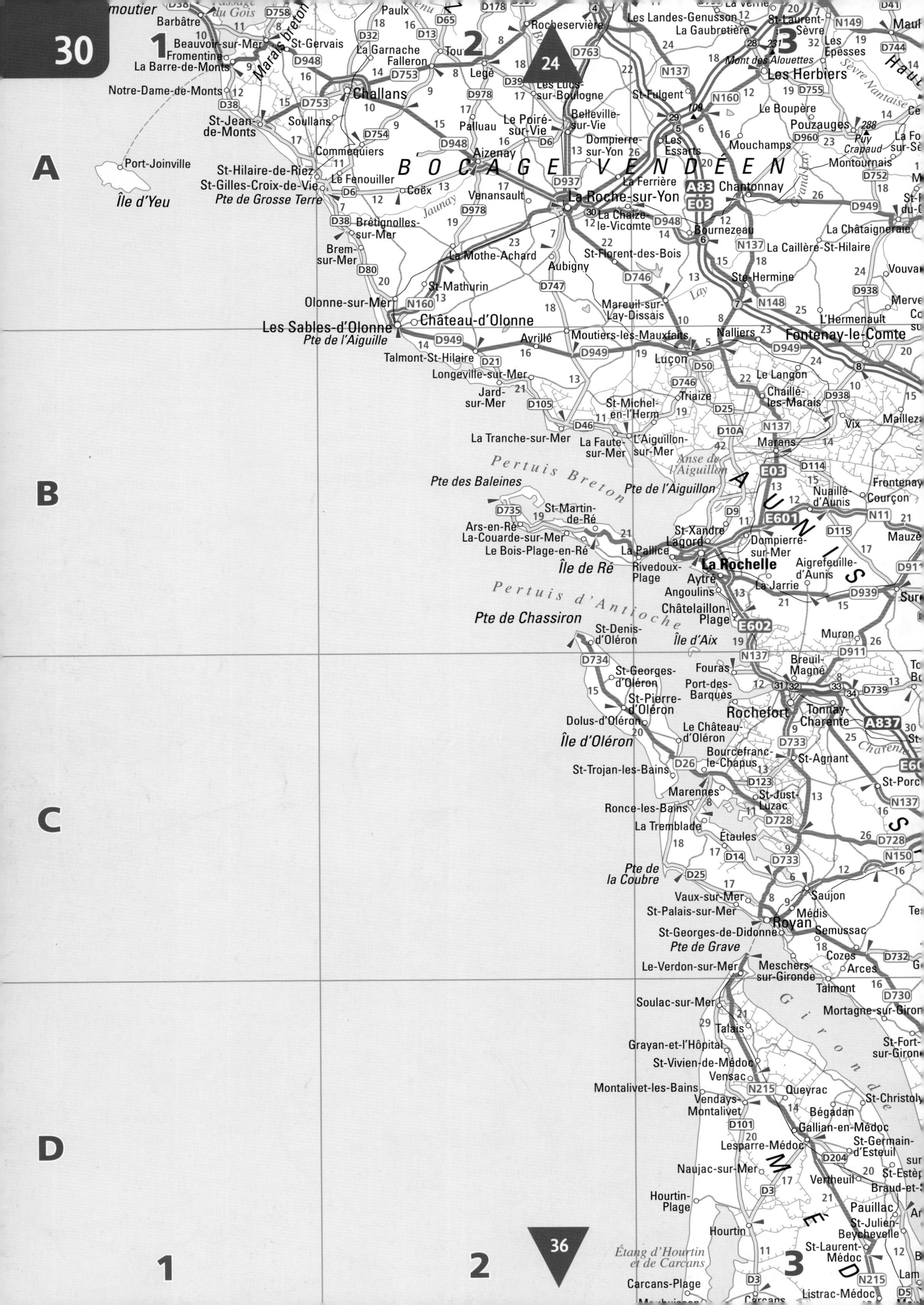

24
36
A
B
C
D
1
2
3
Barbâtre
Beauvoir-sur-Mer
Fromentine
La Barre-de-Monts
St-Gervais
Marais breton
Notre-Dame-de-Monts
St-Jean-de-Monts
Soullans
Port-Joinville
Île d'Yeu
St-Hilaire-de-Riez
St-Gilles-Croix-de-Vie
Pte de Grosse Terre
Le Fenouiller
Commequiers
Challans
Paulx
La Garnache
Falleron
Touvois
Legé
Rocheservière
Les Lucs-sur-Boulogne
Palluau
Le Poiré-sur-Vie
Belleville-sur-Vie
Aizenay
Dompierre-sur-Yon
Les Essarts
BOCAGE VENDÉEN
Coëx
Venansault
La Roche-sur-Yon
La Ferrière
La Chaize-le-Vicomte
Les Landes-Genusson
La Gaubretière
St-Laurent-Sèvre
Mont des Alouettes
Les Herbiers
Les Epesses
St-Fulgent
Le Boupère
Pouzauges
Puy Crapaud
Mouchamps
Montournais
Chantonnay
Bournezeau
La Châtaigneraie
La Caillère-St-Hilaire
Ste-Hermine
L'Hermenault
Fontenay-le-Comte
Brétignolles-sur-Mer
Brem-sur-Mer
La Mothe-Achard
Aubigny
St-Florent-des-Bois
St-Mathurin
Olonne-sur-Mer
Château-d'Olonne
Les Sables-d'Olonne
Pte de l'Aiguille
Mareuil-sur-Lay-Dissais
Avrillé
Moutiers-les-Mauxfaits
Nalliers
Talmont-St-Hilaire
Luçon
Longeville-sur-Mer
Jard-sur-Mer
St-Michel-en-l'Herm
Triaize
Le Langon
Chaillé-les-Marais
Vix
Maillezais
La Tranche-sur-Mer
La Faute-sur-Mer
L'Aiguillon-sur-Mer
Anse de l'Aiguillon
Marans
Pertuis Breton
Pte des Baleines
Pte de l'Aiguillon
AUNIS
Nuaillé-d'Aunis
Courçon
Frontenay
St-Martin-de-Ré
Ars-en-Ré
La Couarde-sur-Mer
Le Bois-Plage-en-Ré
Île de Ré
La Pallice
Rivedoux-Plage
St-Xandre
Lagord
Dompierre-sur-Mer
La Rochelle
Aigrefeuille-d'Aunis
Mauzé
Aytré
Angoulins
La Jarrie
Pertuis d'Antioche
Châtelaillon-Plage
Pte de Chassiron
St-Denis-d'Oléron
Île d'Aix
Muron
Fouras
Breuil-Magné
St-Georges-d'Oléron
Port-des-Barques
Rochefort
Tonnay-Charente
St-Pierre-d'Oléron
Dolus-d'Oléron
Île d'Oléron
Le Château-d'Oléron
Bourcefranc-le-Chapus
St-Agnant
St-Trojan-les-Bains
Marennes
St-Just-Luzac
Ronce-les-Bains
La Tremblade
Étaules
Pte de la Coubre
Vaux-sur-Mer
Saujon
Médis
St-Palais-sur-Mer
Royan
Semussac
St-Georges-de-Didonne
Pte de Grave
Cozes
Arces
Le Verdon-sur-Mer
Meschers-sur-Gironde
Talmont
Soulac-sur-Mer
Talais
Mortagne-sur-Gironde
Gironde
Grayan-et-l'Hôpital
St-Vivien-de-Médoc
Vensac
Montalivet-les-Bains
Vendays-Montalivet
Queyrac
Bégadan
Gaillan-en-Médoc
Lesparre-Médoc
St-Germain-d'Esteuil
Naujac-sur-Mer
Vertheuil
Hourtin-Plage
Pauillac
St-Julien-Beychevelle
Hourtin
St-Laurent-Médoc
Étang d'Hourtin et de Carcans
Carcans-Plage
Listrac-Médoc
MÉDOC

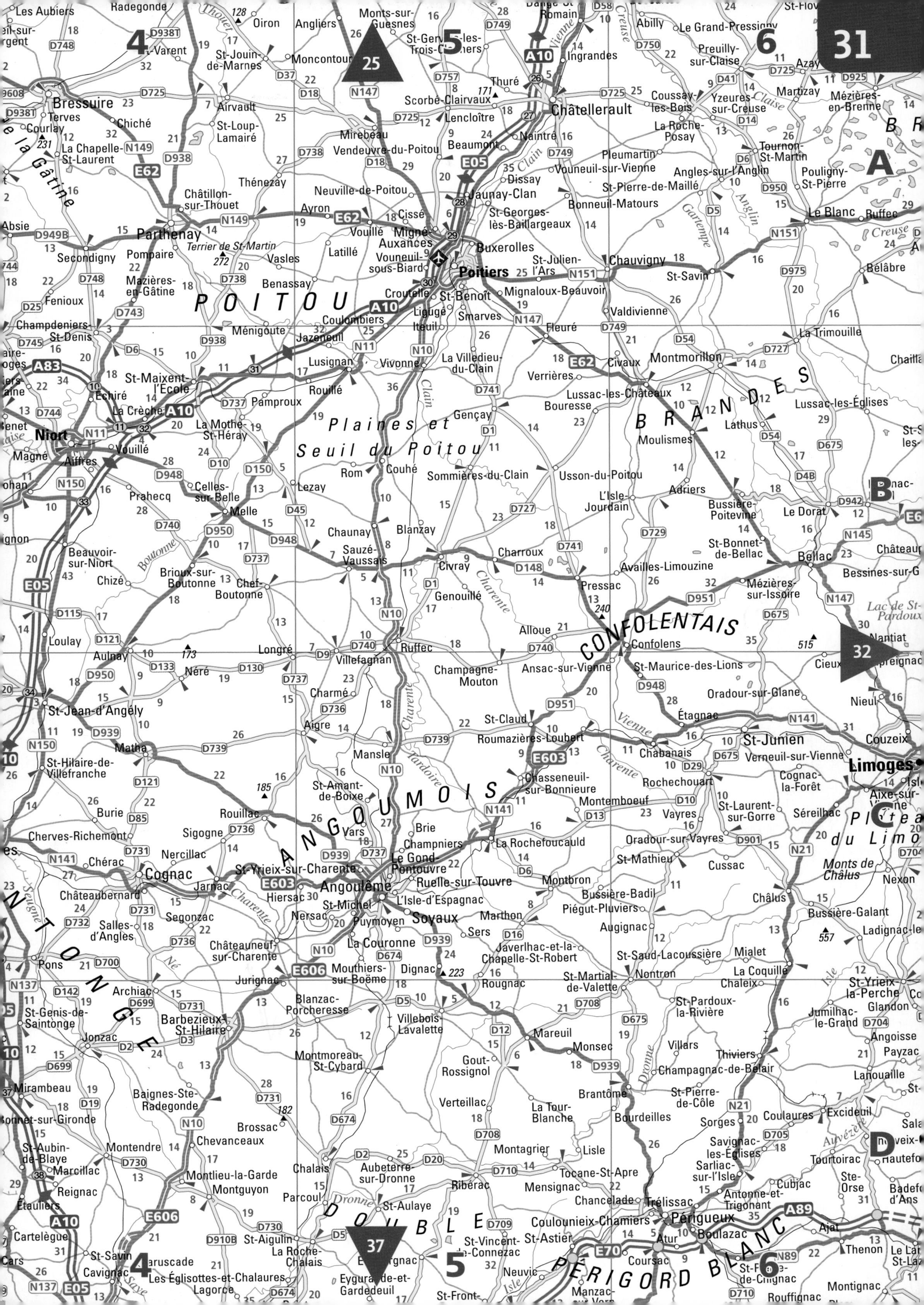31
25
32
37
4
5
6
A
B
C
D
Les Aubiers
Radegonde
Oiron
Angliers
Monts-sur-Guesnes
St-Gervais-les-Trois-Clochers
Romain
Abilly
Le Grand-Pressigny
Preuilly-sur-Claise
Azay
St-Varent
St-Jouin-de-Marnes
Moncontour
Ingrandes
Bressuire
Terves
Courlay
Chiché
Airvault
St-Loup-Lamairé
Mirebeau
Scorbé-Clairvaux
Lencloître
Thuré
Châtellerault
Coussay-les-Bois
Yzeures-sur-Creuse
Martizay
Mézières-en-Brenne
La Chapelle-St-Laurent
Vendeuvre-du-Poitou
Beaumont
Naintré
La Roche-Posay
Tournon-St-Martin
Pleumartin
Vouneuil-sur-Vienne
Angles-sur-l'Anglin
Pouligny-St-Pierre
Gâtine
Thénezay
Neuville-de-Poitou
Dissay
Jaunay-Clan
St-Pierre-de-Maillé
Châtillon-sur-Thouet
Ayron
Cissé
St-Georges-lès-Baillargeaux
Bonneuil-Matours
Le Blanc
Ruffec
Absie
Parthenay
Vouillé
Migné-Auxances
Secondigny
Pompaire
Terrier de St-Martin
Vasles
Latillé
Vouneuil-sous-Biard
Buxerolles
Poitiers
St-Julien-l'Ars
Chauvigny
St-Savin
Bélâbre
Mazières-en-Gâtine
Benassay
Fenioux
Croutelle
St-Benoît
Mignaloux-Beauvoir
Valdivienne
POITOU
Ligugé
Smarves
Coulombiers
Champdeniers-St-Denis
Ménigoute
Jazeneuil
Iteuil
Fleuré
La Trimouille
Lusignan
Vivonne
La Villedieu-du-Clain
Civaux
Montmorillon
St-Maixent-l'École
Échiré
Rouillé
Verrières
Lussac-les-Châteaux
Pamproux
La Crèche
Boloresse
Lussac-les-Églises
La Mothe-St-Héray
Gençay
Plaines et Seuil du Poitou
BRANDES
Lathus
Niort
Moulismes
Magné
Aiffres
Vouillé
Celles-sur-Belle
Prahecq
Melle
Lezay
Rom
Couhé
Sommières-du-Clain
Usson-du-Poitou
L'Isle-Jourdain
Adriers
Bussière-Poitevine
Le Dorat
Chaunay
Blanzay
Beauvoir-sur-Niort
Brioux-sur-Boutonne
Chizé
Chef-Boutonne
Sauzé-Vaussais
Civray
Charroux
Availles-Limouzine
St-Bonnet-de-Bellac
Bellac
Châteauponsac
Bessines-sur-Gartempe
Genouillé
Pressac
Mézières-sur-Issoire
Loulay
Aulnay
Néré
Longré
Villefagnan
Ruffec
Alloue
CONFOLENTAIS
Confolens
Nantiat
St-Jean-d'Angély
Charmé
Champagne-Mouton
Ansac-sur-Vienne
St-Maurice-des-Lions
Oradour-sur-Glane
Nieul
Aigre
St-Claud
Étagnac
Matha
Roumazières-Loubert
Chabanais
St-Junien
Couzeix
St-Hilaire-de-Villefranche
Mansle
Verneuil-sur-Vienne
Limoges
Chasseneuil-sur-Bonnieure
Rochechouart
Cognac-la-Forêt
St-Amant-de-Boixe
ANGOUMOIS
Montembœuf
Burie
Rouillac
Vayres
St-Laurent-sur-Gorre
Séreilhac
Aixe-sur-Vienne
Cherves-Richemont
Sigogne
Vars
Brie
Champniers
La Rochefoucauld
Oradour-sur-Vayres
Plateau du Limousin
Chérac
Nercillac
Le Gond-Pontouvre
St-Mathieu
Cussac
Monts de Châlus
Cognac
Jarnac
St-Yrieix-sur-Charente
Angoulême
Ruelle-sur-Touvre
Montbron
Bussière-Badil
Nexon
Châteaubernard
Hiersac
St-Michel
L'Isle-d'Espagnac
Piégut-Pluviers
Châlus
Segonzac
Nersac
Puymoyen
Soyaux
Marthon
Bussière-Galant
Salles-d'Angles
Châteauneuf-sur-Charente
La Couronne
Sers
Augignac
Javerlhac-et-la-Chapelle-St-Robert
Ladignac-le-Long
Pons
Dignac
St-Saud-Lacoussière
Mialet
Mouthiers-sur-Boëme
La Coquille
Jurignac
Rougnac
St-Martial-de-Valette
Nontron
Chaleix
St-Yrieix-la-Perche
Archiac
SAINTONGE
Blanzac-Porcheresse
Villebois-Lavalette
St-Pardoux-la-Rivière
Glandon
St-Genis-de-Saintonge
Barbezieux-St-Hilaire
Jumilhac-le-Grand
Jonzac
Mareuil
Angoisse
Montmoreau-St-Cybard
Monsec
Payzac
Villars
Thiviers
Gout-Rossignol
Champagnac-de-Belair
Lanouaille
Mirambeau
Baignes-Ste-Radegonde
Brantôme
St-Pierre-de-Côle
Verteillac
La Tour-Blanche
Bourdeilles
Sorges
Coulaures
Excideuil
Brossac
St-Ciers-sur-Gironde
Chevanceaux
St-Aubin-de-Blaye
Montendre
Savignac-les-Églises
Montagrier
Lisle
Tourtoirac
Hautefort
Marcillac
Chalais
Aubeterre-sur-Dronne
Tocane-St-Apre
Sarliac-sur-l'Isle
Ste-Orse
Montlieu-la-Garde
Montguyon
Ribérac
Mensignac
Cubjac
Antonne-et-Trigonant
Badefols-d'Ans
Reignac
Étauliers
Parcoul
St-Aulaye
Chancelade
Trélissac
Coulounieix-Chamiers
Périgueux
Ajat
Cartelègue
St-Savin
St-Aigulin
La Roche-Chalais
DOUBLE
St-Vincent-de-Connezac
St-Astier
Atur
Boulazac
Thenon
PÉRIGORD BLANC
Cars
Cavignac
Les Églisottes-et-Chalaures
Lagorce
Eygurande-et-Gardedeuil
St-Front-
Neuvic
Coursac
St-Pierre-de-Chignac
Montignac
Rouffignac
Manzac
Gartempe
Anglin
Creuse
Claise
Vienne
Clain
Thouet
Charente
Boutonne
Tardoire
Dronne
Isle
Né
Seugne
Auvézère
Lac de St-Pardoux
A10
A83
A89
E05
E62
E603
E606
E70
N10
N11
N21
N141
N145
N147
N149
N150
N151
N137
N89

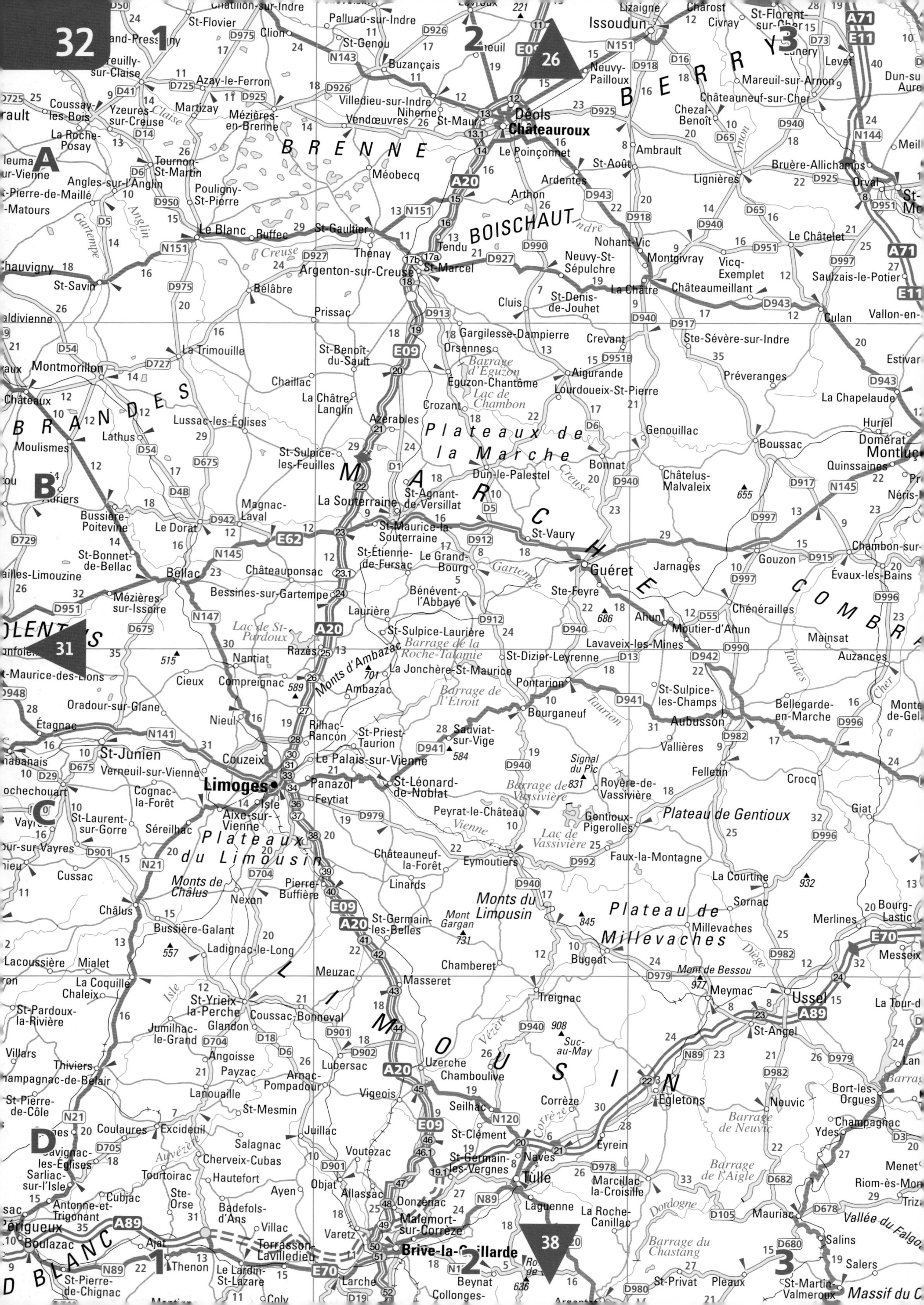

BRENNE
BERRY
BOISCHAUT
BRANDES
MARCHE
COMBRAILLE
LIMOUSIN
Plateaux de la Marche
Plateaux du Limousin
Plateau de Gentioux
Plateau de Millevaches
Monts du Limousin
Monts d'Ambazac
Monts de Châlus
Issoudun
Châteauroux
Déols
St-Flovier
Palluau-sur-Indre
Clion
St-Genou
Buzançais
Azay-le-Ferron
Mézières-en-Brenne
Villedieu-sur-Indre
Niherne
Vendœuvres
St-Maur
Le Poinçonnet
Ardentes
Arthon
Méobecq
Neuvy-Pailloux
Mareuil-sur-Arnon
Châteauneuf-sur-Cher
Chezal-Benoît
Ambrault
St-Août
Lignières
Bruère-Allichamps
Orval
Levet
Dun-sur-Auron
Charost
Civray
St-Florent-sur-Cher
Lizaigne
Coussay-les-Bois
Yzeures-sur-Creuse
Martizay
La Roche-Posay
Tournon-St-Martin
Angles-sur-l'Anglin
Pouligny-St-Pierre
Le Blanc
Ruffec
St-Gaultier
Thenay
Argenton-sur-Creuse
St-Marcel
Tendu
Bélâbre
Prissac
Chauvigny
St-Savin
Neuvy-St-Sépulchre
Nohant-Vic
La Châtre
Montgivray
Vicq-Exemplet
Châteaumeillant
Le Châtelet
Saulzais-le-Potier
Culan
Cluis
St-Denis-de-Jouhet
Gargilesse-Dampierre
Orsennes
Barrage d'Éguzon
Éguzon-Chantôme
Lac de Chambon
Crozant
Aigurande
Lourdoueix-St-Pierre
Crevant
Ste-Sévère-sur-Indre
Préveranges
La Chapelaude
Genouillac
Boussac
Domérat
Montluçon
Quinssaines
Bonnat
Châtelus-Malvaleix
Dun-le-Palestel
St-Agnant-de-Versillat
La Souterraine
St-Maurice-la-Souterraine
St-Benoît-du-Sault
Chaillac
La Châtre-Langlin
Azerables
St-Sulpice-les-Feuilles
La Trimouille
Montmorillon
Lussac-les-Églises
Lathus
Moulismes
Bussière-Poitevine
Le Dorat
Magnac-Laval
St-Bonnet-de-Bellac
Bellac
Châteauponsac
Bessines-sur-Gartempe
Mézières-sur-Issoire
St-Étienne-de-Fursac
Le Grand-Bourg
Bénévent-l'Abbaye
St-Vaury
Guéret
Jarnages
Ste-Feyre
Gouzon
Chambon-sur-Voueize
Évaux-les-Bains
Chénérailles
Ahun
Moutier-d'Ahun
Lavaveix-les-Mines
Mainsat
Auzances
Laurière
St-Sulpice-Laurière
Lac de St-Pardoux
Razès
Barrage de la Roche-Talamie
La Jonchère-St-Maurice
St-Dizier-Leyrenne
Pontarion
Bourganeuf
Barrage de l'Étroit
Ambazac
Nantiat
Compreignac
Cieux
Oradour-sur-Glane
Nieul
Étagnac
St-Junien
Rilhac-Rancon
St-Priest-Taurion
Sauviat-sur-Vige
Couzeix
Limoges
Le Palais-sur-Vienne
Panazol
Feytiat
St-Léonard-de-Noblat
Isle
Aixe-sur-Vienne
Verneuil-sur-Vienne
Cognac-la-Forêt
Rochechouart
St-Laurent-sur-Gorre
Séreilhac
Cussac
Châlus
Nexon
Pierre-Buffière
Bussière-Galant
Ladignac-le-Long
Châteauneuf-la-Forêt
Eymoutiers
Linards
St-Germain-les-Belles
Peyrat-le-Château
Lac de Vassivière
Royère-de-Vassivière
Gentioux-Pigerolles
Faux-la-Montagne
St-Sulpice-les-Champs
Aubusson
Vallières
Felletin
Crocq
Bellegarde-en-Marche
Giat
La Courtine
Sornac
Millevaches
Bugeat
Chamberet
Mont Gargan
Treignac
Meymac
Mont de Bessou
Ussel
St-Angel
Merlines
Messeix
Meuzac
Masseret
St-Yrieix-la-Perche
Coussac-Bonneval
Glandon
Jumilhac-le-Grand
La Coquille
Chaleix
Lacoussière
Mialet
St-Pardoux-la-Rivière
Villars
Thiviers
Angoisse
Payzac
Arnac-Pompadour
Lubersac
Uzerche
Chamboulive
Vigeois
Lanouaille
St-Mesmin
Seilhac
Corrèze
Égletons
Neuvic
Barrage de Neuvic
Bort-les-Orgues
Ydes
Champagnac
Excideuil
Coulaures
Juillac
Salagnac
Cherveix-Cubas
Hautefort
Tourtoirac
Voutezac
St-Clément
St-Germain-les-Vergnes
Naves
Tulle
Eyrein
Marcillac-la-Croisille
Barrage de l'Aigle
Mauriac
Salins
Salers
Ayen
Objat
Allassac
Donzenac
Malemort-sur-Corrèze
Brive-la-Gaillarde
Laguenne
La Roche-Canillac
Barrage du Chastang
Cubjac
Antonne-et-Trigonant
Périgueux
Boulazac
Sarliac-sur-l'Isle
Savignac-les-Églises
St-Pierre-de-Côle
Badefols-d'Ans
Villac
Terrasson-Lavilledieu
Le Lardin-St-Lazare
Thenon
St-Pierre-de-Chignac
Varetz
Larche
Beynat
Collonges-
St-Privat
Pleaux
St-Martin-Valmeroux
Vallée du Falgoux
Massif du C
Riom-ès-Montagnes
Menet
A20
A71
A89
E09
E11
E62
E70
N151
N145
N141
N147
N21
N89
N120
26
31
38

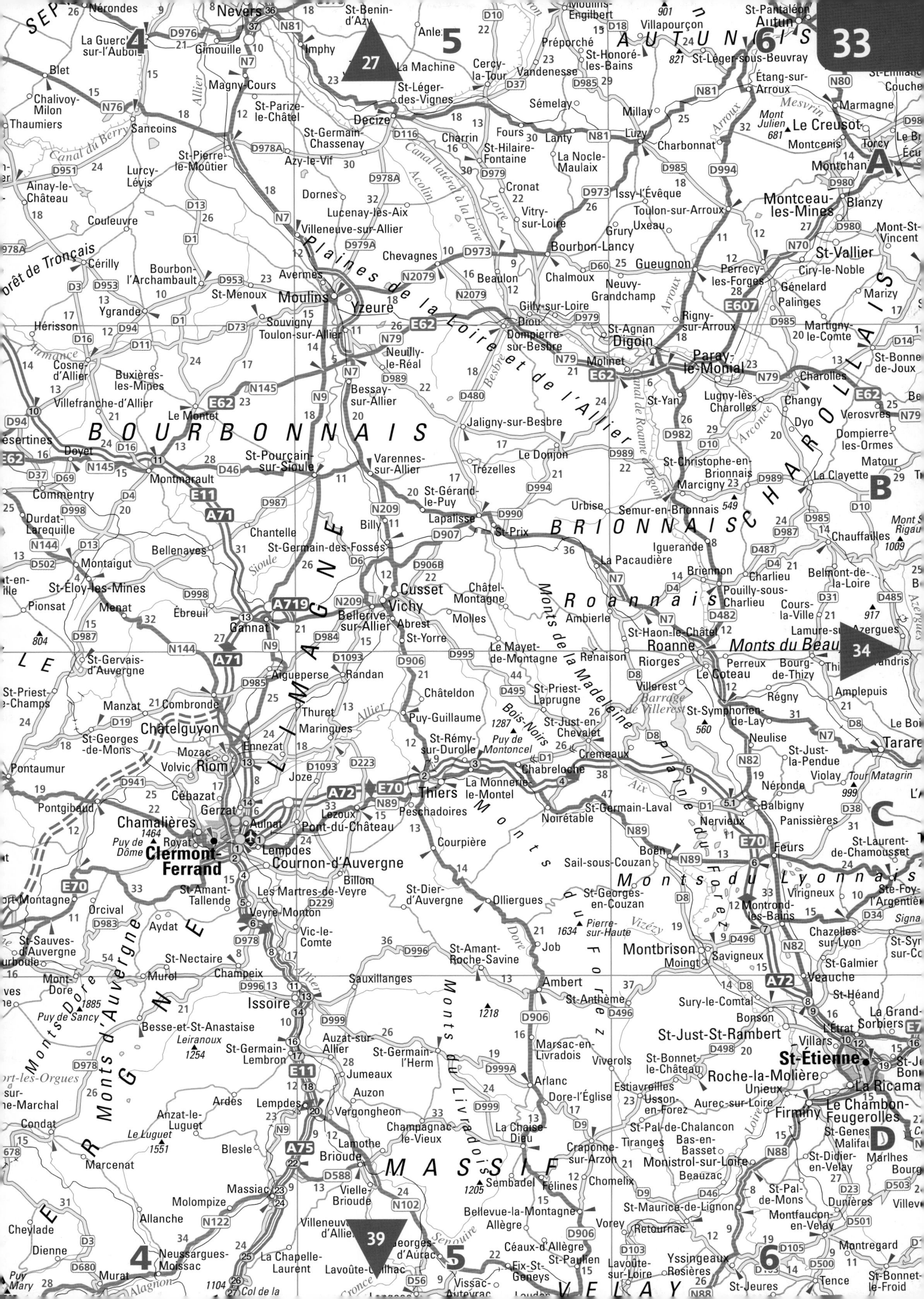33
Nérondes
Nevers
St-Benin-d'Azy
Moulins-Engilbert
Villapourçon
St-Pantaléon
Autun
La Guerche-sur-l'Aubois
Gimouille
Imphy
27
La Machine
Anlezy
5
Cercy-la-Tour
Vandenesse
Préporché
St-Honoré-les-Bains
AUTUNOIS
St-Léger-sous-Beuvray
Blet
Magny-Cours
St-Léger-des-Vignes
Étang-sur-Arroux
Marmagne
Couches
Chalivoy-Milon
Thaumiers
St-Parize-le-Châtel
Decize
Sémelay
Millay
Mont Julien
Le Creusot
Montcenis
Torcy
Sancoins
Canal du Berry
St-Germain-Chassenay
Charrin
Fours
Lanty
Luzy
Charbonnat
St-Pierre-le-Moûtier
Azy-le-Vif
St-Hilaire-Fontaine
La Nocle-Maulaix
Montchanin
A
Ainay-le-Château
Lurcy-Lévis
Dornes
Canal latéral à la Loire
Acolin
Cronat
Issy-l'Évêque
Montceau-les-Mines
Blanzy
Lucenay-lès-Aix
Vitry-sur-Loire
Toulon-sur-Arroux
Couleuvre
Villeneuve-sur-Allier
Grury
Uxeau
Mont-St-Vincent
Forêt de Tronçais
Cérilly
Chevagnes
Bourbon-Lancy
St-Vallier
Ciry-le-Noble
Bourbon-l'Archambault
Plaines de la Loire et de l'Allier
Beaulon
Chalmoux
Gueugnon
Perrecy-les-Forges
Génelard
Marizy
Avermes
Ygrande
St-Menoux
Moulins
Yzeure
Neuvy-Grandchamp
Palinges
Gilly-sur-Loire
Rigny-sur-Arroux
Hérisson
Souvigny
Toulon-sur-Allier
Diou
Dompierre-sur-Besbre
St-Agnan
Digoin
Martigny-le-Comte
Cosne-d'Allier
Buxières-les-Mines
Neuilly-le-Réal
Molinet
Paray-le-Monial
St-Bonnet-de-Joux
Charolles
Villefranche-d'Allier
Le Montet
Bessay-sur-Allier
St-Yan
Lugny-lès-Charolles
Changy
Verosvres
BOURBONNAIS
Jaligny-sur-Besbre
Canal de Roanne à Digoin
Dyo
Dompierre-les-Ormes
Désertines
Doyet
Montmarault
St-Pourçain-sur-Sioule
Varennes-sur-Allier
Le Donjon
St-Christophe-en-Brionnais
Matour
Commentry
Trézelles
Marcigny
La Clayette
B
St-Gérand-le-Puy
Semur-en-Brionnais
Urbise
Durdat-Larequille
Lapalisse
St-Prix
BRIONNAIS
CHAROLLAIS
Mont St-Rigaud
Chantelle
Billy
Chauffailles
Iguerande
Bellenaves
St-Germain-des-Fossés
Montaigut
Sioule
La Pacaudière
Belmont-de-la-Loire
St-Éloy-les-Mines
Cusset
Châtel-Montagne
Briennon
Charlieu
Pouilly-sous-Charlieu
Pionsat
Menat
Ébreuil
Vichy
Bellerive-sur-Allier
Abrest
Molles
Monts de la Madeleine
Roannais
Ambierle
Cours-la-Ville
Gannat
St-Yorre
St-Haon-le-Châtel
Lamure-sur-Azergues
St-Gervais-d'Auvergne
Le Mayet-de-Montagne
Renaison
Roanne
Monts du Beaujolais
34
Riorges
Perreux
Bourg-de-Thizy
Aigueperse
Randan
Villerest
Le Coteau
Barrage de Villerest
St-Priest-des-Champs
Manzat
Combronde
Châteldon
St-Priest-la-Prugne
Amplepuis
Régny
LIMAGNE
Thuret
Puy-Guillaume
Bois-Noirs
St-Just-en-Chevalet
St-Symphorien-de-Lay
Châtelguyon
Maringues
St-Georges-de-Mons
Ennezat
St-Rémy-sur-Durolle
Puy de Montoncel
Neulise
Tarare
Mozac
Riom
Volvic
Joze
Cremeaux
Chabreloche
St-Just-la-Pendue
Pontaumur
Thiers
La Monnerie-le-Montel
Violay
Tour Matagrin
Néronde
Cébazat
Gerzat
Lezoux
Peschadoires
Aix
Balbigny
Pontgibaud
Chamalières
Aulnat
Pont-du-Château
St-Germain-Laval
Noirétable
Nervieux
Panissières
C
Puy de Dôme
Royat
Clermont-Ferrand
Lempdes
Cournon-d'Auvergne
Courpière
Monts du Forez
Boën
Feurs
St-Laurent-de-Chamousset
Sail-sous-Couzan
Billom
Lyonnais
Ste-Foy-l'Argentière
St-Amant-Tallende
Les Martres-de-Veyre
St-Dier-d'Auvergne
Olliergues
St-Georges-en-Couzan
Virigneux
Orcival
Veyre-Monton
Montrond-les-Bains
Aydat
Vic-le-Comte
Pierre-sur-Haute
Vizézy
Chazelles-sur-Lyon
St-Sauves-d'Auvergne
Job
Montbrison
Savigneux
Moingt
St-Galmier
St-Nectaire
Champeix
St-Amant-Roche-Savine
Veauche
Mont-Dore
Murol
Sauxillanges
Ambert
Monts du Livradois
St-Anthème
St-Héand
Issoire
Sury-le-Comtal
Bonson
La Grand-Croix
Sorbiers
Puy de Sancy
Monts Dore
Monts d'Auvergne
Besse-et-St-Anastaise
Auzat-sur-Allier
St-Germain-l'Herm
St-Just-St-Rambert
L'Étrat
Villars
Leiranoux
St-Germain-Lembron
Marsac-en-Livradois
Viverols
St-Bonnet-le-Château
St-Étienne
Jumeaux
Arlanc
Estivareilles
Roche-la-Molière
La Ricamarie
Auzon
Usson-en-Forez
Unieux
Ardes
Lempdes
Vergongheon
Dore-l'Église
Aurec-sur-Loire
Firminy
Le Chambon-Feugerolles
Anzat-le-Luguet
Champagnac-le-Vieux
La Chaise-Dieu
St-Genest-Malifaux
Condat
Le Luguet
Lamothe
St-Pal-de-Chalencon
Tiranges
Bas-en-Basset
D
Blesle
Brioude
Craponne-sur-Arzon
Monistrol-sur-Loire
St-Didier-en-Velay
Marlhes
Marcenat
MASSIF
Beauzac
Massiac
Vieille-Brioude
Sembadel
Félines
Chomelix
Molompize
St-Pal-de-Mons
Dunières
Allanche
Bellevue-la-Montagne
St-Maurice-de-Lignon
Montfaucon-en-Velay
Cheylade
Villeneuve-d'Allier
39
Allègre
Vorey
Retournac
Dienne
4
Neussargues-Moissac
Senouire
Céaux-d'Allègre
Montregard
Murat
La Chapelle-Laurent
Lavoûte-Chilhac
St-Georges-d'Aurac
St-Paulien
Lavoûte-sur-Loire
Yssingeaux
Rosières
Tence
St-Bonnet-le-Froid
Vissac-Auteyrac
Fix-St-Geneys
VELAY
St-Jeures
Alagnon
Col de la
6

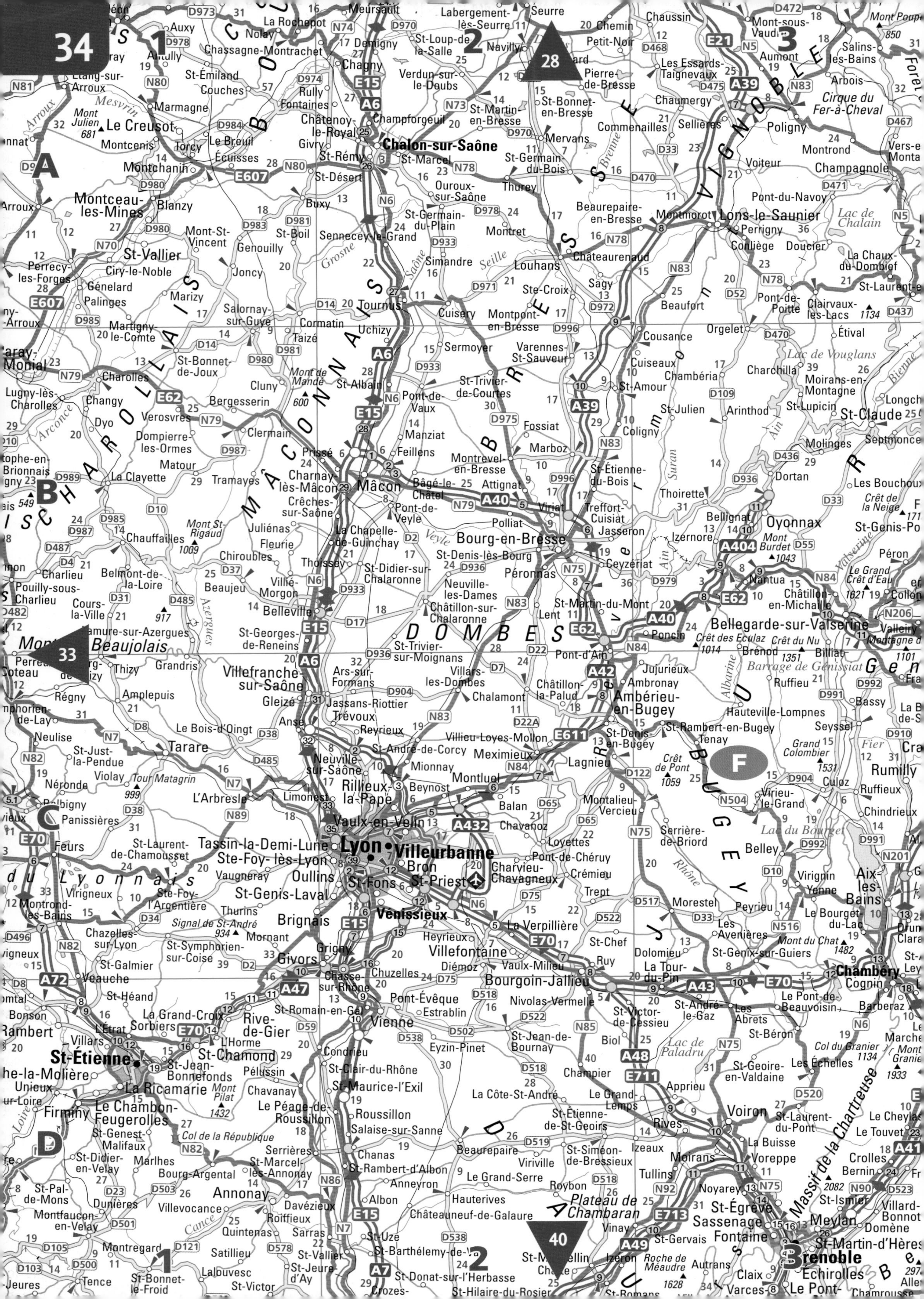
28
33
40
Le Creusot
Montceau-les-Mines
Chalon-sur-Saône
Lons-le-Saunier
Poligny
Champagnole
Louhans
Tournus
Mâcon
Bourg-en-Bresse
Oyonnax
St-Claude
Nantua
Bellegarde-sur-Valserine
Ambérieu-en-Bugey
Villefranche-sur-Saône
Lyon
Villeurbanne
Vénissieux
St-Priest
Bron
Vaulx-en-Velin
Tarare
L'Arbresle
Givors
Vienne
St-Étienne
Firminy
Annonay
Bourgoin-Jallieu
Villefontaine
Voiron
Grenoble
Chambéry
Aix-les-Bains
Belley
Roussillon
St-Chamond
Rive-de-Gier
Paray-le-Monial
Charolles
La Clayette
Digoin
Beaujeu
Belleville
Montluel
Meximieux
Pont-d'Ain
Lagnieu
Rumilly
Seyssel
Culoz
Montbrison
Feurs
Tassin-la-Demi-Lune
Ste-Foy-lès-Lyon
Oullins
St-Fons
St-Genis-Laval
Brignais
Meyzieu
Rillieux-la-Pape
Neuville-sur-Saône
Trévoux
Montrevel-en-Bresse
Pont-de-Vaux
Pont-de-Veyle
Cuisery
Cluny
Buxy
Chagny
Seurre
Arbois
Salins-les-Bains
Sellières
Beaurepaire
La Côte-St-André
St-Marcellin
Tullins
Moirans
Voreppe
Fontaine
Échirolles
Meylan
St-Égrève
Sassenage
St-Martin-d'Hères
Vizille
Le Pont-de-Beauvoisin
Les Abrets
La Tour-du-Pin
Crémieu
Charvieu-Chavagneux
La Verpillière
Heyrieux
Tournon-sur-Rhône
St-Vallier
Chanas
St-Rambert-d'Albon
Le Grand-Serre
Roybon
Châteauneuf-de-Galaure
Hauterives
Plateau de Chambaran
Lac de Paladru
Lac du Bourget
Lac de Vouglans
Lac de Chalain
Mont Pilat 1432
Mont Dore
Crêt de la Neige 1717
Massif de la Chartreuse
Mont du Chat 1482
Col du Granier 1134
Cirque du Fer-à-Cheval
Signal de St-André 934
Mont St-Rigaud 1009
Mont de Mandé 600
Mont Julien 681
Crêt des Eculaz 1014
Crêt du Nu 1351
Grand Colombier 1531
Barrage de Génissiat
Col de la République
Tour Matagrin 999
CHAROLLAIS
MÂCONNAIS
BRESSE
BUGEY
DOMBES
VIGNOBLE
Monts du Lyonnais
Beaujolais
A
B
C
D
F
1
2
3

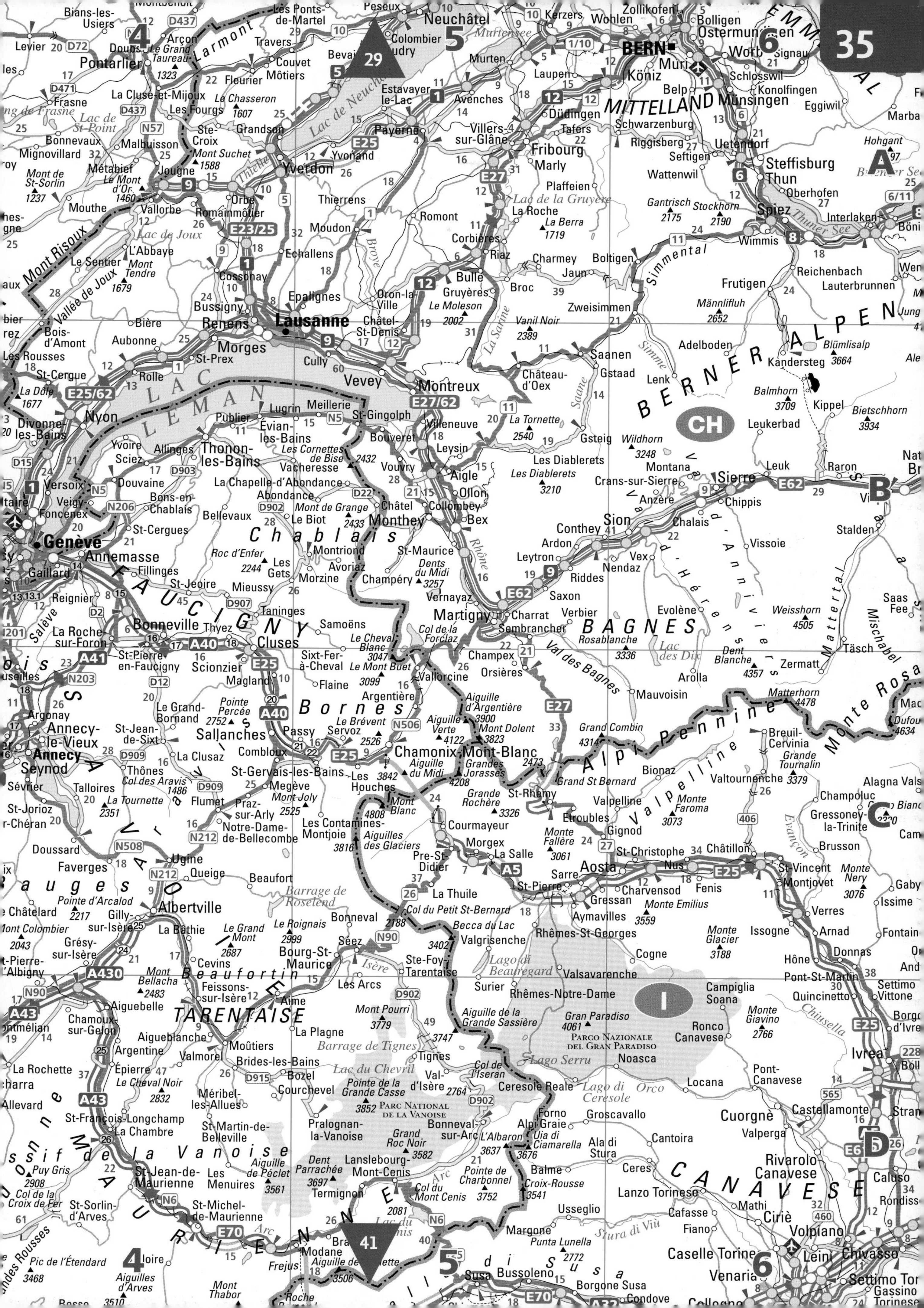
Bians-les-Usiers
Levier
Pontarlier
Doubs
Le Grand Taureau
1323
Arçon
Larmont
Les Ponts-de-Martel
Travers
Couvet
Môtiers
Fleurier
Peseux
Neuchâtel
Colombier
Boudry
Bevaix
29
Lac de Neuchâtel
Murtensee
Kerzers
Wohlen
Zollikofen
Bolligen
Ostermundigen
BERN
Muri
Worb
Signau
Köniz
Belp
Konolfingen
Schlosswil
Münsingen
MITTELLAND
Eggiwil
Marbach
Murten
Laupen
Düdingen
Tafers
Schwarzenburg
Riggisberg
Seftigen
Uetendorf
Steffisburg
Thun
Oberhofen
Hohgant
Estavayer-le-Lac
Avenches
Payerne
Villers-sur-Glâne
Fribourg
Marly
Plaffeien
Lac de la Gruyère
La Roche
La Berra
1719
Gantrisch
2175
Stockhorn
2190
Spiez
Thuner See
Interlaken
Bönigen
Wimmis
La Cluse-et-Mijoux
Les Fourgs
Le Chasseron
1607
Frasne
Lac de St-Point
Bonnevaux
Malbuisson
Mignovillard
Métabief
Mont Suchet
1588
Ste-Croix
Grandson
Yvonand
Yverdon
Jougne
Le Mont d'Or
1460
Mont de St-Sorlin
1237
Mouthe
Vallorbe
Orbe
Romainmôtier
Thierrens
Moudon
Romont
Corbières
Riaz
Bulle
Gruyères
Charmey
Jaun
Boltigen
Simmental
Reichenbach
Frutigen
Lauterbrunnen
Mont Risoux
Lac de Joux
L'Abbaye
Le Sentier
Mont Tendre
1679
Vallée de Joux
Cossonay
Echallens
Broye
Oron-la-Ville
Broc
Zweisimmen
Männlifluh
2652
Bussigny
Renens
Lausanne
Epalignes
Châtel-St-Denis
Le Moleson
2002
Vanil Noir
2389
La Sarine
Bière
Bois-d'Amont
Aubonne
Morges
St-Prex
Cully
Vevey
Montreux
Les Rousses
St-Cergue
Rolle
La Dôle
1677
Nyon
LAC LEMAN
Divonne-les-Bains
Saanen
Gstaad
Château-d'Oex
Simme
Adelboden
Kandersteg
Blümlisalp
3664
Lenk
BERNER ALPEN
Balmhorn
3709
Kippel
Bietschhorn
3934
Leukerbad
CH
Publier
Lugrin
Meillerie
Évian-les-Bains
St-Gingolph
Bouveret
Villeneuve
Leysin
La Tornette
2540
Gsteig
Wildhorn
3248
Les Diablerets
3210
Montana
Crans-sur-Sierre
Sierre
Leuk
Raron
Chippis
Anzère
Yvoire
Sciez
Allinges
Thonon-les-Bains
Les Cornettes de Bise
2432
Vacheresse
Vouvry
Aigle
Ollon
Collombey
Monthey
Bex
Douvaine
La Chapelle-d'Abondance
Abondance
Châtel
Versoix
Veigy-Foncenex
Bons-en-Chablais
Bellevaux
Mont de Grange
2433
Le Biot
Chablais
Conthey
Sion
Chalais
Vissoie
Stalden
Genève
Annemasse
St-Cergues
Roc d'Enfer
2244
Les Gets
Montriond
Avoriaz
Morzine
St-Maurice
Dents du Midi
3257
Champéry
Ardon
Leytron
Vex
Nendaz
Riddes
Saxon
Gaillard
Fillinges
St-Jeoire
Mieussy
FAUCIGNY
Reignier
Taninges
Samoëns
Vernayaz
Martigny
Charrat
Verbier
Sembrancher
BAGNES
Evolène
Weisshorn
4505
Saas Fee
Mischabel
Mattertal
Salève
La Roche-sur-Foron
Bonneville
Thyez
Cluses
Le Cheval Blanc
3047
Col de la Forclaz
Champex
Orsières
Val des Bagnes
Rosablanche
3336
Lac des Dix
Dent Blanche
4357
Arolla
Zermatt
Täsch
St-Pierre-en-Faucigny
Scionzier
Sixt-Fer-à-Cheval
Le Mont Buet
3099
Vallorcine
Mauvoisin
Matterhorn
4478
Monte Rosa
Magland
Flaine
Argentière
Aiguille d'Argentière
3900
Argonay
Annecy-le-Vieux
Annecy
Seynod
Le Grand-Bornand
Pointe Percée
2752
St-Jean-de-Sixt
Sallanches
Bornes
Passy
Le Brévent
2526
Servoz
Aiguille Verte
4122
Mont Dolent
3823
Grand Combin
4314
Alpi Pennine
Breuil-Cervinia
Dufour
4634
Thônes
La Clusaz
Combloux
Chamonix-Mont-Blanc
Aiguille du Midi
3842
Grandes Jorasses
4208
2473
Grand St Bernard
Bionaz
Valpelline
Valtournenche
Grande Tournalin
3379
Alagna Valsesia
Sévrier
Talloires
Col des Aravis
1486
St-Gervais-les-Bains
Les Houches
Grande Rochère
3326
St-Rhémy
Etroubles
Monte Faroma
3073
Champoluc
Gressoney-la-Trinite
St-Jorioz
La Tournette
2351
Flumet
Megève
Mont Joly
2525
Praz-sur-Arly
Notre-Dame-de-Bellecombe
Les Contamines-Montjoie
Aiguilles des Glaciers
3816
Mont Blanc
4808
Courmayeur
Monte Fallère
3061
Gignod
Brusson
Doussard
Faverges
Ugine
Queige
Beaufort
Pre-St-Didier
Morgex
La Salle
St-Christophe
Aosta
Nus
Châtillon
St-Vincent
Montjovet
Monte Nery
3076
Sarre
St-Pierre
Charvensod
Fenis
Gressan
Monte Emilius
3559
Aymavilles
Verres
Issime
Bauges
Pointe d'Arcalod
2217
Albertville
Barrage de Roselend
La Thuile
Col du Petit St-Bernard
2188
Bonneval
Le Roignais
2999
Becca du Lac
3402
Valgrisenche
Rhêmes-St-Georges
Cogne
Monte Glacier
3188
Issogne
Arnad
Donnas
Hône
Pont-St-Martin
Mont Colombier
2043
Gilly-sur-Isère
La Bâthie
Le Grand Mont
2687
Grésy-sur-Isère
Bourg-St-Maurice
Séez
Ste-Foy-Tarentaise
Lago di Beauregard
Valsavarenche
St-Pierre-d'Albigny
Cevins
Mont Bellacha
2483
Beaufortin
Feissons-sur-Isère
Aime
Les Arcs
Isère
Surier
Rhêmes-Notre-Dame
Campiglia Soana
Quincinetto
Settimo Vittone
Aiguebelle
Chamoux-sur-Gelon
Montmélian
TARENTAISE
Mont Pourri
3779
Aiguille de la Grande Sassière
3747
Gran Paradiso
4061
I
Monte Giavino
2766
Ronco Canavese
Chiusella
Aigueblanche
La Plagne
Argentine
Valmorel
Moûtiers
Barrage de Tignes
Tignes
PARCO NAZIONALE DEL GRAN PARADISO
Lago Serru
Noasca
Ivrea
La Rochette
Epierre
Brides-les-Bains
Lac du Chevril
Col de l'Iseran
Pont-Canavese
Le Cheval Noir
2832
Bozel
Pointe de la Grande Casse
Val-d'Isère
2764
Ceresole Reale
Lago di Ceresole
Orco
Locana
Allevard
Méribel-les-Allues
Courchevel
3852
PARC NATIONAL DE LA VANOISE
Forno Alpi Graie
Groscavallo
Castellamonte
Cuorgnè
Valperga
St-François-Longchamp
La Chambre
St-Martin-de-Belleville
Pralognan-la-Vanoise
Grand Roc Noir
3582
Bonneval-sur-Arc
L'Albaron
3637
Uia di Ciamarella
3676
Ala di Stura
Cantoira
Massif de la Vanoise
Puy Gris
2908
St-Jean-de-Maurienne
Les Menuires
Aiguille de Péclet
3561
Dent Parrachée
3697
Lanslebourg-Mont-Cenis
Pointe de Charbonnel
3752
Balme
Croix-Rousse
3541
Ceres
CANAVESE
Rivarolo Canavese
Caluso
Col de la Croix de Fer
St-Sorlin-d'Arves
St-Michel-de-Maurienne
Termignon
Col du Mont Cenis
2081
Lanzo Torinese
Usseglio
Cafasse
Mathi
Ciriè
Rondissone
MAURIENNE
Arc
Margone
Punta Lunella
2772
Stura di Viù
Fiano
Volpiano
Pic de l'Étendard
3468
Aiguilles d'Arves
3510
Modane
41
Aiguille de Scolette
3506
Fréjus
Susa
Bussoleno
Val di Susa
2772
Caselle Torinese
Leini
Chivasso
Venaria
Settimo Torinese
Gassino Torinese
Borgone Susa
Condove
Mont Thabor
Roche
Collegno
E25
E27
E62
E70
A40
A41
A43
A430
A5
N5
N6
N90
N203
N206
N212
N506
N508
D902
D909
D907
D437
D471

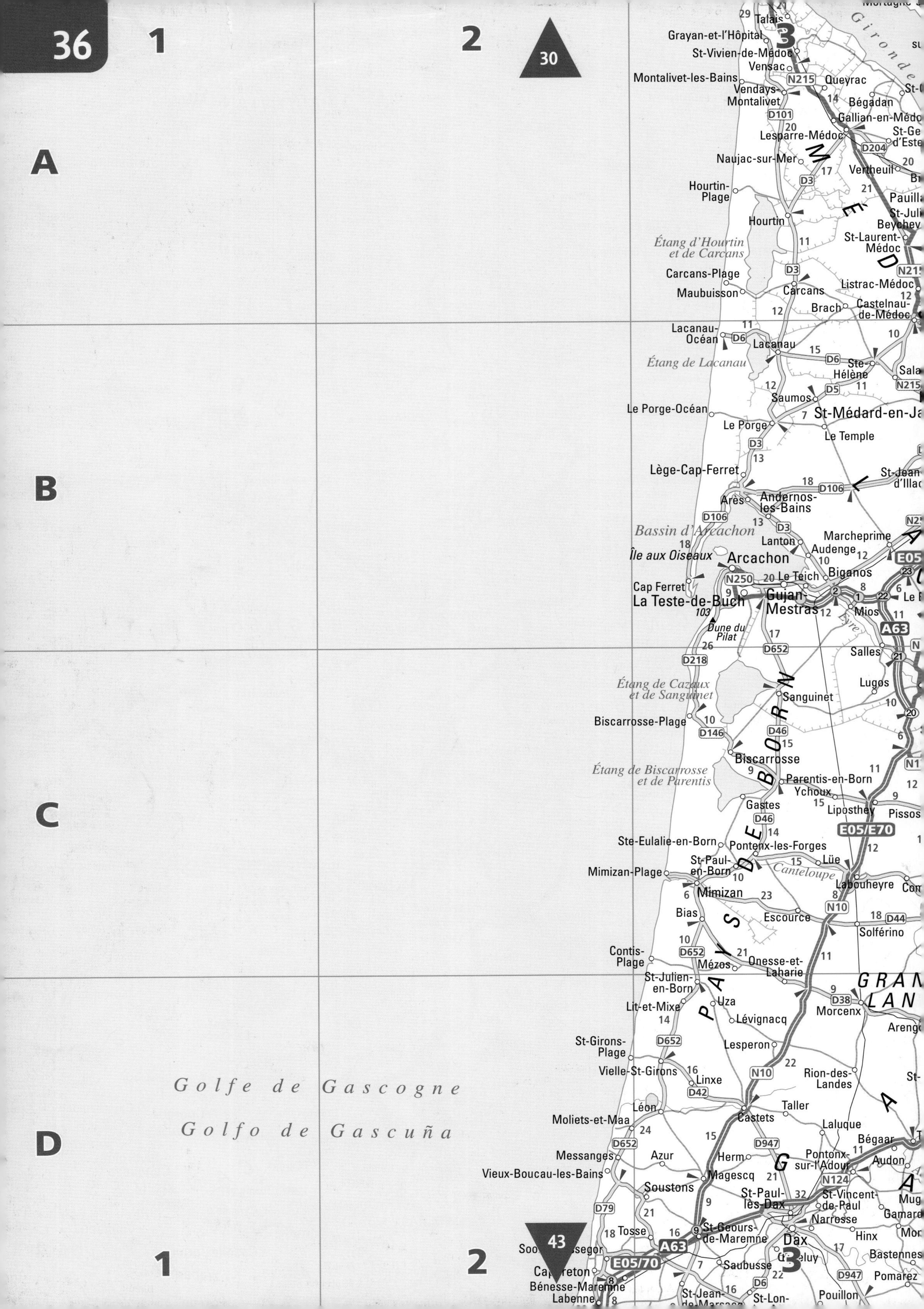
1
2
30
3
A
B
C
D
Gironde
Talais
Grayan-et-l'Hôpital
St-Vivien-de-Médoc
Vensac
Montalivet-les-Bains
Vendays-Montalivet
Queyrac
Bégadan
Gallian-en-Médoc
Lesparre-Médoc
Naujac-sur-Mer
Vertheuil
Hourtin-Plage
Hourtin
MÉDOC
Étang d'Hourtin et de Carcans
St-Laurent-Médoc
Carcans-Plage
Maubuisson
Carcans
Listrac-Médoc
Brach
Castelnau-de-Médoc
Lacanau-Océan
Lacanau
Étang de Lacanau
Ste-Hélène
Saumos
Le Porge-Océan
Le Porge
St-Médard-en-Ja
Le Temple
Lège-Cap-Ferret
Arès
Andernos-les-Bains
Bassin d'Arcachon
Lanton
Marcheprime
Audenge
Île aux Oiseaux
Arcachon
Biganos
Cap Ferret
Le Teich
La Teste-de-Buch
Gujan-Mestras
Mios
Dune du Pilat
Salles
Étang de Cazaux et de Sanguinet
Sanguinet
Lugos
Biscarrosse-Plage
Biscarrosse
Étang de Biscarrosse et de Parentis
Parentis-en-Born
Ychoux
Gastes
Liposthey
Pissos
PAYS DE BORN
Ste-Eulalie-en-Born
Pontenx-les-Forges
St-Paul-en-Born
Lüe
Mimizan-Plage
Canteloupe
Labouheyre
Mimizan
Escource
Bias
Solférino
Contis-Plage
Mézos
Onesse-et-Laharie
St-Julien-en-Born
Morcenx
Uza
Lit-et-Mixe
Lévignacq
St-Girons-Plage
Lesperon
Vielle-St-Girons
Linxe
Rion-des-Landes
Golfe de Gascogne
Golfo de Gascuña
Léon
Taller
Moliets-et-Maa
Castets
Laluque
Bégaar
Messanges
Azur
Herm
Pontonx-sur-l'Adour
Audon
Vieux-Boucau-les-Bains
Magescq
Soustons
St-Paul-lès-Dax
St-Vincent-de-Paul
Narrosse
Tosse
St-Geours-de-Maremne
Hinx
Dax
43
Saubusse
Bastennes
Capbreton
Pomarez
Bénesse-Maremne
Labenne
St-Jean-de-Marsacq
St-Lon-
Pouillon
N215
D101
D204
D3
D6
D5
D106
N250
D218
D652
D146
D46
E05/E70
N10
D44
D38
D652
D42
D947
N124
D79
A63
E05/70
D6
D947
A63

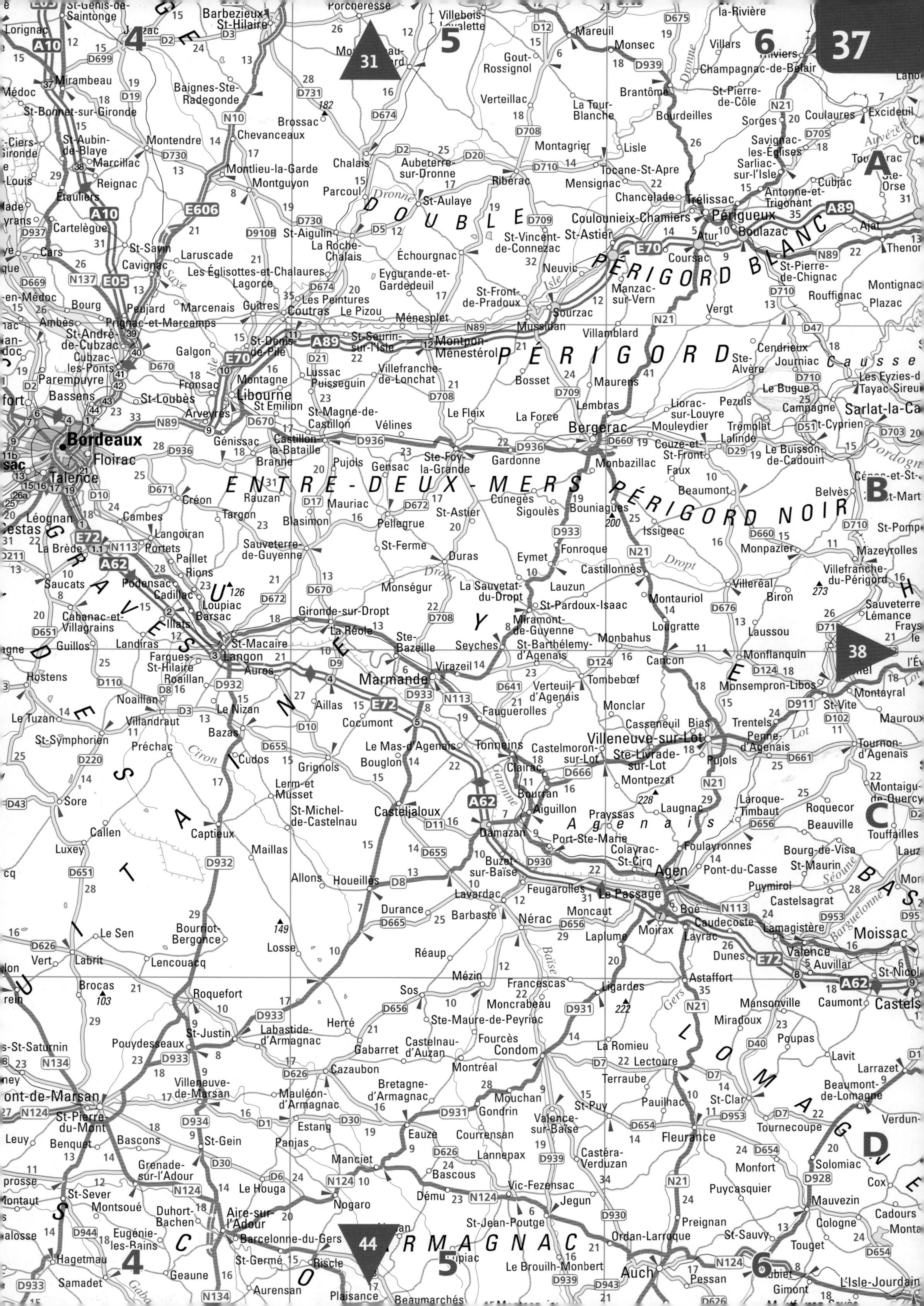

37
31
38
44
4
5
6
A
B
C
D
St-Genis-de-Saintonge
Barbezieux-St-Hilaire
Porcheresse
Villebois-Lavalette
Mareuil
la-Rivière
Lorignac
Monsec
Villars
Thiviers
Mirambeau
Baignes-Ste-Radegonde
Gout-Rossignol
Champagnac-de-Belair
Médoc
St-Bonnet-sur-Gironde
Verteillac
La Tour-Blanche
Brantôme
St-Pierre-de-Côle
Brossac
Bourdeilles
Sorges
Coulaures
Excideuil
St-Ciers-sur-Gironde
St-Aubin-de-Blaye
Montendre
Chevanceaux
Montagrier
Lisle
Savignac-les-Églises
Marcillac
Chalais
Aubeterre-sur-Dronne
Tocane-St-Apre
Sarliac-sur-l'Isle
St-Louis
Reignac
Montlieu-la-Garde
Montguyon
Ribérac
Mensignac
Cubjac
Parcoul
St-Aulaye
Chancelade
Trélissac
Antonne-et-Trigonant
Étauliers
DOUBLE
Coulounieix-Chamiers
Périgueux
Cartelègue
St-Aiguilin
La Roche-Chalais
St-Vincent-de-Connezac
St-Astier
Atur
Boulazac
Ajat
St-Savin
Laruscade
Échourgnac
Coursac
Thenon
Cars
Cavignac
Les Églisottes-et-Chalaures
Eygurande-et-Gardedeuil
Neuvic
PÉRIGORD BLANC
St-Pierre-de-Chignac
Lagorce
Manzac-sur-Vern
Montignac
Bourg
Peujard
Marcenais
Guîtres
Les Peintures
Coutras
Le Pizou
St-Front-de-Pradoux
Sourzac
Vergt
Rouffignac
Plazac
Ambès
Prignac-et-Marcamps
Ménesplet
Mussidan
St-André-de-Cubzac
St-Denis-de-Pile
St-Seurin-sur-l'Isle
Montpon-Ménestérol
Villamblard
Cendrieux
Galgon
PÉRIGORD
Ste-Alvère
Journiac
Causse
Cubzac-les-Ponts
Lussac
Puisseguin
Villefranche-de-Lonchat
Les Eyzies-de-Tayac-Sireuil
Parempuyre
Fronsac
Montagne
Bosset
Maurens
Le Bugue
Bassens
Libourne
St Emilion
Lembras
Liorac-sur-Louyre
Pezuls
Campagne
Sarlat-la-Canéda
St-Loubès
Arveyres
St-Magne-de-Castillon
Le Fleix
La Force
Mouleydier
Trémolat
St-Cyprien
Bordeaux
Génissac
Castillon-la-Bataille
Vélines
Bergerac
Lalinde
Floirac
Branne
Pujols
Gensac
Ste-Foy-la-Grande
Gardonne
Couze-et-St-Front
Le Buisson-de-Cadouin
Talence
ENTRE-DEUX-MERS
Monbazillac
Faux
Rauzan
Beaumont
Belvès
Créon
Mauriac
Cunèges
Sigoulès
Bouniagues
PÉRIGORD NOIR
Léognan
Cestas
Cambes
Targon
Blasimon
Pellegrue
St-Astier
Issigeac
St-Pompont
La Brède
Langoiran
Portets
Sauveterre-de-Guyenne
St-Ferme
Duras
Eymet
Fonroque
Monpazier
Mazeyrolles
Paillet
Rions
Castillonnès
Villefranche-du-Périgord
Saucats
Podensac
Cadillac
Monségur
La Sauvetat-du-Dropt
Lauzun
Villeréal
Biron
Loupiac
Barsac
St-Pardoux-Isaac
Montauriol
Sauveterre-la-Lémance
Cabanac-et-Villagrains
Gironde-sur-Dropt
Miramont-de-Guyenne
Lougratte
Laussou
Illats
La Réole
Ste-Bazeille
Seyches
St-Barthélemy-d'Agenais
Monbahus
Guillos
Landiras
St-Macaire
Langon
Cancon
Monflanquin
Fargues-St-Hilaire
Marmande
Virazeil
Hostens
Roaillan
Auros
Tombebœuf
Monsempron-Libos
Montayral
Noaillan
Aillas
Verteuil-d'Agenais
Le Tuzan
Villandraut
Le Nizan
Cocumont
Fauguerolles
Monclar
St-Vite
Mauroux
Bazas
Casseneuil
Bias
Trentels
St-Symphorien
Préchac
Le Mas-d'Agenais
Tonneins
Castelmoron-sur-Lot
Villeneuve-sur-Lot
Penne-d'Agenais
Tournon-d'Agenais
Ciron
Cudos
Grignols
Bouglon
Clairac
Ste-Livrade-sur-Lot
Pujols
Lerm-et-Musset
Montpezat
Montaigu-de-Quercy
Sore
St-Michel-de-Castelnau
Casteljaloux
Bourran
Aiguillon
Prayssas
Laugnac
Laroque-Timbaut
Roquecor
Callen
Captieux
Damazan
Agenais
Port-Ste-Marie
Beauville
Touffailles
Luxey
Maillas
Colayrac-St-Cirq
Foulayronnes
Bourg-de-Visa
Buzet-sur-Baïse
St-Maurin
Allons
Houeillès
Agen
Pont-du-Casse
Lavardac
Feugarolles
Le Passage
Puymirol
Durance
Barbaste
Castelsagrat
Bourriot-Bergonce
Nérac
Moncaut
Boé
Caudecoste
Lamagistère
Le Sen
Moirax
Layrac
Moissac
Losse
Laplume
Dunes
Valence
Auvillar
Vert
Labrit
Lencouacq
Réaup
St-Nicolas
Brocas
Mézin
Francescas
Astaffort
Roquefort
Sos
Ligardes
Caumont
Castelsarrasin
Moncrabeau
Mansonville
Herré
Ste-Maure-de-Peyriac
Miradoux
Pouydesseaux
St-Justin
Labastide-d'Armagnac
Fourcès
Poupas
Gabarret
Castelnau-d'Auzan
Condom
La Romieu
Lavit
Mont-de-Marsan
Cazaubon
Lectoure
Larrazet
Montréal
Terraube
Villeneuve-de-Marsan
Mauléon-d'Armagnac
Bretagne-d'Armagnac
Mouchan
Pauilhac
St-Clar
Beaumont-de-Lomagne
St-Pierre-du-Mont
Gondrin
St-Puy
Valence-sur-Baïse
Estang
Eauze
Courrensan
Verdun-sur-Garonne
Leuy
Benquet
Bascons
St-Gein
Panjas
Fleurance
Tournecoupe
Grenade-sur-l'Adour
Manciet
Lannepax
Castéra-Verduzan
Solomiac
Bascous
Monfort
Le Houga
Cox
St-Sever
Montsoué
Nogaro
Démù
Vic-Fezensac
Jegun
Puycasquier
Mauvezin
Duhort-Bachen
Aire-sur-l'Adour
St-Jean-Poutge
Cadours
Cologne
Eugénie-les-Bains
Barcelone-du-Gers
ARMAGNAC
Ordan-Larroque
Preignan
St-Sauvy
Hagetmau
St-Germé
Riscle
Le Brouilh-Monbert
Auch
Pessan
Touget
Samadet
Geaune
Aurensan
Plaisance
Beaumarchés
Gimont
L'Isle-Jourdain
LOMAGNE
GRAVES
LANDES
Dronne
Isle
Dropt
Lot
Garonne
Baïse
Gers
Séoune
Dordogne
A10
A62
A89
E05
E70
E72
E606
N10
N21
N89
N113
N124
N134
N137

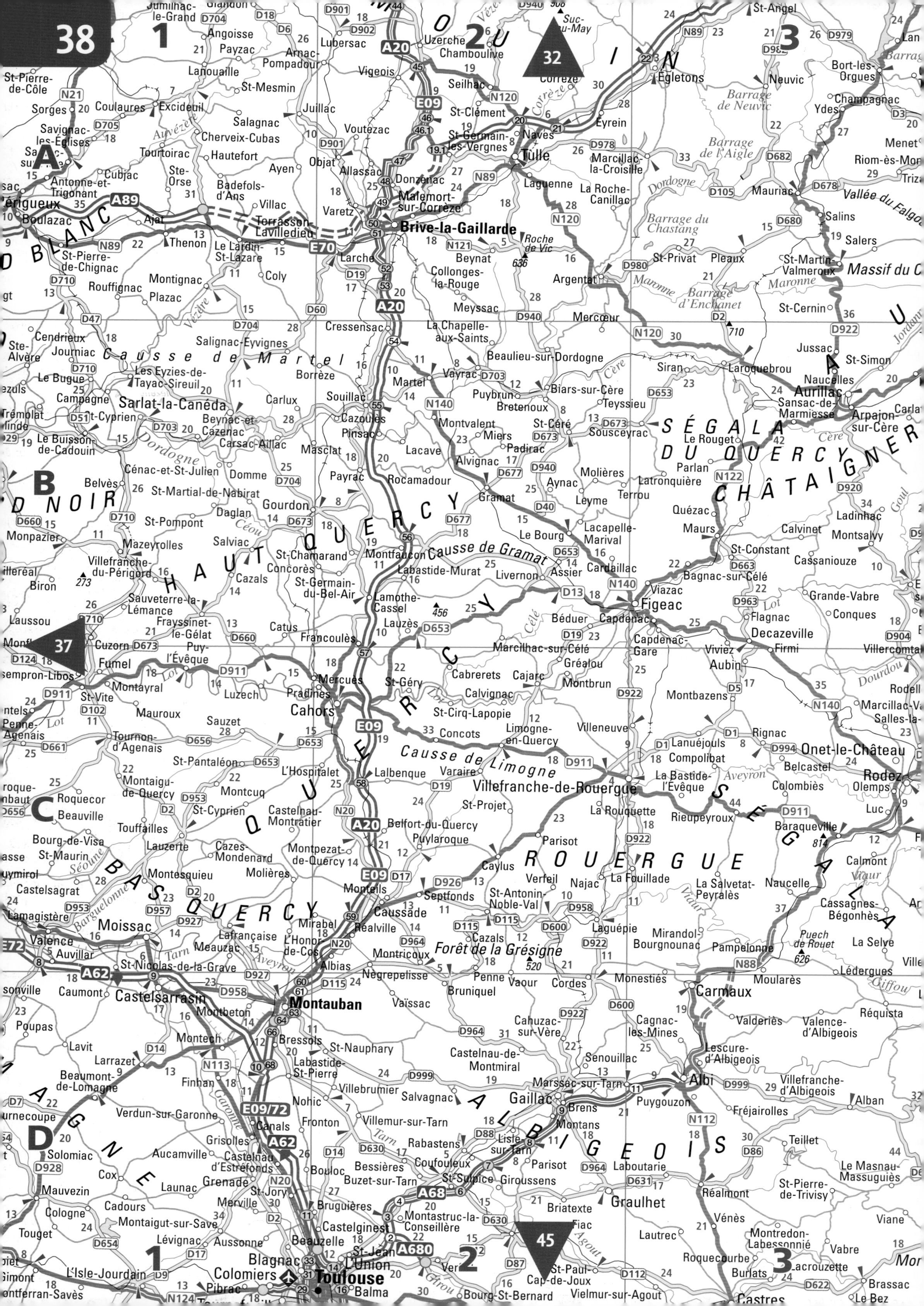
38
1
2
3
A
B
C
D
32
37
45
Jumilhac-le-Grand
Angoisse
Payzac
Lanouaille
St-Mesmin
Excideuil
Coulaures
Sorges
St-Pierre-de-Côle
Savignac-les-Églises
Cherveix-Cubas
Salagnac
Tourtoirac
Hautefort
Cubjac
Antonne-et-Trigonant
Périgueux
Boulazac
Ste-Orse
Badefols-d'Ans
Villac
Ajat
Thenon
Le Lardin-St-Lazare
Terrasson-Lavilledieu
St-Pierre-de-Chignac
Rouffignac
Montignac
Plazac
Coly
Lubersac
Arnac-Pompadour
Vigeois
Juillac
Voutezac
Objat
Allassac
Ayen
Varetz
Donzenac
Malemort-sur-Corrèze
Brive-la-Gaillarde
Larche
Uzerche
Chamboulive
Seilhac
St-Clément
St-Germain-les-Vergnes
Naves
Tulle
Laguenne
Suc-au-May
Corrèze
Égletons
Eyrein
Marcillac-la-Croisille
La Roche-Canillac
Barrage de Neuvic
Barrage de l'Aigle
Barrage du Chastang
Neuvic
St-Angel
Bort-les-Orgues
Champagnac
Ydes
Menet
Riom-ès-Montagnes
Mauriac
Vallée du Falgoux
Salins
Salers
St-Martin-Valmeroux
Massif du Cantal
Pleaux
St-Privat
Argentat
Barrage d'Enchanet
St-Cernin
Mercœur
Beynat
Roche de Vic
Collonges-la-Rouge
Meyssac
La Chapelle-aux-Saints
Beaulieu-sur-Dordogne
Cressensac
Martel
Vayrac
Causse de Martel
Salignac-Eyvignes
Les Eyzies-de-Tayac-Sireuil
Le Bugue
Ste-Alvère
Cendrieux
Journiac
Campagne
Sarlat-la-Canéda
St-Cyprien
Le Buisson-de-Cadouin
Beynac-et-Cazenac
Carsac-Aillac
Carlux
Souillac
Borrèze
Cazoulès
Pinsac
Masclat
Lacave
Payrac
Rocamadour
Montvalent
Miers
Padirac
Alvignac
Gramat
Puybrun
Bretenoux
Biars-sur-Cère
St-Céré
Teyssieu
Siran
Laroquebrou
Jussac
St-Simon
Naucelles
Aurillac
Sansac-de-Marmiesse
Arpajon-sur-Cère
Le Rouget
Parlan
SÉGALA DU QUERCY
CHÂTAIGNERAIE
Sousceyrac
Latronquière
Aynac
Molières
Leyme
Terrou
Quézac
Maurs
Ladinhac
Calvinet
Montsalvy
Cassaniouze
St-Constant
Bagnac-sur-Célé
Grande-Vabre
Conques
Flagnac
Decazeville
Firmi
Viviez
Aubin
Villecomtal
Capdenac-Gare
Capdenac
Figeac
Viazac
Cardaillac
Lacapelle-Marival
Le Bourg
Assier
Livernon
Causse de Gramat
Béduer
Cénac-et-St-Julien
Domme
Belvès
St-Martial-de-Nabirat
Gourdon
Daglan
St-Pompont
BLANC
NOIR
HAUT QUERCY
Monpazier
Mazeyrolles
Villefranche-du-Périgord
Biron
Salviac
St-Chamarand
Concorès
Montfaucon
Labastide-Murat
St-Germain-du-Bel-Air
Lamothe-Cassel
Cazals
Sauveterre-la-Lémance
Frayssinet-le-Gélat
Lauzès
Catus
Francoulès
Cuzorn
Fumel
Puy-l'Évêque
Monsempron-Libos
Laussou
Montayral
St-Vite
Luzech
Mercuès
Pradines
Cahors
St-Géry
Cabrerets
Marcilhac-sur-Célé
Cajarc
Gréalou
Montbrun
Calvignac
St-Cirq-Lapopie
Concots
Limogne-en-Quercy
Causse de Limogne
Varaire
Villefranche-de-Rouergue
Villeneuve
Lanuéjouls
Rignac
Compolibat
La Bastide-l'Évêque
Montbazens
Onet-le-Château
Rodez
Olemps
Belcastel
Colombiès
Luc
Marcillac-Vallon
Salles-la-Source
Rodelle
Baraqueville
Calmont
Naucelle
Rieupeyroux
La Rouquette
St-Projet
Mauroux
Sauzet
Tournon-d'Agenais
Penne-d'Agenais
St-Pantaléon
L'Hospitalet
Lalbenque
Montaigu-de-Quercy
Montcuq
Roquecor
Beauville
St-Cyprien
Castelnau-Montratier
Belfort-du-Quercy
Puylaroque
Touffailles
Lauzerte
Cazes-Mondenard
Montpezat-de-Quercy
Bourg-de-Visa
St-Maurin
Montesquieu
Molières
Castelsagrat
Parisot
Caylus
Verfeil
Najac
La Fouillade
La Salvetat-Peyralès
St-Antonin-Noble-Val
Septfonds
Monteils
Caussade
ROUERGUE
SÉGALA
BAS QUERCY
Lamagistère
Moissac
Valence
Auvillar
Lafrançaise
Meauzac
Mirabel
Réalville
L'Honor-de-Cos
Albias
Montricoux
Forêt de la Grésigne
Cazals
Laguépie
Mirandol-Bourgnounac
Pampelonne
Cassagnes-Bégonhès
Puech de Rouet
La Selve
Lédergues
Moularès
Carmaux
Monestiés
Cordes
Vaour
Penne
Bruniquel
Nègrepelisse
Vaïssac
St-Nicolas-de-la-Grave
Castelsarrasin
Caumont
Montauban
Montbeton
Montech
Bressols
St-Nauphary
Labastide-St-Pierre
Villebrumier
Salvagnac
Castelnau-de-Montmiral
Cahuzac-sur-Vère
Cagnac-les-Mines
Valderiès
Valence-d'Albigeois
Réquista
Lescure-d'Albigeois
Senouillac
Marssac-sur-Tarn
Albi
Villefranche-d'Albigeois
Alban
Puygouzon
Fréjairolles
Gaillac
Brens
Montans
Lisle-sur-Tarn
ALBIGEOIS
Teillet
Le Masnau-Massuguiès
St-Pierre-de-Trivisy
Réalmont
Vénès
Montredon-Labessonnié
Viane
Vabre
Lacrouzette
Brassac
Le Bez
Castres
Burlats
Roquecourbe
Lautrec
Graulhet
Laboutarie
Briatexte
Fiac
Parisot
Giroussens
Coufouleux
Rabastens
St-Sulpice
Villemur-sur-Tarn
Bessières
Buzet-sur-Tarn
Nohic
Fronton
Bouloc
Poupas
Lavit
Larrazet
Beaumont-de-Lomagne
Finhan
Verdun-sur-Garonne
Canals
Grisolles
Aucamville
Castelnau-d'Estrétefonds
Launac
Grenade
St-Jory
Merville
Cox
Solomiac
Mauvezin
Cologne
Cadours
Touget
Montaigut-sur-Save
Lévignac
Aussonne
Beauzelle
Blagnac
Colomiers
Toulouse
Pibrac
L'Isle-Jourdain
Bruguières
Castelginest
Montastruc-la-Conseillère
St-Jean
L'Union
Balma
Verfeil
St-Paul-Cap-de-Joux
Vielmur-sur-Agout
Bourg-St-Bernard
LOMAGNE
A20
A89
E70
E09
A62
A68
A680
E09/72
N20
N120
N121
N122
N124
N140
N88
N112
N113
N89
D940
D911
D999

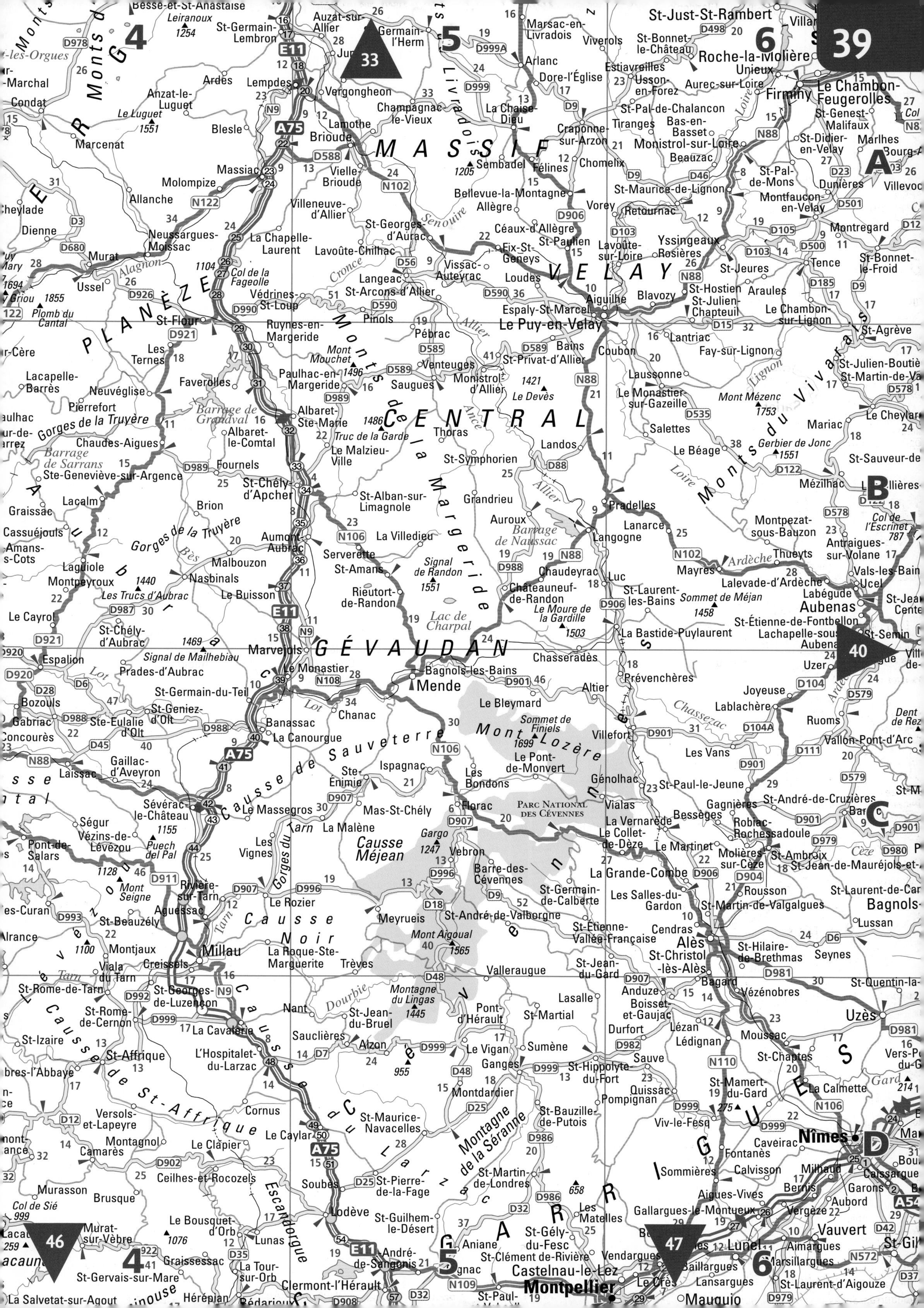

33
40
46
47
4
5
6
A
B
C
D
MASSIF
CENTRAL
VELAY
GÉVAUDAN
PLANÈZE
Monts de la Margeride
Monts du Vivarais
Mont Lozère
Causse de Sauveterre
Causse Méjean
Causse Noir
Causse du Larzac
Causse de St-Affrique
Montagne de la Séranne
Gorges de la Truyère
Gorges du Tarn
PARC NATIONAL DES CÉVENNES
Besse-et-St-Anastaise
Leiranoux 1254
St-Germain-Lembron
Auzat-sur-Allier
St-Germain-l'Herm
Marsac-en-Livradois
Viverols
St-Just-St-Rambert
St-Bonnet-le-Château
Roche-la-Molière
Unieux
Firminy
Le Chambon-Feugerolles
Arlanc
Dore-l'Église
Estivareilles
Usson-en-Forez
Aurec-sur-Loire
St-Pal-de-Chalancon
Tiranges
Bas-en-Basset
Monistrol-sur-Loire
Beauzac
St-Genest-Malifaux
St-Didier-en-Velay
Marlhes
Bourg-Argental
Dunières
St-Pal-de-Mons
Montfaucon-en-Velay
Villevocance
Montregard
St-Bonnet-le-Froid
Tence
Ardes
Lempdes
Vergongheon
Anzat-le-Luguet
Le Luguet 1551
Blesle
Marcenat
Condat
Champagnac-le-Vieux
Lamothe
Brioude
Vieille-Brioude
Massiac
Molompize
Allanche
La Chaise-Dieu
Craponne-sur-Arzon
Sembadel 1205
Félines
Chomelix
Bellevue-la-Montagne
Allègre
Vorey
Retournac
Yssingeaux
Rosières
Villeneuve-d'Allier
St-Georges-d'Aurac
La Chapelle-Laurent
Lavoûte-Chilhac
Neussargues-Moissac
Murat
Dienne
Cheylade
Ussel
Col de la Fageolle
Plomb du Cantal
Griou 1855
Langeac
St-Arcons-d'Allier
Vissac-Auteyrac
Céaux-d'Allègre
Fix-St-Geneys
St-Paulien
Loudes
Lavoûte-sur-Loire
St-Jeures
Araules
St-Hostien
St-Julien-Chapteuil
Blavozy
Aiguilhe
Espaly-St-Marcel
Le Puy-en-Velay
Le Chambon-sur-Lignon
St-Agrève
Védrines-St-Loup
Pinols
St-Flour
Ruynes-en-Margeride
Pébrac
Les Ternes
Lacapelle-Barrès
Neuvéglise
Faverolles
Pierrefort
Mont Mouchet 1496
Paulhac-en-Margeride
Venteuges
Saugues
Monistrol-d'Allier
St-Privat-d'Allier
Bains
Coubon
Lantriac
Fay-sur-Lignon
Laussonne
Le Monastier-sur-Gazeille
Mont Mézenc 1753
St-Julien-Boutières
St-Martin-de-Valamas
Le Cheylard
Mariac
Le Devès 1421
Barrage de Grandval
Albaret-le-Comtal
Chaudes-Aigues
Barrage de Sarrans
Ste-Geneviève-sur-Argence
Albaret-Ste-Marie
Truc de la Garde 1486
Le Malzieu-Ville
Thoras
Landos
Salettes
Le Béage
Gerbier de Jonc 1551
St-Sauveur-de-Montagut
Fournels
St-Chély-d'Apcher
St-Symphorien
Grandrieu
St-Alban-sur-Limagnole
Pradelles
Mézilhac
Lacalm
Brion
Graissac
Cassuéjouls
St-Amans-des-Cots
Aumont-Aubrac
La Villedieu
Auroux
Barrage de Naussac
Langogne
Lanarce
Montpezat-sous-Bauzon
Col de l'Escrinet 787
Antraigues-sur-Volane
Laguiole
Montpeyroux
Les Trucs d'Aubrac 1440
Nasbinals
Malbouzon
Serverette
St-Amans
Signal de Randon 1551
Chaudeyrac
Luc
Mayres
Thueyts
Lalevade-d'Ardèche
Vals-les-Bains
Ucel
Labégude
Aubenas
Le Cayrol
Le Buisson
Rieutort-de-Randon
Châteauneuf-de-Randon
St-Laurent-les-Bains
Sommet de Méjan 1458
St-Étienne-de-Fontbellon
Lachapelle-sous-Aubenas
St-Chély-d'Aubrac
Signal de Mailhebiau 1469
Lac de Charpal
Le Moure de la Gardille 1503
La Bastide-Puylaurent
Espalion
Prades-d'Aubrac
Marvejols
Le Monastier
Bagnols-les-Bains
Mende
Chasseradès
Prévenchères
Uzer
Joyeuse
Bozouls
St-Germain-du-Teil
St-Geniez-d'Olt
Ste-Eulalie-d'Olt
Gabriac
Concourès
Banassac
La Canourgue
Chanac
Le Bleymard
Altier
Sommet de Finiels 1699
Le Pont-de-Monvert
Villefort
Lablachère
Ruoms
Les Vans
Vallon-Pont-d'Arc
Laissac
Gaillac-d'Aveyron
Ste-Énimie
Ispagnac
Les Bondons
Génolhac
St-Paul-le-Jeune
Sévérac-le-Château
Le Massegros
Mas-St-Chély
La Malène
Florac
Vialas
La Vernarède
Le Collet-de-Dèze
Gagnières
Bessèges
Robiac-Rochessadoule
St-André-de-Cruzières
Barjac
Ségur
Vézins-de-Lévézou
Puech del Pal 1155
Pont-de-Salars
Les Vignes
Gargo 1247
Vebron
Barre-des-Cévennes
Le Martinet
Molières-sur-Cèze
St-Ambroix
St-Jean-de-Maruéjols-et-Avéjan
La Grande-Combe
Mont Seigne 1128
Rivière-sur-Tarn
Le Rozier
Aguessac
St-Germain-de-Calberte
Les Salles-du-Gardon
Rousson
St-Martin-de-Valgalgues
St-Laurent-de-Carnols
Bagnols-sur-Cèze
St-Beauzély
Meyrueis
St-André-de-Valborgne
St-Étienne-Vallée-Française
Cendras
Alès
St-Christol-lès-Alès
St-Hilaire-de-Brethmas
Seynes
Lussan
Montjaux
Millau
Creissels
La Roque-Ste-Marguerite
Trèves
Mont Aigoual 1565
Valleraugue
St-Jean-du-Gard
Bagard
Vézénobres
St-Quentin-la-Poterie
Viala-du-Tarn
St-Rome-de-Tarn
St-Georges-de-Luzençon
Nant
Montagne du Lingas 1445
St-Jean-du-Bruel
Pont-d'Hérault
St-Martial
Lasalle
Anduze
Boisset-et-Gaujac
Uzès
St-Rome-de-Cernon
La Cavalerie
Sauclières
Alzon
Le Vigan
Sumène
Durfort
Lézan
Lédignan
Moussac
St-Izaire
St-Affrique
L'Hospitalet-du-Larzac
Ganges
St-Hippolyte-du-Fort
Sauve
St-Chaptes
Vers-Pont-du-Gard
Montdardier
Quissac
Pompignan
St-Mamert-du-Gard
La Calmette
Versols-et-Lapeyre
Cornus
St-Maurice-Navacelles
St-Bauzille-de-Putois
Viv-le-Fesq
Montagnol
Camarès
Le Clapier
Le Caylar
Caveirac
Nîmes
Fontanès
Calvisson
Sommières
Milhaud
Caissargues
Bernis
Garons
Ceilhes-et-Rocozels
Murasson
Brusque
Col de Sié 999
Soubès
St-Pierre-de-la-Fage
St-Martin-de-Londres
Les Matelles
Aigues-Vives
Gallargues-le-Montueux
Vergèze
Aubord
Vauvert
Murat-sur-Vèbre
Le Bousquet-d'Orb
Lunas
Lodève
St-Guilhem-le-Désert
Aniane
St-Gély-du-Fesc
St-Clément-de-Rivière
Vendargues
Lunel
Aimargues
Marsillargues
St-Gilles
Graissessac
La Tour-sur-Orb
St-Gervais-sur-Mare
St-André-de-Sangonis
Clermont-l'Hérault
Castelnau-le-Lez
Montpellier
Le Crès
Baillargues
Lansargues
Mauguio
St-Laurent-d'Aigouze
La Salvetat-sur-Agout
Hérépian
Bédarieux
Escandorgue
Lot
Tarn
Allier
Loire
Ardèche
Dourbie
A75
E11
N88
N9
N102
N106
N122

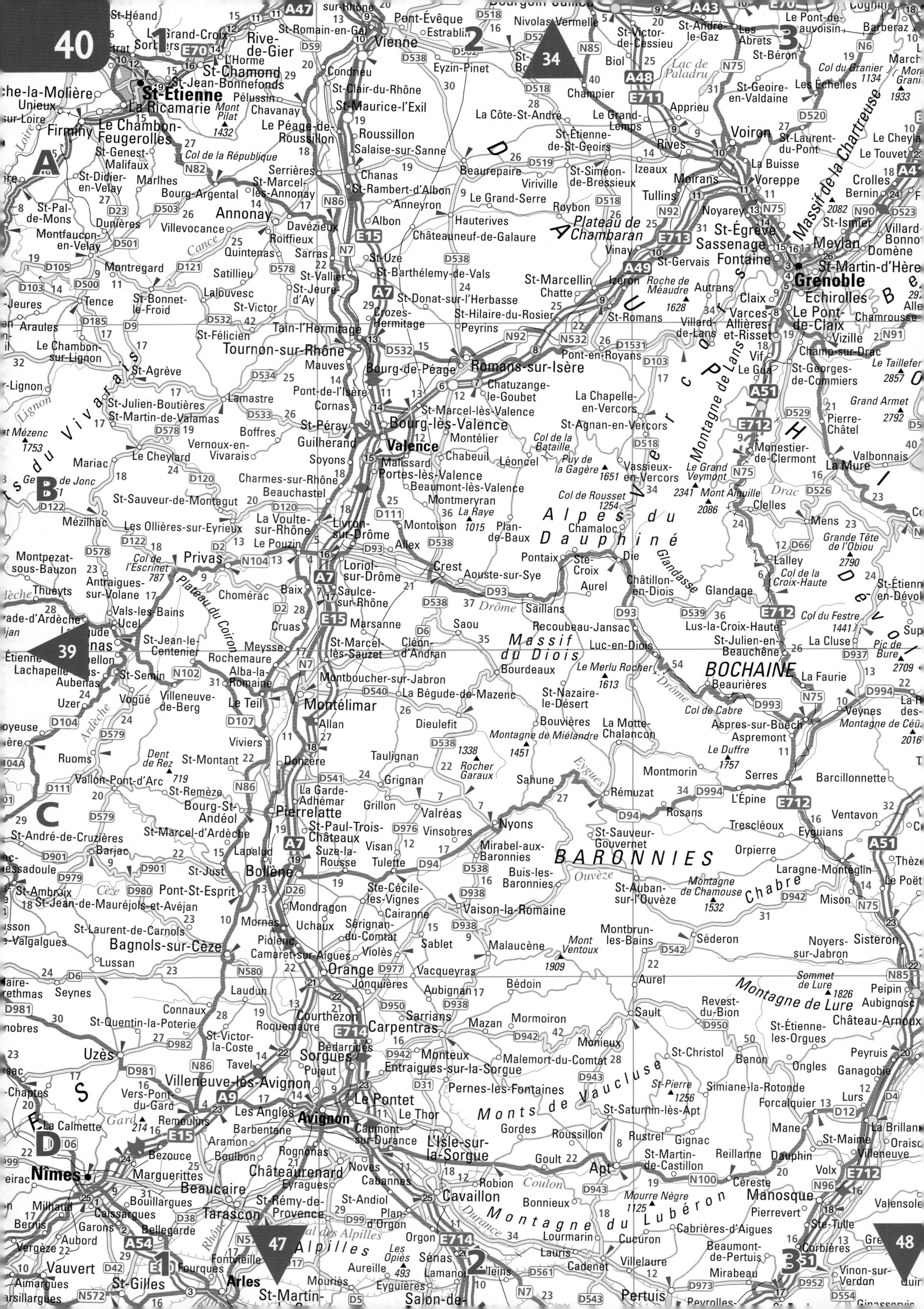
34
39
47
48
St-Étienne
Firminy
Le Chambon-Feugerolles
La Ricamarie
St-Chamond
St-Jean-Bonnefonds
Rive-de-Gier
Vienne
Pont-Évêque
Estrablin
Eyzin-Pinet
Condrieu
St-Clair-du-Rhône
St-Maurice-l'Exil
Roussillon
Salaise-sur-Sanne
Le Péage-de-Roussillon
Chanas
St-Rambert-d'Albon
Anneyron
Albon
Beaurepaire
Hauterives
Châteauneuf-de-Galaure
La Côte-St-André
Le Grand-Lemps
St-Étienne-de-St-Geoirs
Champier
Voiron
Rives
Moirans
Tullins
Voreppe
Grenoble
Meylan
Échirolles
St-Martin-d'Hère
Fontaine
Sassenage
St-Égrève
Le Pont-de-Claix
Vizille
Vif
Massif de la Chartreuse
Col du Granier 1134
Les Échelles
St-Geoire-en-Valdaine
Lac de Paladru
Crolles
Mont Pilat 1432
Col de la République
St-Genest-Malifaux
Bourg-Argental
Annonay
Davézieux
Serrières
St-Marcel-lès-Annonay
Monistrol-sur-Loire
Dunières
Montfaucon-en-Velay
Tence
Le Chambon-sur-Lignon
St-Agrève
Lamastre
Tournon-sur-Rhône
Tain-l'Hermitage
St-Vallier
Sarras
Romans-sur-Isère
Bourg-de-Péage
Chatuzange-le-Goubet
Pont-en-Royans
St-Marcellin
Chatte
Vinay
Izeron
Plateau de Chambaran
Roybon
Viriville
Bourg-lès-Valence
Valence
Guilherand
St-Péray
Cornas
Soyons
Portes-lès-Valence
Beaumont-lès-Valence
Chabeuil
Montélier
Malissard
Montmeyran
Montoison
Plan-de-Baux
Léoncel
Col de la Bataille
La Chapelle-en-Vercors
St-Agnan-en-Vercors
Vassieux-en-Vercors
Col de Rousset 1254
Villard-de-Lans
Autrans
Le Grand Veymont 2341
Mont Aiguille 2086
Monestier-de-Clermont
La Mure
Valbonnais
Mens
Clelles
Alpes du Dauphiné
Massif du Diois
Die
Châtillon-en-Diois
Glandage
Lus-la-Croix-Haute
Col de la Croix-Haute
Grande Tête de l'Obiou 2790
Plateau du Vivarais
Le Cheylard
Vernoux-en-Vivarais
Mézilhac
Les Ollières-sur-Eyrieux
La Voulte-sur-Rhône
Livron-sur-Drôme
Loriol-sur-Drôme
Crest
Aouste-sur-Sye
Saillans
Privas
Chomérac
Col de l'Escrinet 787
Plateau du Coiron
Aubenas
Vals-les-Bains
Montpezat-sous-Bauzon
Thueyts
Le Teil
Villeneuve-de-Berg
Vogüé
Montélimar
Allan
Donzère
Pierrelatte
Viviers
Bourg-St-Andéol
Dieulefit
La Bégude-de-Mazenc
Grignan
Valréas
Nyons
Vinsobres
Rémuzat
BARONNIES
BOCHAINE
Veynes
Aspres-sur-Buëch
Serres
Laragne-Montéglin
Sisteron
Orpierre
Buis-les-Baronnies
Vaison-la-Romaine
Mont Ventoux 1909
Malaucène
Sault
Montbrun-les-Bains
Séderon
Montagne de Lure
Château-Arnoux
Forcalquier
Manosque
Apt
Monts de Vaucluse
Gordes
Roussillon
Cavaillon
Montagne du Lubéron
Pertuis
Orange
Carpentras
Bollène
Pont-St-Esprit
Bagnols-sur-Cèze
Vallon-Pont-d'Arc
Ruoms
Barjac
St-Ambroix
Uzès
Villeneuve-lès-Avignon
Avignon
Le Pontet
Sorgues
L'Isle-sur-la-Sorgue
Châteaurenard
Beaucaire
Tarascon
St-Rémy-de-Provence
Alpilles
Arles
Nîmes
St-Gilles
Vauvert
Salon-de-Provence
A7
A9
A47
A48
A49
A51
A54
E15
E712
E713
E714
N7
N75
N85
N86
N100
D93

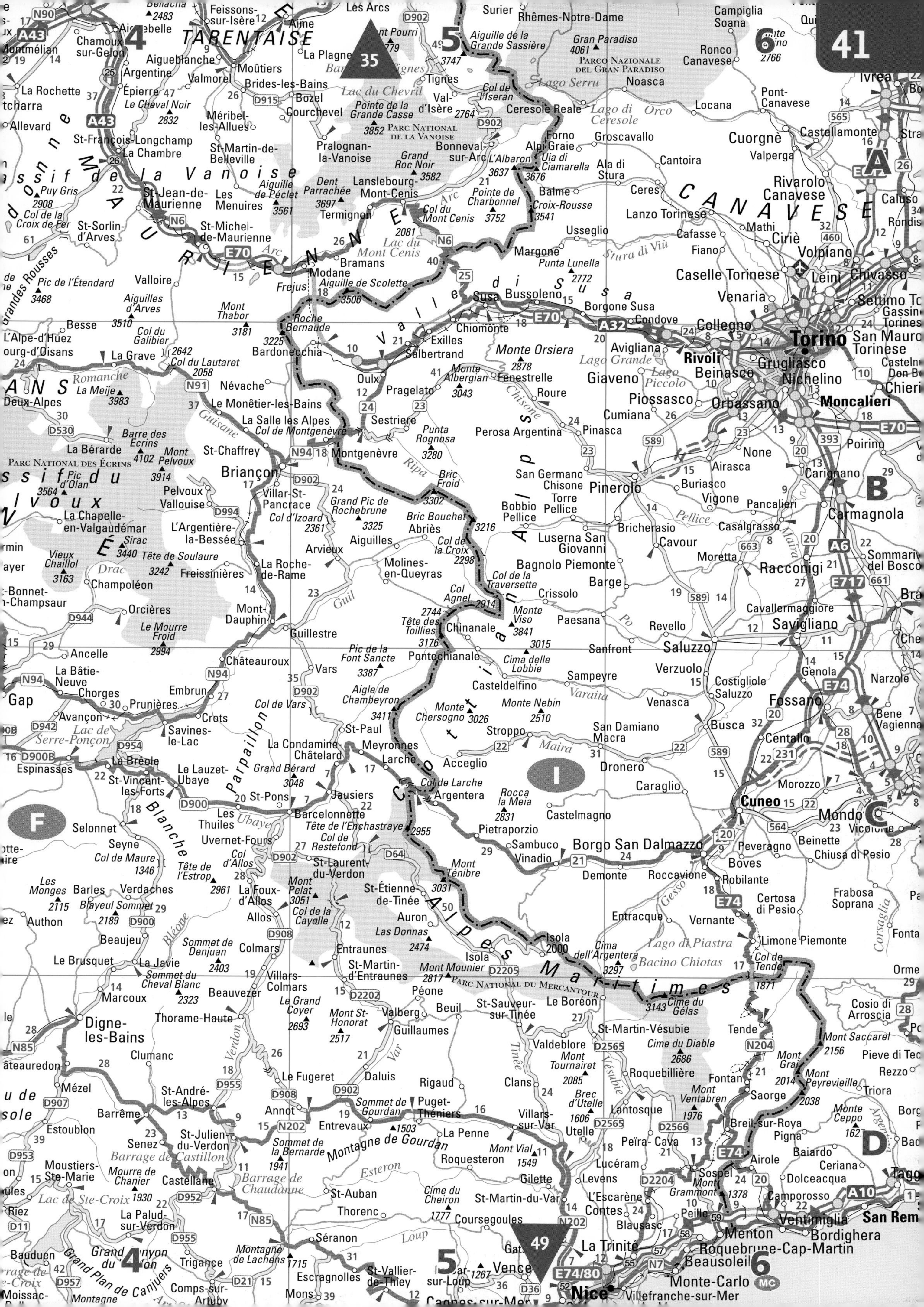
35
49
4
5
6
A
B
C
D
F
I
MC
TARENTAISE
Massif de la Vanoise
MAURIENNE
Valle di Susa
CANAVESE
Alpi Cozie
Alpes Maritimes
Massif du Pelvoux
Parc National de la Vanoise
Parco Nazionale del Gran Paradiso
Parc National des Écrins
Parc National du Mercantour
Montmélian
Chamoux-sur-Gelon
Aiguebelle
Feissons-sur-Isère
Aime
Les Arcs
La Plagne
Surier
Rhêmes-Notre-Dame
Campiglia Soana
Aiguille de la Grande Sassière
Gran Paradiso 4061
Ronco Canavese
Aigueblanche
Argentine
Moûtiers
Valmorel
Brides-les-Bains
Bozel
Courchevel
Tignes
Lac du Chevril
Val-d'Isère
Col de l'Iseran
Ceresole Reale
Lago di Ceresole
Orco
Noasca
Lago Serru
Locana
Pont-Canavese
Ivrea
La Rochette
Épierre
Le Cheval Noir 2832
Méribel-les-Allues
Pointe de la Grande Casse 3852
Allevard
St-François-Longchamp
La Chambre
St-Martin-de-Belleville
Pralognan-la-Vanoise
Bonneval-sur-Arc
Forno Alpi Graie
Uia di Ciamarella 3676
Groscavallo
Cuorgnè
Castellamonte
Valperga
Cantoira
Ala di Stura
L'Albaron 3637
Grand Roc Noir 3582
Puy Gris 2908
Aiguille de Péclet 3561
Dent Parrachée 3697
Lanslebourg-Mont-Cenis
Pointe de Charbonnel 3752
Balme
Ceres
Rivarolo Canavese
Caluso
Rondissone
St-Jean-de-Maurienne
Les Menuires
Termignon
Col du Mont Cenis
Croix-Rousse 3541
Lanzo Torinese
Mathi
Col de la Croix de Fer
St-Sorlin-d'Arves
St-Michel-de-Maurienne
Lac du Mont Cenis
Usseglio
Cafasse
Ciriè
Volpiano
Chivasso
Fiano
Margone
Punta Lunella 2772
Stura di Viù
Grandes Rousses
Pic de l'Étendard 3468
Valloire
Modane
Bramans
Fréjus
Aiguille de Scolette 3506
Caselle Torinese
Leinì
Settimo Torinese
Venaria
Aiguilles d'Arves 3510
Mont Thabor 3181
Roche Bernaude 3225
Susa
Bussoleno
Borgone Susa
Condove
Collegno
Torino
San Mauro Torinese
Gassino Torinese
Besse
L'Alpe-d'Huez
Bourg-d'Oisans
Col du Galibier 2642
Col du Lautaret 2058
La Grave
Bardonecchia
Chiomonte
Exilles
Salbertrand
Monte Orsiera 2878
Avigliana
Lago Grande
Rivoli
Grugliasco
Beinasco
Nichelino
Castelnuovo Don Bosco
Chieri
Romanche
La Meije 3983
Les Deux-Alpes
Névache
Oulx
Pragelato
Monte Albergian 3043
Fenestrelle
Giaveno
Lago Piccolo
Piossasco
Orbassano
Moncalieri
Le Monêtier-les-Bains
Guisane
La Salle les Alpes
Col de Montgenèvre
Sestriere
Chisone
Roure
Cumiana
Pinasca
Perosa Argentina
La Bérarde
Barre des Écrins 4102
Mont Pelvoux 3914
St-Chaffrey
Montgenèvre
Punta Rognosa 3280
Ripa
Poirino
None
Airasca
Carignano
Pic d'Olan 3564
Briançon
Bric Froid 3302
San Germano Chisone
Pinerolo
Buriasco
Vigone
Pancalieri
Carmagnola
Pelvoux
Vallouise
Villar-St-Pancrace
Grand Pic de Rochebrune 3325
Col d'Izoard 2361
Bric Bouchet 3216
Abriès
Bobbio Pellice
Torre Pellice
Bricherasio
Pellice
Casalgrasso
La Chapelle-en-Valgaudémar
L'Argentière-la-Bessée
Aiguilles
Col de la Croix 2298
Luserna San Giovanni
Cavour
Moretta
Sommariva del Bosco
Sirac 3440
Tête de Soulaure 3242
Vieux Chaillol 3163
Drac
Freissinières
La Roche-de-Rame
Arvieux
Molines-en-Queyras
Col de la Traversette
Bagnolo Piemonte
Barge
Racconigi
Champoléon
St-Bonnet-en-Champsaur
Orcières
Guil
Col Agnel 2744
Crissolo
Cavallermaggiore
Mont-Dauphin
Le Mourre Froid 2994
Guillestre
Tête des Toillies 3176
Chinanale
Monte Viso 3841
Paesana
Po
Revello
Savigliano
Ancelle
Pic de la Font Sancte 3387
Pontechianale
Cima delle Lobbie 3015
Sanfront
Saluzzo
La Bâtie-Neuve
Châteauroux
Vars
Casteldelfino
Sampeyre
Verzuolo
Genola
Narzole
Gap
Chorges
Embrun
Aigle de Chambeyron 3411
Varaita
Costigliole Saluzzo
Fossano
Bene Vagienna
Prunières
Col de Vars
Monte Chersogno 3026
Monte Nebin 2510
Venasca
Avançon
Crots
Savines-le-Lac
St-Paul
Stroppo
San Damiano Macra
Busca
Centallo
Lac de Serre-Ponçon
La Condamine-Châtelard
Meyronnes
Maira
Dronero
Espinasses
La Bréole
Le Lauzet-Ubaye
Grand Bérard 3048
Larche
Acceglio
Caraglio
Morozzo
St-Vincent-les-Forts
Parpaillon
Col de Larche
Argentera
St-Pons
Jausiers
Rocca la Meia 2831
Cuneo
Mondovì
Selonnet
Blanche
Les Thuiles
Ubaye
Barcelonnette
Tête de l'Enchastraye 2955
Castelmagno
Pietraporzio
Vicoforte
Seyne
Col de Maure 1346
Uvernet-Fours
Col de Restefond
Sambuco
Vinadio
Borgo San Dalmazzo
Peveragno
Beinette
Chiusa di Pesio
Col d'Allos
Tête de l'Estrop 2961
St-Laurent-du-Verdon
Mont Ténibre 3031
Boves
Robilante
Demonte
Roccavione
Les Monges 2115
Barles
Verdaches
La Foux-d'Allos
Mont Pelat 3051
St-Étienne-de-Tinée
Gesso
Certosa di Pesio
Frabosa Soprana
Blayeul Sommet 2189
Col de la Cayolle
Auron
Entracque
Vernante
Authon
Allos
Las Donnas 2474
Corsaglia
Beaujeu
Bléone
Sommet de Denjuan 2403
Colmars
Entraunes
Isola 2000
Isola
Cima dell'Argentera 3297
Lago di Piastra
Limone Piemonte
Bacino Chiotas
Col de Tende 1871
Le Brusquet
La Javie
St-Martin-d'Entraunes
Mont Mounier 2817
Sommet du Cheval Blanc 2323
Villars-Colmars
Marcoux
Beauvezer
Le Grand Coyer 2693
Péone
Beuil
St-Sauveur-sur-Tinée
Le Boréon
Cime du Gélas 3143
Cosio di Arroscia
Digne-les-Bains
Thorame-Haute
Mont St-Honorat 2517
Valberg
Guillaumes
St-Martin-Vésubie
Tende
Mont Saccarel 2156
Verdon
Var
Tinée
Valdeblore
Cime du Diable 2686
Pieve di Teco
Clumanc
Mont Tournairet 2085
Châteauredon
Le Fugeret
Daluis
Rigaud
Clans
Vésubie
Roquebillière
Fontan
Mont Grai 2014
Mont Pepreville 2038
Rezzo
Triora
Mézel
St-André-les-Alpes
Annot
Sommet de Gourdan
Puget-Théniers
Villars-sur-Var
Brec d'Utelle 1606
Lantosque
Saorge
Mont Ventabren 1976
Barrême
Estoublon
Entrevaux
La Penne
Utelle
Breil-sur-Roya
Pigna
Monte Ceppo 1627
Senez
St-Julien-du-Verdon
Barrage de Castillon
Sommet de la Bernarde 1941
Montagne de Gourdan
Roquesteron
Mont Vial 1549
Peïra-Cava
Airole
Baiardo
Ceriana
Moustiers-Ste-Marie
Mourre de Chanier 1930
Castellane
Barrage de Chaudanne
Esteron
Gilette
Levens
Sospel
Dolceacqua
Riez
Lac de Ste-Croix
La Palud-sur-Verdon
St-Auban
Cime du Cheiron 1777
St-Martin-du-Var
L'Escarène
Mont Grammont 1378
Camporosso
Thorenc
Coursegoules
Contes
Peille
Ventimiglia
San Remo
Bauduen
Grand Canyon du Verdon
Séranon
Loup
Blausasc
Menton
Bordighera
Grand Plan de Canjuers
Trigance
Montagne de Lachens 1715
Roquebrune-Cap-Martin
La Trinité
Beausoleil
Comps-sur-Artuby
Escragnolles
St-Vallier-de-Thiey
Le Bar-sur-Loup
Vence
Monte-Carlo
Nice
Villefranche-sur-Mer
Moissac
Montagne
Mons
Cagnes-sur-Mer
A43
A32
A6
A10
E70
E74
E717
E74/80
N6
N85
N90
N91
N94
N202
N204
D902
D900
D908
D955
D2205
D2565
D2566

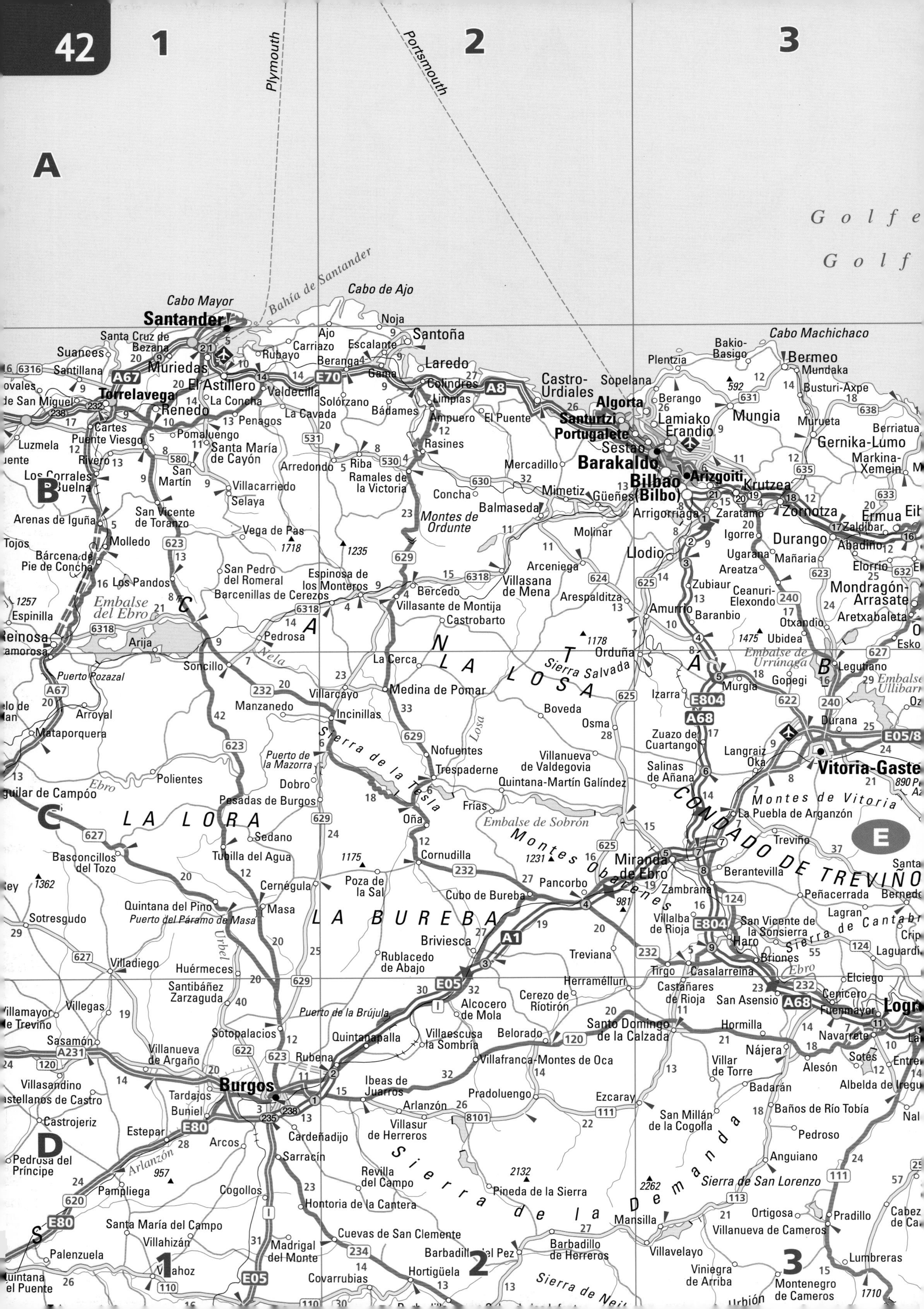
1
2
3
A
B
C
D
E
Plymouth
Portsmouth
Golfe
Golf
Cabo Mayor
Bahía de Santander
Cabo de Ajo
Santander
Noja
Santoña
Santa Cruz de Bezana
Ajo
Carriazo
Escalante
Suances
Rubayo
Beranga
Muriedas
Laredo
Santillana
El Astillero
Gama
Colindres
Castro-Urdiales
Sopelana
Torrelavega
Valdecilla
Limpias
Renedo
La Concha
Solórzano
Bádames
Ampuero
El Puente
Algorta
Santurtzi
Portugalete
Sestao
Barakaldo
Bilbao (Bilbo)
Arizgoiti
Lamiako
Erandio
Berango
Plentzia
Bakio-Basigo
Cabo Machichaco
Bermeo
Mundaka
Mungia
Busturi-Axpe
Murueta
Berriatua
Gernika-Lumo
Markina-Xemein
Cartes
Luzmela
Puente Viesgo
Pomaluengo
Penagos
La Cavada
Santa María de Cayón
Rasines
Rivero
San Martín
Arredondo
Riba
Ramales de la Victoria
Mercadillo
Los Corrales de Buelna
Villacarriedo
Selaya
Concha
Mimetiz
Güeñes
Arrigorriaga
Krutzea
Zaratamo
Zornotza
Ermua
Arenas de Iguña
San Vicente de Toranzo
Balmaseda
Montes de Ordunte
Igorre
Durango
Zaldibar
Abadiño
Tojos
Molledo
Vega de Pas
Molinar
Llodio
Ugarana
Mañaria
Bárcena de Pie de Concha
San Pedro del Romeral
Espinosa de los Monteros
Arceniega
Areatza
Elorrio
Los Pandos
Villasana de Mena
Zubiaur
Ceanuri-Elexondo
Mondragón-Arrasate
Espinilla
Embalse del Ebro
Barcenillas de Cerezos
Bercedo
Villasante de Montija
Arespalditza
Amurrio
Baranbio
Otxandio
Aretxabaleta
Reinosa
Castrobarto
Arija
Pedrosa
Orduña
Ubidea
Esko
Camorosa
Soncillo
Nela
La Cerca
Sierra Salvada
Embalse de Urrúnaga
Legutiano
Puerto Pozazal
Villarcayo
Medina de Pomar
Izarra
Murgia
Gopegi
Embalse Ullibarri
Manzanedo
Incinillas
Boveda
Osma
Durana
Arroyal
Mataporquera
Sierra de la Tesla
Zuazo de Cuartango
Langraiz Oka
Vitoria-Gasteiz
Puerto de la Mazorra
Nofuentes
Villanueva de Valdegovia
Salinas de Añana
Polientes
Dobro
Trespaderne
Quintana-Martín Galíndez
Montes de Vitoria
Aguilar de Campóo
Ebro
Pesadas de Burgos
Frías
La Puebla de Arganzón
LA LORA
Oña
Embalse de Sobrón
Montes Obarenes
Treviño
Sedano
Basconcillos del Tozo
Tubilla del Agua
Cornudilla
Miranda de Ebro
Berantevilla
CONDADO DE TREVIÑO
Pancorbo
Zambrana
Peñacerrada
Cernégula
Poza de la Sal
Cubo de Bureba
Lagran
Quintana del Pino
Puerto del Páramo de Masa
Masa
LA BUREBA
Villalba de Rioja
San Vicente de la Sonsierra
Sierra de Cantabria
Sotresgudo
Briviesca
Haro
Briones
Laguardia
Villadiego
Rublacedo de Abajo
Huérmeces
Treviana
Tirgo
Casalarreina
Elciego
Santibáñez Zarzaguda
Herramélluri
Castañares de Rioja
Cenicero
Villamayor de Treviño
Villegas
Alcocero de Mola
Cerezo de Riotirón
San Asensio
Fuenmayor
Logroño
Puerto de la Brújula
Santo Domingo de la Calzada
Hormilla
Navarrete
Sasamón
Sotopalacios
Quintanapalla
Villaescusa la Sombría
Belorado
Nájera
Villanueva de Argaño
Rubena
Villafranca-Montes de Oca
Villar de Torre
Alesón
Sotés
Villasandino
Castellanos de Castro
Burgos
Tardajos
Ibeas de Juarros
Badarán
Albelda de Iregua
Buniel
Pradoluengo
Ezcaray
Arlanzón
Baños de Río Tobía
Castrojeriz
Estepar
Cardeñadijo
Villasur de Herreros
San Millán de la Cogolla
Arcos
Sarracín
Pedroso
Pedrosa del Príncipe
Sierra de la Demanda
Anguiano
Revilla del Campo
Pineda de la Sierra
Sierra de San Lorenzo
Pampliega
Cogollos
Hontoria de la Cantera
Ortigosa
Pradillo
Santa María del Campo
Mansilla
Villanueva de Cameros
Villahizán
Cuevas de San Clemente
Madrigal del Monte
Barbadillo del Pez
Barbadillo de Herreros
Villavelayo
Palenzuela
Lumbreras
Mahoz
Hortigüela
Viniegra de Arriba
Quintana del Puente
Covarrubias
Sierra de Neila
Urbión
Montenegro de Cameros
A67
A8
E70
E804
A68
E05
A1
E80
A231
E05/80

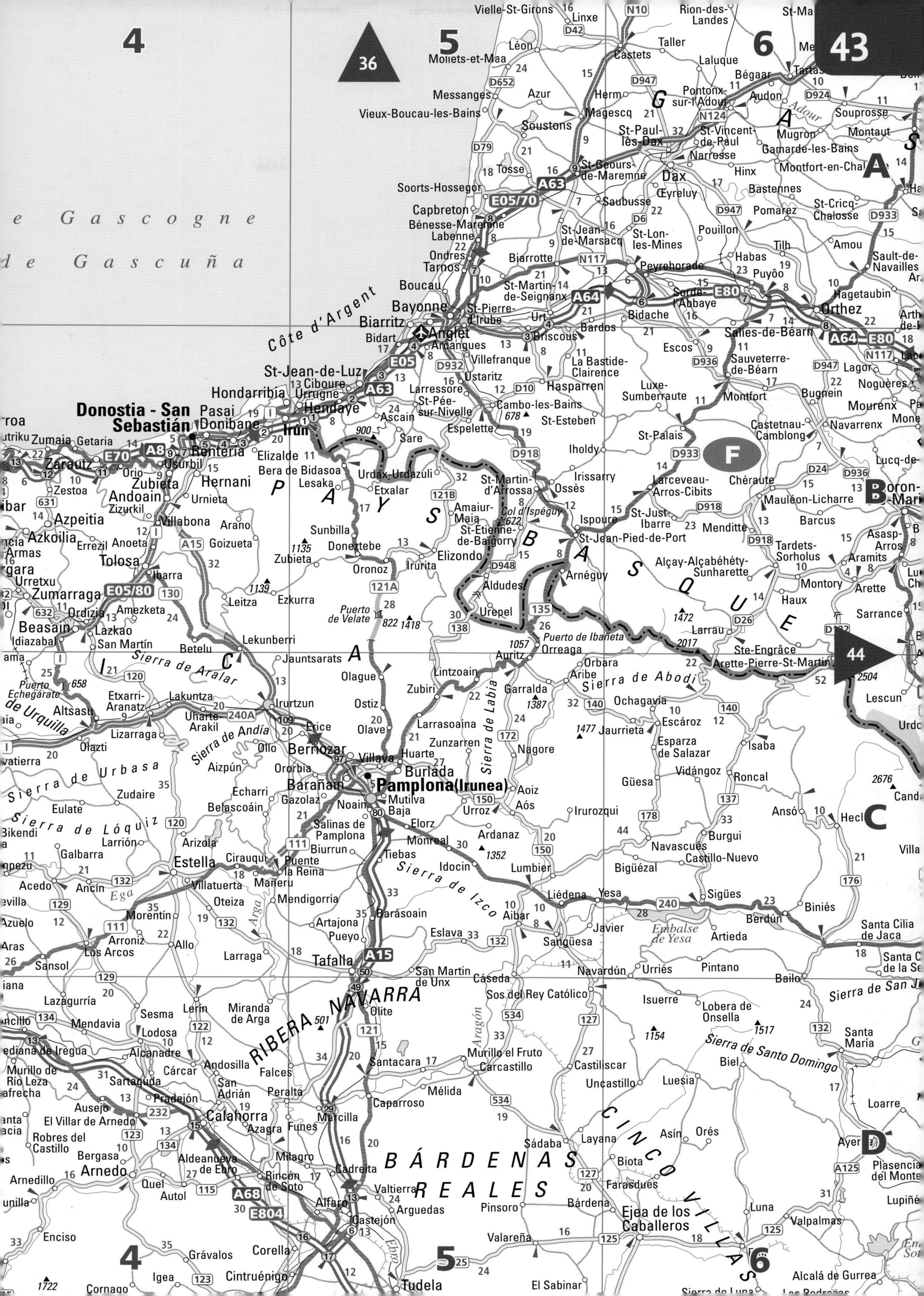
4
5
6
36
44
e Gascogne
de Gascuña
Côte d'Argent
PAYS BASQUE
GASCOGNE
RIBERA NAVARRA
BÁRDENAS REALES
CINCO VILLAS
Vielle-St-Girons
Linxe
Rion-des-Landes
Léon
Castets
Taller
Moliets-et-Maa
Laluque
Bégaar
Tartas
Messanges
Azur
Herm
Pontonx-sur-l'Adour
Audon
Souprosse
Vieux-Boucau-les-Bains
Magescq
Soustons
St-Paul-lès-Dax
St-Vincent-de-Paul
Mugron
Montaut
Gamarde-les-Bains
Narrosse
Tosse
St-Geours-de-Maremne
Dax
Hinx
Montfort-en-Chalosse
Soorts-Hossegor
Œyreluy
Bastennes
Capbreton
Saubusse
Pomarez
St-Cricq-Chalosse
Bénesse-Maremne
Labenne
St-Jean-de-Marsacq
St-Lon-les-Mines
Pouillon
Amou
Ondres
Tarnos
Biarrotte
Peyrehorade
Habas
Puyôo
Sault-de-Navailles
Boucau
St-Martin-de-Seignanx
Sorde-l'Abbaye
Hagetaubin
Bayonne
St-Pierre-d'Irube
Urt
Bidache
Orthez
Biarritz
Anglet
Bardos
Bidart
Arcangues
Briscous
Escos
Salies-de-Béarn
Villefranque
La Bastide-Clairence
Sauveterre-de-Béarn
Lagor
St-Jean-de-Luz
Ciboure
Urrugne
Ustaritz
Hasparren
Luxe-Sumberraute
Montfort
Bugnein
Noguères
Hondarribia
Larressore
St-Pée-sur-Nivelle
Cambo-les-Bains
Mourenx
Donostia - San Sebastián
Pasai Donibane
Hendaye
Irun
Ascain
St-Esteben
Castetnau-Camblong
Navarrenx
Sare
Espelette
St-Palais
Zumaia
Getaria
Errenteria
Elizalde
Iholdy
Lucq-de-Béarn
Zarautz
Orio
Usurbil
Hernani
Bera de Bidasoa
Urdax-Urdazuli
St-Martin-d'Arrossa
Irissarry
Ossès
Larceveau-Arros-Cibits
Chéraute
Zestoa
Zubieta
Lesaka
Etxalar
Mauléon-Licharre
Andoain
Urnieta
Amaiur-Maia
Col d'Ispéguy
St-Etienne-de-Baïgorry
Ispoure
St-Just-Ibarre
Mendite
Barcus
Azpeitia
Zizurkil
Villabona
Arano
St-Jean-Pied-de-Port
Azkoitia
Errezil
Anoeta
Goizueta
Sunbilla
Doneztebe
Elizondo
Tardets-Sorholus
Asasp-Arros
Aramits
Tolosa
Zubieta
Oronoz
Irurita
Arnéguy
Alçay-Alçabéhéty-Sunharette
Ibarra
Aldudes
Montory
Arette
Zumarraga
Leitza
Ezkurra
Puerto de Velate
Urepel
Haux
Ordizia
Amezketa
Sarrance
Beasain
Lazkao
Lekunberri
Larrau
Idiazabal
San Martín
Betelu
Puerto de Ibañeta
Orreaga
Ste-Engrâce
Arette-Pierre-St-Martin
Sierra de Aralar
Jauntsarats
Auritz
Orbara
Aribe
Sierra de Abodi
Olague
Lintzoain
Puerto Echegárate
Etxarri-Aranatz
Lakuntza
Irurtzun
Zubiri
Garralda
Ochagavía
Lescun
Altsasu
Sierra de Urquilla
Uharte-Arakil
Ostiz
Olave
Erice
Larrasoaina
Sierra de Labia
Escároz
Lizarraga
Olazti
Sierra de Andía
Ollo
Berriozar
Villava
Huarte
Zunzarren
Nagore
Jaurrieta
Esparza de Salazar
Isaba
Urdos
Ziordia
Aizpún
Ororbia
Burlada
Vidángoz
Roncal
Sierra de Urbasa
Zudaire
Echarri
Barañain
Pamplona(Irunea)
Aoiz
Güesa
Eulate
Belascoáin
Gazolaz
Noain
Mutilva Baja
Urroz
Aós
Irurozqui
Ansó
Hecho
Sierra de Lóquiz
Larrión
Salinas de Pamplona
Elorz
Ardanaz
Burgui
Arizala
Monreal
Navascués
Castillo-Nuevo
Galbarra
Biurrun
Estella
Cirauqui
Puente la Reina
Tiebas
Idocin
Lumbier
Bigüézal
Acedo
Ancín
Villatuerta
Mañeru
Sierra de Izco
Liédena
Yesa
Sigües
Biniés
Oteiza
Mendigorría
Morentin
Barásoain
Aibar
Berdún
Santa Cilia de Jaca
Arróniz
Artajona
Pueyo
Eslava
Javier
Embalse de Yesa
Artieda
Los Arcos
Allo
Sangüesa
Sansol
Larraga
Tafalla
Navardún
Urriés
Pintano
Bailo
San Martín de Unx
Cáseda
Sos del Rey Católico
Sierra de San Juan de la Peña
Lazagurría
Sesma
Lerín
Miranda de Arga
Olite
Isuerre
Lobera de Onsella
Mendavia
Lodosa
Santa María
Alcanadre
Andosilla
Murillo el Fruto
Carcastillo
Castiliscar
Sierra de Santo Domingo
Biel
Murillo de Río Leza
Cárcar
Falces
Santacara
Uncastillo
Luesia
Sartaguda
San Adrián
Peralta
Mélida
Pradejón
Ausejo
Calahorra
Marcilla
Caparroso
Loarre
El Villar de Arnedo
Azagra
Funes
Sádaba
Layana
Asín
Orés
Robres del Castillo
Aldeanueva de Ebro
Milagro
Biota
Ayerbe
Bergasa
Arnedo
Rincón de Soto
Cadreita
Plasencia del Monte
Arnedillo
Quel
Autol
Valtierra
Farasdués
Alfaro
Arguedas
Pinsoro
Bárdena
Ejea de los Caballeros
Luna
Lupiñén
Castejón
Valpalmas
Enciso
Grávalos
Corella
Valareña
Igea
Cintruénigo
Tudela
El Sabinar
Cornago
Alcalá de Gurrea
A63
E05/70
A64
E80
N117
E05
A8
E70
A15
E05/80
A68
E804
N10
N124
D947
D933
D918
D936
121A
121B
240A
240
111
132
134
129
150
178
137
140
176
534
127
115
123
125
A125
900
678
672
1135
1139
1418
822
1057
2017
1472
2504
2676
1387
1477
1352
501
1154
1517
1722
658

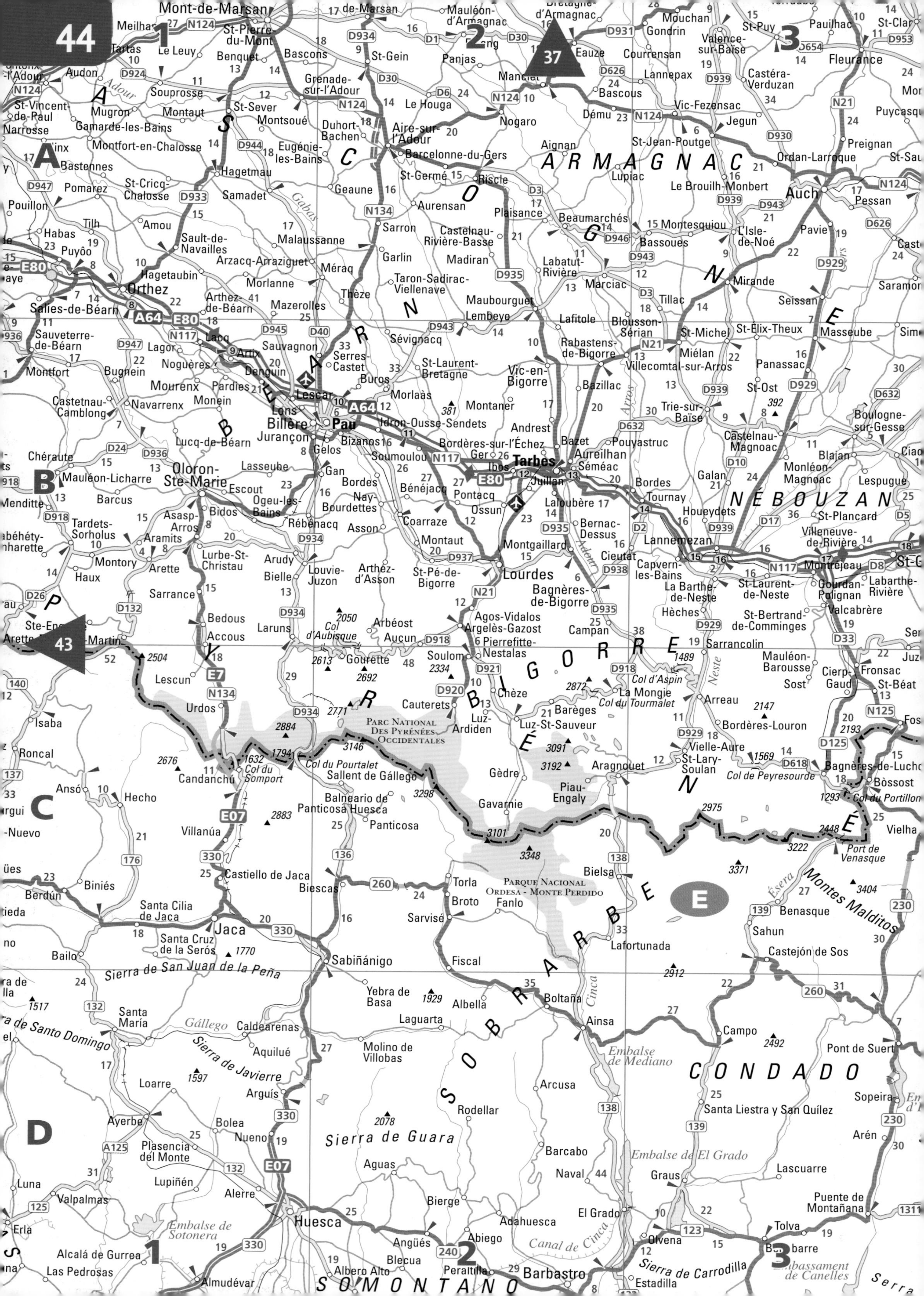
Mont-de-Marsan
Meilhan
Tartas
St-Pierre-du-Mont
Le Leuy
Benquet
Bascons
Mauléon-d'Armagnac
St-Gein
Panjas
Eauze
Gondrin
Mouchan
Courrensan
Valence-sur-Baïse
St-Puy
Pauilhac
Fleurance
Audon
Souprosse
Grenade-sur-l'Adour
Manciet
Lannepax
Castéra-Verduzan
Bascous
St-Vincent-de-Paul
Mugron
Montaut
St-Sever
Montsoué
Le Houga
Nogaro
Vic-Fezensac
Jegun
Puycasquier
Gamarde-les-Bains
Narrosse
Duhort-Bachen
Aire-sur-l'Adour
Démi
Montfort-en-Chalosse
Eugénie-les-Bains
Barcelone-du-Gers
Aignan
St-Jean-Poutge
Preignan
Bastennes
Hagetmau
ARMAGNAC
Ordan-Larroque
Pomarez
St-Cricq-Chalosse
Samadet
Geaune
St-Germé
Riscle
Lupiac
Le Brouilh-Monbert
Auch
Pessan
Pouillon
Amou
Aurensan
Plaisance
Beaumarchés
Montesquiou
L'Isle-de-Noé
Pavie
Habas
Tilh
Puyôo
Sault-de-Navailles
Malaussanne
Sarron
Castelnau-Rivière-Basse
Bassoues
Arzacq-Arraziguet
Méraq
Garlin
Madiran
Labatut-Rivière
Marciac
Mirande
Hagetaubin
Orthez
Morlanne
Taron-Sadirac-Viellenave
Thèze
Maubourguet
Tillac
Seissan
Salies-de-Béarn
Arthez-de-Béarn
Mazerolles
Lembeye
Lafitole
Blousson-Sérian
St-Michel
St-Élix-Theux
Masseube
Sauveterre-de-Béarn
Lagor
Lacq
Artix
Sauvagnon
Serres-Castet
Sévignacq
Rabastens-de-Bigorre
Miélan
Villecomtal-sur-Arros
Panassac
Montfort
Bugnein
Noguères
Denguin
Buros
St-Laurent-Bretagne
Vic-en-Bigorre
St-Ost
Mourenx
Pardies
Lescar
Morlaàs
Bazillac
Castetnau-Camblong
Navarrenx
Monein
Lons
Billère
Pau
Idron-Ousse-Sendets
Montaner
Andrest
Trie-sur-Baïse
Boulogne-sur-Gesse
Lucq-de-Béarn
Jurançon
Bizanos
Bordères-sur-l'Échez
Bazet
Pouyastruc
Castelnau-Magnoac
Chéraute
Gelos
Soumoulou
Ger
Ibos
Tarbes
Aureilhan
Séméac
Blajan
Mauléon-Licharre
Oloron-Ste-Marie
Lasseube
Gan
Bordes
Bénéjacq
Juillan
Galan
Monléon-Magnoac
Lespugue
Barcus
Escout
Ogeu-les-Bains
Nay-Bourdettes
Pontacq
Ossun
Laloubère
Tournay
Houeydets
NÉBOUZAN
Tardets-Sorholus
Asasp-Arros
Bidos
Rébénacq
Asson
Coarraze
Bernac-Dessus
St-Plancard
Aramits
Montory
Arette
Lurbe-St-Christau
Arudy
Montaut
Montgaillard
Cieutat
Lannemezan
Villeneuve-de-Rivière
Haux
Sarrance
Bielle
Louvie-Juzon
Arthez-d'Asson
St-Pé-de-Bigorre
Lourdes
Capvern-les-Bains
La Barthe-de-Neste
St-Laurent-de-Neste
Montréjeau
Gourdan-Polignan
Labarthe-Rivière
Bedous
Accous
Laruns
Col d'Aubisque
Arbéost
Aucun
Agos-Vidalos
Argelès-Gazost
Pierrefitte-Nestalas
Bagnères-de-Bigorre
Campan
Hèches
St-Bertrand-de-Comminges
Valcabrère
Sarrancolin
Mauléon-Barousse
Sost
Cierp-Gaud
Fronsac
St-Béat
Lescun
Gourette
Soulom
Col d'Aspin
La Mongie
Col du Tourmalet
Arreau
Cauterets
Chèze
Barèges
Luz-Ardiden
Luz-St-Sauveur
Bordères-Louron
Urdos
Parc National des Pyrénées Occidentales
Vielle-Aure
St-Lary-Soulan
Col de Peyresourde
Bagnères-de-Luchon
Bòssost
Col du Portillon
Isaba
Roncal
Candanchú
Col du Somport
Col du Pourtalet
Sallent de Gállego
Gèdre
Aragnouet
Piau-Engaly
Ansó
Hecho
Balneario de Panticosa
Huesca
Panticosa
Gavarnie
Villanúa
Vielha
Port de Venasque
Bielsa
Castiello de Jaca
Biescas
Torla
Broto
Fanlo
Parque Nacional Ordesa - Monte Perdido
Biniés
Berdún
Santa Cilia de Jaca
Jaca
Santa Cruz de la Serós
Sarvisé
Benasque
Sahun
Montes Malditos
Lafortunada
Castejón de Sos
Bailo
Sabiñánigo
Fiscal
Sierra de San Juan de la Peña
Yebra de Basa
Albella
Boltaña
Santa María
Caldearenas
Laguarta
Ainsa
Campo
Sierra de Santo Domingo
Aquilué
Molino de Villobas
Embalse de Mediano
Pont de Suert
Sierra de Javierre
CONDADO
Loarre
Arguís
Arcusa
SOBRARBE
Ayerbe
Rodellar
Santa Liestra y San Quílez
Sopeira
Bolea
Nueno
Sierra de Guara
Arén
Plasencia del Monte
Aguas
Barcabo
Embalse de El Grado
Lascuarre
Lupiñén
Naval
Graus
Luna
Alerre
Bierge
Puente de Montañana
Valpalmas
El Grado
Erla
Huesca
Adahuesca
Tolva
Embalse de Sotonera
Abiego
Olvena
Alcalá de Gurrea
Angüés
Canal de Cinca
Benabarre
Las Pedrosas
Blecua
Albero Alto
Peraltilla
Barbastro
Sierra de Carrodilla
Embassament de Canelles
Almudévar
SOMONTANO
Estadilla
CHALOSSE
BÉARN
PYRÉNÉES
BIGORRE
COMMINGES
A
B
C
D
E
1
2
3
37
43

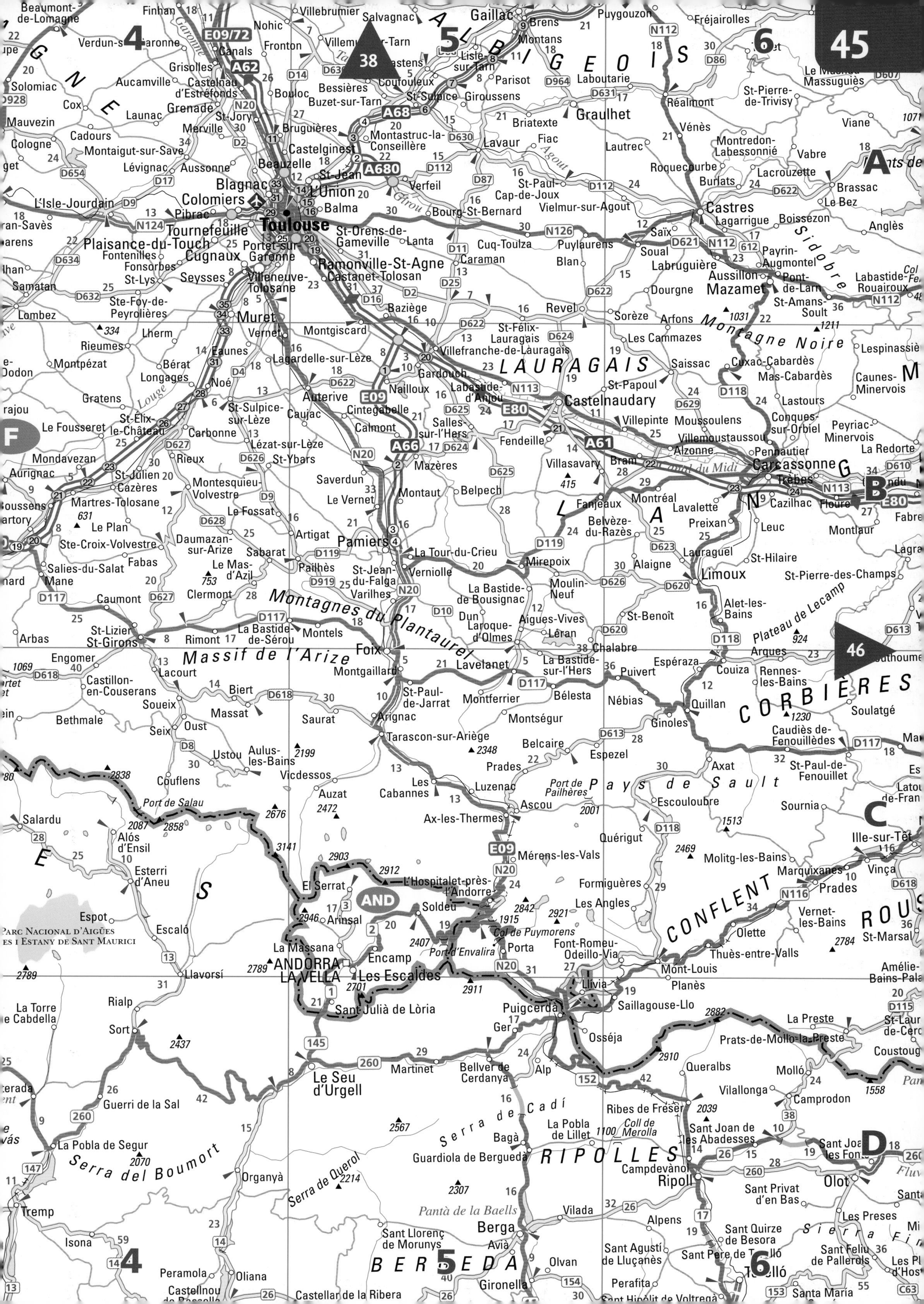
4
5
6
A
B
C
D
F
38
46
ALBIGEOIS
LAURAGAIS
Montagne Noire
Sidobre
Massif de l'Arize
Montagnes du Plantaurel
Plateau de Lecamp
CORBIÈRES
Pays de Sault
CONFLENT
RIPOLLÈS
BERGUEDA
Serra del Boumort
Serra de Cadí
Serra de Querol
Pantà de la Baells
Parc Nacional d'Aigües
es i Estany de Sant Maurici
Beaumont-de-Lomagne
Finhan
Villebrumier
Salvagnac
Gaillac
Brens
Puygouzon
Fréjairolles
Verdun-sur-Garonne
Nohic
Fronton
Montans
Lisle-sur-Tarn
Parisot
Labouitarie
Grisolles
Canals
Castelnau-d'Estrétefonds
Bouloc
Bessières
Coufouleux
St-Sulpice
Giroussens
Graulhet
Réalmont
St-Pierre-de-Trivisy
Le Masnau-Massuguiès
Solomiac
Aucamville
Cox
Launac
Grenade
St-Jory
Buzet-sur-Tarn
Briatexte
Vénès
Viane
Mauvezin
Cadours
Merville
Bruguières
Montastruc-la-Conseillère
Lavaur
Fiac
Lautrec
Montredon-Labessonnié
Vabre
Cologne
Montaigut-sur-Save
Castelginest
Roquecourbe
Lacrouzette
Burlats
Brassac
Lévignac
Aussonne
Beauzelle
St-Jean
L'Union
Verfeil
St-Paul-Cap-de-Joux
Blagnac
Colomiers
Balma
Le Bez
L'Isle-Jourdain
Pibrac
Toulouse
Bourg-St-Bernard
Vielmur-sur-Agout
Castres
Lagarrigue
Boissezon
Anglès
Tournefeuille
Plaisance-du-Touch
Portet-sur-Garonne
St-Orens-de-Gameville
Lanta
Cuq-Toulza
Puylaurens
Saïx
Soual
Payrin-Augmontel
Cugnaux
Fontenilles
Fonsorbes
Ramonville-St-Agne
Caraman
Blan
Labruguière
Aussillon
Mazamet
Pont-de-Larn
Labastide-Rouairoux
Samatan
St-Lys
Seysses
Villeneuve-Tolosane
Castanet-Tolosan
Dourgne
St-Amans-Soult
Ste-Foy-de-Peyrolières
Baziège
Revel
Lombez
Muret
Vernet
Montgiscard
St-Félix-Lauragais
Sorèze
Arfons
Les Cammazes
Lherm
Rieumes
Eaunes
Villefranche-de-Lauragais
Lespinassière
Montpézat
Bérat
Lagardelle-sur-Lèze
Gardouch
Saissac
Cuxac-Cabardès
Mas-Cabardès
Caunes-Minervois
Longages
Noé
Nailloux
Labastide-d'Anjou
St-Papoul
Castelnaudary
Gratens
Auterive
Cintegabelle
Lastours
Conques-sur-Orbiel
St-Élix-le-Château
St-Sulpice-sur-Lèze
Cujac
Calmont
Salles-sur-l'Hers
Villepinte
Moussoulens
Villemoustaussou
Peyriac-Minervois
Le Fousseret
Carbonne
Lézat-sur-Lèze
Fendeille
Alzonne
Pennautier
Mondavezan
Rieux
St-Ybars
Mazères
Villasavary
Bram
Carcassonne
La Redorte
Aurignac
St-Julien
Cazères
Montesquieu-Volvestre
Saverdun
Montaut
Belpech
Fanjeaux
Montréal
Trèbes
Martres-Tolosane
Le Vernet
Lavalette
Cazilhac
Floure
Boussens
Le Plan
Le Fossat
Belvèze-du-Razès
Preixan
Leuc
Fabrezan
Montlaur
Ste-Croix-Volvestre
Daumazan-sur-Arize
Artigat
Pamiers
La Tour-du-Crieu
Mirepoix
Alaigne
Lauraguel
St-Hilaire
Sabarat
Salies-du-Salat
Fabas
Le Mas-d'Azil
Pailhès
St-Jean-du-Falga
Vernioulle
Moulin-Neuf
Limoux
St-Pierre-des-Champs
Mane
Clermont
Varilhes
La Bastide-de-Bousignac
Alet-les-Bains
Caumont
St-Lizier
St-Girons
Rimont
La Bastide-de-Sérou
Montels
Dun
Laroque-d'Olmes
Aigues-Vives
Léran
St-Benoît
Arbas
Chalabre
Arques
Foix
Engomer
Castillon-en-Couserans
Lacourt
Montgaillard
Lavelanet
La Bastide-sur-l'Hers
Puivert
Espéraza
Couiza
Rennes-les-Bains
Biert
St-Paul-de-Jarrat
Montferrier
Bélesta
Nébias
Quillan
Soulatgé
Bethmale
Soueix
Massat
Saurat
Arignac
Montségur
Ginoles
Seix
Oust
Tarascon-sur-Ariège
Belcaire
Espezel
Caudiès-de-Fenouillèdes
Ustou
Aulus-les-Bains
Prades
Axat
St-Paul-de-Fenouillet
Couflens
Vicdessos
Les Cabannes
Luzenac
Port de Pailhères
Escouloubre
Auzat
Ascou
Port de Salau
Ax-les-Thermes
Sournia
Salardu
Quérigut
Ille-sur-Têt
Alós d'Ensil
Mérens-les-Vals
Molitg-les-Bains
Esterri d'Aneu
El Serrat
L'Hospitalet-près-l'Andorre
Formiguères
Marquixanes
Vinça
Prades
AND
Arinsal
Soldeu
Les Angles
Vernet-les-Bains
Espot
Escaló
Col de Puymorens
Olette
La Massana
Encamp
Port d'Envalira
Porta
Font-Romeu-Odeillo-Via
Thuès-entre-Valls
St-Marsal
ANDORRA LA VELLA
Les Escaldes
Mont-Louis
Llavorsí
Planès
Amélie-les-Bains-Palalda
Llívia
Rialp
La Torre de Cabdella
Sant Julià de Lòria
Puigcerdà
Saillagouse-Llo
La Preste
Sort
Ger
Osséja
Prats-de-Mollo-la-Preste
Coustouges
Martinet
Bellver de Cerdanya
Alp
Queralbs
Molló
Le Seu d'Urgell
Gerri de la Sal
Ribes de Freser
Vilallonga
Camprodon
La Pobla de Lillet
Coll de Merolla
Sant Joan de les Abadesses
Sant Joan les Fonts
La Pobla de Segur
Bagà
Guardiola de Berguedà
Campdevànol
Ripoll
Olot
Organyà
Sant Privat d'en Bas
Tremp
Vilada
Alpens
Les Preses
Berga
Avià
Sant Llorenç de Morunys
Sant Quirze de Besora
Sant Pere de Torelló
Sant Feliu de Pallerols
Isona
Sant Agustí de Lluçanès
Peramola
Oliana
Olvan
Torelló
Castellnou
Castellar de la Ribera
Gironella
Perafita
Sant Hipòlit de Voltregà
Santa Maria
Cuzals

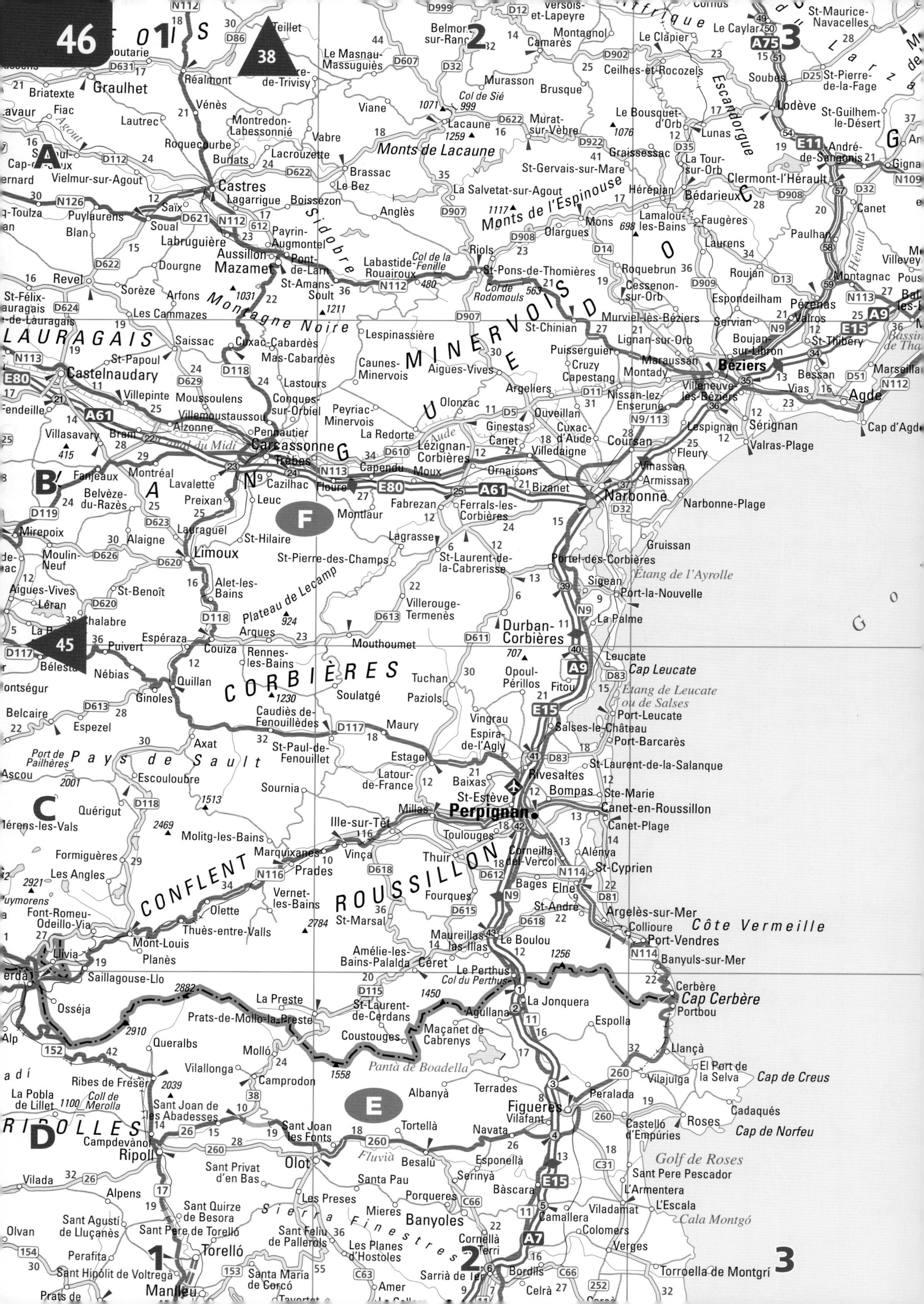

46
38
45
A
B
C
D
E
F
G
1
2
3
Teillet
Réalmont
Graulhet
Briatexte
Fiac
Lautrec
Vénès
Montredon-Labessonnié
Vabre
Roquecourbe
Burlats
Lacrouzette
Cap-de-Joux
Vielmur-sur-Agout
Castres
Lagarrique
Boissezon
Saïx
Soual
Puylaurens
Blan
Labruguière
Payrin-Augmontel
Aussillon
Mazamet
Pont-de-Larn
St-Amans-Soult
Dourgne
Revel
Sorèze
Arfons
Les Cammazes
St-Félix-Lauragais
Montagne Noire
Sidobre
Le Masnau-Massuguiès
Belmont-sur-Rance
Viane
Lacaune
Col de Sié
Monts de Lacaune
Brassac
Le Bez
Anglès
La Salvetat-sur-Agout
Labastide-Rouairoux
Col de la Feuille
Murasson
Brusque
Camarès
Montagnol
Murat-sur-Vèbre
St-Gervais-sur-Mare
Monts de l'Espinouse
Olargues
Mons
Riols
St-Pons-de-Thomières
Col de Rodomouls
Lamalou-les-Bains
Le Clapier
Le Caylar
Ceilhes-et-Rocozels
Escandorgue
Le Bousquet-d'Orb
Lunas
Graissessac
La Tour-sur-Orb
Hérépian
Bédarieux
Faugères
Lodève
Soubès
St-Pierre-de-la-Fage
St-Maurice-Navacelles
St-Guilhem-le-Désert
St-André-de-Sangonis
Gignac
Clermont-l'Hérault
Canet
Paulhan
Laurens
Roujan
Roquebrun
Cessenon-sur-Orb
Murviel-lès-Béziers
Villeveyrac
Montagnac
Pézenas
Valros
Espondeilham
Servian
Lignan-sur-Orb
Boujan-sur-Libron
St-Thibéry
Béziers
Bessan
Marseillan
Agde
Vias
Cap d'Agde
LAURAGAIS
MINERVOIS
Saissac
Cuxac-Cabardès
Mas-Cabardès
St-Papoul
Castelnaudary
Villepinte
Moussoulens
Lastours
Conques-sur-Orbiel
Villemoustaussou
Caunes-Minervois
Aigues-Vives
Lespinassière
St-Chinian
Puisserguier
Cruzy
Capestang
Montady
Maraussan
Villeneuve-lès-Béziers
Nissan-lez-Enserune
Argeliers
Olonzac
Ouveillan
Peyriac-Minervois
Fendeille
Villasavary
Bram
Alzonne
Pennautier
Carcassonne
Trèbes
Canal du Midi
La Redorte
Lézignan-Corbières
Capendu
Moux
Ginestas
Cuxac-d'Aude
Canet
Villedaigne
Coursan
Lespignan
Sérignan
Valras-Plage
Fleury
Vinassan
Armissan
Narbonne
Narbonne-Plage
Fanjeaux
Montréal
Lavalette
Cazilhac
Floure
Belvèze-du-Razès
Preixan
Leuc
Montlaur
Fabrezan
Ferrals-les-Corbières
Ornaisons
Bizanet
Mirepoix
Alaigne
Lauraguel
St-Hilaire
Limoux
Lagrasse
St-Pierre-des-Champs
St-Laurent-de-la-Cabrerisse
Portel-des-Corbières
Gruissan
Étang de l'Ayrolle
Sigean
Port-la-Nouvelle
La Palme
Moulin-Neuf
Aigues-Vives
Léran
St-Benoît
Alet-les-Bains
Plateau de Lecamp
Villerouge-Termenès
Durban-Corbières
Chalabre
Puivert
Espéraza
Arques
Couiza
Rennes-les-Bains
Mouthoumet
Bélesta
Nébias
Quillan
Montségur
Ginoles
CORBIÈRES
Tuchan
Paziols
Opoul-Périllos
Fitou
Leucate
Cap Leucate
Étang de Leucate ou de Salses
Port-Leucate
Soulatgé
Caudiès-de-Fenouillèdes
Maury
Vingrau
Espira-de-l'Agly
Salses-le-Château
Port-Barcarès
Belcaire
Espezel
Axat
St-Paul-de-Fenouillet
Estagel
Port de Pailhères
Pays de Sault
Escouloubre
Latour-de-France
Baixas
Rivesaltes
St-Laurent-de-la-Salanque
Bompas
Ste-Marie
St-Estève
Perpignan
Canet-en-Roussillon
Canet-Plage
Ascou
Quérigut
Sournia
Mérens-les-Vals
Millas
Ille-sur-Têt
Toulouges
Molitg-les-Bains
Formiguères
Les Angles
Marquixanes
Prades
Vinça
Thuir
Corneilla-del-Vercol
Alénya
St-Cyprien
Elne
Bages
CONFLENT
ROUSSILLON
Vernet-les-Bains
Olette
Fourques
St-André
Argelès-sur-Mer
Collioure
Port-Vendres
Côte Vermeille
Font-Romeu-Odeillo-Via
Thuès-entre-Valls
St-Marsal
Mont-Louis
Planès
Llívia
Puymorens
Maureillas-las-Illas
Le Boulou
Amélie-les-Bains-Palalda
Céret
Banyuls-sur-Mer
Saillagouse-Llo
Le Perthus
Col du Perthus
Cerbère
Cap Cerbère
Portbou
Osséja
La Preste
Prats-de-Mollo-la-Preste
St-Laurent-de-Cerdans
Coustouges
La Jonquera
Agullana
Maçanet de Cabrenys
Espolla
Llançà
El Port de la Selva
Cap de Creus
Vilajuïga
Queralbs
Molló
Vilallonga
Camprodon
Pantà de Boadella
Ribes de Freser
La Pobla de Lillet
Coll de Merolla
Sant Joan de les Abadesses
Albanyà
Terrades
Figueres
Vilafant
Peralada
Cadaqués
Roses
Cap de Norfeu
Castelló d'Empúries
RIPOLLES
Campdevànol
Ripoll
Sant Joan les Fonts
Tortellà
Navata
Olot
Besalú
Fluvià
Esponellà
Golf de Roses
Sant Pere Pescador
L'Armentera
Vilada
Sant Privat d'en Bas
Santa Pau
Serinyà
Bàscara
Alpens
Sant Quirze de Besora
Les Preses
Porqueres
Mieres
Viladamat
L'Escala
Cala Montgó
Camallera
Banyoles
Colomers
Sierra Finestres
Sant Agustí de Lluçanès
Sant Pere de Torelló
Sant Feliu de Pallerols
Les Planes d'Hostoles
Cornellà del Terri
Verges
Olvan
Perafita
Torelló
Sant Hipòlit de Voltregà
Manlleu
Santa Maria de Corcó
Amer
Sarrià de Ter
Bordils
Celrà
Torroella de Montgrí
Prats de Lluçanès

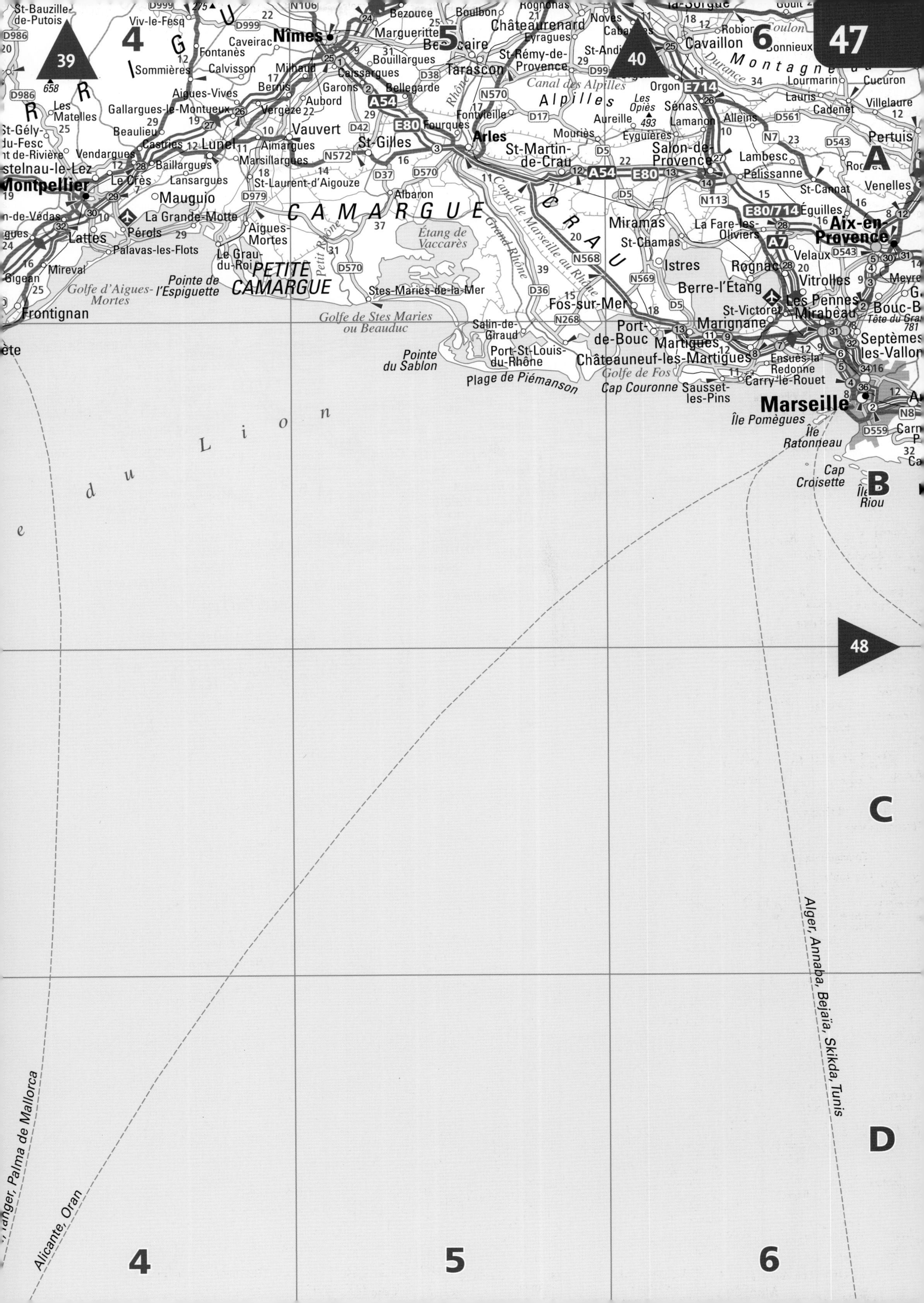
39
40
48
4
5
6
A
B
C
D
St-Bauzille-de-Putois
Viv-le-Fesq
Sommières
Fontanès
Caveirac
Calvisson
Nîmes
Milhaud
Caissargues
Bouillargues
Marguerittes
Bezouce
Beaucaire
Boulbon
Tarascon
Châteaurenard
Eyragues
St-Rémy-de-Provence
Noves
Cavaillon
Robion
Bonnieux
Cucuron
Lourmarin
Lauris
Cadenet
Villelaure
Pertuis
Montagne
Durance
Canal des Alpilles
Alpilles
Les Opiès
493
Orgon
Sénas
Aureille
Mouriès
Eygueires
Lamanon
Alleins
Salon-de-Provence
Lambesc
Pélissanne
St-Cannat
Venelles
Éguilles
Aix-en-Provence
Aigues-Vives
Gallargues-le-Montueux
Vergèze
Aubord
Bernis
Garons
Bellegarde
Fourques
Fontvieille
Arles
St-Martin-de-Crau
Les Matelles
St-Gély-du-Fesc
Beaulieu
Castries
Lunel
Vendargues
Baillargues
Le Crès
Montpellier
Lansargues
Mauguio
Vauvert
Aimargues
Marsillargues
St-Laurent-d'Aigouze
St-Gilles
Albaron
CAMARGUE
CRAU
Lattes
Pérols
La Grande-Motte
Palavas-les-Flots
Aigues-Mortes
Le Grau-du-Roi
PETITE CAMARGUE
Mireval
Gigean
Frontignan
Golfe d'Aigues-Mortes
Pointe de l'Espiguette
Petit Rhône
Étang de Vaccarès
Grand Rhône
Canal de Marseille au Rhône
Stes-Maries-de-la-Mer
Golfe de Stes Maries ou Beauduc
Pointe du Sablon
Salin-de-Giraud
Port-St-Louis-du-Rhône
Plage de Piémanson
Miramas
St-Chamas
Istres
La Fare-les-Oliviers
Rognac
Velaux
Vitrolles
Berre-l'Étang
Fos-sur-Mer
Les Pennes-Mirabeau
St-Victoret
Marignane
Port-de-Bouc
Martigues
Châteauneuf-les-Martigues
Golfe de Fos
Cap Couronne
Sausset-les-Pins
Carry-le-Rouet
Ensuès-la-Redonne
Septèmes-les-Vallons
Bouc-Bel-Air
Marseille
Île Pomègues
Île Ratonneau
Cap Croisette
Île Riou
A54
E80
A7
E80/714
E714
N7
N113
N568
N569
N572
N268
D570
D36
D979
Golfe du Lion
Alger, Annaba, Bejaïa, Skikda, Tunis
Alicante, Oran
Tanger, Palma de Mallorca

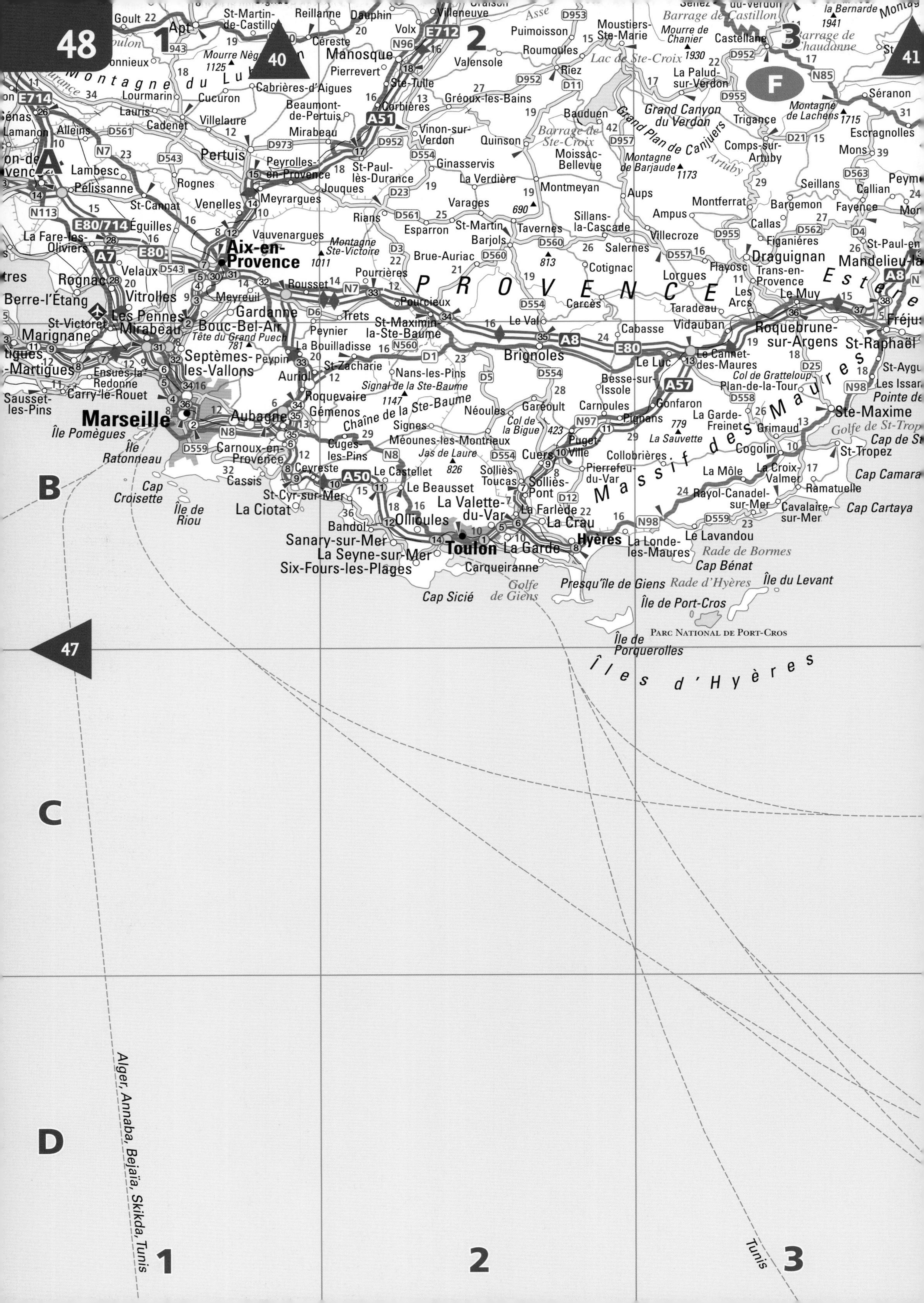

40
41
47
F
A
B
C
D
1
2
3
Apt
St-Martin-de-Castillon
Reillanne
Dauphin
Villeneuve
Céreste
Volx
Manosque
Pierrevert
Ste-Tulle
Corbières
Vinon-sur-Verdon
Valensole
Puimoisson
Roumoules
Riez
Gréoux-les-Bains
Quinson
Moustiers-Ste-Marie
Lac de Ste-Croix
Barrage de Ste-Croix
Bauduen
Moissac-Bellevue
Grand Plan de Canjuers
Montagne de Barjaude
1173
Barrage de Castillon
Mourre de Chanier
1930
Castellane
Barrage de Chaudanne
La Palud-sur-Verdon
Grand Canyon du Verdon
Trigance
Montagne de Lachens
1715
Comps-sur-Artuby
Artuby
Séranon
Escragnolles
Mons
Seillans
Callian
Fayence
Bargemon
Montferrat
Callas
Figanières
Draguignan
Trans-en-Provence
Les Arcs
Le Muy
Taradeau
Vidauban
Lorgues
Flayosc
Ampus
Aups
Villecroze
Salernes
Sillans-la-Cascade
Tavernes
Montmeyan
Varages
La Verdière
Ginasservis
St-Martin
Barjols
813
690
Cotignac
Carcès
Mourre Nègre
1125
Montagne du Luberon
Cabrières-d'Aigues
Beaumont-de-Pertuis
Mirabeau
Lourmarin
Cucuron
Lauris
Cadenet
Villelaure
Pertuis
Peyrolles-en-Provence
St-Paul-lès-Durance
Jouques
Meyrargues
Rians
Esparron
Brue-Auriac
Pourrières
Vauvenargues
Montagne Ste-Victoire
1011
Aix-en-Provence
Venelles
Rognes
St-Cannat
Éguilles
Lambesc
Pélissanne
Alleins
Lamanon
La Fare-les-Oliviers
Velaux
Rognac
Berre-l'Étang
Vitrolles
Les Pennes-Mirabeau
St-Victoret
Marignane
Martigues
Ensuès-la-Redonne
Carry-le-Rouet
Sausset-les-Pins
Rousset
Meyreuil
Gardanne
Bouc-Bel-Air
Tête du Grand Puech
781
Septèmes-les-Vallons
Peypin
Trets
Pourcieux
St-Maximin-la-Ste-Baume
Peynier
La Bouilladisse
Auriol
St-Zacharie
Nans-les-Pins
Signal de la Ste-Baume
1147
Roquevaire
Gémenos
Chaîne de la Ste-Baume
Marseille
Île Pomègues
Île Ratonneau
Aubagne
Carnoux-en-Provence
Cuges-les-Pins
Cassis
Ceyreste
Cap Croisette
Île de Riou
La Ciotat
St-Cyr-sur-Mer
Bandol
Sanary-sur-Mer
La Seyne-sur-Mer
Six-Fours-les-Plages
Cap Sicié
Ollioules
Le Castellet
Le Beausset
Signes
Méounes-lès-Montrieux
Jas de Laure
826
Néoules
Garéoult
Col de la Bigue
423
Solliès-Toucas
Solliès-Pont
Cuers
Puget-Ville
La Valette-du-Var
Toulon
La Garde
Carqueiranne
Golfe de Giens
La Farlède
La Crau
Hyères
Presqu'île de Giens
La Londe-les-Maures
Pierrefeu-du-Var
Collobrières
Pignans
Carnoules
Besse-sur-Issole
Le Luc
Le Cannet-des-Maures
Brignoles
Le Val
Cabasse
PROVENCE
Massif des Maures
Gonfaron
779
La Sauvette
La Garde-Freinet
Grimaud
Plan-de-la-Tour
Col de Gratteloup
Cogolin
La Môle
La Croix-Valmer
Rayol-Canadel-sur-Mer
Cavalaire-sur-Mer
Le Lavandou
Rade de Bormes
Cap Bénat
Rade d'Hyères
Île du Levant
Île de Port-Cros
Parc National de Port-Cros
Île de Porquerolles
Îles d'Hyères
Ramatuelle
St-Tropez
Cap Camarat
Cap Cartaya
Ste-Maxime
Golfe de St-Tropez
Cap de St
Pointe de
Les Issambres
St-Aygulf
Roquebrune-sur-Argens
St-Raphaël
Fréjus
Mandelieu-la
St-Paul-en
Esterel
Alger, Annaba, Bejaïa, Skikda, Tunis
Tunis
A7
A8
A50
A51
A57
E80
E80/714
E712
E714
N7
N8
N85
N96
N97
N98
N113
N560
D1
D3
D4
D5
D6
D11
D12
D21
D23
D25
D543
D554
D557
D558
D559
D560
D561
D562
D563
D952
D953
D955
D957
D973

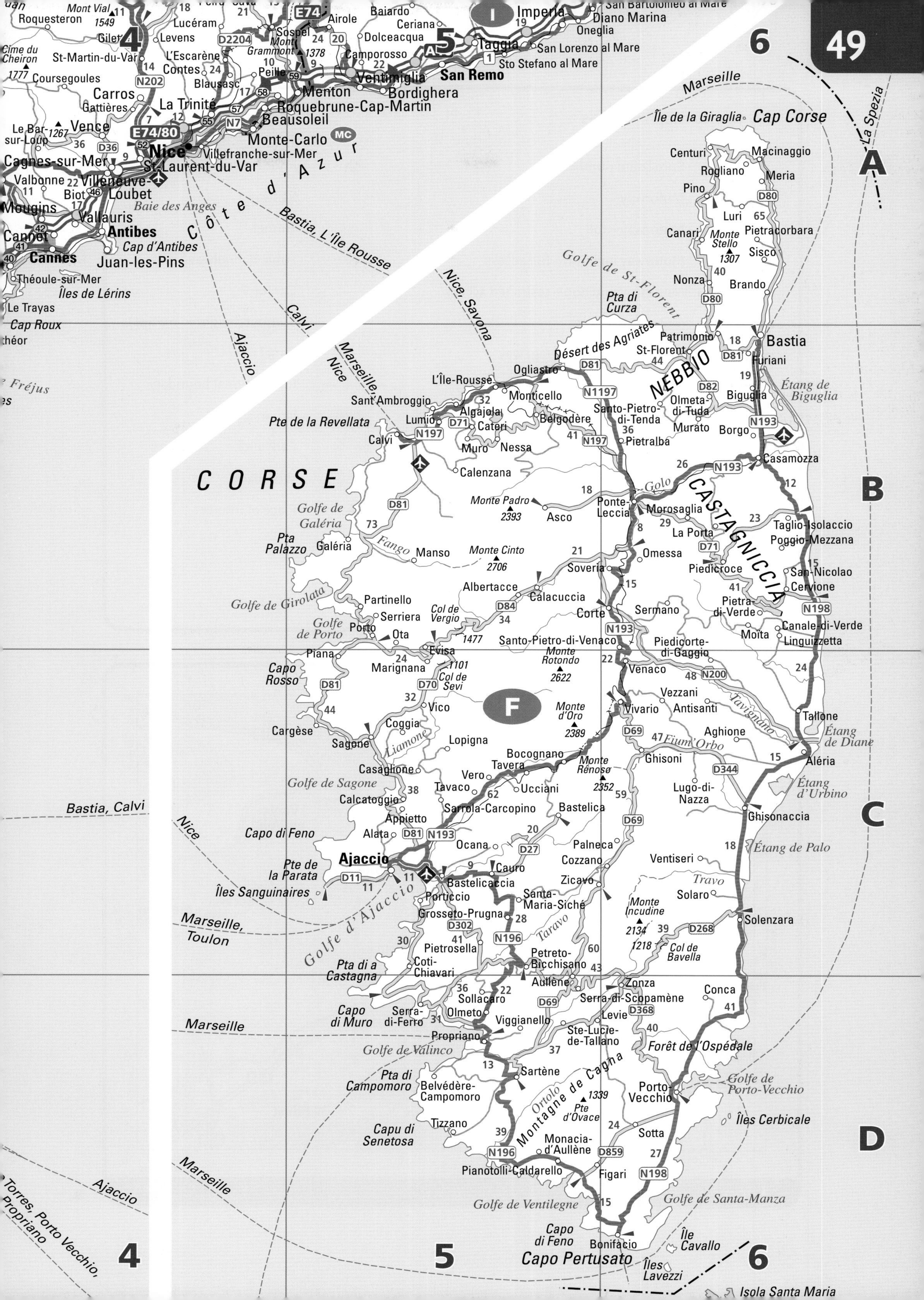
Roquesteron
Mont Vial 1549
Gilet
Cime du Cheiron 1777
St-Martin-du-Var
Coursegoules
Carros
Gattières
Le Bar-sur-Loup
Vence
Cagnes-sur-Mer
Valbonne
Villeneuve-Loubet
Biot
Mougins
Vallauris
Cannet
Antibes
Cap d'Antibes
Cannes
Juan-les-Pins
Théoule-sur-Mer
Îles de Lérins
Le Trayas
Cap Roux
Lucéram
Levens
L'Escarène
Contes
Blausasc
La Trinité
Nice
St-Laurent-du-Var
Villefranche-sur-Mer
Monte-Carlo
Beausoleil
Roquebrune-Cap-Martin
Menton
Peille
Sospel
Monti Grammont 1378
Airole
Baiardo
Ceriana
Dolceacqua
Camporosso
Ventimiglia
Bordighera
San Remo
Taggia
Imperia
Diano Marina
Oneglia
San Lorenzo al Mare
Sto Stefano al Mare
Baie des Anges
Côte d'Azur
Bastia, L'Île Rousse
Nice, Savona
Calvi
Ajaccio
Marseille, Nice
Marseille
La Spezia
Île de la Giraglia
Cap Corse
Centuri
Macinaggio
Rogliano
Meria
Pino
Luri
Canari
Monte Stello 1307
Pietracorbara
Sisco
Nonza
Brando
Golfe de St-Florent
Pta di Curza
Désert des Agriates
Patrimonio
St-Florent
Bastia
Furiani
NEBBIO
Étang de Biguglia
Biguglia
Olmeta-di-Tuda
Murato
Borgo
Ogliastro
L'Île-Rousse
Monticello
Sant'Ambroggio
Algajola
Lumio
Cateri
Belgodère
Santo-Pietro-di-Tenda
Pietralba
Pte de la Revellata
Calvi
Muro
Nessa
Calenzana
Casamozza
CORSE
Golo
CASTAGNICCIA
Monte Padro 2393
Asco
Ponte-Leccia
Morosaglia
La Porta
Taglio-Isolaccio
Poggio-Mezzana
Golfe de Galéria
Pta Palazzo
Galéria
Fango
Manso
Monte Cinto 2706
Omessa
Soveria
Piedicroce
San-Nicolao
Cervione
Albertacce
Calacuccia
Golfe de Girolata
Partinello
Serriera
Col de Vergio
Golfe de Porto
Porto
Ota
Corte
Sermano
Pietra-di-Verde
Moïta
Canale-di-Verde
Linguizzetta
Piana
Evisa
Santo-Pietro-di-Venaco
Piedicorte-di-Gaggio
Capo Rosso
Marignana
Col de Sevi
Monte Rotondo 2622
Venaco
Vico
Vezzani
Antisanti
Tavignano
Tallone
Cargèse
Coggia
Liamone
Monte d'Oro 2389
Vivario
Aghione
Étang de Diane
Sagone
Lopigna
Bocognano
Fium'Orbo
Aléria
Tavera
Monte Renoso 2352
Ghisoni
Casaglione
Golfe de Sagone
Vero
Tavaco
Ucciani
Lugo-di-Nazza
Étang d'Urbino
Calcatoggio
Sarrola-Carcopino
Bastelica
Ghisonaccia
Appietto
Capo di Feno
Alata
Ocana
Palneca
Étang de Palo
Bastia, Calvi
Ajaccio
Cozzano
Ventiseri
Pte de la Parata
Cauro
Zicavo
Îles Sanguinaires
Bastelicaccia
Travo
Porticcio
Santa-Maria-Siché
Solaro
Monte Incudine 2134
Golfe d'Ajaccio
Marseille, Toulon
Grosseto-Prugna
Taravo
Solenzara
Col de Bavella
Pietrosella
Petreto-Bicchisano
Pta di a Castagna
Coti-Chiavari
Aullène
Zonza
Sollacaro
Serra-di-Scopamène
Conca
Capo di Muro
Serra-di-Ferro
Olmeto
Viggianello
Levie
Propriano
Ste-Lucie-de-Tallano
Forêt de l'Ospédale
Golfe de Valinco
Sartène
Pta di Campomoro
Belvédère-Campomoro
Montagne de Cagna
Ortolo
Pte d'Ovace 1339
Porto-Vecchio
Golfe de Porto-Vecchio
Îles Cerbicale
Capu di Senetosa
Tizzano
Monacia-d'Aullène
Sotta
Pianotolli-Caldarello
Figari
Golfe de Ventilegne
Golfe de Santa-Manza
Capo di Feno
Bonifacio
Île Cavallo
Capo Pertusato
Îles Lavezzi
Isola Santa Maria
Torres, Porto Vecchio, Propriano
A
B
C
D
4
5
6

Key to city map symbols

E55	Euro route number		International airport	
A13	Motorway		Railway	
	Motorway – toll		Tunnel	
37	Motorway junction – full access		Funicular railway	
12	Motorway junction – restricted access		Car ferry	
	Motorway services	▲480	Summit (height in metres)	
309	Main road – dual carriageway		Canal	
	Main road – single carriageway		International boundary	
516	Secondary road – dual carriageway		Urban area	
	Secondary road – single carriageway		Parkland	
	Other road		Woodland	
	Motorway tunnel	★	Place of interest	
	Main road tunnel			
	Motorway/road under construction			
	Road toll			

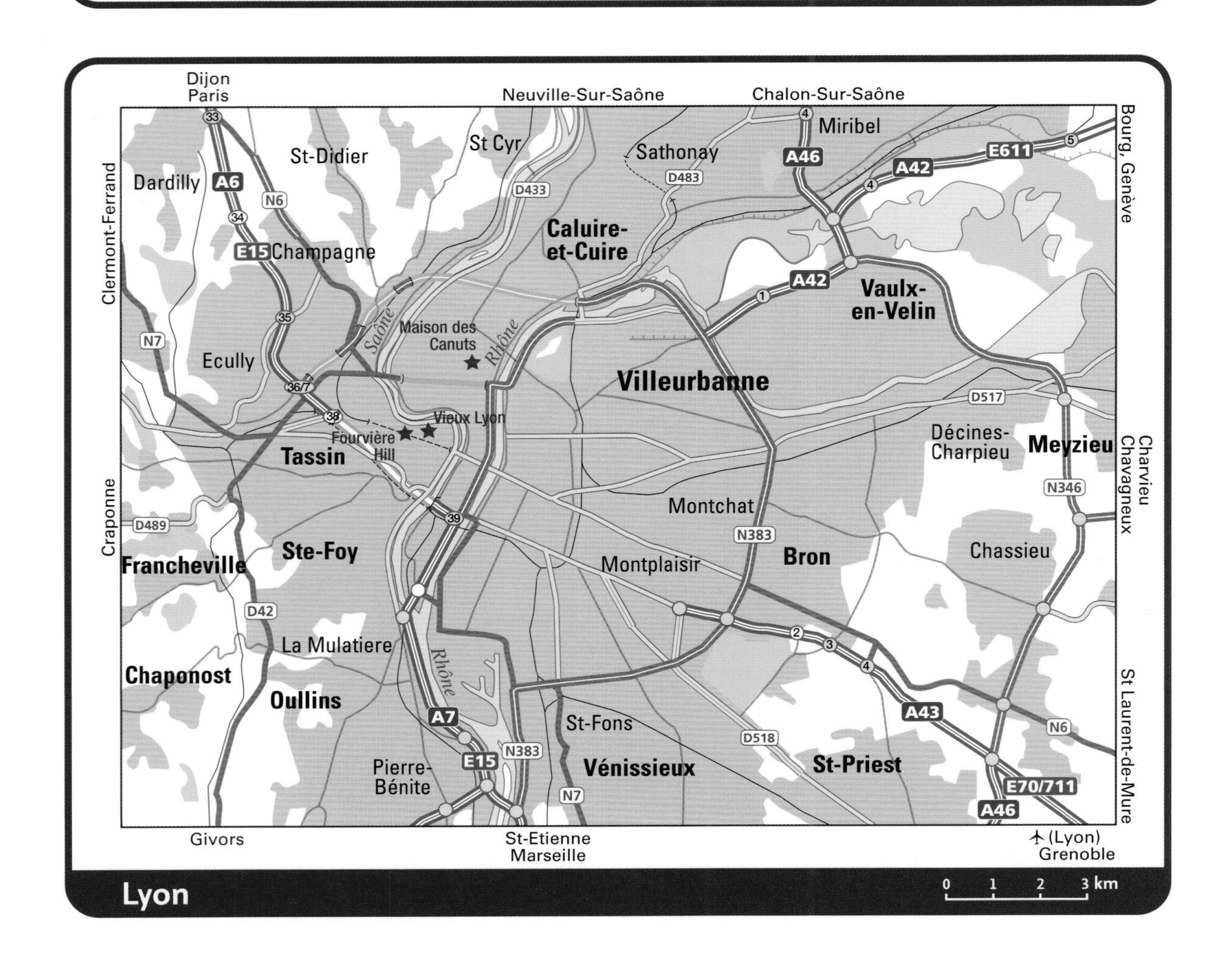

Lyon

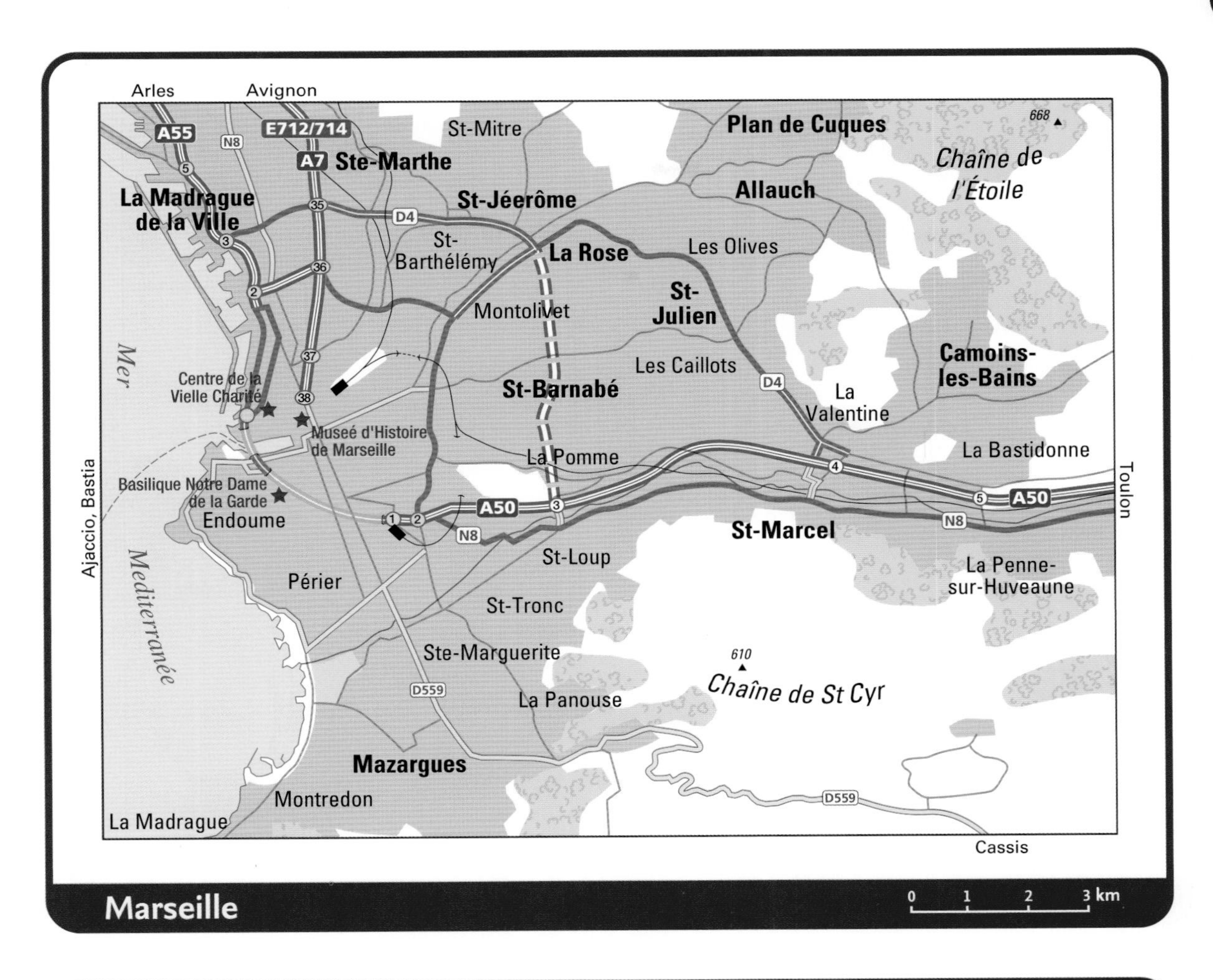
Arles
Avignon
A55
N8
E712/714
A7
St-Mitre
Ste-Marthe
Plan de Cuques
668
Chaîne de l'Étoile
La Madrague de la Ville
St-Jéerôme
D4
Allauch
St-Barthélémy
La Rose
Les Olives
St-Julien
Montolivet
Mer Mediterranée
Centre de la Vielle Charité
Camoins-les-Bains
Les Caillots
D4
La Valentine
St-Barnabé
Museé d'Histoire de Marseille
La Pomme
La Bastidonne
Basilique Notre Dame de la Garde
Endoume
A50
N8
St-Marcel
Toulon
Ajaccio, Bastia
St-Loup
La Penne-sur-Huveaune
Périer
St-Tronc
Ste-Marguerite
610
Chaîne de St Cyr
D559
La Panouse
Mazargues
Montredon
La Madrague
Cassis
0 1 2 3 km

Marseille

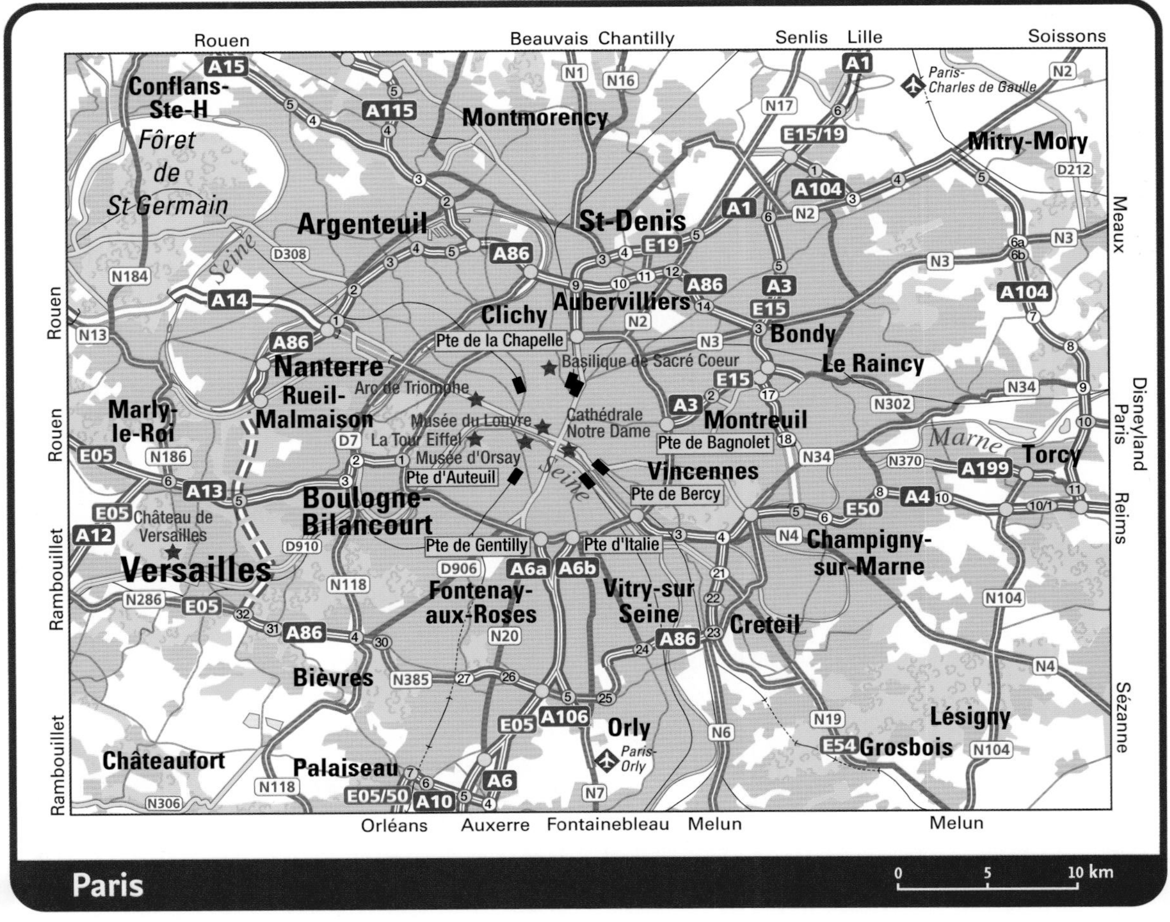
Rouen
Beauvais
Chantilly
Senlis
Lille
Soissons
A15
Conflans-Ste-H
Fôret de St Germain
A115
N1
N16
A1
Paris-Charles de Gaulle
N2
Montmorency
N17
E15/19
Mitry-Mory
D212
A104
Argenteuil
St-Denis
A1
N2
Meaux
Seine
D308
A86
E19
N3
N184
N3
A14
Clichy
Aubervilliers
A86
A3
E15
A104
Rouen
N13
A86
N2
Pte de la Chapelle
N3
Bondy
Nanterre
Basilique de Sacré Coeur
Le Raincy
Rueil-Malmaison
Arc de Triomphe
E15
N34
Marly-le-Roi
Musée du Louvre
Cathédrale Notre Dame
A3
Montreuil
N302
Disneyland Paris
D7
La Tour Eiffel
Musée d'Orsay
Pte de Bagnolet
Rouen
E05
N186
Pte d'Auteuil
N34
N370
Marne
Torcy
A199
Vincennes
A4
A13
Pte de Bercy
Reims
E05
Château de Versailles
Boulogne-Billancourt
E50
A12
D910
Pte de Gentilly
Pte d'Italie
N4
Champigny-sur-Marne
Rambouillet
Versailles
D906
A6a
A6b
N118
Fontenay-aux-Roses
Vitry-sur Seine
N286
E05
N104
A86
Creteil
N20
A86
N4
Bièvres
N385
Sézanne
A106
E05
Orly
N19
Lésigny
N6
E54
Grosbois
N104
Rambouillet
Châteaufort
Palaiseau
Paris-Orly
A6
N118
E05/50
A10
N7
N306
Orléans
Auxerre
Fontainebleau
Melun
Melun
0 5 10 km

Paris

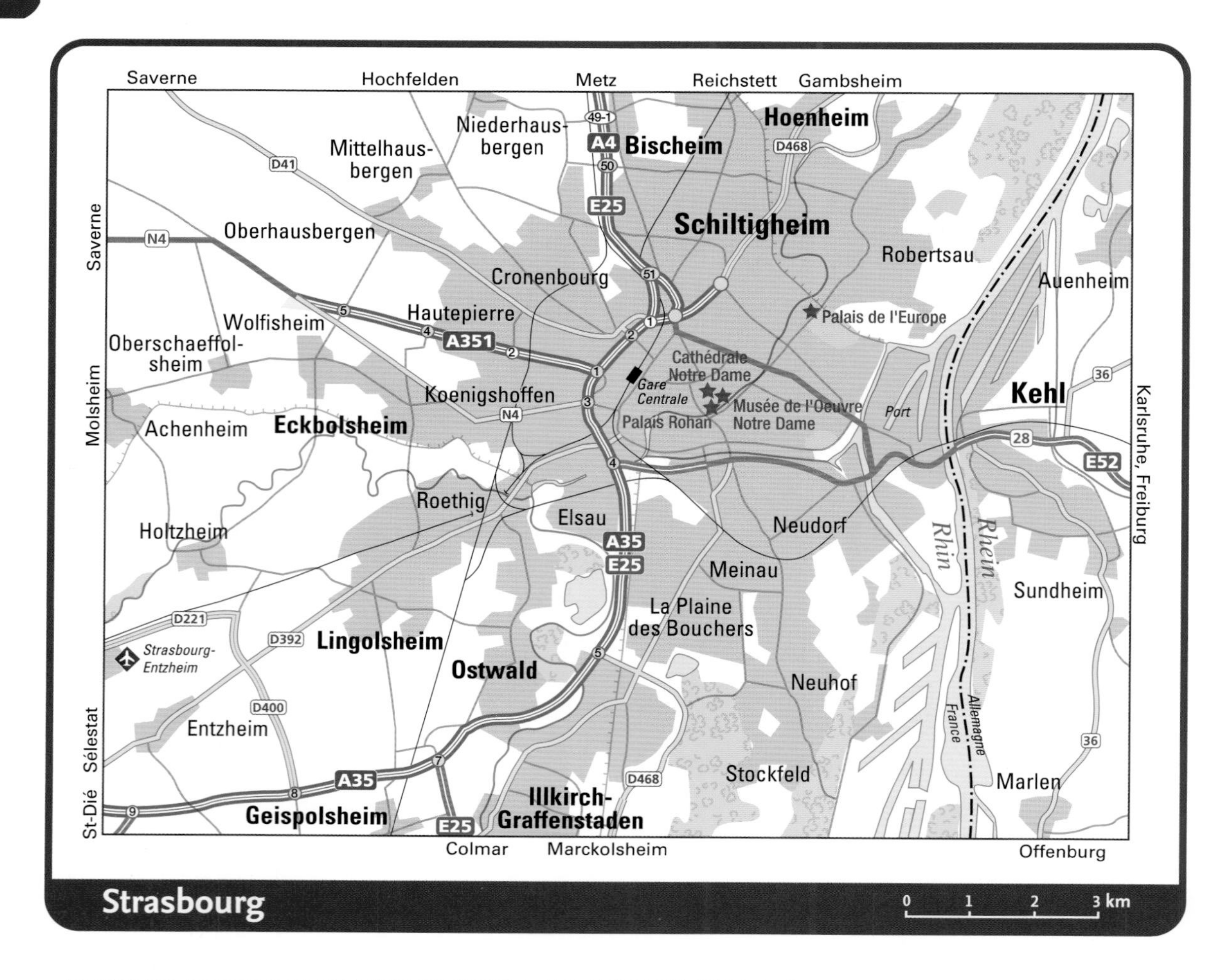
Saverne
Hochfelden
Metz
Reichstett
Gambsheim
Niederhaus-bergen
Mittelhaus-bergen
Bischeim
Hoenheim
Schiltigheim
Oberhausbergen
Robertsau
Cronenbourg
Auenheim
Wolfisheim
Hautepierre
Palais de l'Europe
Oberschaeffol-sheim
Cathédrale Notre Dame
Gare Centrale
Musée de l'Oeuvre Notre Dame
Palais Rohan
Port
Kehl
Koenigshoffen
Achenheim
Eckbolsheim
Roethig
Elsau
Neudorf
Holtzheim
Meinau
Rhin
Rhein
La Plaine des Bouchers
Sundheim
Strasbourg-Entzheim
Lingolsheim
Ostwald
Neuhof
Entzheim
Allemagne
France
Stockfeld
Marlen
Geispolsheim
Illkirch-Graffenstaden
Colmar
Marckolsheim
Offenburg
Saverne
Molsheim
Sélestat
St-Dié
Karlsruhe, Freiburg
A4
E25
A351
A35
E52
N4
D41
D468
D221
D392
D400
0 1 2 3 km

Strasbourg

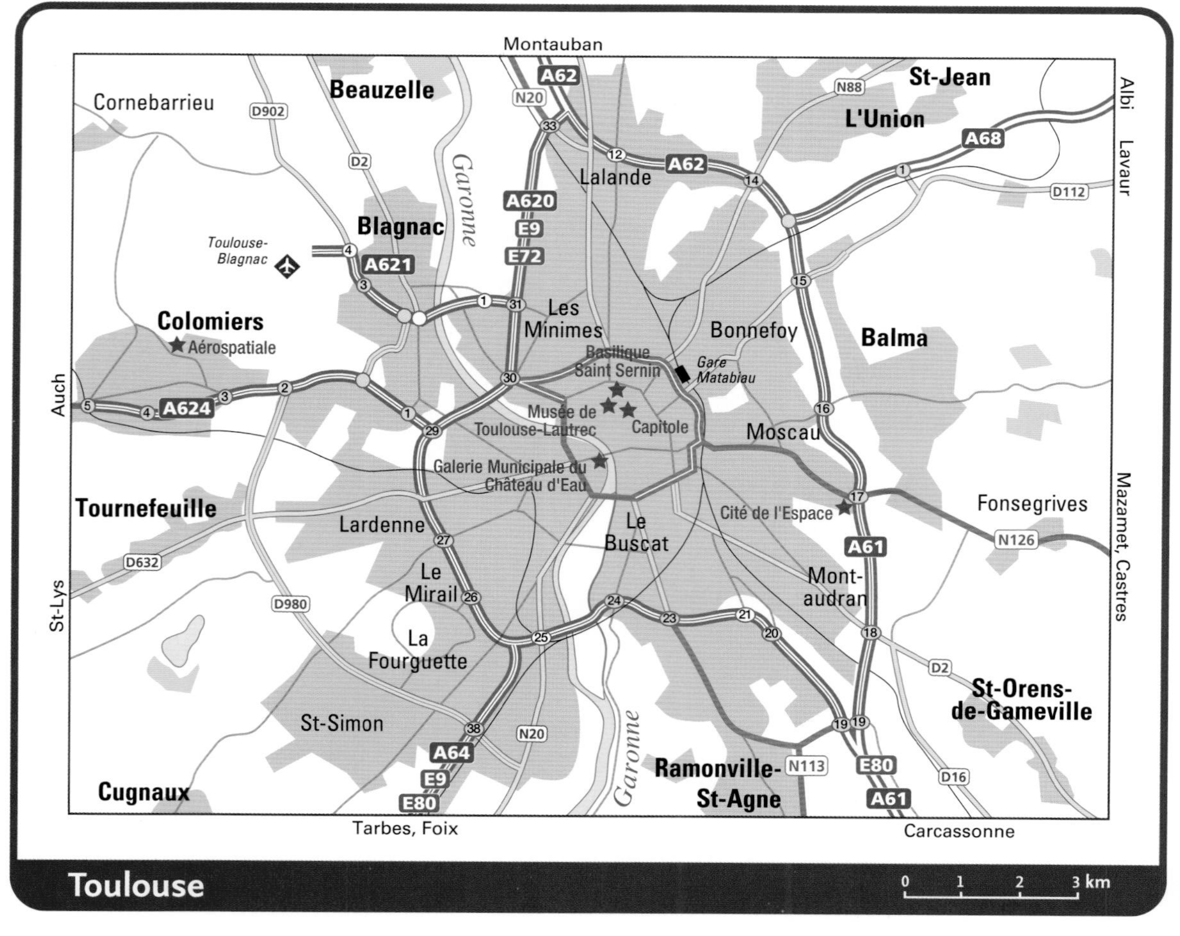
Montauban
Cornebarrieu
Beauzelle
St-Jean
L'Union
Lalande
Garonne
Blagnac
Toulouse-Blagnac
Les Minimes
Bonnefoy
Balma
Colomiers
Aérospatiale
Basilique Saint Sernin
Gare Matabiau
Musée de Toulouse-Lautrec
Capitole
Moscau
Galerie Municipale du Château d'Eau
Tournefeuille
Cité de l'Espace
Fonsegrives
Lardenne
Le Buscat
Le Mirail
Mont-audran
La Fourguette
St-Simon
St-Orens-de-Gameville
Ramonville-St-Agne
Cugnaux
Tarbes, Foix
Carcassonne
Auch
St-Lys
Albi
Lavaur
Mazamet, Castres
A62
A68
A620
E9
E72
A621
A624
A61
A64
E80
N20
N88
N126
N113
D902
D2
D112
D632
D980
D16
0 1 2 3 km

Toulouse

A

Abbeville **14** D2
Abilly **25** D6
Ablis **18** D2
Abondance **35** B5
Abreschviller **21** D4
Abrest **33** B5
Abriès **41** B5
Accous **43** C6
Acheux-en-Amiénois **14** D3
Achicourt **14** C3
Acquigny **17** C6
Adriers **31** B6
Agde **46** B3
Agen **37** C6
Aghione **49** C6
Agneaux **16** C3
Agon-Coutainville **16** C2
Agos-Vidalos **44** B2
Aguessac **39** C4
Ahun **32** B3
Aiffres **31** B4
Aignan **37** D5
Aignay-le-Duc **27** C6
Aigre **31** C5
Aigrefeuille-d'Aunis **30** B3
Aigrefeuille-sur-Maine **24** D2
Aiguebelle **35** D4
Aigueblanche **35** D4
Aigueperse **33** C4
Aigues-Mortes **47** A4
Aigues-Vives **39** D6
Aigues-Vives **45** B5
Aigues-Vives **46** B2
Aiguilhe **39** A5
Aiguilles **41** B5
Aiguillon **37** C5
Aigurande **32** B2
Aillant-sur-Tholon **27** B4
Aillas **37** C5
Aillevillers-et-Lyaumont **28** B3
Ailly-le-Haut-Clocher **14** D2
Ailly-sur-Noye **18** B3
Ailly-sur-Somme **14** D2
Aimargues **39** D6
Aime **35** D4
Ainay-le-Château **33** A4
Airaines **14** D2
Aire-sur-l'Adour **37** D4
Aire-sur-la-Lys **14** C3
Airvault **25** D4
Aisey-sur-Seine **27** B6
Aïssey **28** C3
Aisy-sur-Armançon **27** C5
Aix-en-Othe **27** A5
Aix-en-Provence **48** A1
Aixe-sur-Vienne **31** C6
Aix-les-Bains **34** C3
Aizenay **30** A2
Ajaccio **49** C5
Ajat **31** D6
Alaigne **45** B6
Alata **49** C5
Alba-la-Romaine **40** C1
Alban **38** D3
Albaret-le-Comtal **39** B4
Albaret-Ste-Marie **39** B5
Albaron **39** D6
Albens **34** C3
Albert **14** D3
Albertacce **49** B5
Albertville **35** C4
Albestroff **21** C4
Albi **38** D3
Albias **38** C2
Albon **34** D2
Alby-sur-Chéran **34** C3
Alçay-Alçabéhéty-Sunharette **43** B6
Aldudes **43** B5
Alençon **17** D5
Alénya **46** C2
Aléria **49** C6
Alès **39** C6
Alet-les-Bains **45** B6
Algajola **49** B5
Algrange **20** B3
Allaire **23** C5

Allan **40** C1
Allanche **33** D4
Allarmont **21** D4
Allassac **32** D2
Allègre **33** D5
Alleins **40** D2
Allemond **35** D4
Allevard **35** D4
Allex **40** B2
Allibaudières **19** D5
Alligny-en-Morvan **27** D5
Allinges **35** B4
Allogny **26** D3
Allonnes **25** B5
Allonnes **25** C5
Allons **37** C5
Allos **41** C4
Alloue **31** B5
Alluy **27** D5
Alrance **39** C4
Altier **39** C5
Altkirch **29** C4
Alvignac **38** B2
Alzon **39** D5
Alzonne **45** B6
Amance **28** B3
Amancey **28** D3
Ambazac **32** C2
Ambérieu-en-Bugey **34** C2
Ambert **33** D5
Ambès **37** B4
Ambierle **33** B6
Ambillou **25** C5
Amblainville **18** C2
Ambleteuse **14** B2
Amboise **25** C6
Ambon **23** D4
Ambrault **26** D2
Ambrières-les-Vallées **17** D4
Ambronay **34** C2
Amélie-les-Bains-Palalda **46** D2
Amiens **14** D2
Amilly **26** B3
Amou **43** A6
Amplepuis **33** C6
Ampus **48** A3
Ancelle **41** C4
Ancenis **23** D6
Ancerville **19** D6
Ancy-le-Franc **27** B5
Andelot-Blancheville **28** A1
Andernos-les-Bains **36** B3
Andilly-en-Bassigny **28** B2
Andlau **21** D5
Andolsheim **29** B5
Andorra la Vella *AND* **45** C5
Andouillé **24** B3
Andrest **44** B2
Anduze **39** D6
Anet **18** C1
Angely **27** C5
Angers **25** C4
Angerville **26** A2
Anglade **31** D4
Anglès **45** A6
Angles-sur-l'Anglin **31** A6
Anglet **43** A5
Angliers **25** D5
Anglure **19** D5
Angoisse **31** D6
Angoulême **31** C5
Angoulins **30** B3
Angrie **24** C3
Aniane **39** D5
Aniche **15** C4
Anizy-le-Château **19** B4
Anlezy **27** D4
Annecy **35** C4
Annecy-le-Vieux **35** C4
Annemasse **35** B4
Anneyron **34** D2
Annonay **34** D1
Annot **41** D5
Anor **15** D5
Anould **29** B4
Ansac-sur-Vienne **31** C6
Anse **34** C1
Anthéor **49** B4

Anthien **27** C5
Antibes **49** A4
Antisanti **49** C6
Antonne-et-Trigonant **31** D6
Antony **18** D2
Antraigues-sur-Volane **39** B6
Antrain **16** D2
Antully **27** D6
Anvin **14** C2
Anzat-le-Luguet **33** D4
Anzin **15** C4
Aouste-sur-Sye **40** B2
Appietto **49** C5
Apprieu **34** D3
Apremont-la-Forêt **20** C2
Apt **40** D2
Aragnouet **44** C2
Aramits **43** B6
Aramon **40** D1
Araules **34** D1
Arbas **45** B4
Arbecey **28** B2
Arbois **28** D2
Arcachon **36** B3
Arcangues **43** B5
Arc-en-Barrois **28** B1
Arces **30** C3
Arces-Dilo **27** B4
Arc-et-Senans **28** D2
Archiac **31** D4
Arcis-sur-Aube **19** D5
Arc-lès-Gray **28** C2
Arçon **28** D3
Arçonnay **17** D5
Arc-sur-Tille **28** C1
Ardentes **32** A2
Ardes **33** D4
Ardres **14** B2
Arengosse **36** D3
Arès **36** B3
Arette **43** B6
Arette-Pierre-St-Martin **43** C6
Arfons **45** B6
Argelès-Gazost **44** B2
Argelès-sur-Mer **46** C2
Argeliers **46** B2
Argences **25** B5
Argentan **17** D4
Argentat **32** D2
Argenteuil **18** C2
Argentière **35** C5
Argentine **35** D4
Argenton-Château **25** D4
Argenton-sur-Creuse **32** A2
Argentre **24** B3
Argentré-du-Plessis **23** C6
Argent-sur-Sauldre **26** C3
Argonay **35** C4
Argouges **16** D2
Argueil **18** B1
Arignac **45** C4
Arinsal *AND* **45** C5
Arinthod **34** B3
Arlanc **33** D5
Arles **40** D1
Arleuf **27** D5
Arleux **15** C4
Armentières **14** C3
Armissan **46** B3
Arnac-Pompadour **32** D2
Arnage **25** B5
Arnay-le-Duc **27** D6
Arnéguy **43** B5
Aron **25** A4
Arpajon **18** D2
Arpajon-sur-Cère **38** B3
Arques **14** B3
Arques **45** C6
Arques-la-Bataille **14** D1
Arracourt **20** D3
Arradon **23** C4
Arras **14** C3
Arreau **44** C3
Arrentières **27** A6
Arrigny **19** D6
Arrou **25** B6
Ars-en-Ré **30** B2

Ars-sur-Formans **34** C2
Ars-sur-Moselle **20** C3
Artannes-sur-Indre **25** C5
Artenay **26** B2
Arthez-d'Asson **44** B2
Arthez-de-Béarn **43** B6
Arthon **32** A2
Arthon-en-Retz **24** D2
Artigat **45** B5
Artix **44** B1
Arudy **44** B1
Arveyres **37** B4
Arvieu **39** C4
Arvieux **41** B5
Arzacq-Arraziguet **44** A1
Asasp-Arros **43** B6
Ascain **43** A5
Aschères-le-Marché **26** B2
Asco **49** B5
Ascou **45** C5
Asfeld **19** B5
Aspet **44** B3
Aspremont **40** C3
Aspres-sur-Buëch **40** C3
Assérac **23** D4
Assier **38** B2
Asson **44** B2
Astaffort **37** D6
Athies **14** D3
Athies-sous-Laon **19** B4
Athis-de-l'Orne **17** D4
Attignat **34** B2
Attigny **19** B6
Atur **31** D6
Aubagne **48** B1
Aube **17** D5
Aubenas **39** B6
Aubenton **15** D5
Aubergenville **18** C2
Auberive **28** B1
Aubeterre-sur-Dronne **31** D5
Aubiet **37** D6
Aubignan **40** D2
Aubigné-Racan **25** C5
Aubignosc **40** D3
Aubigny **30** A2
Aubigny-en-Artois **14** C3
Aubigny-sur-Nère **26** C3
Aubin **38** C3
Aubord **39** D6
Auboué **20** C2
Aubusson **32** C3
Auby **15** C4
Aucamville **38** D1
Auch **37** D6
Auchy-au-Bois **14** C3
Aucun **44** B2
Audenge **36** B3
Auderville **16** B2
Audeux **28** C2
Audierne **22** C1
Audincourt **29** C4
Audon **36** D3
Audresselles **14** B2
Audruicq **14** B2
Audun-le-Roman **20** B2
Auffay **17** B6
Augignac **31** C6
Aullène **49** D5
Aulnat **33** C4
Aulnay **31** C4
Aulnay-sous-Bois **18** C3
Aulnois sur-Seille **20** C3
Aulnoye-Aymeries **15** D5
Aulon **44** B3
Ault **14** D1
Aulus-les-Bains **45** C4
Aumale **18** B2
Aumetz **20** B2
Aumont **28** D2
Aumont-Aubrac **39** B5
Aunay-en-Bazois **27** D5
Aunay-sur-Odon **17** C4
Auneau **18** D2
Aups **48** A2
Auray **23** C4
Aurec-sur-Loire **33** D6
Aureilhan **44** B2

Aureille 40 D2
Aurel 40 B2
Aurel 40 D3
Aurensan 37 D4
Aurignac 45 B4
Aurillac 38 B3
Auriol 48 B1
Auron 41 C5
Auros 37 C4
Auroux 39 B5
Aussillon 45 A6
Aussonne 38 D1
Auterive 45 B5
Authon 25 C6
Authon 41 C4
Authon-du-Perche 25 A6
Autrans 34 D3
Autreville 20 D2
Autrey-lès-Gray 28 C2
Autry 19 C6
Autun 27 D6
Auve 19 C6
Auvers-le-Hamon 25 B4
Auvillar 37 C6
Auxerre 27 B4
Auxi-le-Château 14 D2
Auxonne 28 D2
Auxy 27 D6
Auzances 32 C3
Auzat 45 C5
Auzat-sur-Allier 33 D5
Auzon 33 D5
Availles-Limouzine 31 B6
Avallon 27 C5
Avançon 41 C4
Avant-lès-Ramerupt 19 D5
Avenay-Val-d'Or 19 C5
Avermes 33 A5
Avesnes-le-Comte 14 C3
Avesnes-sur-Helpe 15 D5
Avignon 40 D2
Avilley 28 C3
Avion 14 C3
Avioth 20 B2
Avize 19 C5
Avoine 25 D5
Avon 18 D3
Avord 26 D3
Avoriaz 35 B5
Avoudrey 28 D3
Avranches 16 D2
Avril 20 C2
Avrillé 25 C4
Avrillé 30 B2
Axat 45 C6
Ax-les-Thermes 45 C5
Aydat 33 C4
Ayen 32 D1
Aynac 38 B2
Ayron 31 A5
Aytré 30 B3
Azay-le-Ferron 25 D6
Azay-le-Rideau 25 C5
Azé 24 B3
Azerables 32 B2
Azur 36 D3
Azy-le-Vif 27 D4

B

Baâlon 20 B1
Baccarat 21 D4
Bacqueville-en-Caux 14 D1
Badefols-d'Ans 31 D6
Baden 23 D4
Badonviller 21 D4
Bagard 39 D6
Bâgé-le-Châtel 34 B2
Bages 46 C2
Bagnac-sur-Célé 38 B3
Bagneaux-sur-Loing 26 A3
Bagnères-de-Bigorre 44 B2
Bagnères-de-Luchon 44 C3
Bagnols-les-Bains 39 C5
Bagnols-sur-Cèze 40 C1
Baignes-Ste-Radegonde 31 D4
Baigneux-les-Juifs 27 C6

Baillargues 39 D6
Bailleau-le-Pin 17 D6
Bailleul 14 B3
Bain-de-Bretagne 23 C6
Bains 39 B5
Bains-les-Bains 28 B3
Bais 23 C6
Bais 25 A4
Baix 40 B1
Baixas 46 C2
Balan 19 B6
Balan 34 C2
Balaruc-les-Bains 47 A4
Balbigny 33 C6
Ballée 25 B4
Balleroy 16 C3
Ballon 25 B5
Ballots 23 C6
Balma 38 D2
Balot 27 B6
Banassac 39 C4
Bandol 48 B2
Bannalec 22 C3
Bannay 26 C3
Banon 40 D3
Bantheville 20 B1
Banyuls-sur-Mer 46 C3
Bapaume 14 D3
Baraqueville 38 C3
Barbaste 37 C5
Barbâtre 24 D1
Barbentane 40 D1
Barberaz 34 D3
Barbezieux-St-Hilaire 31 D4
Barbonne-Fayel 19 D5
Barcelonne-du-Gers 37 D4
Barcelonnette 41 C4
Barcillonnette 40 C3
Barcus 43 B6
Bardos 43 A5
Barèges 44 C2
Barentin 17 B6
Barenton 16 D3
Barfleur 16 B3
Bargemon 48 A3
Barjac 39 C6
Barjols 48 A2
Bar-le-Duc 20 D1
Barles 41 C4
Barneville-Carteret 16 B2
Baronville 20 C3
Barr 21 D5
Barre-des-Cévennes 39 C5
Barrême 41 D4
Barsac 37 B4
Bar-sur-Aube 27 A6
Bar-sur-Seine 27 B6
Bartenheim 29 C5
Bascons 37 D4
Bascous 37 D5
Bas-en-Basset 33 D6
Basse-Goulaine 23 D6
Bassens 37 B4
Bassoues 44 A3
Bassy 34 C3
Bastelica 49 C5
Bastelicaccia 49 C5
Bastennes 36 D3
Bastia 49 B6
Batz-sur-Mer 23 D4
Baud 23 C4
Bauduen 41 D4
Baugé 25 C4
Baugy 26 D3
Baulon 23 B5
Baume-les-Dames 28 C3
Bavay 15 C5
Bavilliers 29 C4
Baye 19 C5
Bayel 27 B6
Bayeux 16 C3
Bayon 20 D3
Bayonne 43 A5
Bazas 37 C4
Bazet 37 D4
Bazièges 45 A5
Bazillac 44 B2
Bazoches 27 C5

Bazoches-au-Houlme 17 D4
Bazoches-les-Gallerandes 26 B2
Bazoches-sur-Hoëne 17 D5
Bazougers 25 B4
Bazouges 24 B3
Beaucaire 40 D1
Beaucamps-le-Vieux 14 D2
Beauchastel 40 B2
Beaucouzé 25 C4
Beaufay 25 B5
Beaufort 34 A3
Beaufort 35 C4
Beaufort-en-Vallée 25 C4
Beaugency 26 B1
Beaujeu 34 B1
Beaujeu 41 C4
Beaujeu-St-Vallier-Pierrejux-et-Quitteur
28 C2
Beaulieu 39 D6
Beaulieu-lès-Loches 25 D6
Beaulieu-sur-Dordogne 38 B2
Beaulieu-sur-Loire 26 C3
Beaulon 33 A5
Beaumarchés 44 A2
Beaumesnil 17 C5
Beaumetz-lès-Loges 14 D3
Beaumont 16 B2
Beaumont 31 A5
Beaumont 37 B6
Beaumont-de-Lomagne 37 D6
Beaumont-de-Pertuis 40 D3
Beaumont-en-Argonne 19 B6
Beaumont-en-Véron 25 D5
Beaumont-le-Roger 17 C6
Beaumont-lès-Valence 40 B2
Beaumont-sur-Oise 18 C2
Beaumont-sur-Sarthe 25 A5
Beaune 27 D6
Beaune-La Rolande 26 B3
Beaupréau 24 D3
Beauquesne 14 D3
Beaurepaire 34 D2
Beaurepaire-en-Bresse 34 A3
Beaurières 40 C3
Beausite 20 C1
Beausoleil 41 D6
Beautor 19 B4
Beauvais 18 B2
Beauval 14 D3
Beauvezer 41 D4
Beauville 37 C6
Beauvoir-sur-Mer 24 D1
Beauvoir-sur-Niort 31 B4
Beauzac 33 D6
Beauzelle 38 D1
Bécherel 23 B5
Bécon-les-Granits 24 C3
Bédarieux 39 D4
Bédarrides 40 D2
Bédée 23 B5
Bédoin 40 D2
Bedous 43 B6
Béduer 38 B2
Bégaar 36 D3
Bégadan 30 D3
Bégard 22 A3
Behren-lès-Forbach 21 C4
Bélâbre 31 A6
Belcaire 45 C5
Belcastel 38 C3
Bélesta 45 C5
Belfort 29 C4
Belfort-du-Quercy 38 C2
Belgodère 49 B5
Belhomert-Guéhouville 17 D6
Belin-Béliet 36 C3
Bellac 31 B6
Bellegarde 26 B3
Bellegarde 40 D1
Bellegarde-en-Marche 32 C3
Bellegarde-sur-Valserine 34 B3
Belle-Isle-en-Terre 22 B3
Bellême 17 D5
Bellenaves 33 B4
Bellencombre 17 B6
Bellerive-sur-Allier 33 B5
Belles-Forêts 21 D4
Belleu 19 B4

Bellevaux 35 B4
Belleville 34 B1
Belleville-sur-Meuse 20 C2
Belleville-sur-Vie 24 D2
Bellevue-la-Montagne 33 D5
Belley 34 C3
Bellherbe 28 C3
Bellignat 34 B3
Bellou-en-Houlme 17 D4
Belmont-de-la-Loire 33 B6
Belmont-sur-Rance 39 D4
Belpech 45 B5
Belvédère-Campomoro 49 D5
Belvès 37 B6
Belvèze-du-Razès 45 B6
Belz 22 C3
Benassay 31 A5
Bénéjacq 44 B2
Bénesse-Maremne 36 D2
Bénestroff 21 C4
Benet 31 B4
Bénévent-l'Abbaye 32 B2
Benfeld 21 D5
Bénodet 22 C2
Benquet 37 D4
Bérat 45 B4
Berck 14 C1
Bergerac 37 B5
Bergères-lès-Vertus 19 C5
Bergesserin 34 B1
Bergues 14 B3
Bernac-Dessus 44 B2
Bernaville 14 D2
Bernay 17 C5
Bernin 34 D3
Bernis 39 D6
Berre-l'Étang 47 A6
Berrien 22 B2
Berru 19 C5
Berry-au-Bac 19 B5
Bertrichamps 21 D4
Besançon 28 D2
Bessan 46 B3
Bessay-sur-Allier 33 B5
Besse 41 B4
Besse-et-St-Anastaise 33 D4
Bessèges 39 C6
Bessé-sur-Braye 25 B6
Besse-sur-Issole 48 B2
Bessières 38 D2
Bessines-sur-Gartempe 32 B2
Bethmale 45 C4
Bethon 19 D4
Béthune 14 C3
Beton-Bazoches 19 D4
Betton 23 B6
Betz 18 C3
Beuil 41 D5
Beurville 27 A6
Beuvry 14 C3
Beuzeville 17 B5
Béville-le-Comte 18 D2
Beynac-et-Cazenac 38 B1
Beynat 32 D2
Beynost 34 C2
Bèze 28 C1
Béziers 46 B3
Bezouce 40 D1
Bians-les-Usiers 28 D3
Biarritz 43 B5
Biarrotte 43 A5
Biars-sur-Cère 38 B2
Bias 36 C3
Bias 37 C6
Bidache 43 A6
Bidart 43 B5
Bidos 43 B6
Bielle 44 B1
Bierné 25 B4
Biert 45 C4
Biesles 28 B1
Biganos 36 B3
Bignan 23 C4
Biguglia 49 B6
Billère 44 B1
Billiat 34 B3
Billom 33 C5
Billy 33 B5

Binas **26** B1
Binic **23** A4
Biol **34** D2
Biot **49** A4
Biron **37** B6
Biscarrosse **36** C3
Biscarrosse-Plage **36** C3
Bischheim **21** D5
Bischwiller **21** D5
Bitche **21** C5
Bitschwiller-lès-Thann **29** B4
Bizanet **46** B2
Bizanos **44** B2
Blagnac **38** D1
Blain **23** D5
Blainville-sur-Mer **16** C2
Blaiserives **19** D6
Blajan **44** B3
Blâmont **21** D4
Blan **45** A5
Blancafort **26** C3
Blangy-sur-Bresle **14** D2
Blanquefort **37** B4
Blanzac-Porcheresse **31** D5
Blanzay **31** B5
Blanzy **33** A6
Blasimon **37** B5
Blausasc **41** D6
Blavozy **39** A6
Blaye **30** D3
Bléneau **26** C3
Blénod-lès-Toul **20** D2
Blérancourt **19** B4
Bléré **25** C6
Blesle **33** D4
Blet **26** D3
Bligny **27** B6
Bligny-sur-Ouche **27** D6
Blois **26** C1
Blousson-Sérian **44** A2
Bocognano **49** C5
Boé **37** C6
Boën **33** C6
Boffres **40** B1
Bohain-en-Vermandois **15** D4
Bohars **22** B1
Boiscommun **26** B3
Bois-d'Amont **35** B4
Boisgervilly **23** B5
Bois-Guillaume **17** B6
Boisset-et-Gaujac **39** D6
Boissezon **45** A6
Bolandoz **28** D3
Bolbec **17** B5
Bollène **40** C1
Bologne **28** B1
Bompas **46** C2
Bona **27** D4
Bonboillon **28** C2
Bonchamp-lès-Laval **24** B3
Bonifacio **49** D6
Bonnat **32** B2
Bonnétable **25** B5
Bonneuil-Matours **31** A5
Bonneval **26** B1
Bonneval **35** C5
Bonneval-sur-Arc **35** D5
Bonnevaux **28** D3
Bonneville **35** B4
Bonnieux **40** D2
Bonny-sur-Loire **26** C3
Bono **23** C4
Bons-en-Chablais **35** B4
Bonson **33** D6
Boos **17** B6
Bordeaux **37** B4
Bordères-Louron **44** C3
Bordères-sur-l'Échez **44** B2
Bordes **44** B2
Bordes **44** B3
Borgo **49** B6
Borrèze **38** B2
Bort-les-Orgues **32** D3
Bosset **37** B5
Bouafles **17** C6
Boucau **43** A5
Bouc-Bel-Air **47** A6
Boucé **17** D4

Bouchain **15** C4
Bouchemaine **25** C4
Bouchoir **18** B3
Boué **15** D5
Bouglon **37** C5
Bouguenais **23** D6
Bouillargues **39** D6
Bouilly **27** B5
Bouin **24** D1
Boujailles **28** D3
Boujan-sur-Libron **46** B3
Boulay-Moselle **20** C3
Boulazac **31** D6
Boulbon **40** D1
Bouligny **20** C2
Bouloc **38** D1
Boulogne-Billancourt **18** D2
Boulogne-sur-Gesse **44** B3
Boulogne-sur-Mer **14** C2
Bouloire **25** B5
Boulouris **48** B3
Boult-aux-Bois **19** B6
Boulzicourt **19** B6
Bouniagues **37** B6
Bourbon-Lancy **33** A5
Bourbon-l'Archambault **33** A4
Bourbonne-les-Bains **28** B2
Bourbourg **14** B2
Bourbriac **22** B3
Bourcefranc-le-Chapus **30** C3
Bourdeaux **40** C2
Bourdeilles **31** D6
Bourdonnay **21** D4
Bouresse **31** B5
Bourg **37** A4
Bourg-Achard **17** B6
Bourganeuf **32** C2
Bourg-Argental **34** D1
Bourg-de-Péage **40** B2
Bourg-de-Thizy **33** C6
Bourg-de-Visa **37** C6
Bourg-Dun **17** A6
Bourg-en-Bresse **34** B2
Bourges **26** D3
Bourg-et-Comin **19** B4
Bourg-Lastic **32** C3
Bourg-lès-Valence **40** B2
Bourgneuf-en-Mauges **24** C3
Bourgneuf-en-Retz **24** D1
Bourgogne **19** B5
Bourgoin-Jallieu **34** C2
Bourg-St-Andéol **40** C1
Bourg-St-Bernard **38** D2
Bourg-St-Maurice **35** C5
Bourgtheroulde-Infreville **17** B6
Bourguébus **17** C4
Bourgueil **25** C5
Bourmont **28** B2
Bournezeau **30** A3
Bourran **37** C5
Bourriot-Bergonce **37** C4
Bourron-Marlotte **26** A3
Boussac **32** B3
Boussens **45** B4
Boussières **28** D2
Boussois **15** C5
Bouvières **40** C2
Bouvron **23** D5
Bouxières-aux-Dames **20** D3
Bouxwiller **21** D5
Bouy **19** C5
Bouzonville **20** C3
Boves **14** D3
Boynes **26** B3
Bozel **35** D4
Bozouls **39** C4
Brach **36** A3
Bracieux **26** C1
Braine **19** B4
Bram **45** B6
Bramans **35** D5
Brando **49** A6
Branne **37** B4
Brantôme **31** D6
Brassac **38** D3
Brassy **27** C5
Braud-et-St-Louis **31** D4
Bray-sur-Seine **19** D4

Bray-sur-Somme **14** D3
Brazey-en-Plaine **28** D1
Brécey **16** C3
Brech **23** C4
Bréhal **16** C2
Bréhan **23** C4
Breidenbach **21** C5
Breil-sur-Roya **41** D6
Brélès **22** B1
Brem-sur-Mer **30** A2
Brénod **34** B3
Brens **38** D2
Bressols **38** D1
Bressuire **25** D4
Brest **22** B1
Bretagne-d'Armagnac **37** D5
Breteil **23** B5
Bretenoux **38** B2
Breteuil **17** C6
Breteuil **18** B2
Brétignolles-sur-Mer **30** A2
Bretoncelles **17** D6
Brettville-sur-Laize **17** C4
Breuches **28** B3
Breuil-Magné **30** C3
Breuilpont **18** C1
Breuvannes-en-Bassigny **28** B2
Brézolles **17** D6
Briançon **41** B4
Briare **26** C3
Briatexte **38** D2
Bricon **28** B1
Bricquebec **16** B2
Brides-les-Bains **35** D4
Brie **31** C5
Brie-Comte-Robert **18** D3
Brienne-le-Château **19** D6
Briennon **33** B6
Brienon-sur-Armançon **27** B4
Briey **20** C2
Brignais **34** C1
Brignogan-Plage **22** A2
Brignoles **48** B2
Brillon-en-Barrois **20** D1
Brinon-sur-Beuvron **27** C4
Brinon-sur-Sauldre **26** C2
Brin-sur-Seille **20** D3
Brion **39** B4
Brionne **17** C5
Brioude **33** D5
Brioux-sur-Boutonne **31** B4
Briouze **17** D4
Briscous **43** B5
Brissac-Quincé **25** C4
Brive-la-Gaillarde **32** D2
Brix **16** B2
Brocas **37** D4
Broglie **17** C5
Broin **28** D1
Bron **34** C2
Broons **23** B5
Broquiès **39** D4
Brossac **31** D4
Brottes **28** B1
Brou **25** A6
Brousseval **19** D6
Brouvelieures **29** A4
Bruay-la-Bussière **14** C3
Brue-Auriac **48** A2
Bruère-Allichamps **32** A3
Bruguières **38** D2
Brûlon **25** B4
Brumath **21** D5
Brunehamel **15** D5
Bruniquel **38** D2
Brusque **39** D4
Bruyères **29** A4
Bruz **23** C5
Bû **18** D1
Buais **16** D3
Bubry **22** C3
Bucey-lès-Gy **28** C2
Buchy **17** B6
Bucy-lès-Pierrepont **19** B5
Bugeat **32** C2
Bugnein **43** B6
Buis-les-Baronnies **40** C2

Bulgnéville **28** A2
Bully-les-Mines **14** C3
Burie **31** C4
Burlats **38** D3
Buros **44** B2
Busigny **15** D4
Bussang **29** B4
Bussière-Badil **31** C5
Bussière-Galant **31** C6
Bussière-Poitevine **31** B6
Bussy-en-Othe **27** B4
Bussy-le-Grand **27** C6
Buxerolles **31** A5
Buxières-les-Mines **33** B4
Buxy **34** A1
Buzançais **26** D1
Buzancy **19** B6
Buzet-sur-Baïse **37** C5
Buzet-sur-Tarn **38** D2

C

Cabanac-et-Villagrains **37** B4
Cabannes **40** D2
Cabasse **48** B2
Cabrerets **38** C2
Cabrières-d'Aigues **40** D3
Cadenet **40** D2
Cadillac **37** B4
Cadours **37** D6
Caen **17** C4
Cagnac-les-Mines **38** D3
Cagnes-sur-Mer **49** A4
Cahors **38** C2
Cahuzac-sur-Vère **38** D2
Cairanne **40** C2
Caissargues **39** D6
Cajarc **38** C2
Calacuccia **49** B5
Calais **14** B2
Calcatoggio **49** C5
Calenzana **49** B5
Callac **22** B3
Callas **48** A3
Callen **37** C4
Callian **48** A3
Calmont **38** C3
Calmont **45** B5
Calvi **49** B5
Calvignac **38** C2
Calvinet **38** B3
Calvisson **39** D6
Camarès **39** D4
Camaret-sur-Aigues **40** C2
Camaret-sur-Mer **22** B1
Cambes **37** B4
Cambo-les-Bains **43** B5
Cambrai **15** D4
Cambron **14** D2
Camon **14** D3
Camors **23** C4
Campagne **37** B6
Campagne-lès-Hesdin **14** C2
Campan **44** B2
Campbon **23** D5
Campénéac **23** C5
Canale-di-Verde **49** B6
Canals **38** D1
Canaples **14** D2
Canari **49** A6
Cancale **16** D2
Cancon **37** C6
Candé **24** C3
Canet **46** A3
Canet **46** B2
Canet-en-Roussillon **46** C2
Canet-Plage **46** C2
Cannes **49** A4
Cantenac **37** A4
Cany-Barville **17** A5
Capbreton **36** D2
Cap d'Agde **46** B3
Capdenac **38** B3
Capdenac-Gare **38** B3
Capendu **45** B6
Capestang **46** B2
Cap Ferret **36** B3

Captieux 37 C4
Capvern-les-Bains 44 B3
Caraman 45 A5
Carantec 22 A2
Carbonne 45 B4
Carcans 30 D3
Carcans-Plage 30 D3
Carcassonne 45 B6
Carcès 48 A2
Cardaillac 38 B2
Carentan 16 C3
Carentoir 23 C5
Cargèse 49 C5
Carhaix-Plouguer 22 B3
Carignan 20 B1
Carlat 38 B3
Carlux 38 B1
Carmaux 38 D3
Carnac 22 D3
Carnières 15 D4
Carnoules 48 B2
Carnoux-en-Provence 48 B1
Carolles 16 D2
Carpentras 40 D2
Carpiquet 17 C4
Carquefou 23 D6
Carqueiranne 48 B2
Carros 41 D5
Carrouges 17 D4
Carry-le-Rouet 47 B6
Cars 31 D4
Carsac-Aillac 38 B1
Carspach 29 C4
Cartelègue 31 D4
Carteret 16 B2
Carvin 14 C3
Casaglione 49 C5
Casamozza 49 B6
Cassagnes-Bégonhès 38 C3
Cassaniouze 38 B3
Cassel 14 B3
Casseneuil 37 C6
Cassis 48 B1
Cassuéjouls 39 B4
Castanet-Tolosan 45 A5
Castelginest 38 D2
Casteljaloux 37 C5
Castellane 41 D4
Castelmoron-sur-Lot 37 C5
Castelnau-Barbarens 44 A3
Castelnaudary 45 B5
Castelnau-d'Auzan 37 D5
Castelnau-de-Médoc 36 B3
Castelnau-de-Montmiral 38 D2
Castelnau d'Estréfonds 38 D1
Castelnau-le-Lez 39 D6
Castelnau-Magnoac 44 B3
Castelnau-Montratier 38 C1
Castelnau-Rivière-Basse 44 A2
Castelsagrat 37 C6
Castelsarrasin 37 D6
Castéra-Verduzan 37 D5
Castetnau-Camblong 43 B6
Castets 36 D3
Castillon-en-Couserans 45 C4
Castillon-la-Bataille 37 B5
Castillonnès 37 B6
Castres 45 A6
Castries 39 D6
Cateri 49 B5
Cattenom 20 B3
Catus 38 B1
Caudan 22 C3
Caudebec-lès-Elbeuf 17 C6
Caudecoste 37 C6
Caudiès-de-Fenouillèdes 45 C6
Caudry 15 D4
Caujac 45 B5
Caulnes 23 B5
Caumont 37 D6
Caumont 45 B4
Caumont-l'Éventé 16 C3
Caumont-sur-Durance 40 D2
Caunes-Minervois 45 B6
Cauro 49 C5
Caussade 38 C2
Cauterets 44 C2
Cavaillon 40 D2

Cavalaire-sur-Mer 48 B3
Caveirac 39 D6
Cavignac 31 D4
Cayeux-sur-Mer 14 D1
Caylus 38 C2
Cazals 38 B1
Cazals 38 C2
Cazaubon 37 D5
Cazères 45 B4
Cazes-Mondenard 38 C1
Cazilhac 45 B6
Cazoulès 38 B2
Ceaucé 17 D4
Céaux-d'Allègre 33 D5
Cébazat 33 C4
Ceilhes-et-Rocozels 39 D4
Ceintrey 20 D3
Celles-sur-Belle 31 B4
Celles-sur-Ource 27 B6
Cellettes 26 C1
Cénac-et-St-Julien 38 B1
Cendras 39 C6
Cendrieux 37 B6
Centuri 49 A6
Cérans-Foulletourte 25 B5
Cerbère 46 D3
Cercy-la-Tour 27 D5
Cerdon 26 C3
Cérences 16 C2
Céreste 40 D3
Céret 46 C2
Cergy 18 C2
Cérilly 33 A4
Cerisiers 27 B4
Cerisy-la-Forêt 16 C3
Cerisy-la-Salle 16 C3
Cerizay 24 D3
Cernay 29 B4
Cernay-en-Dormois 19 C6
Cersay 25 D4
Cervione 49 B6
Cervon 27 D5
Cessenon-sur-Orb 46 A2
Cesson 18 D3
Cesson-Sévigné 23 B6
Cestas 37 B4
Ceton 25 A6
Cevins 35 C4
Ceyreste 48 B1
Ceyzériat 34 B2
Chabanais 31 C6
Chabeuil 40 B2
Chablis 27 B5
Chabreloche 33 C5
Chabris 26 C1
Chagny 27 D6
Chaillac 32 B1
Chailland 24 A3
Chaillé-les-Marais 30 B3
Chailley 27 B5
Chaintrix-Bierges 19 C5
Chalabre 45 B5
Chalais 31 D5
Chalamont 34 C2
Chalampé 29 B5
Chaleix 31 D6
Châlette-sur-Loing 26 B3
Chaligny 20 D3
Chalindrey 28 B2
Chalivoy-Milon 26 D3
Challans 24 D2
Challerange 19 B6
Challes-les-Eaux 34 D3
Chalmoux 33 A5
Chalonnes-sur-Loire 24 C3
Châlons-en-Champagne 19 C6
Chalon-sur-Saône 27 D6
Châlus 31 C6
Chamalières 33 C4
Chamaloc 40 B2
Chamberet 32 C2
Chambéria 34 B3
Chambéry 34 D3
Chambley-Bussières 20 C2
Chambois 17 D5
Chambon-sur-Voueize 32 B3
Chambord 26 C1
Chamboulive 32 D2

Chambray-lès-Tours 25 C6
Chambry 19 B4
Chamesson 27 B6
Chamonix-Mont-Blanc 35 C5
Chamoux-sur-Gelon 35 D4
Champagnac 32 D3
Champagnac-de-Belair 31 D6
Champagnac-le-Vieux 33 D5
Champagne-Mouton 31 C5
Champagne-sur-Seine 18 D3
Champagney 28 C3
Champagnole 34 A3
Champaubert 19 C5
Champdeniers-St-Denis 31 B4
Champ-d'Oiseau 27 C6
Champeix 33 C4
Champforgeuil 27 D6
Champgenéteux 25 A4
Champier 34 D2
Champigné 25 C4
Champignelles 27 B4
Champigny 27 A4
Champlemy 27 C4
Champlitte 28 C2
Champniers 31 C5
Champoléon 41 B4
Champsecret 17 D4
Champs-sur-Tarentaine-Marchal 32 D3
Champs-sur-Yonne 27 B4
Champ-sur-Drac 40 B3
Champtoceaux 23 D6
Chamrousse 34 D3
Chanac 39 C5
Chanas 34 D2
Chanceaux 27 C6
Chanceaux-sur-Choiselle 25 C6
Chancelade 31 D6
Changé 24 B3
Changé 25 B5
Changy 33 B6
Chantelle 33 B4
Chantilly 18 C3
Chantonnay 30 A3
Chanu 16 D3
Chaource 27 B5
Charbonnat 27 D5
Charcenne 28 C2
Charchilla 34 B3
Charenton-du-Cher 33 A4
Chargey-lès-Gray 28 C2
Charleville-Mézières 15 D6
Charlieu 33 B6
Charly 19 C4
Charmé 31 C5
Charmes 28 A3
Charmes-sur-Rhône 40 B2
Charmoy 27 B4
Charnay-lès-Mâcon 34 B2
Charny 27 B4
Charolles 33 B6
Chârost 26 D2
Charquemont 29 D4
Charrey-sur-Seine 27 B6
Charrin 27 D4
Charroux 31 B5
Chartres 18 D1
Charvieu-Chavagneux 34 C2
Chassagne-Montrachet 27 D6
Chasseneuil-sur-Bonnieure 31 C5
Chasseradès 39 C5
Chasse-sur-Rhône 34 C2
Chassigny-Aisey 28 C2
Chassillé 25 B4
Château-Arnoux 40 D3
Châteaubernard 31 C4
Châteaubourg 23 B6
Châteaubriant 23 C6
Château-Chinon 27 D5
Château-d'Olonne 30 A2
Château-du-Loir 25 C5
Châteaudun 25 B6
Châteaugiron 23 C6
Château-Gontier 24 B3
Château-Landon 26 B3
Château-la-Vallière 25 C5
Châteaulin 22 B2
Châteaumeillant 32 A3
Châteauneuf-de-Galaure 34 D2

Châteauneuf-de-Randon 39 B5
Châteauneuf-d'Ille-et-Vilaine 16 D2
Châteauneuf-du-Faou 22 B2
Châteauneuf-en-Thymerais 17 D6
Châteauneuf-la-Forêt 32 C2
Châteauneuf-les-Martigues 47 B6
Châteauneuf-sur-Charente 31 C4
Châteauneuf-sur-Cher 26 D3
Châteauneuf-sur-Loire 26 B2
Châteauneuf-sur-Sarthe 25 C4
Châteauneuf-Val-de-Bargis 27 C4
Châteauponsac 31 B6
Château-Porcien 19 B5
Châteauredon 41 D4
Châteaurenard 26 B3
Châteaurenard 40 D2
Châteaurenaud 34 A2
Château-Renault 25 C6
Châteauroux 26 D2
Châteauroux 41 C4
Château-Salins 20 D3
Château-Thierry 19 C4
Châteauvillain 27 B6
Châtel 35 B5
Châtelaillon-Plage 30 B3
Châtelaudren 23 B4
Châtel-Censoir 27 C5
Châteldon 33 C5
Châtel-Gérard 27 C5
Châtelguyon 33 C4
Châtellerault 25 D5
Châtel-Montagne 33 B5
Châtel-sur-Moselle 28 A3
Châtelus-Malvaleix 32 B3
Châtenois 28 A2
Châtenois 29 A5
Châtenois-les-Forges 29 C4
Châtenoy-le-Royal 27 D6
Châtillon-Coligny 26 B3
Châtillon-en-Bazois 27 D5
Châtillon-en-Diois 40 B3
Châtillon-en-Michaille 34 B3
Châtillon-la-Palud 34 C2
Châtillon-sur-Chalaronne 34 B2
Châtillon-sur-Colmont 24 A3
Châtillon-sur-Indre 25 D6
Châtillon-sur-Loire 26 C3
Châtillon-sur-Marne 19 C5
Châtillon-sur-Seine 27 B6
Châtillon-sur-Thouet 31 A4
Chatte 34 D2
Chatuzange-le-Goubet 40 B2
Chaudenay 28 B2
Chaudes-Aigues 39 B4
Chaudeyrac 39 B5
Chauffailles 33 B6
Chauffayer 40 B3
Chaulnes 14 D3
Chaumergy 28 D2
Chaumont 28 B1
Chaumont-en-Vexin 18 C2
Chaumont-Porcien 19 B5
Chaumont-sur-Aire 20 C1
Chaumont-sur-Loire 25 C6
Chaunay 31 B5
Chauny 19 B4
Chaussin 28 D2
Chauvigny 31 A5
Chavanay 34 D1
Chavanges 19 D6
Chavanoz 34 C2
Chavelot 28 A3
Chazelles-sur-Lyon 33 C6
Chécy 26 B2
Chef-Boutonne 31 B4
Chemazé 24 B3
Chémery 26 C1
Chémery-sur-Bar 19 B6
Chemillé 24 D3
Chemin 28 D1
Cheminon 19 D6
Chemiré-le-Gaudin 25 B4
Chenecey-Buillon 28 D2
Chénérailles 32 B3
Cheniménil 28 B3
Chenôve 28 C1
Cheny 27 B4
Chepy 19 C6

Chérac 31 C4
Chéraute 43 B6
Cherbourg 16 B2
Chéroy 27 B4
Cherveix-Cubas 31 D6
Cherves-Richemont 31 C4
Chesley 27 B5
Chessy-les-Prés 27 B5
Chevagnes 33 A5
Chevanceaux 31 D4
Chevillon 20 D1
Chevilly 26 B2
Chevreuse 18 D2
Cheylade 33 D4
Chezal-Benoît 26 D2
Chèze 44 C2
Chiché 25 D4
Chilleurs-aux-Bois 26 B2
Chindrieux 34 C3
Chinon 25 D5
Chiroubles 34 B1
Chizé 31 B4
Cholet 24 D3
Chomelix 33 D5
Chomérac 40 B1
Chooz 15 D6
Chorges 41 C4
Chouilly 19 C5
Chouzy-sur-Cisse 25 C6
Choye 28 C2
Chuzelles 34 C2
Ciadoux 44 B3
Ciboure 43 B5
Cierp-Gaud 44 C3
Cieutat 44 B3
Cieux 31 C6
Cinq-Mars-la-Pile 25 C5
Cintegabelle 45 B5
Cintrey 28 B2
Cirey-sur-Blaise 27 A6
Cirey-sur-Vezouze 21 D4
Ciry-le-Noble 33 A6
Cissé 31 A5
Civaux 31 B6
Civray 26 D2
Civray 31 B5
Clairac 37 C5
Clairoix 18 B3
Clairvaux-les-Lacs 34 A3
Claix 34 D3
Clamecy 27 C4
Clans 41 D5
Claret 40 C3
Clary 15 D4
Clécy 17 C4
Cléder 22 A2
Clefmont 28 B2
Cléguérec 22 B3
Clelles 40 B3
Cléon 17 B6
Cléon-d'Andran 40 C2
Cléré-les-Pins 25 C5
Clères 17 B6
Cléry 27 A5
Clermain 34 B1
Clermont 18 B3
Clermont 45 B4
Clermont-en-Argonne 20 C1
Clermont-Ferrand 33 C4
Clermont-l'Hérault 39 D5
Clerval 28 C3
Cléry-St-André 26 B2
Clion 25 D6
Clisson 24 D3
Clohars-Carnoët 22 C3
Cloyes-sur-le-Loir 25 B6
Cluis 32 A2
Clumanc 41 D4
Cluny 34 B1
Cluses 35 C4
Coarraze 44 B2
Cocumont 37 C5
Coëx 30 A2
Coggia 49 C5
Cognac 31 C4
Cognac-la-Forêt 31 C6
Cognin 34 D3
Cogolin 48 B3

Coincy 19 C4
Colayrac-St-Cirq 37 C6
Coligny 34 B2
Collinée 23 B4
Collioure 46 C2
Collobrières 48 B3
Collonges 34 B3
Collonges-la-Rouge 38 A2
Colmar 29 B4
Colmars 41 C4
Colméry 27 C4
Cologne 37 D6
Colombelles 17 C4
Colombey-les-Belles 20 D2
Colombey-les Deux-Églises 27 A6
Colombiès 38 C3
Colomiers 38 D1
Colroy-la-Grande 29 A4
Coly 32 D1
Combeaufontaine 28 C2
Comblanchien 27 D6
Combles 14 D3
Combloux 35 C4
Combourg 16 D2
Combronde 33 C4
Commenailles 28 D2
Commentry 33 B4
Commequiers 24 D2
Commer 25 A4
Commercy 20 D2
Compiègne 18 B3
Compolibat 38 C3
Compreignac 31 C6
Comps-sur-Artuby 41 D4
Conca 49 D6
Concarneau 22 C2
Conches-en-Ouche 17 C6
Concorès 38 B2
Concots 38 C2
Condat 33 D4
Condé-en-Brie 19 C4
Condé-sur-Huisne 17 D6
Condé-sur-Noireau 17 C4
Condé-sur-Vire 16 C3
Condom 37 D5
Condrieu 34 D1
Conflans-en-Jarnisy 20 C2
Conflans-sur-Lanterne 28 B3
Confolens 31 B6
Congrier 23 C6
Conlie 25 B4
Conliège 34 A3
Connantre 19 D5
Connaux 40 D1
Connerré 25 B5
Conques 38 B3
Conques-sur-Orbiel 45 B6
Contes 41 D6
Contis-Plage 36 C3
Contres 26 C1
Contrexéville 28 B2
Conty 18 B2
Coole 19 D6
Coray 22 C2
Corbeil-Essonnes 18 D3
Corbeilles 26 B3
Corbeny 19 B5
Corbie 14 D3
Corbières 40 D3
Corbigny 27 C5
Corcelles-lès-Cîteaux 28 D1
Corcieux 29 B4
Cordemais 23 D5
Cordes 38 D2
Corlay 22 B3
Cormatin 34 A1
Cormeilles 17 C5
Cormicy 19 B5
Cormontreuil 19 C5
Cornas 40 B2
Corneilla-del-Vercol 46 C2
Cornimont 29 B4
Cornus 39 D4
Coron 25 D4
Corps 40 B3
Corps-Nuds 23 C6
Corre 28 B2

Corrèze 32 D2
Corrobert 19 C4
Corseul 16 D1
Corte 49 B6
Cosne-Cours-sur-Loire 26 C3
Cosne-d'Allier 33 B4
Cossé-le-Vivien 24 B3
Coti-Chiavari 49 D5
Cotignac 48 A2
Coubon 39 B6
Couches 27 D6
Coucy-le-Château-Auffrique 19 B4
Coudekerque-Branche 14 B3
Couëron 23 D6
Couflens 45 C4
Coufouleux 38 D2
Couhé 31 B5
Couiza 45 C6
Coulaines 25 B5
Coulanges-la-Vineuse 27 C4
Coulanges-sur-Yonne 27 C4
Coulaures 31 D6
Couleuvre 33 A4
Coullons 26 C3
Coulmier-le-Sec 27 B6
Coulmiers 26 B2
Coulogne 14 B2
Coulombiers 31 B5
Coulombs 18 D1
Coulommiers 19 D4
Coulonges-sur-l'Autize 31 B4
Coulounieix-Chamiers 31 D6
Couptrain 17 D4
Courcelles-Chaussy 20 C3
Courchaton 28 C3
Courchevel 35 D4
Cour-Cheverny 26 C1
Courcité 25 A4
Courçon 30 B3
Courcy 19 B5
Courgains 25 A5
Courgenay 27 A4
Courlay 25 D4
Courmelles 19 B4
Cournon-d'Auvergne 33 C4
Courpière 33 C5
Courrensan 37 D5
Coursac 31 D6
Coursan 46 B2
Coursegoules 41 D5
Courseulles-sur-Mer 17 B4
Cours-la-Ville 33 B6
Courson-les-Carrières 27 C4
Courtalain 25 B6
Courtenay 27 B4
Courthézon 40 D2
Courtomer 17 D5
Courville-sur-Eure 17 D6
Cousance 34 B3
Cousances-les-Forges 20 D1
Coussac-Bonneval 32 D1
Coussay-les-Bois 25 D6
Coussegrey 27 B5
Coussey 20 D2
Coustouges 46 D2
Coutances 16 C2
Couterne 17 D4
Coutras 37 A4
Couze-et-St-Front 37 B6
Couzeix 31 C6
Cox 37 D6
Cozes 30 C3
Cozzano 49 C6
Crach 23 D4
Cran-Gevrier 35 C4
Craon 24 B3
Craonne 19 B5
Craponne-sur-Arzon 33 D5
Cravant 27 C5
Créances 16 C2
Créancey 37 B5
Crêches-sur-Saône 34 B2
Crécy-en-Ponthieu 14 C2
Crécy-la-Chapelle 18 C3
Crécy-sur-Serre 19 B4
Creil 18 C3
Creissels 39 C4
Cremeaux 33 C6

Crémieu 34 C2
Créon 37 B4
Crépey 20 D2
Crépy 19 B4
Crépy-en-Valois 18 C3
Cressensac 38 B2
Crest 40 B2
Créteil 18 D3
Creutzwald 20 C3
Crevant 32 B2
Crévéchamps 20 D3
Crèvecœur-le-Grand 18 B2
Criel-sur-Mer 14 D1
Criquetot-l'Esneval 17 B5
Crocq 32 C3
Croisilles 14 D3
Crolles 34 D3
Cronat 33 A5
Crots 41 C4
Croutelle 31 A5
Crouy 19 B4
Crouy-sur-Ourcq 19 C4
Crozant 32 B2
Crozes-Hermitage 34 D2
Crozon 22 B1
Cruas 40 B1
Cruseilles 35 C4
Crusnes 20 B2
Cruzy 46 B2
Cruzy-le-Châtel 27 B5
Cubjac 31 D6
Cubzac-les-Ponts 37 B4
Cucuron 40 D3
Cudos 37 C4
Cuers 48 B2
Cugand 24 D3
Cuges-les-Pins 48 B2
Cugnaux 45 A4
Cuguen 16 D2
Cuiseaux 34 B3
Cuise-la-Motte 19 B4
Cuisery 34 A2
Culan 32 A3
Culoz 34 C3
Cunault 25 C4
Cunegès 37 B5
Cunfin 27 B6
Cuq-Toulza 45 A5
Curgy 27 D6
Cussac 31 C6
Cusset 33 B5
Cussy-les-Forges 27 C5
Custines 20 D3
Cuxac-Cabardès 45 B6
Cuxac-d'Aude 46 B2
Cuzorn 37 B6

D

Dabo 21 D4
Daglan 38 B1
Dainville 14 C3
Dainville-Berthéléville 20 D2
Dalstein 20 C3
Daluis 41 D5
Damas-aux-Bois 20 D3
Damazan 37 C5
Damelevières 20 D3
Damery 19 C5
Damgan 23 D4
Damigny 17 D5
Dammarie 26 A1
Dammartin-en-Goële 18 C3
Dampierre 28 D2
Dampierre-sur-Linotte 28 C3
Dampierre-sur-Salon 28 C2
Damprichard 29 D4
Damville 17 C6
Damvillers 20 B2
Dangé-St-Romain 25 D5
Danjoutin 29 C4
Dannemarie 29 C4
Daon 25 B4
Daoulas 22 B2
Darney 28 B3
Darnieulles 28 B3
Daumazan-sur-Arize 45 B4

Daumeray 25 C4
Dauphin 40 D3
Davézieux 34 D1
Dax 36 D3
Deauville 17 B5
Decazeville 38 B3
Decize 27 D4
Delle 29 C4
Delme 20 C3
Demange-aux-Eaux 20 D2
Demigny 27 D6
Dému 37 D5
Denain 15 C4
Denguin 44 B1
Déols 26 D2
Derval 23 C6
Descartes 25 D6
Désertines 33 B4
Desvres 14 C2
Die 40 B2
Diémoz 34 C2
Dienne 33 D4
Dienville 19 D6
Dieppe 14 D1
Dieue-sur-Meuse 20 C2
Dieulefit 40 C2
Dieulouard 20 C3
Dieuze 21 D4
Dignac 31 C5
Digne-les-Bains 41 D4
Digny 17 D6
Digoin 33 B6
Dijon 28 C1
Dinan 16 D1
Dinard 16 D1
Dingé 16 D2
Diou 33 A5
Dissay 31 A5
Dissay-sous-Courcillon 25 C5
Dives-sur-Mer 17 C4
Divion 14 C3
Divonne-les-Bains 35 B4
Dixmont 27 B4
Dizy 19 C5
Dizy-le-Gros 19 B5
Dol-de-Bretagne 16 D2
Dole 28 D2
Dollon 25 B5
Dolomieu 34 C3
Dolus-d'Oléron 30 C3
Domart-en-Ponthieu 14 D2
Domats 27 B4
Dombasle-en-Xaintois 28 A2
Domène 34 D3
Domérat 32 B3
Domèvre-en-Haye 20 D2
Domèvre-sur-Vezouze 21 D4
Domfront 16 D3
Domgermain 20 D2
Dommartin-le-Franc 19 D6
Dommartin-Varimont 19 C6
Domme 38 B1
Domont 18 C3
Dompcevrin 20 C2
Dompierre-les-Ormes 33 B6
Dompierre-sur-Besbre 33 B5
Dompierre-sur-Mer 30 B3
Dompierre-sur-Yon 30 A2
Domrémy-la-Pucelle 20 D2
Donchery 19 B6
Donges 23 D5
Donjeux 20 D1
Donnemarie-Dontilly 19 D4
Donville-les-Bains 16 C2
Donzenac 32 D2
Donzère 40 C1
Donzy 27 C4
Dordives 26 B3
Dore-l'Église 33 D5
Dormans 19 C4
Dornes 33 A5
Dortan 34 B3
Douai 15 C4
Douarnenez 22 C2
Doubs 28 D3
Douchy 27 B4
Douchy-les-Mines 15 C4
Doucier 34 A3

Doudeville 17 B6
Doué-la-Fontaine 25 D4
Doulaincourt-Saucourt 28 A1
Doullens 14 D3
Dourdan 18 D2
Dourgne 45 A6
Douriez 14 C2
Doussard 35 C4
Douvaine 35 B4
Douvres-la-Délivrande 17 C4
Douzy 19 B6
Doyet 33 B4
Dozulé 17 C4
Draguignan 48 A3
Dreux 18 D1
Droué 25 B6
Drulingen 21 C4
Drumettaz-Clarafond 34 C3
Drusenheim 21 D5
Druyes-les-Belles-Fontaines 27 C4
Ducey 16 D3
Duclair 17 B6
Dugny-sur-Meuse 20 C2
Duhort-Bachen 37 D4
Dun 45 B5
Dunes 37 C6
Dunières 33 D6
Dunkerque 14 B3
Dun-le-Palestel 32 B2
Dun-les-Places 27 C5
Dun-sur-Auron 26 D3
Dun-sur-Meuse 20 B1
Durance 37 C5
Duras 37 B5
Durban-Corbières 46 B2
Durdat-Larequille 33 B4
Durfort 39 D6
Durtal 25 C4
Dyo 33 B6

E

Eaunes 45 B4
Eauze 37 D5
Ébreuil 33 B4
Échauffour 17 D5
Échenoz-la-Méline 28 C3
Échiré 31 B4
Échirolles 34 D3
Échourgnac 31 D5
Éclaron-Braucourt-Ste-Livière 19 D6
Écommoy 25 B5
Écos 18 C1
Écouché 17 D4
Écouflant 25 C4
Écouis 18 C1
Écrouves 20 D2
Écueillé 26 D1
Écuisses 33 A6
Écury-sur-Coole 19 C5
Égletons 32 D3
Éguilles 47 A6
Eguisheim 29 B4
Éguzon-Chantôme 32 B2
Einville-au-Jard 20 D3
Elbeuf 17 C6
Elne 46 C2
Éloyes 28 B3
El Serrat AND 45 C5
Elven 23 C4
Embrun 41 C4
Encamp AND 45 C5
Englefontaine 15 D4
Engomer 45 C4
Ennezat 33 C4
Ensisheim 29 B5
Ensuès-la-Redonne 47 B6
Entraigues-sur-la-Sorgue 40 D2
Entrains-sur-Nohain 27 C4
Entrammes 24 B3
Entraunes 41 C5
Entraygues-sur-Truyère 38 B3
Entrevaux 41 D5
Envermeu 14 D1
Épaignes 17 C5
Épernay 19 C5
Épernon 18 D2

Épieds-en-Beauce 26 B1
Épierre 35 D4
Épinac 27 D6
Épinal 28 B3
Epiry 27 D5
Époisses 27 C5
Eppeville 19 B4
Épuisay 25 B6
Équeurdreville-Hainneville 16 B2
Erbray 23 C6
Erdeven 22 C3
Éréac 23 B3
Ergué-Gabéric 22 C2
Ermenonville 18 C3
Ernée 24 A3
Erquy 16 D1
Erstein 21 D5
Ervillers 14 D3
Ervy-le-Châtel 27 B5
Escos 43 B6
Escouloubre 45 C6
Escource 36 C3
Escout 44 B1
Escragnolles 41 D5
Esnes 15 D4
Espalion 39 C4
Espaly-St-Marcel 39 A5
Esparron 48 A2
Espelette 43 B5
Espéraza 45 C6
Espezel 45 C5
Espinasses 41 C4
Espira-de-l'Agly 46 C2
Espondeilham 46 A3
Esprels 28 C3
Essay 17 D5
Essert 29 C4
Essoyes 27 B6
Estagel 46 C2
Estaing 39 B4
Estaires 14 C3
Estang 37 D5
Esternay 19 D4
Estiavreilles 33 D6
Estissac 27 A5
Estivareilles 33 B4
Estoublon 41 D4
Estrablin 34 D2
Estrées-St-Denis 18 B3
Esvres 25 C6
Étables-sur-Mer 23 A4
Étagnac 31 C6
Étain 20 C2
Étais-la-Sauvin 27 C4
Étalante 27 C6
Étampes 18 D2
Étang-sur-Arroux 27 D5
Étaples 14 C2
Étaules 30 C3
Étauliers 31 D4
Éternoz 28 D3
Étival 34 B3
Étival-Clairefontaine 21 D4
Étivey 27 C5
Étréchy 18 D2
Étrépagny 18 C1
Étretat 17 B5
Étreux 15 D4
Étupes 29 C4
Étuz 28 C2
Eu 14 D1
Eugénie-les-Bains 37 D4
Eurville-Bienville 20 D1
Euville 20 D2
Évaux-les-Bains 32 B3
Évian-les-Bains 35 B4
Evisa 49 C5
Évran 16 D2
Évrecy 17 C4
Évreux 17 C6
Évron 25 B4
Évry 18 D3
Excideuil 31 D6
Exmes 17 D5
Eyguians 40 C3
Eyguières 40 D2
Eygurande-et-Gardeuil 31 D5
Eymet 37 B5

Eymoutiers 32 C2
Eyragues 40 D2
Eyrans 31 D3
Eyrein 32 D2
Eyzin-Pinet 34 D2
Ézy-sur-Eure 18 C1

F

Fabas 45 B4
Fabrègues 44 A4
Fabrezan 46 B2
Fagnières 19 C5
Fain-lès-Montbard 27 C6
Fains-Véel 20 D1
Faissault 19 B6
Falaise 17 C4
Falleron 24 D2
Fameck 20 C3
Fanjeaux 45 B5
Faremoutiers 18 D3
Fargues-St-Hilaire 37 C4
Faucogney-et-la-Mer 28 B3
Faugères 46 A3
Fauguerolles 37 C5
Faulquemont 20 C3
Fauquembergues 14 C2
Fauville-en-Caux 17 B5
Faux 37 B6
Faux-la-Montagne 32 C2
Faverges 35 C4
Faverney 28 B3
Faverolles 39 B4
Fay-de-Bretagne 23 D5
Fayence 48 A3
Fayl-la-Forêt 28 B2
Fay-sur-Lignon 39 B6
Fécamp 17 B5
Fégréac 23 D5
Feillens 34 B2
Feissons-sur-Isère 35 D4
Félines 33 D5
Felletin 32 C3
Fénay 28 D1
Fendeille 45 B5
Fénétrange 21 C4
Feneu 25 C4
Fenioux 31 A4
Fépin 15 D6
Fère-Champenoise 19 D5
Fère-en-Tardenois 19 C4
Férel 23 D5
Ferney-Voltaire 35 B4
Ferrals-les-Corbières 46 B2
Ferrette 29 C4
Ferrières 26 B3
Fessenheim 29 B5
Festieux 19 B5
Feugarolles 37 C5
Feuquières 18 B2
Feuquières-en-Vimeu 14 D2
Feurs 33 C6
Feytiat 32 C1
Fiac 38 D2
Figanières 48 A3
Figari 49 D5
Figeac 38 B3
Fillinges 35 B4
Finhan 38 D1
Firmi 38 C3
Firminy 33 D6
Fismes 19 C5
Fitou 46 C2
Fitz-James 18 B3
Fix-St-Geneys 33 D5
Flagnac 38 B3
Flaine 35 C5
Flamanville 16 B2
Flavigny-sur-Moselle 20 D3
Flavigny-sur-Ozerain 27 C6
Flavin 38 C3
Flayosc 48 A3
Flers 17 D4
Fleurance 37 D6
Fleuré 31 B5
Fleurie 34 B1
Fleury 46 B3

Fleury-les-Aubrais 26 B2
Fleury-sur-Andelle 17 B6
Fléville-Lixières 20 C2
Flirey 20 C2
Flixecourt 14 D2
Flize 19 B6
Flogny-la-Chapelle 27 B5
Floing 19 B6
Floirac 37 B4
Florac 39 C5
Florange 20 C3
Floure 45 B6
Flumet 35 C4
Foëcy 26 D2
Foix 45 C5
Folschviller 20 C3
Fonroque 37 B5
Fonsorbes 45 A4
Fontaine 29 C4
Fontaine 34 D3
Fontainebleau 18 D3
Fontaine-Française 28 C2
Fontaine-le-Bourg 17 B6
Fontaine-le-Dun 17 A6
Fontaine-lès-Dijon 28 C1
Fontaine-lès-Luxeuil 28 B3
Fontaines 27 C4
Fontaines 27 D6
Fontan 41 D6
Fontanès 39 D6
Fontenay-le-Comte 30 B3
Fontenilles 45 A4
Fontenoy 27 C4
Fontenoy-le-Château 28 B3
Fontevraud-l'Abbaye 25 D5
Font-Romeu-Odeillo-Via 45 C6
Fontvieille 40 D1
Forbach 21 C4
Forcalquier 40 D3
Forges-les-Eaux 18 B1
Formerie 18 B2
Formiguères 45 C6
Fort-Mahon-Plage 14 C1
Fos 44 C3
Fossiat 34 B2
Fos-sur-Mer 47 A6
Foucarmont 14 D1
Fouesnant 22 C2
Foug 20 D2
Fougères 16 D3
Fougerolles 28 B3
Fougerolles-du-Plessis 16 D3
Fouilloy 14 D3
Foulain 28 B1
Foulayronnes 37 C6
Fouras 30 C3
Fourcès 37 D5
Fourchambault 27 D4
Fourmies 15 D5
Fournels 39 B4
Fourques 40 D1
Fourques 46 C2
Fours 27 D5
Fraize 29 B4
Francescas 37 D5
Francoulès 38 B2
Frangy 34 C3
Franois 28 D2
Frasne 28 D3
Frayssinet-le-Gélat 38 B1
Fréhel 16 D1
Freissinières 41 B4
Freistroff 20 C3
Fréjairolles 38 D3
Fréjus 48 B3
Frencq 14 C2
Fresnay-sur-Sarthe 25 A4
Fresnes-en-Woëvre 20 C2
Fresnes-sur-Apance 28 B2
Fresne-St-Mamès 28 C2
Fresnoy-Folny 14 D1
Fresnoy-le-Grand 15 D4
Fresse-sur-Moselle 29 B4
Fretigney-et-Velloreille 28 C2
Frévent 14 C2
Freyming-Merlebach 21 C4
Friville-Escarbotin 14 D1
Froges 34 D3

Froideconche 28 B3
Froissy 18 B2
Fromentine 24 D1
Fronsac 37 B4
Fronsac 44 C3
Frontenard 28 D1
Frontenay-Rohan-Rohan 31 B4
Frontignan 47 A4
Fronton 38 D1
Frouard 20 D3
Fruges 14 C2
Fumay 15 D6
Fumel 37 C6
Furiani 49 B6
Fussy 26 D3
Futeau 19 C6

G

Gabarret 37 D5
Gabriac 39 C4
Gacé 17 D5
Gagnières 39 C6
Gaillac 38 D2
Gaillac-d'Aveyron 39 C4
Gaillard 35 B4
Gaillon 17 C6
Galan 44 B3
Galéria 49 B5
Galgon 37 B4
Gallardon 18 D2
Gallargues-le-Montueux 39 D6
Gallian-en-Médoc 30 D3
Gamaches 14 D1
Gamarde-les-Bains 36 D3
Gambsheim 21 D5
Gan 44 B2
Ganagobie 40 D3
Ganges 39 D5
Gannat 33 B4
Gap 41 C4
Garchizy 27 D4
Gardanne 47 A6
Gardonne 37 B5
Gardouch 45 B5
Garein 37 D4
Garéoult 48 B2
Gargilesse-Dampierre 32 B2
Garlin 44 A2
Garons 39 D6
Gasny 18 C1
Gastes 36 C3
Gattières 41 D5
Gauchy 15 D4
Gavarnie 44 C2
Gavray 16 C2
Geaune 37 D4
Gèdre 44 C2
Geispolsheim 21 D5
Gelos 44 B2
Gemeaux 28 C1
Gémenos 48 B1
Gémozac 30 C3
Gençay 31 B5
Gendrey 28 D2
Génelard 33 A6
Genêts 16 D2
Génissac 37 B4
Genlis 28 D1
Gennes 25 C4
Gennes-sur-Seiche 23 C6
Génolhac 39 C6
Genouillac 32 B3
Genouillé 31 B5
Genouilly 26 D2
Genouilly 34 A1
Gensac 37 B5
Gentioux-Pigerolles 32 C3
Ger 16 D3
Ger 44 B2
Gérardmer 29 B4
Géraudot 27 A6
Germay 20 D2
Gerzat 33 C4
Gespunsart 15 D6
Gesté 23 D6
Gétigné 24 D3

Gévezé 23 B5
Gevrey-Chambertin 28 D1
Gex 35 B4
Ghisonaccia 49 C6
Ghisoni 49 C6
Ghyvelde 14 B3
Giat 32 C3
Gien 26 C3
Gièvres 26 C2
Gigean 47 A4
Gignac 39 D5
Gignac 40 D3
Gilette 41 D5
Gilly-sur-Isère 35 C4
Gilly-sur-Loire 33 A5
Gimont 37 D6
Gimouille 27 D4
Ginasservis 48 A2
Ginestas 46 B2
Ginoles 45 C6
Girancourt 28 B3
Giromagny 29 B4
Gironde-sur-Dropt 37 B5
Giroussens 38 D2
Gisors 18 C2
Givet 15 D6
Givors 34 C2
Givry 27 D6
Givry-en-Argonne 19 C6
Gizeux 25 C5
Glainans 28 C3
Glandage 40 B3
Glandon 31 D6
Gleizé 34 C1
Glère 29 C4
Glos-la-Ferrière 17 C5
Goderville 17 B5
Golbey 28 B3
Golinhac 38 B3
Goncelin 34 D3
Gondrecourt-le-Château 20 D2
Gondreville 20 D2
Gondrin 37 D5
Gonfaron 48 B3
Gonfreville-l'Orcher 17 B5
Gonsans 28 D3
Gordes 40 D2
Gorron 16 D3
Gorze 20 C3
Gosné 23 B6
Gouarec 22 B3
Gouesnou 22 B1
Gouhenans 28 C3
Goult 40 D2
Goumois 29 C4
Gourdan-Polignan 44 B3
Gourdon 38 B1
Gourette 44 C2
Gourgançon 19 D5
Gourin 22 B3
Gournay-en-Bray 18 B2
Goussainville 18 C3
Gout-Rossignol 31 D5
Gouvieux 18 C3
Gouzon 32 B3
Goven 23 C5
Graçay 26 D2
Grâces 22 B3
Graissac 39 B4
Graissessac 39 D4
Gramat 38 B2
Grancey-le-Château-Nouvelle 28 C1
Grandcamp-Maisy 16 B3
Grand-Champ 23 C4
Grand-Couronne 17 B6
Grande-Synthe 14 B2
Grande-Vabre 38 B3
Grand-Fort-Philippe 14 B2
Grand-Fougeray 23 C5
Grandpré 19 B6
Grandpuits-Bailly-Carrois 18 D3
Grandrieu 39 B5
Grandris 33 B6
Grandvelle-et-le-Perrenot 28 C2
Grandvillars 29 C4
Grandvillers 28 A3
Grandvilliers 18 B2
Granges-sur-Vologne 29 B4

Granville 16 C2
Grasse 49 A4
Gratens 45 B4
Graulhet 38 D2
Gravelines 14 B2
Gravelotte 20 C3
Gravigny 17 C6
Gray 28 C2
Grayan-et-l'Hôpital 30 D3
Gréalou 38 C2
Grenade 38 D1
Grenade-sur-l'Adour 37 D4
Grenant 28 C2
Grenoble 40 A3
Gréoux-les-Bains 40 D3
Grésy-sur-Aix 34 C3
Grésy-sur-Isère 35 C4
Greux 20 D2
Grez-en-Bouère 25 B4
Gries 21 D5
Grignan 40 C2
Grignols 37 C5
Grigny 34 C2
Grillon 40 C2
Grimaud 48 B3
Grisolles 38 D1
Groix 22 C3
Grosseto-Prugna 49 C5
Grostenquin 21 C4
Gruey-lès-Surance 28 B3
Gruissan 46 B3
Grury 33 A6
Gudmont-Villiers 28 A1
Guebwiller 29 B4
Guégon 23 C4
Guémar 29 B5
Guémené-Penfao 23 C5
Guémené-sur-Scorff 22 C3
Guénange 20 C3
Guenrouet 23 D5
Guer 23 C5
Guérande 23 D4
Guéret 32 B2
Guérigny 27 D4
Guéthary 33 A6
Guichen 23 C5
Guidel 22 C3
Guignen 23 C5
Guignes 18 D3
Guignicourt 19 B5
Guilers 22 B1
Guilherand 40 B2
Guillaumes 41 D5
Guillestre 41 B4
Guilliers 23 C4
Guillon 27 C5
Guillos 37 B4
Guilvinec 22 C2
Guînes 14 B2
Guingamp 22 B3
Guipavas 22 B1
Guipry 23 C5
Guiscard 19 B4
Guise 15 D4
Guissény 22 A1
Guîtres 37 A4
Gujan-Mestras 36 B3
Gundershoffen 21 C5
Gy 28 C2
Gyé-sur-Seine 27 B6

H

Habas 43 A6
Habsheim 29 C5
Hadol 28 B3
Hagetaubin 43 A6
Hagetmau 37 D4
Hagondange 20 C3
Haguenau 21 D5
Hallencourt 14 D2
Halstroff 20 B3
Ham 19 B4
Hambach 21 C4
Hambye 16 C3
Hampont 20 D3
Han-sur-Nied 20 C3

Hanvec 22 B2
Hardelot-Plage 14 C1
Harfleur 17 B5
Hargnies 15 D6
Harly 15 D4
Harnes 14 C3
Haroué 20 D3
Hasparren 43 B5
Haubourdin 14 C3
Haute-Amance 28 B2
Hautefort 31 D6
Hauterives 34 D2
Hauteville-Lompnes 34 C3
Hautmont 15 C5
Haux 43 B6
Hayange 20 B3
Hazebrouck 14 C3
Hèches 44 B3
Hédé 23 B5
Heiltz-le-Maurupt 19 D6
Hénanbihen 16 D1
Hendaye 43 B5
Hénin-Beaumont 14 C3
Hennebont 22 C3
Hennezel 28 B3
Henrichemont 26 C3
Herbault 25 C6
Herbignac 23 D5
Hérépian 46 A3
Héric 23 D6
Héricourt 29 C4
Hérimoncourt 29 C4
Hérisson 33 B4
Herm 36 D3
Herment 32 C3
Hérouville-St-Clair 17 C4
Herré 37 D5
Herry 26 D3
Hesdin 14 C2
Heuchin 14 C2
Heudicourt-sous-les-Côtes 20 C2
Heyrieux 34 C2
Hiersac 31 C5
Hinx 36 D3
Hirsingue 29 C4
Hirson 15 D5
Hochfelden 21 D5
Homécourt 20 C2
Hondschoote 14 B3
Honfleur 17 B5
Hornoy-le-Bourg 14 D2
Hostens 37 C4
Houdain 14 C3
Houdan 18 D1
Houdelaincourt 20 D2
Houécourt 28 A2
Houeillès 37 C5
Houeydets 44 B3
Houlgate 17 C4
Hourtin 30 D3
Hourtin-Plage 30 D3
Hucqueliers 14 C2
Huelgoat 22 B2
Hunspach 21 C5
Huriel 32 B3
Hyères 48 B2
Hymont 28 A3

I

Ibos 44 B2
Idron-Ousse-Sendets 44 B2
Iffendic 23 B5
Ifs 17 C4
Igé 25 A5
Igney 28 A3
Igornay 27 D6
Iguerande 33 B6
Iholdy 43 B5
Illats 37 B4
Ille-sur-Têt 45 C6
Illiers-Combray 25 A6
Illkirch-Graffenstaden 21 D5
Illzach 29 B4
Imphy 27 D4
Incheville 14 D1
Ingersheim 29 B4

Ingrandes 24 C3
Ingrandes 25 D5
Inguiniel 22 C3
Ingwiller 21 C5
Insming 21 C4
Inzinzac-Lochrist 22 C3
Irancy 27 C5
Irissarry 43 B5
Irodouër 23 B5
Isbergues 14 C3
Isches 28 B2
Isdes 26 C2
Is-en-Bassigny 28 B2
Isigny-sur-Mer 16 B3
Isle 31 C6
Isles-sur-Suippe 19 B5
Isola 41 C5
Isola 2000 41 C5
Ispagnac 39 C5
Ispoure 43 B5
Issigeac 37 B6
Issoire 33 D4
Issoudun 26 D2
Is-sur-Tille 28 C1
Issy-l'Évêque 33 A6
Istres 47 A6
Iteuil 31 B5
Ivry-la-Bataille 18 C1
Ivry-sur-Seine 18 D3
Izeaux 34 D3
Izernore 34 B3
Izeron 34 D2

J

Jaligny-sur-Besbre 33 B5
Jallais 24 D3
Jametz 20 B2
Janville 26 B2
Janzé 23 C6
Jard-sur-Mer 30 B2
Jargeau 26 B2
Jarménil 28 B3
Jarnac 31 C4
Jarnages 32 B3
Jarny 20 C2
Jarville-la-Malgrange 20 D3
Jarzé 25 C4
Jassans-Riottier 34 C2
Jasseron 34 B2
Jaunay-Clan 31 A5
Jausiers 41 C5
Javerlhac-et-la-Chapelle-St-Robert 31 C5
Javron-les-Chapelles 17 D4
Jazeneuil 31 B5
Jegun 37 D5
Jeumont 15 C5
Job 33 C5
Jœuf 20 C3
Joigny 27 B4
Joinville 20 D1
Joncy 34 A1
Jonquières 40 D2
Jonzac 31 D4
Josnes 26 B1
Josselin 23 C4
Jouarre 19 C4
Joué-lès-Tours 25 C5
Joué-sur-Erdre 23 D6
Jougne 35 A4
Jouques 48 A1
Journiac 37 B6
Joux-la-Ville 27 C5
Jouy 18 D1
Jouy-aux-Arches 20 C3
Jouy-le-Potier 26 B2
Joyeuse 39 C6
Joze 33 C5
Juan-les-Pins 49 A4
Jublains 25 A4
Jugon-les-Lacs 16 D1
Juillac 32 D1
Juillan 44 B2
Jujurieux 34 C3
Juliénas 34 B1
Jullouville 16 D2
Jumeaux 33 D5

Jumilhac-le-Grand 31 D6
Juniville 19 B6
Jupilles 25 B5
Jurançon 44 B1
Jurignac 31 D4
Jussac 38 B3
Jussey 28 B2
Juvigné 23 B6
Juvigny-le-Tertre 16 D3
Juvigny-sous-Andaine 17 D4
Juzennecourt 27 B6
Juzet-d'Izaut 44 C3

K

Kaysersberg 29 B4
Kerlouan 22 A2
Kernascléden 22 C3

L

La Baconnière 24 B3
La Balme-de-Sillingy 35 C4
La Barre-de-Monts 24 D1
La Barre-en-Ouche 17 C5
La Barthe-de-Neste 44 B3
Labarthe-Rivière 44 B3
La Bassée 14 C3
La Bastide-Clairence 43 B5
Labastide-d'Anjou 45 B5
Labastide-d'Armagnac 37 D4
La Bastide-de Bousignac 45 B5
La Bastide-de-Sérou 45 B5
La Bastide-l'Évêque 38 C3
Labastide-Murat 38 B2
La Bastide-Puylaurent 39 B6
Labastide-Rouairoux 45 A6
Labastide-St-Pierre 38 D1
La Bastide-sur-l'Hers 45 C5
La Bâthie 35 C4
La Bâtie-Neuve 41 C4
Labatut-Rivière 44 A2
La Baule-Escoublac 23 D4
La Bazoche-Gouet 25 B6
La Bazoge 25 B5
Labégude 39 B6
La Bégude-de-Mazenc 40 C2
Labenne 43 A5
La Bérarde 41 B4
Labergement-lès-Seurre 28 D1
La Bernerie-en-Retz 24 D1
Lablachère 39 C6
La Bonneville-sur-Iton 17 C6
La Bouëxière 23 B6
Labouheyre 36 C3
La Bouilladisse 48 B1
La Bourboule 33 C4
Laboutarie 38 D3
La Brède 37 B4
La Bréole 41 C4
La Bresse 29 B4
La Brillanne 40 D3
Labrit 37 C4
La Broque 21 D4
La Bruffière 24 D3
Labruguière 45 A6
L'Absie 31 A4
La Buisse 34 D3
La Bussière 26 B3
La Caillère-St-Hilaire 30 A3
Lacalm 39 B4
La Calmette 39 D6
Lacanau 36 B3
Lacanau-Océan 36 B3
Lacanche 27 D6
La Canourgue 39 C4
La Capelle 15 D5
Lacapelle-Barrès 39 B4
Lacapelle-Marival 38 B2
Lacaune 39 D4
La Cavalerie 39 D4
Lacave 38 B2
La Celle-St-Avant 25 D5
La Chaise-Dieu 33 D5
La Chaize-le-Vicomte 30 A2
La Chambre 35 D4

La Chapelaude 32 B3
La Chapelle 19 B6
La Chapelle-aux-Bois 28 B3
La Chapelle-aux-Saints 38 B2
La Chapelle-d'Abondance 35 B5
La Chapelle-d'Aligné 25 B4
La Chapelle-d'Angillon 26 C3
La Chapelle-de-Guinchay 34 B2
La Chapelle-des-Fougeretz 23 B5
La Chapelle-en-Valgaudémar 41 B4
La Chapelle-en-Vercors 40 B3
La Chapelle-la-Reine 26 A3
La Chapelle-Laurent 33 D4
Lachapelle-sous-Aubenas 39 B6
La Chapelle-St-André 27 C4
La Chapelle-St-Laurent 31 A4
La Chapelle-St-Luc 27 A5
La Chapelle-St-Quillain 28 C2
La Chapelle-St-Ursin 26 D2
La Chapelle-sur-Erdre 23 D6
La Charité-sur-Loire 27 D4
La Chartre-sur-le-Loir 25 B5
La Châtaigneraie 30 A3
La Châtre 32 A3
La Châtre-Langlin 32 B2
La Chaume 27 B6
La Chaussée-St-Victor 26 C1
La Chaussée-sur-Marne 19 D6
La Chaux-du-Dombief 34 A3
La Cheppe 19 C6
La Chèze 23 B4
La Ciotat 48 B1
La Clayette 33 B6
La Clusaz 35 C4
La Cluse 40 B3
La Cluse-et-Mijoux 28 D3
La Condamine-Châtelard 41 C5
La Coquille 31 C6
La Côte-St-André 34 D2
La-Couarde-sur-Mer 30 B2
La Couronne 31 C5
Lacourt 45 C4
La Courtine 32 C3
La Couture-Boussey 18 C1
Lacq 43 B6
La Crau 48 B2
La Crèche 31 B4
Lacroix-Barrez 39 B4
La Croixille 23 B6
La Croix-Valmer 48 B3
Lacrouzette 38 D3
Ladignac-le-Long 31 C6
Ladinhac 38 B3
Ladon 26 B3
La Fare-les-Oliviers 47 A6
La Farlède 48 B2
La Faurie 40 C3
La Faute-sur-Mer 30 B2
La Fère 19 B4
La Ferrière 30 A2
La Ferrière-aux-Étangs 17 D4
La Ferté-Alais 18 D3
La Ferté-Bernard 25 B5
La Ferté-Frênel 17 C5
La Ferté-Gaucher 19 D4
La Ferté-Imbault 26 C2
La Ferté-Loupière 27 B4
La Ferté-Macé 17 D4
La-Ferté-Milon 19 C4
La Ferté-sous-Jouarre 19 C4
La Ferté-St-Aubin 26 C2
La Ferté-St-Cyr 26 C2
Laferté-sur-Amance 28 B2
Laferté-sur-Aube 27 B6
La Férté-Vidame 17 D6
La Ferté-Villeneuil 25 B6
Lafitole 44 B2
La Flèche 25 C4
La Fontaine-St-Martin 25 B5
La Force 37 B5
La Forêt-sur-Sèvre 24 D3
La Forge 29 B4
La Fouillade 38 C3
La Foux-d'Allos 41 C4
Lafrançaise 38 C1
Lafrimbolle 21 D4
La Gacilly 23 C5
La Garde 48 B2

La Garde-Adhémar **40** C1
La Garde-Freinet **48** B3
Lagardelle-sur-Lèze **45** B4
La Garnache **24** D2
Lagarrigue **45** A6
La Gaubretière **24** D3
La Glacerie **16** B2
Lagnieu **34** C2
Lagny-sur-Marne **18** C3
Lagor **43** B6
Lagorce **31** D4
Lagord **30** B3
La Grand-Croix **34** D1
La Grande-Combe **39** C6
La Grande-Motte **47** A4
Lagrasse **45** B6
La Grave **41** B4
Laguenne **32** D2
Laguépie **38** C2
La Guerche-de-Bretagne **23** C6
La Guerche-sur-l'Aubois **26** D3
Laguiole **39** B4
La Haye-du-Puits **16** C2
La Haye-Pesnel **16** D2
Laheycourt **19** C6
L'Aigle **17** D5
Laignes **27** B6
L'Aiguillon-sur-Mer **30** B2
Lailly-en-Val **26** B2
Laimont **20** D1
Laissac **39** C4
La Jarrie **30** B3
La Javie **41** C4
La Jonchère-St-Maurice **32** C2
La Jumellière **24** C3
Lalbenque **38** C2
Lalevade-d'Ardèche **39** B6
Lalinde **37** B6
Lallaing **15** C4
Lalley **40** B3
La Londe-les-Maures **48** B2
Laloubère **44** B2
La Loupe **17** D6
Lalouvesc **34** D1
La Loye **28** D2
L'Alpe-d'Huez **41** B4
Laluque **36** D3
La Machine **27** D4
Lamagistère **37** C6
La Malène **39** C5
Lamalou-les-Bains **46** A3
Lamanon **40** D2
La Marche **27** D4
Lamarche **28** B2
Lamarche-sur-Saône **28** C2
Lamargelle **27** C6
Lamarque **30** D3
La Massana *AND* **45** C5
Lamastre **40** B1
Lamballe **16** D1
Lambesc **47** A6
La Meilleraye-de-Bretagne **23** D6
La Milesse **25** B5
La Môle **48** B3
La Mongie **44** C2
La Monnerie-le-Montel **33** C5
Lamothe **33** D5
La Mothe-Achard **30** A2
Lamothe-Cassel **38** B2
La Mothe-St-Héray **31** B4
Lamotte-Beuvron **26** C2
La Motte-Chalancon **40** C2
La Motte-du-Caire **40** C3
Lampaul-Guimiliau **22** B2
Lampaul-Plouarzel **22** B1
La Mure **40** B3
Lamure-sur-Azergues **33** B6
Lanarce **39** B6
Landeleau **22** B2
Landerneau **22** B2
Landersheim **21** D5
Landévant **22** C3
Landiras **37** B4
Landivisiau **22** B2
Landivy **16** D3
Landos **39** B5
Landrecies **15** D5

Landres **20** C2
Landudec **22** C2
Lanester **22** C3
La Neuve-Lyre **17** C6
La Neuville-au-Pont **19** C6
Laneuville-sur-Meuse **20** B1
Langeac **33** D5
Langeais **25** C5
Langogne **39** B5
Langoiran **37** B4
Langon **37** C4
Langres **28** B1
Langueux **23** B4
Languidic **22** C3
Lanloup **23** A4
Lanmeur **22** A2
Lannemezan **44** B3
Lannepax **37** D5
Lannilis **22** B1
Lannion **22** A3
Lannoy **15** C4
Lanobre **32** D3
La Nocle-Maulaix **27** D5
Lanouaille **31** D6
Lansargues **39** D6
Lanslebourg-Mont-Cenis **35** D5
Lanta **45** A5
Lanton **36** B3
Lantosque **41** D6
Lantriac **39** B6
Lanty **27** D5
Lanuéjouls **38** C3
Lanvollon **23** A4
Laon **19** B4
Laons **17** D6
La Pacaudière **33** B5
Lapalisse **33** B5
La Pallice **30** B3
La Palme **46** B2
Lapalud **40** C1
La Palud-sur-Verdon **41** D4
La Pellerine **23** B6
La Penne **41** D5
La Petite-Pierre **21** C4
La Plagne **35** D5
Laplume **37** C6
La Pommeraye **24** C3
La Porta **49** B6
La Pouëze **24** C3
Lapoutroie **29** B4
La Preste **45** D6
Laragne-Montéglin **40** C3
La Ravoire **34** D3
L'Arbresle **34** C1
Larceveau-Arros-Cibits **43** B6
Larchamp **16** D3
Larchant **26** A3
Larche **32** D2
Larche **41** C5
La Redorte **45** B6
La Réole **37** B5
L'Argentière-la-Bessée **41** B4
La Ricamarie **33** D6
La Riche **25** C5
Larmor-Plage **22** C3
La Roche-Bernard **23** D5
La Roche-Canillac **32** D2
La Roche-Chalais **31** D5
La Roche-de-Rame **41** B4
La Roche-Derrien **22** A3
La Roche-des-Arnauds **40** C3
La Rochefoucauld **31** C5
La Rochelle **30** B3
Larochemillay **27** D5
La Roche-Posay **25** D6
La Rochepot **27** D6
La Roche-sur-Foron **35** B4
La Roche-sur-Yon **30** A2
La Rochette **35** D4
La Roë **23** C6
La Romieu **37** D6
Laroquebrou **38** B3
Laroque-d'Olmes **45** B5
La Roque-Ste-Marguerite **39** C4
Laroque-Timbaut **37** C6
La Rouquette **38** C2
Larrau **43** B6
Larrazet **37** D6

Larressore **43** B5
Laruns **44** B1
Laruscade **31** D4
Lasalle **39** D5
La Salle les Alpes **41** B4
La Salvetat-Peyralès **38** C3
La Salvetat-sur-Agout **46** A2
La Sauvetat-du-Dropt **37** B5
La Séguinière **24** D3
La Selve **38** C3
La Seyne-sur-Mer **48** B2
La Souterraine **32** B2
Lassay-les-Châteaux **17** D4
Lasseube **44** B1
Lassigny **18** B3
Lastours **45** B6
La Suze-sur-Sarthe **25** B5
La Teste-de-Buch **36** B3
Lathus **31** B6
Latillé **31** A5
La Tour-Blanche **31** D5
La Tour-d'Auvergne **33** D4
Latour-de-France **46** C2
La Tour-du-Crieu **45** B5
La Tour-du-Pin **34** D3
La Tour-sur-Orb **39** D4
La Tranche-sur-Mer **30** B2
La Tremblade **30** C3
La Trimouille **31** B6
La Trinité **41** D6
La Trinité-Porhoët **23** C4
La Trinité-sur-Mer **23** D4
Latronquière **38** B3
Lattes **47** A4
La Turballe **23** D4
Laudun **40** D1
Laugnac **37** C6
Launac **38** D1
Lauraguel **45** B6
Laurens **46** A3
Laurière **32** B2
Lauris **40** D2
Laussonne **39** B6
Laussou **37** B6
Lauterbourg **21** C6
Lautrec **38** D3
Lauzerte **38** C1
Lauzès **38** B2
Lauzun **37** B5
Laval **24** B3
Lavalette **45** B6
La Valette-du-Var **48** B2
Lavardac **37** C5
Lavaur **38** D2
Lavaveix-les-Mines **32** B3
Lavelanet **45** C5
La Verdière **48** A2
La Vernarède **39** C6
La Verpillière **34** C2
La Verrie **24** D3
La Veuve **19** C5
La Ville-aux-Clercs **25** B6
La Villedieu **39** B5
La Villedieu-du-Clain **31** B5
La Villedieu-en-Fontenette **28** B3
Laviron **28** D3
Lavit **37** D6
La Voulte-sur-Rhône **40** B1
Lavoûte-Chilhac **33** D5
Lavoûte-sur-Loire **33** D6
Laxou **20** D3
Layrac **37** C6
Le Barp **36** B3
Le Bar-sur-Loup **41** D5
Le Béage **39** B6
Le Beausset **48** B2
Le Bez **38** D3
Lebiez **14** C2
Le Biot **35** B4
Le Blanc **31** A6
Le Bleymard **39** C5
Le Bois-d'Oingt **34** C1
Le Bois-Plage-en-Ré **30** B2
Le Boréon **41** D5
Le Boulou **46** C2
Le Boupère **24** D3
Le Bourg **38** B2
Le Bourg-d'Oisans **41** B4

Le Bourget-du-Lac **34** C3
Le Bousquet-d'Orb **39** D4
Le Breuil **19** C4
Le Breuil **27** D6
Le Brouilh-Monbert **37** D5
Le Brusquet **41** C4
Le Bugue **37** B6
Le Buisson **39** B4
Le Buisson-de-Cadouin **37** B6
Le Cannet **49** A4
Le Cannet-des-Maures **48** B3
Le Castellet **48** B2
Le Cateau-Cambrésis **15** D4
Le Catelet **15** D4
Le Caylar **39** D5
Le Cayrol **39** B4
Le Chambon-Feugerolles **33** D6
Le Chambon-sur-Lignon **39** A6
Le Château-d'Oléron **30** C3
Le Châtelard **35** C4
Le Châtelet **32** A3
Le Chêne **19** D5
Le Chesne **19** B6
Le Cheylard **39** B6
Le Cheylas **34** D3
Le Clapier **39** D4
Le Collet-de-Dèze **39** C6
Le Conquet **22** B1
Le Coteau **33** C6
Le Coudray-St-Germer **18** B2
Lécousse **16** D3
Le Crès **39** D6
Le Creusot **27** D6
Le Croisic **23** D4
Le Crotoy **14** D2
Lectoure **37** D6
Lédergues **38** C3
Lédignan **39** D6
Le Donjon **33** B5
Le Dorat **31** B6
Le Faou **22** B2
Le Faouët **22** C3
Le Fenouiller **30** A2
Le Fleix **37** B5
Le Folgoët **22** B2
Le Fossat **45** B4
Le Fousseret **45** B4
Le Fugeret **41** D4
Le Fuilet **23** D6
Le Gault-Soigny **19** D4
Le Gault-St-Denis **26** A1
Legé **24** D2
Lège-Cap-Ferret **36** B3
Le Genest-St-Isle **24** B3
Le Gond-Pontouvre **31** C5
Le Grand-Bornand **35** C4
Le Grand-Bourg **32** B2
Le Grand-Lemps **34** D3
Le Grand-Lucé **25** B5
Le Grand-Pressigny **25** D6
Le Grand-Quevilly **17** B6
Le Grand-Serre **34** D2
Le Grau-du-Roi **47** A4
Le Gros Theil **17** C6
Le Gua **40** B3
Le Havre **17** B5
Le Hohwald **21** D4
Léhon **16** D1
Le Horps **17** D4
Le Houga **37** D4
Le Langon **30** B3
Le Lardin-St-Lazare **31** D6
Le Lauzet-Ubaye **41** C4
Le Lavandou **48** B3
Le Leuy **37** D4
Le Lion-d'Angers **24** C3
Le Louroux-Béconnais **24** C3
Le Luc **48** B3
Le Lude **25** C5
Le Malzieu-Ville **39** B5
Le Mans **25** B5
Le Markstein **29** B4
Le Martinet **39** C6
Le Mas-d'Agenais **37** C5
Le Mas-d'Azil **45** B4
Le Masnau-Massuguiès **38** D3
Le Massegros **39** C4
Le Mayet-de-Montagne **33** B5

Le May-sur-Èvre 24 D3
Lemberg 21 C5
Lembeye 44 B2
Lembras 37 B6
Le Mêle-sur-Sarthe 17 D5
Le Merlerault 17 D5
Le Mesnil-sur-Oger 19 C5
Le Molay-Littry 16 C3
Le Monastier 39 C4
Le Monastier-sur-Gazeille 39 B6
Le Monêtier-les-Bains 41 B4
Le Montet 33 B4
Lempdes 33 C4
Lempdes 33 D5
Le Muy 48 A3
Lencloître 25 D5
Lencouacq 37 C4
Le Neubourg 17 C6
Léning 21 C4
Le Nizan 37 C4
Le Nouvion-en-Thiérache 15 D5
Lens 14 C3
Lent 34 B2
Léognan 37 B4
Léon 36 D3
Léoncel 40 B2
Le Palais 22 D3
Le Palais-sur-Vienne 32 C1
Le Pallet 24 D2
Le Parcq 14 C2
Le Passage 37 C6
Le Pavillon-Ste-Julie 19 D5
Le Péage-de-Roussillon 34 D2
Le Pellerin 23 D5
Le Périer 40 B3
Le Perthus 46 D2
Le Pertre 23 C6
Le Petit-Quevilly 17 B6
Le Pian-Médoc 37 B4
Le Pin-au-Haras 17 D5
L'Épine 40 C3
Le Pin-la-Garenne 17 D5
Le Pizou 37 A5
Le Plan 45 B4
Le Plessis-Belleville 18 C3
Le Poët 40 C3
Le Poinçonnet 32 A2
Le Poiré-sur-Vie 24 D2
Le Pont-de-Beauvoisin 34 D3
Le Pont-de-Claix 34 D3
Le Pont-de-Monvert 39 C5
Le Pontet 40 D2
Le Porge 36 B3
Le Porge-Océan 36 B3
Le Portel 14 C1
Le Pouldu 22 C3
Le Pouliguen 23 D4
Le Pouzin 40 B1
Le Puy-en-Velay 39 A5
Le Puy-Notre-Dame 25 D4
Le Quesnoy 15 D4
Le Raincy 18 C3
Léran 45 B5
Léré 26 C3
Le Relecq-Kerhuon 22 B1
Lerm-et Musset 37 C4
Le Rouget 38 B3
Lérouville 20 D2
Le Rozier 39 C4
Le Russey 29 D4
Les Abrets 34 D3
Les Aix-d'Angillon 26 D3
Les Andelys 18 C1
Les Angles 40 D1
Les Angles 45 C6
Les Arcs 35 D5
Les Arcs 48 A3
Les Aubiers 25 D4
Les Avenières 34 C3
Les Bondons 39 C5
Les Bordes 26 B3
Les Bouchoux 34 B3
Les Cabannes 45 C5
L'Escale 40 D3
Les Cammazes 45 B6
Lescar 44 B1
L'Escarène 41 D6
Lesconil 22 C2

Les Contamines-Montjoie 35 C5
Lescun 43 C6
Lescure-d'Albigeois 38 D3
Les Deux-Alpes 41 B4
Les Échelles 34 D3
Les Églisottes-et-Chalaures 31 D4
Le Sel-de-Bretagne 23 C6
Le Sen 37 C4
Les Éparges 20 C2
Les Epesses 24 D3
Les Escaldes AND 45 C5
Les Essards-Taignevaux 28 D2
Les Essarts 24 D3
Les Eyzies-de-Tayac-Sireuil 37 B6
Les Fins 28 D3
Les Forges 28 B3
Les Fourgs 28 D3
Les Gets 35 B4
Les Herbiers 24 D3
Les Houches 35 C5
Les Issambres 48 B3
Les Landes-Genusson 24 D3
Les Lucs-sur-Boulogne 24 D2
Les Maillys 28 D1
Les Marches 34 D3
Les Martres-de-Veyre 33 C4
Les Matelles 39 D5
Les Mées 40 D3
Les Menuires 35 D4
Lesmont 19 D6
Les Mureaux 18 C2
Lesneven 22 B2
Les Ollières-sur-Eyrieux 40 B1
Lesparre-Médoc 30 D3
Les Peintures 31 D4
Les Pennes-Mirabeau 47 B6
Lesperon 36 D3
Les Pieux 16 B2
Lespignan 46 B3
Lespinassière 45 B6
Les Planches-en-Montagne 34 A3
Les Ponts-de-Cé 25 C4
Lespugue 44 B3
Les Rosiers-sur-Loire 25 C4
Les Rousses 35 B4
Les Sables-d'Olonne 30 B2
Les Salles-du-Gardon 39 C6
Lessay 24 C2
Les Sièges 27 B4
Les Sorinières 23 D6
Les Ternes 39 B4
Les Thuiles 41 C4
Lestrade 39 D4
Les Trois-Moutiers 25 D5
Les Vans 39 C6
Les Vignes 39 C4
Le Teich 36 B3
Le Teil 40 C1
Le Teilleul 16 D3
Le Temple 36 B3
Le Theil 25 A5
Le-Theil-de-Bretagne 23 C6
Le Thillot 29 B4
Le Tholy 29 B4
Le Thor 40 D2
Le Touquet-Paris-Plage 14 C2
Le Touvet 34 D3
L'Étrat 33 D6
Le Trayas 49 A4
Le Tréport 14 D1
Le Tuzan 37 C4
Leuc 45 B6
Leucate 46 C2
Leuglay 27 B6
Le Val 48 B2
Le Vallinot-Longeau-Percey 28 B1
Levens 41 D5
Le-Verdon-sur-Mer 30 C3
Le Vernet 45 B5
Lèves 18 D1
Levet 26 D3
Levie 49 D5
Levier 28 D3
Le Vigan 39 D5
Lévignac 38 D1
Lévignacq 36 D3
Le-Vivier-sur-Mer 16 D2
Levroux 26 D1

Leyme 38 B2
Lézan 39 D6
Lézat-sur-Lèze 45 B4
Lezay 31 B4
Lézignan-Corbières 46 B2
Lezoux 33 C5
Lherm 45 B4
L'Hermenault 30 A3
L'Honor-de-Cos 38 C1
L'Horme 34 D1
L'Hospitalet 38 C2
L'Hospitalet-du-Larzac 39 D4
L'Hospitalet-près-l'Andorre 45 C5
L'Huisserie 24 B3
Lhuître 19 D5
Liancourt 18 B3
Liart 15 D5
Libourne 37 B4
Licques 14 B2
Liernais 27 C5
Liffol-le-Grand 28 A2
Liffré 23 C6
Ligardes 37 D5
Lignan-sur-Orb 46 B3
Ligné 23 D6
Lignières 32 A3
Ligny-en-Barrois 20 D1
Ligny-le-Châtel 27 B5
Ligueil 25 D6
Ligugé 31 A5
L'Île-Bouchard 25 D5
L'Île-Rousse 49 B5
Lille 15 C4
Lillebonne 17 B5
Lillers 14 C3
Limay 18 C2
Limoges 32 C1
Limogne-en-Quercy 38 C2
Limonest 34 C2
Limoux 45 B6
Linards 32 C2
Lingolsheim 21 D5
Linguizzetta 49 C6
Linxe 36 D3
Lion-sur-Mer 17 B4
Liorac-sur-Louyre 37 B6
Liposthey 36 C3
Liré 23 D6
Lisieux 17 C5
Lisle 31 D5
L'Isle-Adam 18 C2
L'Isle-de-Noé 44 A3
L'Isle-d'Espagnac 31 C5
L'Isle-en-Dodon 45 B4
L'Isle-Jourdain 31 B6
L'Isle-Jourdain 37 D6
L'Isle-sur-la-Sorgue 40 D2
L'Isle-sur-le-Doubs 28 C3
L'Isle-sur-Serein 27 C5
Lisle-sur-Tarn 38 D2
Listrac-Médoc 30 D3
Lit-et-Mixe 36 D3
Livarot 17 C5
Livernon 38 B2
Livron-sur-Drôme 40 B2
Lizy-sur-Ourcq 19 C4
Loches 25 D6
Locmaria-Plouzané 22 B1
Locmariaquer 23 D4
Locminé 23 C4
Locquirec 22 C2
Locronan 22 C2
Loctudy 22 C2
Lodève 39 D5
Logron 25 B6
Lohéac 23 C5
Loigny-la-Bataille 26 B2
Loiré 24 C3
Loiron 24 B3
Loisy-sur-Marne 19 D6
Lombez 45 A4
Lomme 14 C3
Londinières 14 D1
Long 14 D2
Longages 45 B4
Longchaumois 34 B3
Longecourt-en-Plaine 28 D1
Longeville-en-Barrois 20 D1

Leyme 38 B2
Longeville-sur-Mer 30 B2
Longny-au-Perche 17 D6
Longré 31 C4
Longueau 14 D3
Longué-Jumelles 25 C4
Longuenesse 14 B2
Longueville 19 D4
Longueville-sur-Scie 14 D1
Longuyon 20 B2
Longwy 20 B2
Lonlay-l'Abbaye 16 D3
Lons 44 B1
Lons-le-Saunier 34 A3
Lopigna 49 C5
Lorgues 48 A3
Lorient 22 C3
Lorignac 30 D3
Loriol-sur-Drôme 40 B2
Lormes 27 C5
Lorrez-le-Bocage-Préaux 26 A3
Lorris 26 B3
Losse 37 C5
Louannec 22 A3
Loudéac 23 B4
Loudes 39 A5
Loudun 25 D5
Loué 25 B4
Lougratte 37 B6
Louhans 34 A2
Loulans 28 C3
Loulay 31 B4
Loupiac 37 B4
Lourdes 44 B2
Lourdoueix-St-Pierre 32 B2
Lourmarin 40 D2
Loury 26 B2
Louverné 24 B3
Louvie-Juzon 44 B1
Louviers 17 C6
Louvigné-du-Désert 16 D3
Louvroil 15 C5
Louze 19 D6
Loyettes 34 C2
Lubersac 32 D2
Luc 38 C3
Luc 39 B5
Luçay-le-Mâle 26 D1
Lucé 18 D1
Lucenay-lès-Aix 33 A5
Lucenay-l'Évêque 27 D5
Luc-en-Diois 40 C3
Lucéram 41 D6
Lucey 20 D2
Luché-Pringé 25 C5
Lucheux 14 D3
Luchy 18 B2
Luçon 30 B3
Lucq-de-Béarn 43 B6
Luc-sur-Mer 17 B4
Lucy-le-Bois 27 C5
Lüe 36 C3
Luglon 37 D4
Lugny-lès-Charolles 33 B6
Lugo-di-Nazza 49 C6
Lugos 36 C3
Lugrin 35 B5
Luisant 18 D1
Lumbres 14 C2
Lumio 49 B5
Lunas 39 D4
Lunel 39 D6
Lunery 26 D2
Lunéville 20 D3
L'Union 38 D2
Lupiac 37 D5
Luppy 20 C3
Lurbe-St-Christau 43 B6
Lurcy-Lévis 33 A4
Lure 28 C3
Luri 49 A6
Lurs 40 D3
Lury-sur-Arnon 26 D2
Lusignan 31 B5
Lusigny-sur-Barse 27 A5
Lus-la-Croix-Haute 40 B3
Lussac 37 B5
Lussac-les-Châteaux 31 B6
Lussac-les-Églises 31 B6

Lussan 39 C6
Lutterbach 29 B4
Lux 28 C1
Luxe-Sumberraute 43 B6
Luxeuil-les-Bains 28 B3
Luxey 37 C4
Luzarches 18 C3
Luz-Ardiden 44 C2
Luzech 38 C1
Luzenac 45 C5
Luz-St-Sauveur 44 C2
Luzy 27 D5
Lyon 34 C2
Lyons-la-Forêt 18 B1

M

Machault 19 B6
Machecoul 24 D2
Macinaggio 49 A6
Mâcon 34 B2
Madiran 44 A2
Maël-Carhaix 22 B3
Magescq 36 D3
Magland 35 C4
Magnac-Laval 31 B6
Magné 31 B4
Magnières 20 D3
Magny-Cours 27 D4
Magny-en-Vexin 18 C2
Maîche 29 D4
Maignelay-Montigny 18 B3
Maillas 37 C4
Maillebois 17 D6
Maillezais 30 B3
Mailly-la-Ville 27 C5
Mailly-le-Camp 19 D5
Mailly-Maillet 14 D3
Mainsat 32 B3
Maintenon 18 D1
Mainvilliers 18 D1
Maisse 18 D3
Malancourt 20 C1
Malansac 23 C5
Malaucène 40 C2
Malaunay 17 B6
Malaussanne 44 A1
Malbouzon 39 B4
Malbuisson 28 D3
Malemort-du-Comtat 40 D2
Malemort-sur-Corrèze 32 D2
Malesherbes 26 A3
Malestroit 23 C4
Malicorne-sur-Sarthe 25 B4
Malijai 40 D3
Malissard 40 B2
Mamers 17 D5
Mamirolle 28 D3
Manciet 37 D5
Mandelieu-la-Napoule 49 A4
Mandeure 29 C4
Mandres-en-Barrois 20 D2
Mane 40 D3
Mane 45 B4
Mangiennes 20 B2
Manhuelles 20 C2
Manlay 27 D6
Manosque 40 D3
Mansle 31 C5
Manso 49 B5
Mansonville 37 D6
Mantes-la-Jolie 18 C2
Mantes-la-Ville 18 C2
Manthelan 25 D6
Mantoche 28 C2
Manzac-sur-Vern 31 D5
Manzat 33 C4
Manziat 34 B2
Marac 28 B1
Marans 30 B3
Maranville 27 B6
Maraussan 46 B3
Maraye-en-Othe 27 B5
Marboz 34 B2
Marcenais 37 A4
Marcenat 33 D4
Marchaux 28 C3

Marchenoir 26 B1
Marcheprime 36 B3
Marchiennes 15 C4
Marciac 44 A2
Marcilhac-sur-Célé 38 B2
Marcillac 31 D4
Marcillac-la-Croisille 32 D3
Marcillac-Vallon 38 C3
Marcillat-en-Combraille 33 B4
Marcilly-en-Gault 26 C2
Marcilly-en-Villette 26 B2
Marcilly-le-Hayer 27 A4
Marcilly-sur-Eure 17 C6
Marck 14 B2
Marckolsheim 29 B5
Marcoing 15 D4
Marcoux 41 D4
Marcq-en-Barœul 15 C4
Mardeuil 19 C5
Marennes 30 C3
Mareuil 31 D5
Mareuil-sur-Arnon 26 D2
Mareuil-sur-Ay 19 C5
Mareuil-sur-Lay-Dissais 30 A3
Marey-sur-Tille 28 C1
Margerie-Hancourt 19 D6
Marguerittes 39 D6
Margut 20 B1
Mariac 39 B6
Marignana 49 C5
Marignane 47 B6
Marigné-Laillé 25 B5
Marigny 16 C3
Marigny-le-Châtel 19 D5
Marines 18 C2
Maringues 33 C5
Marizy 33 A6
Marle 14 B5
Marlenheim 21 D5
Marlhes 33 D6
Marly 15 C4
Marly 20 C3
Marmagne 26 D2
Marmagne 27 D6
Marmande 37 C5
Marmoutier 21 D5
Marnay 28 C2
Marne-la-Vallée 18 C3
Marolles-les-Braults 25 A5
Maromme 17 B6
Maroué 16 D1
Marquion 15 D4
Marquise 14 B2
Marquixanes 45 C6
Marsac-en-Livradois 33 D5
Marsac-sur-Don 23 D6
Marsal 20 D3
Marsannay-la-Côte 28 C1
Marsanne 40 B2
Marseillan 46 B3
Marseille 48 B1
Marseille-en-Beauvaisis 18 B2
Marsillargues 39 D6
Marssac-sur-Tarn 38 D3
Martel 38 B2
Marthon 31 C5
Martigné-Briand 25 D4
Martigné-Ferchaud 23 C6
Martigné-sur-Mayenne 24 B3
Martigny-le-Comte 33 A6
Martigny-les-Bains 28 B2
Martigny-les-Gerbonvaux 20 D2
Martigues 47 B6
Martizay 25 D6
Martres-Tolosane 45 B4
Marvejols 39 C5
Marville 20 B2
Marzan 23 D5
Mas-Cabardès 45 B6
Masclat 38 B1
Masevaux 29 B4
Massat 45 C4
Massay 26 D2
Masseret 32 D2
Masseube 44 B3
Massiac 33 D4
Mas-St-Chély 39 C5

Matha 31 C4
Mathay 29 C4
Matignon 16 D1
Matigny 15 D4
Matour 33 B6
Mattaincourt 28 A3
Maubert-Fontaine 15 D6
Maubeuge 15 C5
Maubourguet 44 A2
Maubuisson 30 D3
Mauguio 39 D6
Mauléon 24 D3
Mauléon-Barousse 44 C3
Mauléon-d'Armagnac 37 D4
Mauléon-Licharre 43 B6
Maulévrier 24 D3
Maure-de-Bretagne 23 C5
Maureillas-las-Illas 46 C2
Maurens 37 B5
Mauriac 32 D3
Mauriac 37 B5
Mauron 23 C5
Mauroux 37 C6
Maurs 38 B3
Maury 45 C6
Mauves 40 B2
Mauvezin 37 D6
Mauzé-sur-le-Mignon 30 B3
Maxent 23 C5
Mayenne 25 A4
Mayet 25 B5
Mayres 39 B6
Mazagran 19 B6
Mazamet 45 A6
Mazan 40 D2
Mazé 25 C4
Mazères 45 B5
Mazerolles 44 A1
Mazeyrolles 38 A2
Mazières-en-Gâtine 31 A4
Meaulne 33 A4
Méaulte 14 D3
Meaux 18 C3
Meauzac 38 C1
Médis 30 C3
Megève 35 C4
Mehun-sur-Yèvre 26 D2
Meilhan 37 D4
Meillac 16 D2
Meillant 26 D3
Meillerie 35 B5
Melay 24 D3
Melay 28 B2
Melgven 22 C2
Mélisey 28 B3
Mellac 22 C3
Melle 31 B4
Melrand 22 C3
Melun 18 D3
Membrey 28 C2
Menars 26 C1
Menat 33 B4
Mende 39 C5
Menditte 43 B6
Ménéac 23 B4
Ménesplet 37 B5
Ménessaire 27 D5
Menet 32 D3
Menetou-Salon 26 D3
Ménigoute 31 B4
Ménil-la-Tour 20 D2
Ménil-sur-Belvitte 21 D4
Mennecy 18 D3
Mennetou-sur-Cher 26 C2
Menou 27 C4
Mens 40 B3
Mensignac 31 D5
Menton 41 D6
Méobecq 32 A2
Méounes-les-Montrieux 48 B2
Mer 26 C1
Méraq 44 A2
Mercœur 38 B2
Mercuès 38 C2
Merdrignac 23 B4
Méreau 26 D2
Mérens-les-Vals 45 C5
Méréville 26 A2

Meria 49 A6
Méribel-les-Allues 35 D4
Merlevenez 22 C1
Merlines 32 C3
Merrey 28 B2
Mers-les-Bains 14 D1
Méru 18 C2
Mervans 28 D1
Mervent 30 A3
Merville 14 C3
Merville 38 D1
Méry-sur-Seine 19 D5
Mésanger 23 D6
Meschers-sur-Gironde 30 C3
Mesgrigny 19 D5
Meslay-du-Maine 25 B4
Mesquer 23 C5
Messac 23 C5
Messanges 36 D2
Messei 17 D4
Messeix 32 C3
Messincourt 20 B1
Mesves-sur-Loire 27 D4
Métabief 35 A4
Mettray 25 C5
Metz 20 C3
Metzervisse 20 C3
Meulan 18 C2
Meung-sur-Loire 26 B2
Meursault 27 D6
Meuzac 32 D2
Meximieux 34 C2
Meylan 34 D3
Meymac 32 C3
Meyrargues 48 A1
Meyreuil 48 A1
Meyronnes 41 C5
Meyrueis 39 C5
Meyssac 38 A2
Meysse 40 C1
Meythet 35 C4
Mèze 46 B3
Mézel 41 D4
Mézidon-Canon 17 C4
Mézières-en-Brenne 25 D6
Mézières-sur-Issoire 31 B6
Mézilhac 39 B6
Mézilles 27 C4
Mézin 37 D5
Mézos 36 C3
Mialet 31 C6
Miélan 44 B3
Miers 38 B2
Mieussy 35 B4
Migennes 27 B4
Mignaloux-Beauvoir 31 A5
Migné-Auxances 31 A5
Mignovillard 28 D3
Milhaud 39 D6
Milizac 22 B1
Millas 46 C2
Millau 39 C4
Millay 27 D5
Millevaches 32 C3
Millières 28 B2
Milly-la-Forêt 18 D3
Mimizan 36 C3
Mimizan-Plage 36 C3
Miniac-Morvan 16 D2
Minot 27 C6
Mionnay 34 C2
Mios 36 B3
Mirabeau 40 D3
Mirabel 38 C2
Mirabel-aux-Baronnies 40 C2
Miradoux 37 D6
Miramas 47 A6
Mirambeau 31 D4
Miramont-de-Guyenne 37 B5
Mirande 44 A3
Mirandol-Bourgnounac 38 C3
Mirebeau 25 D5
Mirebeau 28 C1
Mirecourt 28 A3
Mirepoix 45 B5
Mireval 47 A4
Miserey-Salines 28 C2
Mison 40 C3

Missillac **23** D5
Mitry-Mory **18** C3
Mittersheim **21** C4
Modane **35** D5
Moëlan-sur-Mer **22** C3
Moingt **33** C6
Moirans **34** D3
Moirans-en-Montagne **34** B3
Moirax **37** C6
Moisdon-la-Rivière **23** C6
Moislains **14** D3
Moissac **37** C6
Moissac-Bellevue **48** A2
Moissey **28** D2
Moïta **49** B6
Molesmes **27** B6
Molières **38** B2
Molières **38** C1
Molières-sur-Cèze **39** C6
Moliets-et-Maa **36** D2
Molines-en-Queyras **41** B5
Molinet **33** B6
Molinges **34** B3
Molitg-les-Bains **45** C6
Molles **33** B5
Molliens-Dreuil **14** D2
Molompize **33** D4
Moloy **27** C6
Monacia-d'Aullène **49** D5
Monbahus **37** B6
Monbazillac **37** B5
Moncaut **37** C6
Moncel-sur-Seille **20** D3
Monclar **37** C6
Moncontour **16** D1
Moncontour **25** D4
Moncoutant **31** A4
Moncrabeau **37** D5
Mondavezan **45** B4
Mondeville **17** C4
Mondoubleau **25** B6
Mondragon **40** C1
Monein **43** B6
Monestier-de-Clermont **40** B3
Monestiés **38** C3
Monéteau **27** B4
Monflanquin **37** C6
Monfort **37** D6
Monieux **40** D2
Monistrol-d'Allier **39** B5
Monistrol-sur-Loire **33** D6
Monléon-Magnoac **44** B3
Monnaie **25** C6
Monpazier **37** B6
Mons **41** D5
Mons **46** A2
Monsec **31** D5
Monségur **37** B5
Monsempron-Libos **37** C6
Montady **46** B3
Montagnac **46** A3
Montagne **37** B4
Montagney **28** C2
Montagnol **39** D4
Montagrier **31** D5
Montaigu **24** D2
Montaigu-de-Quercy **37** C6
Montaigut **33** B4
Montaigut-sur-Save **38** D1
Montalieu-Vercieu **34** C3
Montalivet-les-Bains **30** D3
Montaner **44** B2
Montans **38** D2
Montargis **26** B3
Montastruc-la-Conseillère **38** D2
Montataire **18** C3
Montauban **38** D1
Montauban-de-Bretagne **23** B5
Montaudin **16** D3
Montauriol **37** B6
Montauroux **48** A3
Montaut **37** D4
Montaut **44** B2
Montaut **45** B5
Montayral **37** C6
Montbard **27** C6
Montbarrey **28** D2
Montbazens **38** C3
Montbazin **47** A4
Montbazon **25** C6
Montbéliard **29** C4
Montbenoît **28** D3
Montbeton **38** D1
Montboucher-sur-Jabron **40** C2
Montbozon **28** C3
Montbrison **33** C6
Montbron **31** C5
Montbrun **38** C2
Montbrun-les-Bains **40** C3
Montcavrel **14** C2
Montceau-les-Mines **33** A6
Montcenis **27** D6
Montchanin **33** A6
Montcornet **19** B5
Montcresson **26** B3
Montcuq **38** C1
Montcy-Notre-Dame **15** D6
Montdardier **39** D5
Mont-Dauphin **41** B4
Mont-de-Marsan **37** D4
Montdidier **18** B3
Mont-Dore **33** D4
Montebourg **16** B2
Monte-Carlo *MC* **41** D6
Montech **38** D1
Monteils **38** C2
Montel-de-Gelat **32** C3
Montélier **40** B2
Montélimar **40** C1
Montels **45** B5
Montemboeuf **31** C5
Montenay **24** A3
Montendre **31** D4
Monterblanc **23** C4
Montereau-fault-Yonne **18** D3
Montesquieu **37** C6
Montesquieu-Volvestre **45** B4
Montesquiou **44** A3
Monteux **40** D2
Montfaucon **24** D3
Montfaucon **38** B2
Montfaucon-d'Argonne **20** C1
Montfaucon-en-Velay **33** D6
Montferran-Savès **37** D6
Montferrat **48** A3
Montferrier **45** C5
Montfort **23** B5
Montfort **43** B6
Montfort-en-Chalosse **36** D3
Montfort-l'Amaury **18** D2
Montfort-le-Gesnois **25** B5
Montfort-sur-Risle **17** B5
Montgaillard **44** B2
Montgaillard **45** C5
Montgenèvre **41** B5
Montgeron **18** D3
Montgiscard **45** B5
Montgivray **32** A3
Montguyon **31** D4
Monthermé **15** D6
Monthois **19** C6
Monthureux-sur-Saône **28** B2
Monticello **49** B5
Montier-en-Der **19** D6
Montiers-sur-Saulx **20** D1
Montignac **31** D6
Montigny **21** D4
Montigny-la-Resie **27** B5
Montigny-lès-Metz **20** C3
Montigny-Mornay-Villeneuve-sur-Vingeanne **28** C2
Montigny-sur-Aube **27** B6
Montivilliers **17** B5
Montjaux **39** C4
Montjean **24** B3
Montlaur **45** B6
Montlieu-la-Garde **31** D4
Mont-Louis **45** C6
Montluçon **32** B3
Montluel **34** C2
Montmarault **33** B4
Montmartin-sur-Mer **16** C2
Montmédy **20** B2
Montmélian **35** D4
Montmeryran **40** B2
Montmeyan **48** A2
Montmirail **19** C4
Montmirail **25** B6
Montmirey-le-Château **28** D2
Montmoreau-St-Cybard **31** D5
Montmorillon **31** B6
Montmorin **40** C3
Montmorot **34** A3
Montmort-Lucy **19** C5
Montoir-de-Bretagne **23** D5
Montoire-sur-le-Loir **25** B6
Montoison **40** B2
Montory **43** B6
Montournais **30** A3
Montpellier **39** D6
Montpeyroux **39** B4
Montpezat **37** C6
Montpézat **45** B4
Montpezat-de-Quercy **38** C2
Montpezat-sous-Bauzon **39** B6
Montpon-Ménestérol **37** B5
Montpont-en-Bresse **34** A2
Montréal **27** C5
Montréal **37** D5
Montréal **45** B6
Montredon-Labessonnié **38** D3
Montregard **33** D6
Montréjeau **44** B3
Montrésor **25** D6
Montret **34** A2
Montreuil **14** C2
Montreuil-Bellay **25** D4
Montreuil-Juigné **25** C4
Montrevault **24** C3
Montrevel-en-Bresse **34** B2
Montrichard **25** C6
Montricoux **38** C2
Montriond **35** B5
Montrond **28** D2
Montrond-les-Bains **33** C6
Monts **25** C5
Montsalvy **38** B3
Montsauche-les-Settons **27** D5
Montségur **45** C5
Montsoué **37** D4
Mont-sous-Vaudrey **28** D2
Monts-sur-Guesnes **25** D5
Mont-St-Aignan **17** B6
Mont-St-Jean **27** C6
Mont-St-Martin **20** B2
Mont-St-Vincent **33** A6
Montsûrs **25** B4
Montsuzain **19** D5
Montvalent **38** B2
Montville **17** B6
Montzéville **20** C1
Morbier **34** A3
Morcenx **36** D3
Mordelles **23** C5
Moréac **23** C4
Morée **25** B6
Morestel **34** C3
Moret-sur-Loing **18** D3
Moreuil **14** D3
Morez **35** B4
Morgat **22** B1
Morhange **20** C3
Morienval **18** C3
Morlaàs **44** B2
Morlaix **22** B2
Morlanne **44** A1
Morley **20** D1
Mormant **18** D3
Mormoiron **40** D2
Mornant **34** C1
Mornas **40** C1
Morosaglia **49** B6
Mortagne-au-Perche **17** D5
Mortagne-sur-Gironde **30** D3
Mortagne-sur-Sèvre **24** D3
Mortain **16** D3
Morteau **28** D3
Morteaux-Coulibœuf **17** C4
Mortrée **17** D5
Morzine **35** B5
Mouchamps **24** D3
Mouchan **37** D5
Mougins **49** A4
Moularès **38** C3
Moulay **25** A4
Mouleydier **37** B6
Mouliherne **25** C4
Moulin-Neuf **45** B5
Moulins **33** A5
Moulins-Engilbert **27** D5
Moulins-la-Marche **17** D5
Moulis-en-Médoc **36** A3
Moulismes **31** B6
Moult **17** C4
Mourenx **43** B6
Mouriès **40** D2
Moussac **39** D6
Moussey **21** D4
Moussoulens **45** B6
Moussy **27** D4
Moustéru **22** B3
Moustey **36** C3
Moustiers-Ste-Marie **41** D4
Mouthe **35** A4
Mouthier-Haute-Pierre **28** D3
Mouthiers-sur-Boëme **31** C5
Mouthoumet **45** C6
Moutier-d'Ahun **32** B3
Moûtiers **35** D4
Moutiers-les-Mauxfaits **30** B2
Moux **45** B6
Moux-en-Morvan **27** D5
Mouy **18** C2
Mouzay **20** B1
Mouzon **20** B1
Moy-de-l'Aisne **19** B4
Moyenmoutier **21** D4
Moyenneville **14** D2
Mozac **33** C4
Mugron **36** D3
Muizon **19** C5
Mulhouse **29** B4
Mulsanne **25** B5
Mundolsheim **21** D5
Munster **29** B4
Murasson **39** D4
Murat **33** D4
Murato **49** B6
Murat-sur-Vèbre **39** D4
Mur-de-Barrez **39** B4
Mûr-de-Bretagne **23** B4
Mur-de-Sologne **26** C1
Muret **45** A4
Muro **49** B5
Murol **33** D4
Muron **30** B3
Mûrs-Erigné **25** C4
Murviel-lès-Béziers **46** A3
Mussidan **37** A5
Mussy-sur-Seine **27** B6
Mutzig **21** D5
Muzillac **23** D4
Myon **28** D2

N

Nailloux **45** B5
Naintré **25** D5
Naives-Rosières **20** D1
Naizin **23** C4
Najac **38** C2
Nalliers **30** B3
Nançay **26** C2
Nancy **20** D3
Nangis **19** D4
Nans-les-Pins **48** B2
Nant **39** D5
Nanterre **18** C2
Nantes **23** D6
Nanteuil-le-Haudouin **18** C3
Nantiat **31** B6
Nantua **34** B3
Narbonne **46** B2
Narbonne-Plage **46** B3
Narcy **27** D4
Narrosse **36** D3
Nasbinals **39** B4
Naucelle **38** C3
Naucelles **38** B3
Naujac-sur-Mer **30** D3
Navarrenx **43** B6

Naves 32 D2
Navilly 28 D1
Nay-Bourdettes 44 B2
Nazelles-Négron 25 C6
Nébias 45 C6
Nègrepelisse 38 C2
Nemours 26 A3
Néoules 48 B2
Nérac 37 C5
Nercillac 31 C4
Néré 31 C4
Néris-les-Bains 33 B4
Néronde 33 C6
Nérondes 26 D3
Nersac 31 C5
Nervieux 33 C6
Nesle 18 B3
Nessa 49 B5
Nettancourt 19 C6
Neufchâteau 28 A2
Neufchâtel-en-Bray 18 B1
Neufchâtel-Hardelot 14 C2
Neufchâtel-sur-Aisne 19 B5
Neuillé-Pont-Pierre 25 C5
Neuilly 27 D4
Neuilly-en-Thelle 18 C2
Neuilly-le-Réal 33 B5
Neuilly-l'Évêque 28 B2
Neuilly-St-Front 19 C4
Neulise 33 C6
Neung-sur-Beuvron 26 C2
Neussargues-Moissac 33 D4
Neuvéglise 39 B4
Neuvic 31 D5
Neuvic 32 D3
Neuville-aux-Bois 26 B2
Neuville-de-Poitou 31 A5
Neuville-les-Dames 34 B2
Neuville-lès-Dieppe 14 D1
Neuville-sur-Saône 34 C2
Neuvilly-en-Argonne 20 C1
Neuvy-Grandchamp 33 A6
Neuvy-le-Roi 25 C5
Neuvy-Pailloux 26 D2
Neuvy-St-Sépulchre 32 A2
Neuvy-sur-Barangeon 26 C2
Névache 41 B4
Nevers 27 D4
Névez 22 C2
Néville 17 A5
Nexon 31 C6
Nice 49 A4
Niederbronn-les-Bains 21 C5
Nieul 31 C6
Niherne 26 D1
Nilvange 20 B3
Nîmes 40 D1
Niort 31 B4
Nissan-lez-Enserune 46 B3
Nitry 27 C5
Nivillac 23 D5
Nivillers 18 B2
Nivolas-Vermelle 34 D2
Noaillan 37 C4
Noailles 18 B2
Nocé 17 D5
Nods 28 D3
Noé 45 B4
Nœux-les-Mines 14 C3
Nogaro 37 D5
Nogent 28 B1
Nogent-le-Bernard 25 A5
Nogent-le-Roi 18 D1
Nogent-le-Rotrou 25 A6
Nogent-sur-Aube 19 D5
Nogent-sur-Oise 18 C3
Nogent-sur-Seine 19 D4
Nogent-sur-Vernisson 26 B3
Noguères 43 B6
Nohant-Vic 32 A3
Nohic 38 D2
Noidans-lès-Vesoul 28 C3
Noilhan 45 A4
Noirétable 33 C5
Noirmoutier-en-l'Île 24 D1
Noisseville 20 C3
Nolay 27 D6
Nomeny 20 C3

Nomexy 28 A3
Nonancourt 17 D6
Nontron 31 D6
Nonza 49 A6
Noroy-le-Bourg 28 C3
Norrent-Fontes 14 C3
Nort-sur-Erdre 23 D6
Notre-Dame-de-Bellecombe 35 C4
Notre-Dame-de-Gravenchon 17 B5
Notre-Dame-de-Monts 24 D1
Notre-Dame-d'Oé 25 C6
Nouan-le-Fuzelier 26 C2
Nouans-les-Fontaines 25 D6
Nouart 19 B6
Nouvion 14 D2
Nouzilly 25 C6
Nouzonville 15 D6
Noves 40 D2
Novillars 28 C3
Novion-Porcien 19 B6
Novy-Chevrières 19 B6
Noyal-Muzillac 23 D4
Noyalo 23 D4
Noyal-Pontivy 23 C4
Noyant 25 C5
Noyarey 34 D3
Noyen-sur-Sarthe 25 B4
Noyers 27 C5
Noyers-sur-Cher 26 C1
Noyers-sur-Jabron 40 C3
Noyon 18 B3
Nozay 23 D6
Nozeroy 28 D3
Nuaillé-d'Aunis 30 B3
Nueil-sur-Argent 25 D4
Nuillé-sur-Vicoin 24 B3
Nuits 27 B5
Nuits-St-Georges 28 D1
Nyoiseau 24 B3
Nyons 40 C2

O

Obernai 21 D5
Objat 32 D2
Ocana 49 C5
Octeville 16 B2
Octeville-sur-Mer 17 B5
Œyreluy 36 D3
Offemont 29 C4
Offranville 14 D1
Oger 19 C5
Ogeu-les-Bains 44 B1
Ogéviller 21 D4
Ogliastro 49 B5
Oignies 15 C4
Oiron 25 D4
Oiselay-et-Grachaux 28 C2
Oisemont 14 D2
Oisseau 24 A3
Oissel 17 B6
Oizon 26 C3
Olargues 46 A2
Olemps 38 C3
Olette 45 C6
Olivet 26 B2
Olliergues 33 C5
Ollioules 48 B2
Olmeta-di-Tuda 49 B6
Olmeto 49 D5
Olonne-sur-Mer 30 A2
Olonzac 46 B2
Oloron-Ste-Marie 43 B6
Omessa 49 B6
Omont 19 B6
Ondres 43 A5
Onesse-et-Laharie 36 D3
Onet-le-Château 38 C3
Ongles 40 D3
Onzain 25 C6
Opoul-Périllos 46 C2
Oradour-sur-Glane 31 C6
Oradour-sur-Vayres 31 C6
Oraison 40 D3
Orange 40 C2
Orbais-l'Abbaye 19 C5
Orbec 17 C5

Orchamps-Vennes 28 D3
Orchies 15 C4
Orcières 41 B4
Orcival 33 C4
Ordan-Larroque 37 D6
Orgelet 34 B3
Orgères-en-Beauce 26 B2
Orgon 40 D2
Origny-Ste-Benoîte 15 D4
Orléans 26 B2
Ornaisons 46 B2
Ornans 28 D3
Orpierre 40 C3
Orsay 18 D2
Orsennes 32 B2
Orthez 43 A6
Orval 32 A3
Orvault 23 D6
Osny 18 C2
Osséja 45 D5
Ossès 43 B5
Ossun 44 B2
Ottmarsheim 29 B5
Ouanne 27 C4
Ouarville 26 A2
Oucques 25 B6
Oudon 23 D6
Ougney 28 D2
Ouistreham 17 C4
Oulchy-le-Château 19 C4
Oullins 34 C2
Ouroux-en-Morvan 27 D5
Ouroux-sur-Saône 34 A2
Ourville-en-Caux 17 B5
Oust 45 C4
Outarville 26 A2
Outreau 14 C2
Ouveillan 46 B2
Ouzouer-le-Marché 26 B1
Ouzouer-sur-Loire 26 B3
Oyonnax 34 B3
Ozoir-la-Ferrière 18 D3

P

Pabu 22 A3
Pacy-sur-Eure 17 C6
Padirac 38 B2
Padoux 28 A3
Pagny-sur-Moselle 20 C2
Pailhès 45 B5
Paillet 37 B4
Paimbœuf 23 D5
Paimpol 22 A3
Paimpont 23 C5
Palaiseau 18 D2
Palavas-les-Flots 47 A4
Palinges 33 A6
Palis 27 A5
Palluau 24 D2
Palluau-sur-Indre 26 D1
Palneca 49 C6
Paluel 17 A5
Pamiers 45 B5
Pampelonne 38 C3
Pamproux 31 B4
Panassac 44 B3
Panazol 32 C1
Panissières 33 C6
Panjas 37 D5
Pannes 26 B3
Paramé 16 D2
Paray-le-Monial 33 B6
Parcé-sur-Sarthe 25 B4
Parcoul 31 D5
Pardies 44 B1
Parempuyre 37 B4
Parentis-en-Born 36 C3
Pargny-sur-Saulx 19 D6
Parigné-l'Évêque 25 B5
Paris 18 C3
Parisot 38 C2
Parisot 38 D2
Parlan 38 B3
Paron 27 B4
Parthenay 31 A4

Partinello 49 B5
Pas-en-Artois 14 D3
Passais 16 D3
Passy 35 C5
Patay 26 B2
Patrimonio 49 B6
Pau 44 B2
Pauilhac 37 D6
Pauillac 30 D3
Paulhac-en-Margeride 39 B5
Paulhan 46 A3
Paulx 24 D2
Pauvres 19 B6
Pavie 37 D6
Pavilly 17 B6
Payrac 38 B2
Payrin-Augmontel 45 A6
Payzac 31 D6
Paziols 46 C2
Péaule 23 D5
Pébrac 39 B5
Peillac 23 C5
Peille 41 D6
Peipin 40 D3
Peïra-Cava 41 D6
Pélissanne 47 A6
Pellegrue 37 B5
Pellevoisin 26 D1
Pélussin 34 D1
Pelvoux 41 B4
Pénestin 23 D4
Penly 14 D1
Penmarch 22 C2
Pennautier 45 B6
Penne 38 C2
Penne-d'Agenais 37 C6
Penvénan 22 A3
Péone 41 D5
Percy 16 C3
Périers 16 C2
Périgueux 31 D6
Pernes-les-Fontaines 40 D2
Pérols 47 A4
Péron 34 B3
Péronnas 34 B2
Péronne 14 D3
Perpignan 46 C2
Perrecy-les-Forges 33 A6
Perreux 33 C6
Perrigny 34 A3
Perrogney-les-Fontaines 28 B1
Perros-Guirec 22 A3
Persan 18 C2
Perthes 18 D3
Pertuis 40 D3
Pervenchères 17 D5
Peschadoires 33 C5
Pesmes 28 C2
Pessac 37 B4
Pessan 37 D6
Petit-Mars 23 D6
Petit-Noir 28 D1
Petreto-Bicchisano 49 D5
Peujard 37 A4
Pexonne 21 D4
Peymeinade 49 A4
Peynier 48 B1
Peypin 48 B1
Peyrat-le-Château 32 C2
Peyrehorade 43 A6
Peyriac-Minervois 45 B6
Peyrieu 34 C3
Peyrins 33 B2
Peyrolles-en-Provence 48 A1
Peyruis 40 D3
Pézenas 46 A3
Pezuls 37 B6
Pfaffenhoffen 21 C5
Phalsbourg 21 D4
Piana 49 C5
Pianotolli-Caldarello 49 D5
Piau-Engaly 44 C2
Pibrac 38 D1
Picauville 16 B2
Picquigny 14 D2
Piedicorte-di-Gaggio 49 C6
Piedicroce 49 B6
Piégut-Pluviers 31 C6

Piennes 20 C2
Pierre-Buffière 32 C2
Pierre-Châtel 40 B3
Pierre-de-Bresse 28 D1
Pierrefeu-du-Var 48 B2
Pierrefitte-Nestalas 44 C2
Pierrefitte-sur-Aire 20 C2
Pierrefonds 18 B3
Pierrefontaine-les-Varans 28 D3
Pierrefort 39 B4
Pierrelatte 40 C1
Pierrepont 20 B2
Pierres 18 D1
Pierrerevert 40 D3
Pietracorbara 49 A6
Pietra-di-Verde 49 B6
Pietralba 49 B6
Pietrosella 49 C5
Piffonds 27 B4
Pignans 48 B2
Piney 19 D5
Pino 49 A6
Pinols 39 A5
Pinsac 38 B2
Piolenc 40 C1
Pionsat 33 B4
Pipriac 23 C5
Piriac-sur-Mer 23 D4
Pissos 36 C3
Pithiviers 26 B2
Pîtres 17 B6
Plabennec 22 B1
Plaintel 23 B4
Plaisance 37 D5
Plaisance-du-Touch 45 A4
Plaisir 18 D2
Plancher-Bas 29 C4
Plancoët 16 D1
Plancy-l'Abbaye 19 D5
Plan-de-Baux 40 B2
Plan-de-la-Tour 48 B3
Plan-d'Orgon 40 D2
Planès 45 D6
Plazac 37 A6
Pleaux 32 D3
Pleine-Fougères 16 D2
Plélan-le-Grand 23 C5
Plélo 23 B4
Plémet 23 B4
Plénée-Jugon 16 D1
Pléneuf-Val-André 16 D1
Plérin 23 B4
Plescop 23 C4
Plessé 23 D5
Plestin-les-Grèves 22 A3
Pleubian 22 A3
Pleudihen-sur-Rance 16 D2
Pleumartin 31 A6
Pleumeur-Bodou 22 A3
Pleurs 19 D5
Pleuven 22 C2
Pleyben 22 B2
Pleyber-Christ 22 B2
Plobannalec 22 C2
Ploemeur 22 C3
Ploeren 23 C4
Ploërmel 23 C4
Plœuc-sur-Lié 23 B4
Plogonnec 22 C2
Plombières-les-Bains 28 B3
Plomeur 22 C2
Plomodiern 22 B2
Plonéour-Lanvern 22 C2
Plonévez-du-Faou 22 B2
Plonevez-Porzay 22 B2
Plouagat 23 B4
Plouaret 22 A3
Plouarzel 22 B1
Plouay 22 C3
Ploubalay 16 D1
Ploubazlanec 23 A4
Ploubezre 22 A3
Ploudalmézeau 22 B1
Ploudiry 22 B2
Plouescat 22 A2
Plouézec 23 A4
Ploufragan 23 B4
Plougasnou 22 A2

Plougastel-Daoulas 22 B2
Plougonven 22 B3
Plougonver 22 B3
Plougrescant 22 A3
Plouguenast 23 B4
Plouguerneau 22 A1
Plouguernével 22 B3
Plouguiel 22 A3
Plouguin 22 B1
Plouha 23 A4
Plouharnel 22 D3
Plouhinec 22 C1
Plouhinec 22 C3
Plouigneau 22 B3
Ploumagoar 22 B3
Ploumilliau 22 A3
Plounévez-Moëdec 22 B3
Plounévez-Quintin 22 B3
Plouray 22 B3
Plouvorn 22 B2
Plouyé 22 B2
Plouzané 22 B1
Plouzévédé 22 A2
Plozévet 22 C1
Plumelec 23 C4
Pluméliau 23 C4
Plumergat 23 C4
Pluneret 23 C4
Pluvigner 23 C4
Pluzunet 22 A3
Podensac 37 B4
Poggio-Mezzana 49 B6
Pogny 19 C6
Poinçon-lès-Larrey 27 B6
Pointis-Inard 44 B3
Poiseux 27 D4
Poissons 20 D1
Poissy 18 C2
Poitiers 31 A5
Poix-de-Picardie 14 D2
Poix-Terron 19 B6
Polaincourt-et-Clairefontaine 28 B3
Poligny 28 D2
Polisot 27 B6
Polliat 34 B2
Polminhac 38 B3
Pomarez 36 D3
Pommard 27 D6
Pompaire 31 A4
Pompey 20 D3
Pompignan 39 D5
Poncin 34 B3
Pons 31 C4
Pontacq 44 B2
Pontailler-sur-Saône 28 C2
Pontaix 40 B2
Pont-à-Marcq 15 C4
Pont-à-Mousson 20 C3
Pontarion 32 C2
Pontarlier 28 D3
Pontaubault 16 D2
Pont-Audemer 17 B5
Pontault-Combault 18 D3
Pontaumur 33 C4
Pont-Aven 22 C2
Pontcharra 34 D3
Pontchâteau 23 D5
Pont-Croix 22 C1
Pont-d'Ain 34 C2
Pont-de-Buis-lès-Quimerch 22 B2
Pont-de-Chéruy 34 C2
Pont-de-Larn 45 A6
Pont-de-l'Isère 40 B2
Pont-de-Poitte 34 A3
Pont-de-Roide 29 C4
Pont-de-Salars 39 C4
Pont-de-Vaux 34 B2
Pont-de-Veyle 34 B2
Pont-d'Hérault 39 D5
Pont-d'Ouilly 17 C4
Pont-du-Casse 37 C6
Pont-du-Château 33 C5
Pont-du-Navoy 34 A3
Ponte-Leccia 49 B6
Pont-en-Royans 40 B2
Pontenx-les-Forges 36 C3
Pont-Évêque 34 D2
Pont-Farcy 16 C3

Pontfaverger-Moronvilliers 19 C5
Pontgibaud 33 C4
Pont-Hébert 16 C3
Pontivy 22 C3
Pont-l'Abbé 22 C2
Pont-la-Ville 27 B6
Pont-les-Moulins 28 C3
Pont-l'Évêque 17 C5
Pontlevoy 25 C6
Pontoise 18 C2
Pontonx-sur-l'Adour 36 D3
Pontorson 16 D2
Pontpoint 18 C3
Pontrieux 22 A3
Pont-Ste-Marie 27 A5
Pont-Ste-Maxence 18 C3
Pont-St-Esprit 40 C1
Pont-sur-Yonne 27 A4
Pontvallain 25 B5
Pornic 24 D1
Pornichet 23 D5
Porspoder 22 B1
Porta 45 C5
Portbail 16 B2
Port-Barcarès 46 C2
Port Brillet 23 B4
Port-de-Bouc 47 B6
Port-de-Piles 25 D5
Port-des-Barques 30 C3
Portel-des-Corbières 46 B2
Port-en-Bessin-Huppain 16 B3
Portes-lès-Valence 40 B2
Portets 37 B4
Portet-sur-Garonne 45 A4
Porticcio 49 C5
Portieux 28 A3
Port-Joinville 30 A1
Port-la-Nouvelle 46 B2
Port-Leucate 46 C2
Port-Louis 22 C3
Port-Navalo 23 D4
Porto 49 C5
Porto-Vecchio 49 D6
Port-Ste-Marie 37 C5
Port-St-Louis-du-Rhône 47 B5
Port-St-Père 24 D2
Port-sur-Saône 28 C3
Port-Vendres 46 C3
Possesse 19 C6
Potigny 17 C4
Pouancé 23 C6
Pougny 27 C4
Pougues-les-Eaux 27 D4
Pougy 19 D6
Pouillon 43 A6
Pouilly-en-Auxois 27 C6
Pouilly-sous-Charlieu 33 B6
Pouilly-sur-Loire 27 C3
Pouilly-sur-Saône 28 D1
Poulaines 26 D1
Pouldreuzic 22 C2
Pouligny-St-Pierre 31 A6
Poullaouen 22 B3
Poupas 37 D6
Pourcieux 48 A2
Pourrain 27 B4
Pourrières 48 A2
Poussan 46 A3
Poussay 28 A3
Pouxeux 28 B3
Pouyastruc 44 B2
Pouydesseaux 37 D5
Pouzauges 24 D3
Pouzay 25 D5
Pradelles 39 B5
Prades 45 C5
Prades 45 C6
Prades-d'Aubrac 39 C4
Pradines 38 C2
Prahecq 31 B4
Pralognan-la-Vanoise 35 D5
Prats-de-Mollo-la-Preste 45 D6
Prauthoy 28 C1
Prayssas 37 C6
Praz-sur-Arly 35 C4
Préchac 37 C4
Précigné 25 B4
Précy-sous-Thil 27 C6

Pré-en-Pail 17 D4
Préfailles 24 D1
Preignan 37 D6
Preixan 45 B5
Prémery 27 D4
Prémilhat 32 B3
Préporché 27 D5
Pressac 31 B5
Preuilly-sur-Claise 25 D6
Prévenchères 39 C6
Préveranges 32 B3
Prez-sous-Lafauche 28 A2
Prignac-et-Marcamps 37 A4
Prissac 32 A1
Prissé 34 B2
Privas 40 B1
Propriano 49 D5
Provenchères-sur-Fave 29 A4
Provins 19 D4
Prunières 41 C4
Pruniers-en-Sologne 26 C2
Publier 35 B4
Puget-Théniers 41 D5
Puget-Ville 48 B2
Puimoisson 41 D4
Puiseaux 26 B3
Puisieux 14 D3
Puisseguin 37 B4
Puisseguin 37 B5
Puisserguier 46 B2
Puivert 45 C6
Pujaut 40 D1
Pujols 37 B5
Pujols 37 C6
Pulversheim 29 B4
Putanges-Pont-Écrepin 17 D4
Puttelange-aux-Lacs 21 C4
Puybrun 38 B2
Puycasquier 37 D6
Puygouzon 38 C2
Puylaroque 38 C2
Puylaurens 45 A5
Puy-l'Évêque 38 C1
Puymirol 37 C6
Puymoyen 31 C5
Puyôo 43 A6

Q

Quarré-les-Tombes 27 C5
Quatre-Champs 19 B6
Queige 35 C4
Quelaines-St-Gault 24 B3
Quend 14 C2
Quérigut 45 C6
Querrieu 14 D3
Quesnoy-sur-Deûle 15 C4
Quessoy 16 D1
Questembert 23 C4
Quettehou 16 B3
Quettreville-sur-Sienne 16 C2
Quevauvillers 14 D2
Queyrac 30 D3
Quézac 38 B3
Quiberon 22 D3
Quillan 45 C6
Quillebeuf-sur-Seine 17 B5
Quimper 22 C2
Quimperlé 22 C3
Quincy-Voisins 18 C3
Quingey 28 D2
Quinson 40 D3
Quinssaines 32 B3
Quintenas 34 D1
Quintin 23 B4
Quissac 39 D6
Quittebeuf 17 C6

R

Rabastens 38 D2
Rabastens-de-Bigorre 44 B2
Rachecourt-sur-Marne 20 D1
Raismes 15 C4
Ramatuelle 48 B3
Rambervillers 28 A3

Rambouillet **18** D2
Rambucourt **20** D2
Ramonville-St-Agne **45** A5
Randan **33** C5
Randonnai **17** D5
Rânes **17** D4
Raon-l'Étape **21** D4
Raulhac **39** B4
Rauzan **37** B4
Ravières **27** B5
Rayol-Canadel-sur-Mer **48** B3
Razès **32** C2
Réalmont **38** D3
Réalville **38** C2
Réaup **37** C5
Rebais **19** C4
Rébénacq **44** B1
Recey-sur-Ource **27** B6
Réchicourt-le-Château **21** D4
Recoubeau-Jansac **40** B3
Réding **21** D4
Redon **23** C5
Régny **33** C6
Reichshoffen **21** C5
Reignac **31** D4
Reignier **35** B4
Reillanne **40** D3
Reims **19** C5
Rémalard **17** D6
Rembercourt-Sommaisne **20** C1
Remiremont **28** B3
Remoulins **40** D1
Remungol **23** C4
Rémuzat **40** C2
Renaison **33** C6
Renazé **23** C6
Rennes **23** B6
Rennes-les-Bains **45** C6
Renwez **15** D6
Réquista **38** D3
Ressons-sur-Matz **18** B3
Rethel **19** B5
Retiers **23** C6
Retournac **33** D6
Reuilly **26** D2
Revel **45** A5
Revest-du-Bion **40** D3
Revigny-sur-Ornain **19** D6
Revin **15** D6
Reyrieux **34** C2
Rezé **23** D6
Rhinau **29** A5
Riaillé **23** D6
Rians **48** A2
Riantec **22** C3
Ribeauvillé **29** B4
Ribécourt-Dreslincourt **18** B3
Ribemont **15** D4
Ribérac **31** D5
Richardménil **20** D3
Richelieu **25** D5
Riec-sur-Belon **22** C3
Rieumes **45** B4
Rieupeyroux **38** C3
Rieutort-de-Randon **39** B5
Rieux **23** D5
Rieux **45** B4
Riez **41** D4
Rigaud **41** D5
Rignac **38** C3
Rigny-le-Ferron **27** A4
Rigny-sur-Arroux **33** A6
Rigny-Ussé **25** C5
Rilhac-Rancon **32** C1
Rillé **25** C5
Rillieux-la-Pape **34** C2
Rimont **45** B4
Riols **46** A2
Riom **33** C4
Riom-ès-Montagnes **33** D4
Rion-des-Landes **36** D3
Rions **37** B4
Riorges **33** C6
Rioz **28** C3
Riquewihr **29** B4
Riscle **37** D5
Rive-de-Gier **34** D1
Rivedoux-Plage **30** B3

Rivery **14** D3
Rives **34** D3
Rivesaltes **46** C2
Rivière-sur-Tarn **39** C4
Rixheim **29** B5
Roaillan **37** C4
Roanne **33** C6
Robert-Espagne **20** D1
Robiac-Rochessadoule **39** C6
Robion **40** D2
Rocamadour **38** B2
Rochechouart **31** C6
Rochefort **30** C3
Rochefort-en-Terre **23** C5
Rochefort-Montagne **33** C4
Rochefort-sur-Nenon **28** D2
Roche-la-Molière **33** D6
Rochemaure **40** C1
Roches-Bettaincourt **28** A1
Rocheservière **24** D2
Rochetaillée **28** B1
Rochin **15** C4
Rocourt-St-Martin **19** C4
Rocroi **15** D6
Rodelle **38** C3
Rodez **38** C3
Rogliano **49** A6
Rognac **47** A6
Rognes **47** A6
Rognonas **40** D1
Rohan **23** C4
Rohrbach-lès-Bitche **21** C4
Roiffieux **34** D1
Roisel **15** D4
Rolampont **28** B1
Rom **31** B5
Romagné **23** B6
Romans-sur-Isère **40** B2
Romazy **16** D2
Rombas **20** C3
Romillé **23** B5
Romilly-sur-Seine **19** D5
Romorantin-Lanthenay **26** C2
Ronce-les-Bains **30** C3
Ronchamp **28** C3
Roquebillière **41** D6
Roquebrun **46** A2
Roquebrune-Cap-Martin **41** D6
Roquebrune-sur-Argens **48** B3
Roquecor **37** C6
Roquecourbe **38** D3
Roquefort **37** D4
Roquemaure **40** D1
Roquesteron **41** D5
Roquevaire **48** B1
Rosans **40** C3
Roscanvel **22** B1
Roscoff **22** A2
Rosheim **21** D5
Rosières **33** D6
Rosières-en-Santerre **14** D3
Rosoy **27** B4
Rosporden **22** C2
Rostrenen **22** B3
Rothéneuf **16** D2
Rouans **23** D5
Roubaix **15** C4
Rouen **17** B6
Rouffach **29** B4
Rouffignac **37** A6
Rougé **23** C6
Rougemont **28** C3
Rougemont-le-Château **29** B4
Rougnac **31** C5
Rouillac **31** C4
Rouillé **31** B5
Roujan **46** A3
Roulans **28** C3
Roumazières-Loubert **31** C5
Roumoules **41** D4
Rousset **48** A1
Roussillon **34** D2
Roussillon **40** D2
Rousson **39** C6
Routot **17** B6
Rouvroy-sur-Audry **15** D6
Rouy **27** D4
Royan **30** C3

Royat **33** C4
Roybon **34** D2
Roye **18** B3
Royère-de-Vassivière **32** C2
Rozay-en-Brie **18** D3
Rozoy-sur-Serre **19** B5
Ruaudin **25** B5
Rue **14** C2
Rueil-Malmaison **18** C2
Ruelle-sur-Touvre **31** C5
Ruffec **31** A6
Ruffec **31** B5
Ruffey-lès-Echirey **28** C1
Ruffiac **23** C5
Ruffieu **34** C3
Ruffieux **34** C3
Rugles **17** D6
Rully **27** D6
Rumigny **15** D5
Rumilly **34** C3
Rumont **20** D1
Ruoms **39** C6
Rupt-sur-Moselle **28** B3
Rustrel **40** D3
Ruy **34** C2
Ruynes-en-Margeride **39** B4
Ryes **17** B4

S

Saales **29** A4
Sabarat **45** B4
Sables-d'Or-les-Pins **16** D1
Sablé-sur-Sarthe **25** B4
Sablet **40** C2
Sabres **36** C3
Sacquenay **28** C1
Saffré **23** D6
Sagone **49** C5
Sagy **34** A2
Sahune **40** C2
Saillagouse-Llo **45** D6
Saillans **40** B2
Sail-sous-Couzan **33** C6
Sains-Richaumont **15** D5
St-Affrique **39** D4
St-Agnan **33** B5
St-Agnan-en-Vercors **40** B3
St-Agnant **30** C3
St-Agnant-de-Versillat **32** B2
St-Agrève **39** B6
St-Aignan **26** C1
St-Aignan-sur-Roë **23** C6
St-Aigulin **31** D4
St-Albain **34** B2
St-Alban **16** D1
St-Alban-Leysse **34** D3
St-Alban-sur-Limagnole **39** B5
St-Amand-en-Puisaye **27** C4
St-Amand-les-Eaux **15** C4
St-Amand-Longpré **25** C6
St-Amand-Montrond **32** A3
St-Amand-sur-Fion **19** D6
St-Amans **39** B5
St-Amans-des-Cots **39** B4
St-Amans-Soult **45** A6
St-Amant-de-Boixe **31** C5
St-Amant-Roche-Savine **33** C5
St-Amant-Tallende **33** C4
St-Amarin **29** B4
St-Ambroix **39** C6
St-Amour **34** B2
St-Andiol **40** D2
St-André **46** C2
St-André-de-Corcy **34** C2
St-André-de-Cruzières **39** C6
St-André-de-Cubzac **37** B4
St-André-de-l'Eure **17** C6
St-André-de-Sangonis **39** D5
St-André-de-Valborgne **39** C5
St-André-le-Gaz **34** D3
St-André-les-Alpes **41** D4
St-André-les-Vergers **27** A5
St-Angel **32** D3
St-Anthème **33** D6
St-Antonin-Noble-Val **38** C2
St-Août **32** A3

St-Apollinaire **28** C1
St-Arcons-d'Allier **39** A5
St-Arnoult-en-Yvelines **18** D2
St-Astier **31** D5
St-Astier **37** B5
St-Auban **41** D5
St-Auban-sur-l'Ouvèze **40** C3
St-Aubin **28** D1
St-Aubin-Château-Neuf **27** B4
St-Aubin-d'Aubigné **23** B6
St-Aubin-de-Blaye **31** D4
St-Aubin-du-Cormier **23** B6
St-Aubin-lès-Elbeuf **17** B6
St-Aubin-sur-Mer **17** B4
St-Aulaye **31** D5
St-Avé **23** C5
St-Avertin **25** C6
St-Avold **21** C4
St-Ay **26** B2
St-Aygulf **48** B3
St-Barthélemy-d'Agenais **37** C5
St-Barthélemy-de-Vals **34** D2
St-Bauzille-de-Putois **39** D5
St-Béat **44** C3
St-Beauzély **39** C4
St-Benin-d'Azy **27** D4
St-Benoît **31** A5
St-Benoît **45** B6
St-Benoît-du-Sault **32** B2
St-Benoît-sur-Loire **26** B3
St-Béron **34** D3
St-Berthevin **24** B3
St-Bertrand-de-Comminges **44** B3
St-Blaise-la-Roche **21** D4
St-Blin-Semilly **28** A2
St-Boil **34** A1
St-Bonnet-de-Bellac **31** B6
St-Bonnet-de-Joux **33** B6
St-Bonnet-en-Bresse **28** D1
St-Bonnet-en-Champsaur **41** B4
St-Bonnet-le-Château **33** D6
St-Bonnet-le-Froid **33** D6
St-Bonnet-sur-Gironde **30** D3
St-Branchs **25** D6
St-Brevin-les-Pins **23** D5
St-Briac-sur-Mer **16** D1
St-Brice-en-Coglès **16** D2
St-Brieuc **23** B4
St-Bris-le-Vineux **27** B5
St-Brisson **27** C5
St-Broing-les-Moines **27** C6
St-Calais **25** B6
St-Cannat **47** A6
St-Céré **38** B2
St-Cergues **35** B4
St-Cernin **38** A3
St-Chaffrey **41** B4
St-Chamarand **38** B2
St-Chamas **47** A6
St-Chamond **33** D6
St-Chaptes **39** D6
St-Chef **34** C2
St-Chély-d'Apcher **39** B5
St-Chély-d'Aubrac **39** B4
St-Chinian **46** B2
St-Christol **40** D3
St-Christol-lès-Alès **39** C6
St-Christoly-Médoc **30** D3
St-Christophe-en-Bazelle **26** D2
St-Christophe-en-Brionnais **33** B6
St-Ciers-sur-Gironde **31** D4
St-Cirq-Lapopie **38** C2
St-Clair-du-Rhône **34** D2
St-Clar **37** D6
St-Claud **31** C5
St-Claude **34** B3
St-Clément **20** D3
St-Clément **27** A4
St-Clément **32** D2
St-Clément de-Rivière **39** D5
St-Constant **38** B3
St-Cosme-en-Vairais **25** A5
St-Cricq-Chalosse **37** D4
St-Cyprien **37** B6
St-Cyprien **38** C1
St-Cyprien **46** C2
St-Cyr-sur-Loire **25** C5
St-Cyr-sur-Mer **48** B2

St-Denis 18 C3
St-Denis-d'Anjou 25 B4
St-Denis-de-Gastines 24 A3
St-Denis-de-Jouhet 32 A2
St-Denis-de-Pile 37 B4
St-Denis-d'Oléron 30 B2
St-Denis-en-Bugey 34 C2
St-Denis-lès-Bourg 34 B2
St-Désert 34 A1
St-Didier-en-Velay 33 D6
St-Didier-sur-Chalaronne 34 B2
St-Dié 29 A4
St-Dier-d'Auvergne 33 C5
St-Dizier 19 D6
St-Dizier-Leyrenne 32 C2
St-Dolay 23 D5
St-Donat-sur-l'Herbasse 34 D2
St-Doulchard 26 D3
Ste-Adresse 17 B5
Ste-Alvère 37 B6
Ste-Bazeille 37 C5
Ste-Cécile-les-Vignes 40 C2
Ste-Croix 34 A2
Ste-Croix 40 B2
Ste-Croix-Volvestre 45 B4
Ste-Engrâce 43 B6
Ste-Énimie 39 C5
Ste-Eulalie d'Olt 39 C4
Ste-Eulalie-en-Born 36 C3
Ste-Feyre 32 B2
Ste-Foy-de-Peyrolières 45 A4
Ste-Foy-la-Grande 37 B5
Ste-Foy-l'Argentière 33 C6
Ste-Foy-lès-Lyon 34 C2
Ste-Foy-Tarentaise 35 C5
Ste-Geneviève 18 C2
Ste-Geneviève-sur-Argence 39 B4
St-Égrève 34 D3
Ste-Hélène 36 B3
Ste-Hermine 30 A3
Ste-Livrade-sur-Lot 37 C6
St-Élix-le-Château 45 B4
St-Élix-Theux 44 B3
Ste-Lizaigne 26 D2
St-Éloy-les-Mines 33 B4
Ste-Lucie-de-Tallano 49 D5
Ste-Marie 46 C2
Ste-Marie-aux-Mines 29 A4
Ste-Maure-de-Peyriac 37 D5
Ste-Maure-de-Touraine 25 D5
Ste-Maxime 48 B3
Ste-Menehould 19 C6
Ste-Mère-Église 16 B3
St-Émiland 27 D6
Ste-Orse 31 D6
Ste-Pazanne 24 D2
Ste-Radegonde 25 D4
St-Erme-Outre-et-Ramecourt 19 B5
Saintes 31 C4
Ste-Sabine 27 D6
Ste-Savine 27 A5
Ste-Sévère-sur-Indre 32 B3
St-Esteben 43 B5
St-Estèphe 30 D3
St-Estève 46 C2
Ste-Suzanne 25 B4
Ste-Étienne 33 D6
St-Étienne-de-Baïgorry 43 B5
St-Étienne-de-Fontbellon 39 B6
St-Étienne-de-Fursac 32 B2
St-Étienne-de-Montluc 23 D5
St-Étienne-de-St-Geoirs 34 D2
St-Étienne-de-Tinée 41 C5
St-Étienne-du-Bois 34 B2
St-Étienne-du-Rouvray 17 B6
St-Étienne-en-Dévoluy 40 B3
St-Étienne-les-Orgues 40 D3
St-Étienne-lès-Remiremont 28 B3
St-Étienne-Vallée-Française 39 C5
Ste-Tulle 40 D3
Ste-Vertu 27 B5
St-Fargeau 27 C4
St-Félicien 40 B1
St-Félix-Lauragais 45 A5
St-Ferme 37 B5
St-Firmin 20 D3
St-Firmin 40 B3
St-Flavy 19 D5

St-Florent 49 B6
St-Florent-des-Bois 30 A2
St-Florentin 27 B5
St-Florent-le-Vieil 24 C3
St-Florent-sur-Cher 26 D2
St-Flour 39 B4
St-Flovier 25 D6
St-Fons 34 C2
St-Fort-sur-Gironde 30 D3
St-Frajou 45 B4
St-François-Longchamp 35 D4
St-Front-de-Pradoux 31 D5
St-Fulgent 24 D3
St-Galmier 33 C6
St-Gaudens 44 B3
St-Gaultier 32 A2
St-Gein 37 D4
St-Gély-du-Fesc 39 D5
St-Genest-Malifaux 33 D6
St-Geniez 41 C4
St-Geniez-d'Olt 39 C4
St-Genis-de-Saintonge 31 D4
St-Genis-Laval 34 C2
St-Genis-Pouilly 34 B3
St-Genix-sur-Guiers 34 C3
St-Genou 26 D1
St-Geoire-en-Valdaine 34 D3
St-Georges-Buttavent 24 A3
St-Georges-d'Aurac 33 D5
St-Georges-de-Commiers 40 B3
St-Georges-de-Didonne 30 C3
St-Georges-de-Luzençon 39 D4
St-Georges-de-Mons 33 C4
St-Georges-de-Reneins 34 B1
St-Georges-des-Groseillers 17 D4
St-Georges-d'Oléron 30 C2
St-Georges-du-Vièvre 17 C5
St-Georges-en-Couzan 33 C6
St-Georges-lès-Baillargeaux 31 A5
St-Georges-sur-Baulche 27 B4
St-Georges-sur-Cher 25 C6
St-Georges-sur-Loire 24 C3
St-Geours-de-Maremne 36 D3
St-Gérand-le-Puy 33 B5
St-Germain-Chassenay 27 D4
St-Germain-de-Calberte 39 C5
St-Germain-de-la-Coudre 25 A5
St-Germain-des-Fossés 33 B5
St-Germain-d'Esteuil 30 D3
St-Germain-du-Bel-Air 38 B2
St-Germain-du-Bois 34 A2
St-Germain-du-Corbéis 17 D5
St-Germain-du-Plain 34 A2
St-Germain-du-Puy 26 D3
St-Germain-du-Teil 39 C4
St-Germain-en-Laye 18 C2
St-Germain-Laval 33 C6
St-Germain-Lembron 33 D4
St-Germain-les-Belles 32 C2
St-Germain-les-Vergnes 32 D2
St-Germain-l'Herm 33 D5
St-Germé 37 D4
St-Gervais 24 D1
St-Gervais 34 D3
St-Gervais-d'Auvergne 33 C4
St-Gervais-la-Forêt 26 C1
St-Gervais-les-Bains 35 C5
St-Gervais-les-Trois-Clochers 25 D5
St-Gervais-sur-Mare 39 D4
St-Géry 38 C2
St-Gildas-de-Rhuys 23 D4
St-Gildas-des-Bois 23 D5
St-Gilles 39 D6
St-Gilles-Croix-de-Vie 30 A2
St-Gingolph 35 B5
St-Girons 40 B3
St-Girons-Plage 36 D2
St-Gobain 19 B4
St-Guénolé 22 C1
St-Guilhem-le-Désert 39 D5
St-Haon-le-Châtel 33 B6
St-Héand 33 D6
St-Herblain 23 D6
St-Hilaire 45 B6
St-Hilaire-de-Brethmas 39 C6
St-Hilaire-de-Riez 30 A2
St-Hilaire-des-Loges 30 B3
St-Hilaire-de-Villefranche 31 C4

St-Hilaire-du-Harcouët 16 D3
St-Hilaire-du-Rosier 34 D2
St-Hilaire-Fontaine 33 A5
St-Hilaire-le-Grand 19 C6
St-Hilaire-St-Florent 25 C4
St-Hippolyte 29 A5
St-Hippolyte 29 C4
St-Hippolyte-du-Fort 39 D5
St-Honoré-les-Bains 27 D5
St-Hostien 39 A6
St-Ismier 34 D3
St-Izaire 39 D4
St-Jacques-de-la-Lande 23 C5
St-James 16 D2
St-Jean 38 D2
St-Jean-Bonnefonds 33 D6
St-Jean-Brévelay 23 C4
St-Jean-d'Angély 31 C4
St-Jean-d'Assé 25 B5
St-Jean-de-Bournay 34 D2
St-Jean-de-Braye 26 B2
St-Jean-de-Daye 16 C3
St-Jean-de-la-Ruelle 26 B2
St-Jean-de-Losne 28 D1
St-Jean-de-Luz 43 B5
St-Jean-de-Marsacq 36 D3
St-Jean-de-Mauréjols-et-Avéjan 39 C6
St-Jean-de-Maurienne 35 D4
St-Jean-de-Monts 24 D1
St-Jean-de-Sixt 35 C4
St-Jean-de-Védas 47 A4
St-Jean-d'Illac 36 B3
St-Jean-du-Bruel 39 D5
St-Jean-du-Falga 45 B5
St-Jean-du-Gard 39 C6
St-Jean-le-Centenier 40 C1
St-Jean-Pied-de-Port 43 B5
St-Jean-Poutge 37 D5
St-Jean-sur-Erve 25 B4
St-Jeoire 35 B4
St-Jeure-d'Ay 34 D1
St-Jeures 33 D6
St-Joachim 23 D5
St-Jores 16 C2
St-Jorioz 35 C4
St-Jory 38 D1
St-Jouan-des-Guérets 16 D2
St-Jouin-Bruneval 17 B5
St-Jouin-de-Marnes 25 D4
St-Julien 34 B3
St-Julien 45 B4
St-Julien-Beychevelle 30 D3
St-Julien-Boutières 39 B6
St-Julien-Chapteuil 39 A6
St-Julien-de-Concelles 23 D6
St-Julien-de-Vouvantes 23 C6
St-Julien-du-Sault 27 B4
St-Julien-du-Verdon 41 D4
St-Julien-en-Beauchêne 40 C3
St-Julien-en-Born 36 D3
St-Julien-en-Genevois 35 B4
St-Julien-l'Ars 31 A5
St-Junien 31 C6
St-Just 40 C1
St-Just-en-Chaussée 18 B3
St-Just-en-Chevalet 33 C5
St-Just-Ibarre 43 B6
St-Justin 37 D4
St-Just-la-Pendue 33 C6
St-Just-Luzac 30 C3
St-Just-Sauvage 19 D5
St-Just-St-Rambert 33 D6
St-Lambert-des-Levées 25 C4
St-Lary-Soulan 44 C3
St-Laurent-Bretagne 44 B2
St-Laurent-d'Aigouze 39 D6
St-Laurent-de-Carnols 40 C1
St-Laurent-de-Cerdans 45 D6
St-Laurent-de-Chamousset 33 C6
St-Laurent-de-la-Cabrerisse 46 B2
St-Laurent-de-la-Salanque 46 C2
St-Laurent-de-Neste 44 B3
St-Laurent-des-Autels 23 D6
St-Laurent-du-Pont 34 D3
St-Laurent-du-Var 41 D5
St-Laurent-du-Verdon 41 C5
St-Laurent-en-Caux 17 B6
St-Laurent-en-Grandvaux 34 A3

St-Laurent-les-Bains 39 B6
St-Laurent-Médoc 30 D3
St-Laurent-Nouan 26 C1
St-Laurent-sur-Gorre 31 C6
St-Laurent-sur-Sèvre 24 D3
St-Léger-des-Vignes 27 D4
St-Léger-en-Yvelines 18 D2
St-Léger-sous-Beuvray 27 D5
St-Léonard 29 A4
St-Léonard-de-Noblat 32 C2
St-Lizier 45 B4
St-Lô 16 C3
St-Lon-les-Mines 36 D3
St-Loubès 37 B4
St-Loup-de-la-Salle 27 D6
St-Loup-Lamairé 25 D4
St-Loup-sur-Semouse 28 B3
St-Lubin-des-Joncherets 17 D6
St-Lunaire 16 D1
St-Lupicin 34 B3
St-Lyé 19 D5
St-Lys 45 A4
St-Macaire 37 B4
St-Macaire-en-Mauges 24 D3
St-Magne 37 C4
St-Magne-de-Castillon 37 B5
St-Maime 40 D3
St-Maixent-l'École 31 B4
St-Malo 16 D1
St-Malo-de-la-Lande 16 C2
St-Mamert-du-Gard 39 D6
St-Marcel 18 C1
St-Marcel 27 D6
St-Marcel 32 A2
St-Marcel-d'Ardèche 40 C1
St-Marcel-lès-Annonay 34 D1
St-Marcel-lès-Sauzet 40 C2
St-Marcel-lès-Valence 40 B2
St-Marcellin 34 D2
St-Marc-sur-Seine 27 C6
St-Mards-en-Othe 27 B5
St-Marsal 45 C6
St-Mars-d'Outillé 25 B5
St-Mars-du-Désert 23 D6
St-Mars-la-Brière 25 B5
St-Mars-la-Jaille 23 D6
St-Martial 39 D5
St-Martial-de-Nabirat 38 B1
St-Martial-de-Valette 31 D6
St-Martin 48 A2
St-Martin-Boulogne 14 C2
St-Martin-d'Ablois 19 C5
St-Martin-d'Arrossa 43 B5
St-Martin-d'Auxigny 26 D3
St-Martin-de-Belleville 35 D4
St-Martin-de-Castillon 40 D3
St-Martin-de-Crau 47 A5
St-Martin-de-Landelles 16 D3
St-Martin-de-Londres 39 D5
St-Martin-d'Entraunes 41 D5
St-Martin-de-Ré 30 B2
St-Martin-des-Besaces 16 C3
St-Martin-des-Champs 22 A2
St-Martin-de-Seignanx 43 A5
St-Martin-de-Valamas 39 B6
St-Martin-de-Valgalgues 39 C6
St-Martin-d'Hères 40 B3
St-Martin-d'Oney 37 D4
St-Martin-du-Mont 34 B2
St-Martin-du-Var 41 D5
St-Martin-en-Bresse 28 D1
St-Martin-le-Beau 25 C6
St-Martin-sur-Ouanne 27 B4
St-Martin-Valmeroux 32 D3
St-Martin-Vésubie 41 D5
St-Martory 45 B4
St-Mathieu 31 C6
St-Mathurin 30 A2
St-Maur 26 D1
St-Maurice-de-Lignon 33 D6
St-Maurice-des-Lions 31 C6
St-Maurice-la-Souterraine 32 B2
St-Maurice-l'Exil 34 D2
St-Maurice-Navacelles 39 D5
St-Maurin 37 C6
St-Max 20 D3
St-Maximin-la-Ste-Baume 48 A2
St-Médard-en-Jalles 37 B4

St-Méen-le-Grand 23 B5
St-Méloir-des-Ondes 16 D2
St-Memmie 19 C6
St-Menoux 33 A4
St-Mesmin 19 D5
St-Mesmin 31 D6
St-Michel 15 D5
St-Michel 31 C5
St-Michel 44 B3
St-Michel-Chef-Chef 23 D5
St-Michel-de-Castelnau 37 C4
St-Michel-de-Maurienne 35 D4
St-Michel-en-l'Herm 30 B3
St-Michel-sur-Meurthe 29 A4
St-Mihiel 20 C2
St-Montant 40 C1
St-Nabord 28 B3
St-Nauphary 38 D2
St-Nazaire 23 D5
St-Nazaire-le-Désert 40 C2
St-Nectaire 33 C4
St-Nicolas 14 C3
St-Nicolas-d'Aliermont 14 D1
St-Nicolas-de-la-Grave 37 C6
St-Nicolas-de-Port 20 D3
St-Nicolas-de-Redon 23 C5
St-Nicolas-du-Pélem 22 B3
St-Omer 14 B2
St-Orens-de-Gameville 45 A5
St-Ost 44 B3
St-Ouen 14 D2
St-Ouen 25 B6
St-Ouen-des-Toits 24 B3
St-Pair-sur-Mer 16 D2
St-Palais 43 B6
St-Palais-sur-Mer 30 C3
St-Pal-de-Chalancon 33 D6
St-Pal-de-Mons 33 D6
St-Pantaléon 27 D6
St-Pantaléon 38 C1
St-Papoul 45 B5
St-Pardoux-Isaac 37 B5
St-Pardoux-la-Rivière 31 D6
St-Parize-le-Châtel 27 D4
St-Parres-lès-Vaudes 27 B5
St-Paterne 17 D5
St-Paterne-Racan 25 C5
St-Paul 41 C5
St-Paul-Cap-de-Joux 38 D2
St-Paul-de-Fenouillet 45 C6
St-Paul-de-Jarrat 45 C5
St-Paul-en-Born 36 C3
St-Paul-en-Forêt 48 A3
St-Paul-et-Valmalle 39 D5
St-Paulien 33 D5
St-Paul-le-Jeune 39 C6
St-Paul-lès-Dax 36 D3
St-Paul-lès-Durance 40 D3
St-Paul-Trois-Châteaux 40 C1
St-Pé-de-Bigorre 44 B2
St-Pée-sur-Nivelle 43 B5
St-Péray 40 B2
St-Père 27 C5
St-Père-en-Retz 23 D5
St-Phal 27 B5
St-Philbert-de-Bouaine 24 D2
St-Philbert-de-Grand-Lieu 24 D2
St-Pierre-d'Albigny 35 D4
St-Pierre-de-Chignac 31 D6
St-Pierre-de-Côle 31 D6
St-Pierre-de-la-Fage 39 D5
St-Pierre-de-Maillé 31 A6
St-Pierre-de-Plesguen 16 D2
St-Pierre-des-Champs 45 B6
St-Pierre-des-Corps 25 C6
St-Pierre-des-Échaubrognes 24 D3
St-Pierre-des-Landes 23 B6
St-Pierre-des-Nids 17 D4
St-Pierre-de-Trivisy 38 D3
St-Pierre-d'Irube 43 B5
St-Pierre-d'Oléron 30 C2
St-Pierre-du-Chemin 30 A3
St-Pierre-du-Mont 37 D4
St-Pierre-Église 16 B2
St-Pierre-en-Faucigny 35 B4
St-Pierre-en-Port 17 A5
St-Pierre-le-Moûtier 27 D4
St-Pierre-lès-Elbeuf 17 C6

St-Pierre-lès-Nemours 26 A3
St-Pierre-Montlimart 24 C3
St-Pierre-Quiberon 22 D3
St-Pierre-sur-Dives 17 C4
St-Plancard 44 B3
St-Pois 16 D3
St-Poix 24 B3
St-Pol-de-Léon 22 A2
St-Pol-sur-Mer 14 B3
St-Pol-sur-Ternoise 14 C3
St-Pompont 38 B1
St-Pons 41 C4
St-Pons-de-Thomières 46 A2
St-Porchaire 30 C3
St-Pourçain-sur-Sioule 33 B5
St-Priest 34 C2
St-Priest-de-Champs 33 C4
St-Priest-Laprugne 33 C5
St-Priest-Taurion 32 C2
St-Privat 32 D3
St-Privat-d'Allier 39 B5
St-Prix 33 B5
St-Projet 38 C2
St-Puy 37 D6
St-Quentin 15 D4
St-Quentin-la-Poterie 39 D6
St-Quirin 21 D4
St-Rambert-d'Albon 34 D2
St-Rambert-en-Bugey 34 C3
St-Raphaël 48 B3
St-Remèze 39 C6
St-Rémy 27 D6
St-Rémy-de-Provence 40 D2
St-Remy-en-Bouzemont-St-Genest-et-
Isson 19 D6
St-Rémy-sur-Avre 17 D6
St-Rémy-sur-Durolle 33 C5
St-Renan 22 B1
St-Révérien 27 D4
St-Riquier 14 D2
St-Romain-en-Gal 34 D2
St-Romain-sur-Cher 26 C1
St-Romans 34 D2
St-Rome-de-Cernon 39 D4
St-Rome-de-Tarn 39 D4
St-Saëns 17 B6
St-Saturnin-lès-Apt 40 D2
St-Saud-Lacoussière 31 C6
St-Saulge 27 D4
St-Sauves-d'Auvergne 33 C4
St-Sauveur 22 B2
St-Sauveur 28 B3
St-Sauveur-de-Montagut 40 B1
St-Sauveur-en-Puisaye 27 C4
St-Sauveur-Gouvernet 40 C2
St-Sauveur-Lendelin 16 C2
St-Sauveur-le-Vicomte 16 B2
St-Sauveur-sur-Tinée 41 D5
St-Sauvy 37 D6
St-Savin 31 A6
St-Savin 31 D4
St-Savinien 30 C3
St-Sébastien-de-Morsent 17 C6
St-Sébastien-sur-Loire 23 D6
St-Seine-l'Abbaye 27 C6
St-Semin 39 B6
St-Sernin-sur-Rance 38 D3
St-Seurin-sur-l'Isle 37 B5
St-Sever 37 D4
St-Sever-Calvados 16 C3
St-Siméon-de-Bressieux 34 D2
St-Simon 19 B4
St-Simon 38 B3
St-Sorlin-d'Arves 35 D4
St-Soupplets 18 C3
St-Sulpice 38 D2
St-Sulpice-Laurière 32 B2
St-Sulpice-les-Champs 32 C3
St-Sulpice-les-Feuilles 32 B2
St-Sulpice-sur-Lèze 45 B4
St-Sulpice-sur-Risle 17 D5
St-Sylvain 17 C4
St-Symphorien 37 C4
St-Symphorien 39 B5
St-Symphorien-de-Lay 33 C6
St-Symphorien-sur-Coise 33 C6
St-Thégonnec 22 B2
St-Thibéry 46 B3

St-Thiébault 28 B2
St-Thurien 22 C3
St-Trivier-de-Courtes 34 B2
St-Trivier-sur-Moignans 34 B2
St-Trojan-les-Bains 30 C3
St-Tropez 48 B3
St-Uze 34 D2
St-Valérien 27 B4
St-Valery-en-Caux 17 A5
St-Valery-sur-Somme 14 D2
St-Vallier 33 A6
St-Vallier 34 D2
St-Vallier-de-Thiey 41 D5
St-Varent 25 D4
St-Vaury 32 B2
St-Victor 34 C2
St-Victor-de-Cessieu 34 D2
St-Victoret 47 A6
St-Victor-la-Coste 40 D1
St-Vigor-le-Grand 16 C3
St-Vincent-de-Connezac 31 D5
St-Vincent-de-Paul 36 D3
St-Vincent-les-Forts 41 C4
St-Vit 28 D2
St-Vite 37 C6
St-Vivien-de-Médoc 30 D3
St-Xandre 30 B3
St-Yan 33 B6
St-Ybars 45 B4
St-Yorre 33 C5
St-Yorre 33 C5
St-Yrieix-la-Perche 31 D6
St-Yrieix-sur-Charente 31 C5
St-Yvy 22 C2
St-Zacharie 48 B2
Sainville 18 D2
Saissac 45 B6
Saïx 45 A6
Salagnac 31 D6
Salaise-sur-Sanne 34 D2
Salaunes 36 B3
Salbris 26 C2
Salernes 48 A2
Salers 32 D3
Salettes 39 B6
Saleux 14 D2
Salies-de-Béarn 43 A6
Salies-du-Salat 45 B4
Salignac-Eyvignes 38 B1
Salin-de-Giraud 47 B5
Salins 32 D3
Salins-les-Bains 28 D2
Sallanches 35 C4
Salles 36 C3
Salles-Curan 39 C4
Salles-d'Angles 31 C4
Salles-la-Source 35 A2
Salles-sur-l'Hers 45 B5
Salon 19 D5
Salon-de-Provence 47 A6
Salornay-sur-Guye 34 B1
Salouël 14 D2
Salses-le-Château 46 C2
Salvagnac 38 D2
Salviac 38 B1
Samadet 37 D4
Samatan 45 A4
Samer 14 C2
Samoëns 35 B5
Sampigny 20 D2
Sanary-sur-Mer 48 B2
Sancergues 26 D3
Sancerre 26 C3
Sancey-le-Grand 28 C3
Sancheville 26 B1
Sancoins 26 D3
Sandillon 26 B2
Sangatte 14 B2
Sanguinet 36 C3
San-Nicolao 49 B6
Sansac-de-Marmiesse 38 B3
Santa-Maria-Siché 49 C5
Sant'Ambroggio 49 B5
Sant Julià de Lòria AND 45 D5
Santo-Pietro-di-Tenda 49 B6
Santo-Pietro-di-Venaco 49 C6
Saône 28 D3
Saorge 41 D6

Saou 40 B2
Saramon 44 A3
Saran 26 B2
Sarcelles 18 C3
Sare 43 B5
Sarlat-la-Canéda 38 B1
Sarliac-sur-l'Isle 31 D6
Sarralbe 21 C4
Sarrance 43 B6
Sarrancolin 44 C3
Sarras 34 D2
Sarrebourg 21 D4
Sarreguemines 21 C4
Sarre-Union 21 C4
Sarrians 40 D2
Sarrola-Carcopino 49 C5
Sarron 44 A2
Sarry 19 C6
Sartène 49 D5
Sartilly 16 D2
Sarzeau 23 D4
Sassenage 34 D3
Satillieu 34 D1
Saubusse 36 D3
Saucats 37 B4
Sauclières 39 D5
Saugnacq-et-Muret 36 C3
Saugues 39 B5
Saujon 30 C3
Saulce-sur-Rhône 40 B2
Saulieu 27 C5
Sault 40 D2
Sault-de-Navailles 43 A6
Sault-lès-Rethel 19 B5
Saulx 28 C3
Saulxures-sur-Moselotte 29 B4
Saulzais-le-Potier 32 A3
Saumos 36 B3
Saumur 25 C4
Saurat 45 C5
Sausset-les-Pins 47 B6
Saussy 28 C1
Sautron 23 D6
Sauvagnon 44 B2
Sauve 39 D6
Sauveterre-de-Béarn 43 B6
Sauveterre-de-Guyenne 37 B5
Sauveterre-la-Lémance 37 B6
Sauviat-sur-Vige 32 C2
Sauxillanges 33 D5
Sauzet 38 C1
Sauzé-Vaussais 31 B5
Sauzon 22 D3
Savenay 23 D5
Saverdun 45 B5
Saverne 21 D5
Savières 19 D5
Savignac-les-Églises 31 D6
Savigné-l'Évêque 25 B5
Savigneux 33 C6
Savigny-en-Sancerre 26 C3
Savigny-lès-Beaune 27 D6
Savigny-sur-Braye 25 B6
Savines-le-Lac 41 C4
Savoisy 27 B6
Scaër 22 C3
Scey-sur-Saône-et-St-Albin 28 C2
Scherwiller 29 A5
Schiltigheim 21 D5
Schirmeck 21 D4
Sciez 35 B4
Scionzier 35 C4
Scorbé-Clairvaux 25 D5
Sébazac-Concourès 38 C3
Seclin 15 C4
Secondigny 31 A4
Sedan 19 B6
Séderon 40 C3
Sées 17 D5
Séez 35 C5
Séglien 22 C3
Segonzac 31 C4
Segré 24 C3
Ségrie 25 A4
Ségur 39 C4
Seiches-sur-le-Loir 25 C4
Seignelay 27 B4
Seilhac 32 D2

Seillans **48** A3
Seissan **44** A3
Seix **45** C4
Sélestat **29** A5
Selles-St-Denis **26** C2
Selles-sur-Cher **26** C1
Sellières **28** D2
Selommes **25** B6
Selongey **28** C1
Selonnet **41** C4
Seltz **21** C6
Sembadel **33** D5
Séméac **44** B2
Sémelay **27** D5
Semoutiers-Montsaon **28** B1
Semur-en-Auxois **27** C6
Semur-en-Brionnais **33** B6
Semussac **30** C3
Senarpont **14** D2
Sénas **40** D2
Senez **41** D4
Sengouagnet **44** B3
Senlis **18** C3
Sennecey-le-Grand **34** A2
Senonches **17** D6
Senones **21** D4
Senouillac **38** D2
Sens **27** B4
Sens-de-Bretagne **23** B6
Sentein **45** C4
Senuc **19** B6
Seppois-le-Bas **29** C4
Septèmes-les-Vallons **47** B6
Septeuil **18** C2
Septfonds **38** C2
Septmoncel **34** B3
Seraincourt **19** B5
Séranon **41** D5
Séreilhac **31** C6
Sérent **23** C4
Sergines **27** A4
Sérifontaine **18** B2
Sérignan **46** B3
Sérignan-du-Comtat **40** C2
Sermaises **26** A2
Sermano **49** B6
Sermoyer **34** B2
Serqueux **28** B2
Serquigny **17** C5
Serra-di-Ferro **49** D5
Serra-di-Scopamène **49** D5
Serres **40** C3
Serres-Castet **44** B2
Serriera **49** B5
Serrière-de-Briord **34** C3
Serrières **34** D1
Sers **31** C5
Servance **28** B3
Serverette **39** B5
Servian **46** B3
Servon-sur-Vilaine **23** B6
Servoz **35** C4
Sery **19** B5
Sète **47** B4
Seuil-d'Argonne **20** C1
Seurre **28** D1
Sévérac-le-Château **39** C4
Sévignacq **44** B2
Sévrier **35** C4
Seyches **37** B5
Seyne **41** C4
Seynes **39** C6
Seynod **35** C4
Seyssel **34** C3
Seysses **45** A4
Sézanne **19** D5
Sierck-les-Bains **20** B3
Sierentz **29** C5
Sigean **46** B2
Signes **48** B2
Signy-l'Abbaye **19** B6
Signy-le-Petit **15** D5
Sigogne **31** C4
Sigoulès **37** B5
Silfiac **22** B3
Sillans-la-Cascade **48** A2
Sillé-le-Guillaume **25** B4
Simandre **34** A2

Simiane-la-Rotonde **40** D3
Simorre **44** B3
Sin-le-Noble **15** C4
Siran **38** B3
Sirod **34** A3
Sisco **49** A6
Sissonne **19** B5
Sisteron **40** C3
Sivry-sur-Meuse **20** B1
Six-Fours-les-Plages **48** B2
Sixt-Fer-à-Cheval **35** C5
Sizun **22** B2
Smarves **31** A5
Sochaux **29** C4
Soing **28** C2
Soings-en-Sologne **26** C1
Soissons **19** B4
Soizy-aux-Bois **19** D5
Solaro **49** C6
Soldeu *AND* **45** C5
Solenzara **49** C6
Solesmes **15** D4
Solesmes **25** B4
Solférino **36** C3
Sollacaro **49** D5
Solliès-Pont **48** B2
Solliès-Toucas **48** B2
Solomiac **37** D6
Solre-le-Château **15** D5
Somain **15** C4
Sombernon **27** C6
Sommepy-Tahure **19** C6
Sommesous **19** D5
Somme-Suippe **19** C6
Sommevoire **19** D6
Sommières **39** D6
Sommières-du-Clain **31** B5
Songeons **18** B2
Soorts-Hossegor **36** D2
Sorbiers **33** D6
Sorcy-St-Martin **20** D2
Sorde-l'Abbaye **43** A6
Sore **37** C4
Sorèze **45** A6
Sorges **31** D6
Sorgues **40** D2
Sornac **32** C3
Sos **37** D5
Sospel **41** D6
Sost **44** C3
Sotta **49** D6
Sotteville-lès-Rouen **17** B6
Soual **45** A6
Soubès **39** D5
Soucy **27** A4
Soudan **23** C6
Soueix **45** C4
Souesmes **26** C2
Soufflenheim **21** D5
Souillac **38** B2
Souilly **20** C1
Soulac-sur-Mer **30** D3
Soulaines-Dhuys **19** D6
Soulatgé **45** C6
Soullans **24** D2
Soulom **44** C2
Soultz-Haut-Rhin **29** B4
Soultz-sous-Forêts **21** C5
Soumoulou **44** B2
Souppes-sur-Loing **26** B3
Souprosse **37** D4
Sourdeval **16** D3
Sournia **45** C6
Sours **18** D1
Sourzac **37** A5
Sousceyrac **38** B3
Soustons **36** D3
Souvigny **33** A4
Soveria **49** B6
Soyaux **31** C5
Soye **28** C3
Soyons **40** B2
Spincourt **20** B2
Stainville **20** D1
Steenvoorde **14** B3
Stenay **20** B1
Stes-Maries-de-la-Mer **47** A5
Stiring-Wendel **21** C4

Strasbourg **21** D5
Sts-Geosmes **28** B1
Sturzelbronn **21** C5
Suèvres **26** C1
Suilly-la-Tour **27** C4
Suippes **19** C6
Sully **27** D6
Sully-sur-Loire **26** B3
Sulniac **23** C4
Sumène **39** D5
Superdévoluy **40** B3
Surgères **30** B3
Sury-le-Comtal **33** D6
Surzur **23** D4
Suze-la-Rousse **40** C2

T

Taglio-Isolaccio **49** B6
Tagnon **19** B5
Tain-l'Hermitage **40** B2
Taintrux **29** A4
Taizé **34** B1
Talais **30** D3
Talant **28** C1
Talence **37** B4
Talensac **23** C5
Taliard **41** C4
Taller **36** D3
Talloires **35** C4
Tallone **49** C6
Talmay **28** C2
Talmont **30** D3
Talmont-St-Hilaire **30** B2
Tamnay-en-Bazois **27** D5
Tancarville **17** B5
Taninges **35** B4
Tanlay **27** B5
Tannay **19** B6
Tannay **27** C4
Tantonville **20** D3
Taradeau **48** A3
Tarare **33** C6
Tarascon **40** D1
Tarascon-sur-Ariège **45** C5
Tarbes **44** B2
Tardets-Sorholus **43** B6
Targon **37** B4
Tarnos **43** A5
Taron-Sadirac-Viellenave **44** A2
Tartas **36** D3
Tassin-la-Demi-Lune **34** C2
Taulé **22** A2
Taulignan **40** C2
Tauves **33** D4
Tavaco **49** C5
Tavant **25** D5
Tavaux **28** D2
Tavel **40** D1
Tavera **49** C5
Tavernay **27** D5
Tavernes **48** A2
Taverny **18** C2
Teillay **23** C6
Teillet **38** D3
Tellancourt **20** B2
Tenay **34** C3
Tence **33** D6
Tende **41** D6
Tendu **37** A2
Tergnier **19** B4
Termignon **35** D5
Terminiers **26** B2
Terrasson-Lavilledieu **32** D1
Terraube **37** D6
Terrou **38** B2
Terves **25** D4
Tesson **30** C3
Tessy-sur-Vire **16** C3
Teyssieu **38** B3
Thann **29** B4
Thaon-les-Vosges **28** A3
Thaumiers **26** D3
Theillay **25** C2
Theix **23** C4
Thenay **32** A2
Thénezay **31** A4

Thenon **31** D6
Théoule-sur-Mer **49** A4
Thérouanne **14** C2
Thèze **40** C3
Thèze **44** A2
Thiaucourt-Regniéville **20** C2
Thiberville **17** C5
Thibie **19** C5
Thiéblemont-Farémont **19** D6
Thiers **33** C5
Thiézac **39** B4
Thimert-Gâtelles **17** D6
Thin-le-Moutier **19** B6
Thionville **20** B3
Thiron Gardais **25** A6
Thivars **18** D1
Thiviers **31** D6
Thizy **33** C6
Thoirette **34** B3
Thoiry **18** C2
Thoissey **34** B2
Thônes **35** C4
Thonnance-lès-Joinville **20** D1
Thonon-les-Bains **35** B4
Thorame-Haute **41** D4
Thoras **39** B5
Thoré-la-Rochette **25** B6
Thorenc **41** D5
Thorigny-sur-Oreuse **27** A4
Thouarcé **25** C4
Thouaré-sur-Loire **23** D6
Thouars **25** D4
Thourotte **18** B3
Thuès-entre-Valls **45** C6
Thueyts **39** B6
Thuir **46** C2
Thuré **25** D5
Thuret **33** C5
Thurey **34** A2
Thurins **34** C1
Thury-Harcourt **17** C4
Thyez **35** B4
Tiercé **25** C4
Tignes **35** D5
Tigy **26** B2
Til-Châtel **28** C1
Tilh **43** A6
Tillac **44** A3
Tillières-sur-Avre **17** D6
Tilloy-et-Bellay **19** C6
Tilly-sur-Seulles **17** C4
Tinchebray **17** D3
Tinqueux **19** C5
Tinténiac **23** B5
Tiranges **33** D6
Tizzano **49** D5
Tocane-St-Apre **31** D5
Tombebœuf **37** C5
Tonnay-Boutonne **30** C3
Tonnay-Charente **30** C3
Tonneins **37** C5
Tonnerre **27** B5
Torcy **27** D6
Torigni-sur-Vire **16** C3
Tosse **36** D3
Tôtes **17** B6
Toucy **27** B4
Touffailles **37** C6
Touget **37** D6
Toul **20** D2
Toulon **48** B2
Toulon-sur-Allier **33** B5
Toulon-sur-Arroux **33** A6
Toulouges **46** C2
Toulouse **38** D2
Touques **17** B5
Tourch **22** C2
Tourcoing **15** C4
Tourlaville **16** B2
Tournan-en-Brie **18** D3
Tournay **44** B3
Tournecoupe **37** D6
Tournefeuille **45** A4
Tournon-d'Agenais **37** C6
Tournon-St-Martin **31** A6
Tournon-sur-Rhône **40** B2
Tournus **34** A2
Tourny **18** C1

Tourouvre **17** D5
Tours **25** C6
Tourteron **19** B6
Tourtoirac **31** D6
Toury **26** B2
Touvois **24** D2
Traînel **19** D4
Traînou **26** B2
Tramayes **34** B1
Trannes **27** A6
Trans **16** D2
Trans-en-Provence **48** A3
Trappes **18** D2
Trèbes **45** B6
Trébeurden **22** A3
Treffort-Cuisiat **34** B2
Trégastel **22** A3
Trégueux **23** B4
Tréguier **22** A3
Trégunc **22** C2
Treignac **32** D2
Treigny **27** C4
Trélazé **25** C4
Trélissac **31** D6
Trélon **15** D5
Tremblay-les-Villages **18** D1
Trémentines **24** D3
Tréméven **22** C3
Trémolat **37** B6
Trémouilles **39** C4
Trensacq **36** C3
Trentels **37** C6
Tréon **17** D6
Trept **34** C2
Trescléoux **40** C3
Trets **48** A2
Trévé **23** B4
Tréveray **20** D2
Trèves **39** C5
Trévières **16** C3
Trévillers **29** C4
Trévoux **34** C2
Trézelles **33** B5
Triaize **30** B3
Tribehou **16** C3
Tricot **18** B3
Trie-Château **18** C2
Trie-sur-Baïse **44** B3
Trieux **20** C2
Trigance **41** D4
Trignac **23** D5
Triguères **27** B4
Trilport **18** C3
Trizac **32** D3
Troarn **17** C4
Troissereux **18** B2
Trois-Vèvres **27** D4
Tronville-en-Barrois **20** D1
Troo **25** B6
Trouville-sur-Mer **17** B5
Trouy **26** D3
Troyes **27** A5
Troyon **20** C2
Truchtersheim **21** D5
Trun **17** C5
Tuchan **46** C2
Tuffé **25** B5
Tulette **40** C2
Tulle **32** D2
Tullins **34** D3

U

Ucciani **49** C5
Ucel **39** B6
Uchaux **40** C2
Uchizy **34** B2
Ugine **35** C4
Unieux **33** D6
Unverre **25** A6
Urbise **33** B5
Urdos **44** C1
Urepel **43** B5
Uriménil **28** B3
Urrugne **43** B5
Urt **43** A5
Urville Nacqueville **16** B2
Urzy **27** D4
Ussel **32** D3
Ussel **39** A4
Usson-du-Poitou **31** B5
Usson-en-Forez **33** D6
Ustaritz **43** B5
Ustou **45** C4
Utelle **41** D5
Uvernet-Fours **41** C4
Uxeau **33** A6
Uza **36** D3
Uzel **23** B4
Uzer **39** C6
Uzerche **32** D2
Uzès **39** D6

V

Vaas **25** C5
Vabre **38** D3
Vabres-l'Abbaye **39** D4
Vacheresse **35** B4
Vacqueyras **40** D2
Vagney **29** B4
Vaiges **25** B4
Vailly-sur-Aisne **19** B4
Vailly-sur-Sauldre **26** C3
Vaison-la-Romaine **40** C2
Vaïssac **38** D2
Vaivre-et-Montoille **28** C3
Valanjou **25** D4
Valberg **41** D5
Valbonnais **40** B3
Valbonne **49** A4
Valcabrère **44** B3
Valdahon **28** D3
Valdeblore **41** D5
Val-de-Meuse **28** B2
Val-de-Reuil **17** C6
Valderiès **38** D3
Val-d'Isère **35** D5
Valdivienne **31** A5
Val-d'Izé **23** B6
Valdoie **29** C4
Valençay **26** D1
Valence **37** C6
Valence **40** B2
Valence-d'Albigeois **38** D3
Valence-sur-Baïse **37** D5
Valenciennes **15** C4
Valensole **40** D3
Valentigney **29** C4
Valernes **40** C3
Valfroicourt **28** B3
Vallauris **49** A4
Valleiry **34** B3
Valleraugue **39** D5
Vallet **23** D6
Vallières **32** C3
Valloire **35** D4
Vallon-en-Sully **33** A4
Vallon-Pont-d'Arc **39** C6
Vallorcine **35** C5
Vallouise **41** B4
Valmont **17** B5
Valmorel **35** D4
Valmy **19** C6
Valognes **16** B2
Valras-Plage **46** B3
Valréas **40** C2
Valros **46** A3
Vals-les-Bains **39** B6
Val-Suzon **27** C6
Vanault-les-Dames **19** C6
Vandenesse **27** D5
Vandenesse-en-Auxois **27** D6
Vannes **23** C4
Vanvey **27** B6
Vaour **38** D2
Varades **24** C3
Varages **48** A2
Varaire **38** C2
Varces-Allières-et-Risset **40** B3
Varengeville-sur-Mer **14** D1
Varennes-en-Argonne **20** C1
Varennes-St-Sauveur **34** B2
Varennes-sur-Allier **33** B5
Varennes-Vauzelles **27** D4
Varetz **32** D2
Varilhes **45** B5
Vars **31** C5
Vars **41** C5
Varzy **27** C4
Vasles **31** A4
Vassieux-en-Vercors **40** B2
Vassy **16** C3
Vatan **26** D2
Vaubadon **16** C3
Vaubecourt **20** C1
Vauchassis **27** A5
Vauclaix **27** D5
Vauconcourt-Nervezain **28** C2
Vaucouleurs **20** D2
Vaudémont **20** D3
Vaugneray **34** C1
Vaulx-en-Velin **34** C2
Vaulx-Milieu **34** C2
Vauvenargues **48** A1
Vauvert **39** D6
Vauvillers **28** B3
Vaux-le-Pénil **18** D3
Vaux-sur-Mer **30** C3
Vayrac **38** B2
Vayres **31** C6
Veauche **33** D6
Vebron **39** C5
Védrines-St-Loup **39** A5
Veigy-Foncenex **35** B4
Velaux **47** A6
Vélines **37** B5
Vellevans **28** C3
Velosnes **20** B2
Venaco **49** C6
Venansault **30** A2
Venarey-les-Laumes **27** C6
Vence **41** D5
Vendargues **39** D6
Vendays-Montalivet **30** D3
Vendeuvre-du-Poitou **31** A5
Vendeuvre-sur-Barse **27** A6
Vendœuvres **26** D1
Vendôme **25** B6
Venelles **47** A6
Vénès **38** D3
Vénissieux **34** C2
Venizel **19** B4
Venoy **27** B4
Vensac **30** D3
Ventavon **40** C3
Venteuges **39** B5
Ventiseri **49** C6
Verberie **18** C3
Vercel-Villedieu-le-Camp **28** D3
Verdaches **41** C4
Verdun **20** C2
Verdun-sur-Garonne **38** D1
Verdun-sur-le-Doubs **28** D1
Verfeil **38** C2
Verfeil **38** D2
Vergaville **21** D4
Vergèze **39** D6
Vergigny **27** B5
Vergongheon **33** D5
Vergt **37** A6
Vermand **15** D4
Vermenton **27** C5
Vernantes **25** C5
Vern-d'Anjou **24** C3
Vernet **45** B4
Vernet-les-Bains **45** C6
Verneuil-sur-Avre **17** D6
Verneuil-sur-Vienne **31** C6
Verniolle **45** B5
Vernon **18** C1
Vernouillet **17** D6
Vernoux-en-Vivarais **40** B1
Vern-sur-Seiche **23** C6
Verny **20** C3
Vero **49** C5
Verosvres **33** B6
Verrières **31** B5
Versailles **18** D2
Vers-en-Montage **28** D2
Versols-et-Lapeyre **39** D4
Verson **17** C4
Vers-Pont-du-Gard **40** D1
Vert **37** C4
Verteillac **31** D5
Verteuil-d'Agenais **37** C5
Vertheuil **30** D3
Verton **14** C2
Vertou **23** D6
Vertus **19** C5
Vervins **15** D5
Verzy **19** C5
Vesoul **28** C3
Vétheuil **18** C2
Veulettes-sur-Mer **17** A5
Veynes **40** C3
Veyre-Monton **33** C4
Vézelay **27** C5
Vézelise **20** D3
Vézénobres **39** D6
Vezins **24** D3
Vézins-de-Lévézou **39** C4
Vezzani **49** C6
Viala du Tarn **39** C4
Vialas **39** C5
Viane **38** D3
Viarmes **18** C3
Vias **46** B3
Viazac **38** B3
Vibraye **25** B6
Vicdessos **45** C5
Vic-en-Bigorre **44** B2
Vic-Fezensac **37** D5
Vichy **33** B5
Vic-le-Comte **33** C4
Vico **49** C5
Vicq-Exemplet **32** A3
Vic-sur-Cère **38** B3
Vic-sur-Seille **20** D3
Vidauban **48** B3
Vielle-Aure **44** C3
Vielle-Brioude **33** D5
Vielle-St-Girons **36** D3
Vielmur-sur-Agout **38** D3
Vielverge **28** C2
Vienne **34** D2
Vierville-sur-Mer **16** B3
Vierzon **26** D2
Vieux-Boucau-les-Bains **36** D2
Vif **40** B3
Vigeois **32** D2
Viggianello **49** D5
Vignacourt **14** D2
Vigneulles-les-Hattonchâtel **20** C2
Vignory **28** A1
Vigny **18** C2
Vigy **20** C3
Vihiers **25** D4
Villac **32** D1
Villaines-en-Duesmois **27** C6
Villaines-la-Juhel **25** A4
Villamblard **37** B6
Villandraut **37** C4
Villapourçon **27** D5
Villard-Bonnot **34** D3
Villard-de-Lans **40** B3
Villars **31** D6
Villars **33** D6
Villars-Colmars **41** C4
Villars-les-Dombes **34** C2
Villars-sur-Var **41** D5
Villar-St-Pancrace **41** B4
Villasavary **45** B5
Villé **29** A4
Villebois-Lavalette **31** D5
Villebrumier **38** D2
Villecomtal-sur-Arros **44** B2
Villecomte **28** C1
Villecroze **48** A3
Villedaigne **46** B2
Villedieu-la-Blouère **24** D3
Villedieu-les-Poêles **16** C3
Villedieu-sur-Indre **26** D1
Ville-en-Tardenois **19** C5
Villefagnan **31** C5
Villefontaine **34** C2
Villefort **39** C6
Villefranche-d'Albigeois **38** D3
Villefranche-d'Allier **33** B4
Villefranche-de-Lauragais **45** B5

Villefranche-de-Lonchat **37** B5
Villefranche-de-Panat **39** C4
Villefranche-de-Rouergue **38** C3
Villefranche-du-Périgord **37** B6
Villefranche-sur-Cher **26** C2
Villefranche-sur-Mer **41** D6
Villefranche-sur-Saône **34** C1
Villefranque **43** B5
Villelaure **40** D2
Villemandeur **26** B3
Villemorien **27** B5
Villemoustaussou **45** B6
Villemur-sur-Tarn **38** D2
Villenauxe-la-Grande **19** D4
Villeneuve **38** C3
Villeneuve **40** D3
Villeneuve-au-Chemin **27** B5
Villeneuve-d'Allier **33** D5
Villeneuve-d'Ascq **15** C4
Villeneuve-de-Berg **39** B6
Villeneuve-de-Marsan **37** D4
Villeneuve-de-Rivière **44** B3
Villeneuve-la-Guyard **27** A4
Villeneuve-l'Archevêque **27** A4
Villeneuve-lès-Avignon **40** D1
Villeneuve-lès-Béziers **46** B3
Villeneuve-Loubet **49** A4
Villeneuve-sur-Allier **33** A5
Villeneuve-sur-Lot **37** C6
Villeneuve-sur-Yonne **27** B4
Villeneuve-Tolosane **45** A4
Villepinte **45** B6
Villercomtal **38** C3
Villeréal **37** B6
Villerest **33** C6
Villerouge-Termenès **45** B6
Villers-Bocage **14** D3
Villers-Bocage **16** C3
Villers-Bretonneux **14** D3
Villers-Carbonnel **14** D3
Villers-Cotterêts **19** C4
Villers-Écalles **17** B6
Villers-en-Argonne **19** C6
Villersexel **28** C3
Villers-Farlay **28** D2
Villers-le-lac **28** D3
Villers-lès-Nancy **20** D3
Villers-Outréaux **15** D4
Villers-Semeuse **19** B6
Villers-sur-Mer **17** B4

Villerville **17** B5
Villery **27** B5
Villeseneux **19** C5
Ville-sur-Tourbe **19** C6
Villeurbanne **34** C2
Villeveyrac **46** A3
Villevocance **34** D1
Villié-Morgon **34** B1
Villiers-Charlemagne **24** B3
Villiers-en-Lieu **19** D6
Villiers-en-Plaine **31** B4
Villiers-le-Sec **28** B1
Villiers-St-Benôit **27** B4
Villiers-St-Georges **19** D4
Villieu-Loyes-Mollon **34** C2
Villotte-sur-Aire **20** C2
Vimory **26** B3
Vimoutiers **17** C5
Vimy **14** C3
Vinassan **46** B3
Vinay **34** D3
Vinça **45** C6
Vincey **28** A3
Vineuil **26** C1
Vineuil **26** D1
Vingrau **46** C2
Vinon-sur-Verdon **40** D3
Vinsobres **40** C2
Violay **33** C6
Violès **40** C2
Virazeil **37** C5
Vire **16** C3
Vireux-Wallerand **15** D6
Virey-sous-Bar **27** B5
Viriat **34** B2
Virieu-le-Grand **34** C3
Virigneux **33** C6
Virignin **34** C3
Viriville **34** D2
Viry **35** B4
Visan **40** C2
Vissac-Auteyrac **33** D5
Viterne **20** D3
Vitré **23** B6
Vitrey-sur-Mance **28** B2
Vitrolles **47** A6
Vitry-en-Artois **14** C3
Vitry-en-Perthois **19** D6
Vitry-le-François **19** D6
Vitry-sur-Loire **33** A5

Vitteaux **27** C6
Vittel **28** B2
Vivario **49** C6
Viverols **33** D6
Vivier-au-Court **19** B6
Viviers **40** C1
Viviez **38** B3
Viv-le-Fesq **39** D6
Vivonne **31** B5
Vix **27** B6
Vix **30** B3
Vizille **40** B3
Vogelgrun **29** B5
Vogüé **39** C6
Void-Vacon **20** D2
Voillecomte **19** D6
Voiron **34** D3
Voiteur **34** A3
Volmunster **21** C4
Volonne **40** D3
Volvic **33** C4
Volx **40** D3
Vonges **28** C2
Voreppe **34** D3
Vorey **33** D6
Vougeot **28** D1
Vouillé **31** A5
Vouillé **31** B4
Voulaines-les-Templiers **27** B6
Voulx **27** A4
Vouneuil-sous-Biard **31** A5
Vouneuil-sur-Vienne **31** A5
Voutenay-sur-Cure **27** C5
Voutezac **32** D2
Vouvant **30** A3
Vouvray **25** C6
Vouziers **19** B6
Vouzon **26** C2
Voves **26** A2
Vrécourt **28** B2
Vrizy **19** B6
Vron **14** C2
Vy-lès-Lure **28** C3

W

Warcq **20** C2
Warloy-Baillon **14** D3
Warmeriville **19** B5

Wasigny **19** B5
Wasselonne **21** D5
Wassigny **15** D4
Wassy **19** D6
Watten **14** B2
Wavrin **14** C3
Weyersheim **21** D5
Wimereux **14** B2
Wingen-sur-Moder **21** C5
Wintzenheim **29** B4
Wissant **14** B2
Wissembourg **21** C5
Witry-lès-Reims **19** C5
Wittenheim **29** B4
Wizernes **14** C2
Wœrth **21** C5
Wormhout **14** B3
Woippy **20** C3
Woustviller **21** C4

X

Xertigny **28** B3
Xonrupt-Longemer **29** B4

Y

Ychoux **36** C3
Ydes **32** D3
Yenne **34** C3
Yerville **17** B6
Ygos-St-Saturnin **37** D4
Ygrande **33** A4
Ymonville **26** A2
Yport **17** B5
Yssingeaux **33** D6
Yutz **20** B3
Yvetot **17** B6
Yvignac **16** D1
Yvoire **35** B4
Yzeure **33** A5
Yzeures-sur-Creuse **25** D6

Z

Zicavo **49** C5
Zonza **49** D6